THE PERMANENT WAR ECONOMY

American Capitalism in Decline

REVISED AND UPDATED

by SEYMOUR MELMAN

A TOUCHSTONE BOOK
Published by Simon & Schuster, Inc.
NEW YORK

TO *Senator George McGovern*

For his early (1963) courage and foresight in sponsoring the
first bill in the United States Congress for planning
conversion from a military to a civilian economy. He did not
fear to stand, even alone, for the common good.

Copyright © 1974, 1985 by Seymour Melman

Revised Touchstone Edition, 1985

Published by Simon & Schuster, Inc.
Simon & Schuster Building
Rockefeller Center
1230 Avenue of the Americas
New York, New York 10020

TOUCHSTONE and colophon are registered trademarks
of Simon & Schuster, Inc.

Designed by Irving Perkins

Manufactured in the United States of America

10 9 8 7 6 5 4 3 2 1 Pbk.

Library of Congress Cataloging in Publication Data

Melman, Seymour.
    The permanent war economy.

    (A Touchstone book)
    Bibliography: p.
    Includes index.
    1. United States—Economic conditions—1945-
2. Disarmament—Economic aspects—United States.
3. War—Economic aspects—United States. I. Title.
HC106.5.M434   1985   338.4'76234'0973   85-18428

ISBN 0-671-60643-3 Pbk.

CONTENTS

PREFACE

THE DECLINE of the United States as an economic and industrial system is now well under way. This is a consequence of the normal operation of a thirty-year military economy fashioned under government control at the side of civilian capitalism. The new state-controlled economy, whose unique features include maximization of costs and of government subsidies, has been made into the dominant economic form in American capitalism.

Traditional economic competence of every sort is being eroded by the state capitalist directorate that elevates inefficiency into a national purpose, that disables the market system, that destroys the value of the currency, and that diminishes the decision power of all institutions other than its own. Industrial productivity, the foundation of every nation's economic growth, is eroded by the relentlessly predatory effects of the military economy.

All this began in the circumstances of World War II that made a war economy look like a boon to economy and society, apparently solving the economic problems of the Great Depression. But the self-assured operators of the military economy that burgeoned from 1950 on never reckoned with the possibility that a permanent war economy would function as a parasite, weakening the larger host economy that feeds it. The very perception of such developments has been made difficult by an ideological consensus about war economy that classifies this as a source of economic health. Such ideology, by filtering what we look at, prevents us from seeing both the quality and the depth of the deterioration of American productive competence.

The unintended effects of war economy have made it a prime cause of the stagnation it was invoked to solve.

Since the source of the main negative effects of war economy is the sustained nonproductive use of capital and labor, this process is not unique to the United States. It is shared by all states that try to sustain permanent war economies.

This book has evolved from a series that began with *Our Depleted Society* and was followed by *Pentagon Capitalism*. In these earlier works I focused, first, on the facts of a depletion process in American industrial life traceable to military preemption of capital and technology, and second, on the formation of a government-based central management over the operations of military industry. While the analyses developed in these studies are building blocks in the present work, they are now placed in a more comprehensive framework. This framework delineates the workings of a new economy—in the firm and in the aggregate—that has been spawned by the military system, and that has resulted finally in a military form of state capitalism.

The characterization of the United States economy as state capitalism will be met with dismay by some readers, for the central role of the state that is implied in such a formulation has often been thought of by Americans as foreign to American tradition and belief. However, this is no longer the case. The political-economic ideology that has emerged, especially since the Great Depression, tends to value government economic initiative in general and military activity in particular. In this book, a consideration of this newer ideological consensus is a major point of departure for analyzing the actual as against the idealized picture of the "mixed economy."

As an opponent of the militarization of American society, I have tried to make a contribution toward change by providing in this book a treatment of the economic and industrial problems of moving from military to civilian economy. An understanding of both the feasibility and the difficulties of such moves, I judge, is an essential aspect of the capability for change.

As you will see, I did not conclude with any rosy-hued estimate of the near future prospects for American society. I have become much impressed with the importance of ideological fetters for determining public behavior. Therefore I do not exclude the possibility that the war economy and its economic consequences may endure for some time. In fact, this same judgment of the importance of ideology has led me to do this book as a contribution to the demystification of the conventional wisdom that justifies war economy, an indispensable prelude to changing it.

As this book went to the printer I saw Franz Schurmann's new work on *The Logic of World Power*, Pantheon, 1974. In this highly innovative and wide-ranging volume, Schurman has included an analysis of the growth and functioning of state capitalist and bureaucratic controls in several countries, their relation to each other, and the role of military economy and power in these developments. His political analysis amplifies and supports the development that is portrayed here and makes a valuable intellectual companion piece for the present volume.

Finding out about war economy requires anyone who is not an insider to operate within important constraints. Secrecy is a major feature of a war economy because of the military uses of the main product. Therefore security walls limit information on research, development, production, storage and utilization of many military-industry products. Trying to define the characteristics of military economy therefore encounters some of the problems faced by scholars trying to explore the nature of Soviet industry and Soviet economy. When Western scholars became interested in understanding how Soviet industry works, they could draw upon the newspapers and periodicals of the Soviet Union with their carefully controlled reports on industrial events and the performance of industries and the economy. When students wanted to get a closer view of the performing Soviet industrial units, they had to resort, for many years, to indirect devices. They drew upon the recollections of refugees who had once been a part of the Soviet industrial system and had left the country. They found bits and pieces of information in local papers. Researching Soviet industry had many of the characteristics of detective work: trying to make up a portrait out of jigsaw-puzzle pieces, usually with parts left out. So the scholar had to try to deduce the probable contents of empty spaces in terms of consistency with the rest.

Researching the war economy of the United States has some of the same characteristics. It is not possible, without military security clearances (and controls), to inspect the premises of military-industry plants. For the same reason it is not possible to talk on many levels of detail with managers or engineers currently in military industry. The products cannot be independently examined, because these are, in the main, weapons held by the military. Therefore preparing this book has involved operating under the constraints of observing large systems from the outside. Of course, it is possible to learn quite a bit from the newspapers, from military and military-industry journals, from public addresses and reports of government officials, and from hearings before committees of Congress. "Refugees" from military industry, men who have abandoned careers in those fields and who are prepared to talk about some conditions of their work, are important sources. Nevertheless, this all adds up to only a partial picture, without access to many aspects of the internal operation of enterprises and government departments. For all that, there is quite a bit we do know and it is worth spelling it out for evidence on the formation and operation of a new state capitalist economy that has grown to dominate the American economy as a whole while undermining its competence as a productive system.

In the preparation of this book I benefited beyond measure from sustained discussion with JoAnne Melman and from her numerous contributions to content and form. My graduate assistants at Columbia University, Stephen Tencer, William Hooper and Tom Boucher, did yeoman work in supporting and speeding diverse research and analysis operations since 1970. During this time I enjoyed the loyal and efficient support of Marsha Dennis in the research operations and preparation of successive drafts of the manuscript. My warm thanks to Sue Alexion, Megan Mery and Pat Williams for their willing help in the preparation of manuscript.

I am indebted to several colleagues for helpful comments on parts of the manuscript: Professors Alexander Erlich, Sidney Morgenbesser, Mark Kesselman, Michael Edelstein, Lloyd J. Dumas and Derek Shearer, contributing editor of "Ramparts," contributed generously in critically reviewing the manuscript.

SEYMOUR MELMAN

Columbia University
New York, New York

PREFACE TO THE REVISED EDITION

THE PERMANENT WAR ECONOMY: 1985 AND AFTER

THE MILITARY plans of the Carter and Reagan administrations promise to enlarge the military economy of the United States to unprecedented size. From 1946 to 1980 the federal government expended $2,001,000,000,000 ($2,001 billion) for military purposes. Since the military budgets of the United States are now forecast five years ahead, it is prudent to expect that military budgets recommended by presidents will exceed $2,500 billion from 1980 to 1990.

Such an intensification of military activity, and the parallel enlargement of nuclear and conventional forces, evokes the prospect of greater danger both of small wars (Vietnam) and even of the ultimate catastrophe, a general nuclear war. There is no science or body of experience on the basis of which to predict that the accumulation of increasingly machine-controlled weapons of great lethality can proceed indefinitely without catastrophe by design or accident. Therefore the following economic prognoses are based upon a "best case" perspective of no major war and no nuclear war.

The special microeconomy features of the military-industry firms will be intensified: hence, more intensive cost- and subsidy-maximizing. This is owing to the sustained specialized work of managers, engineers, and production workers in the service of the Pentagon. The trained incapacity of the military-serving occupations for civilian work will, therefore, be intensified. From time to time one may expect further exposés of numbers of "horror stories" that depict seemingly extraordinary cost and price levels for military goods. Such portrayals are misleading, for the important condition is their ordinariness, the direct result of operations of military-industry firms in accordance with the standard regulation and preferred procedures of the top managers in the Department of Defense.

The long-term consequences for the rest of the economy will continue, as described in the main text. As before, these long-term developments, featuring decay in civilian production competence, will be "unseen" by all those who have been trained to the under-standing that the cost of an economic product is denoted simply by its price. For, in that case, military goods bearing prices will appear as part of an enlarging stream of money-valued goods and services.

Since the main text of this book appeared in 1974, the main macroeconomic effects on the civilian economy have proceeded as diagnosed. There have been some shifts of intensity and emphasis. The inflation process, for example, has been relocated. A principal consequence of domestic price inflation from 1965 to 1980 was the rise in price of U.S.-produced goods, so sharp as to make them noncompetitive, vs. imported goods from many countries. The same effect continued, however, after the U.S. domestic price inflation was diminished.

The new form of inflation effect was obtained as the price of the dollar, the means of exchange itself, was raised in relation to other currencies. The average price of the U.S. dollar in relation to other currencies rose 70 percent from 1980 to 1985. This was a conse-quence of the federal government's manipulation of the U.S. dollar in the service of its policies. Thus, to facilitate payment for rapidly enlarging military budgets between 1980 and 1990, the federal government has borrowed lavishly in American and in world markets. The currency borrowed was dollars, including those offered by foreigners after they had exchanged their own currencies in ever larger quantities for the dollars desired by the U.S. Treasury. The result was a worldwide rise in the price of the dollar relative to many other currencies, and an automatic rise in the relative prices of U.S.-produced goods compared with foreign goods. U.S.-produced goods were made less salable, just as they were with the former domesti-cally located price inflation.

Two considerations are critical, in my judgment, for appreciating the future course of the U.S. military economy and of the larger society that contains it. The first is the institutionalization of military economy, notably its top control mechanism. As industries, profes-sional societies, major universities, trade unions, and whole regions of the country become accustomed to depending for livelihood on the

Pentagon dollar, there is an automatic hardening of political commitment among these people. For example: Every person trained in the
sciences and technologies knows that there are limits to the reliability
of mechanisms. Accordingly, there is no prospect for defense, in the
sense of a shield, from the "star wars" program, however designed. In
the presence of forty times overkill capability on each American and
Soviet city, even a 90 percent effective defense (an unheard-of
effectiveness) leaves overkill. Nevertheless, the network of war-
making institutions marches as a solid phalanx in approving the "star
wars" project. For its managers, laboratory staffs, construction firms,
and manufacturing contractors, the "star wars" program promises a
bonanza of money flow for more than a decade.

It is also crucial to monitor, continuously, the operation of the top
management of the military economy, always keeping in mind that
this managerial group, with the normal managerial imperative for
enlarging the scope and intensity of its decision-making power, has
been controlling—by Congressional grant—the largest finance capital
fund in the American economy.

The reader should be alert to the connection between the military
economy and the larger corporate industrial and finance system. The
pattern of cost- and subsidy-maximizing that was formally installed in
the military economy during the long reign of Robert McNamara
(1961–1968) was not a social invention uniquely designed for the
service of the war economy, for cost-maximizing had long been in
place in the industrial and other firms of the American economy.

Until the mid-1960s, *cost-minimizing* in production was the primary pattern of decision-making in American industrial firms, the
better to maximize profit. But alongside the production operation
there has been the growing realm of administrative activity, in which
decisions on production and routines for the enlargement of managerial control have been formulated and implemented. In 1899 there
were ten administrative, technical, and clerical persons for every one
hundred production workers. By 1978 there were forty-two of the
administrative, technical, and clerical group per hundred production
workers. The managerial and related occupations had grown without
any correlation to an increase in productivity, and without correlation
to increases in profit. The enlargement of managerial activity did
expand the scope and intensity of managerial control—but that has
not been part of the formal, explicit criteria for production decision-
making in the capitalist industrial enterprise.

The enlargement of administrative and related activity (far beyond the requirements of decision-making on production) has entailed a process of cost-maximizing, which is offset by growing subsidy drawn from the wealth creation of the production occupations.

Against that background we may understand the appearance of a formal cost- and subsidy-maximizing microeconomy in military industry as a transfer and extension of these modes of microeconomy: from the realm of administration to the wider realm of both administrative and production operations in the military economy.

Finally, I call the reader's attention to the importance of planning and executing the conversion from military to civilian economy. This political-economic transformation is made the more urgent by the intensification of both the short- and long-term consequences of the permanent war economy. Moreover, a society that has made itself economically dependent on military economy will also be incapable of embarking on the necessary planning and negotiations for reversing the arms race. Economic conversion planning is therefore a precondition for significant political moves for peace.

Columbia University   SEYMOUR MELMAN
March, 1985

One

WAR ECONOMY
AND PROSPERITY

WAR BRINGS PROSPERITY. This was the conclusion drawn by Americans who watched the war economy of World War II bring an end to the Great Depression. The ten-year pall of massive unemployment and economic decline was dramatically lifted by the fresh opportunities provided by the large-scale industrial expansion needed to supply the Allied war effort. Employed Americans numbered 46 million in 1939 and 53 million by 1945. Simultaneously, the armed forces were swiftly enlarged from 370,000 to 11,400,000 persons, absorbing a sizable segment of the employable population.

The main focus of American economic effort from 1939 on was, of course, war work of every kind. The government's orders for goods and services soared from $11 billion in 1939 to $117 billion by 1945. At the same time, however, there was a marked increase in civilian personal consumption, which rose 25 percent, from $137 billion in 1939 to $171 billion by 1945. This 25 percent increased spending brought personal consumption to the highest level in American experience.[1] Everyone saw the economy producing more guns *and* more butter. Economically speaking, Americans had never had it so good.

War work ended the Great Depression. War work made business boom and brought economic opportunity, better living and money in the bank to almost all who participated in it. From their experience with World War II, Americans drew the inference that the economy could produce guns and butter, that military spending could boost the economy and that war work could be used to create full employment. They observed that these results had not been achieved by the efforts of President Franklin Roosevelt's civilian New Deal. To be sure, there were some reservations about the desirability or inevitability of using military spending as the road to prosperity. Nevertheless, these shared perceptions among Americans spurred the development of an ideological consensus about war economy that has permeated the thinking especially of intellectuals and political leaders since the end of World War II. The ideological consensus that evolved from World War II transformed the justification for military spending from a time-limited economic effort to achieve a political goal (winning World War II) to a sustaining means for governmental control of the economy. It is a central thesis of this book that this consensus on the economic benefits of military spending has played a vital role in marshaling the commitment of the American people to a permanent war economy.

There was hardly any interregnum between the end of World War II and the start of the political, economic and military confrontations that soon were defined as the Cold War.[2] From the outset, methods of military containment, nuclear and nonnuclear, were given high priority by American planners. The concept of a "permanent war economy" formulated in 1944 was soon made a reality. Once the Soviets exploded an atomic bomb in 1949 and the Korean War was fought (1950–53), a regular annual portion of the American national product (7–10 percent) was spent on the military. Military industry was enlarged and mobilized to win an arms race that has no foreseeable end at this writing.*

---

* The ideology of the Cold War itself has supported the idea of a war economy operating into an indefinite future. In conventional understanding, World War II had a definable end. During World War II everyone expected it to end through an agreed cease-fire, or surrender, or an armistice, or a ceremonial treaty. The idea of the Cold War has not included any defined time or condition of termination.

The operation of a war economy in the United States from 1945 on required more than the decisions of leaders to operate a Cold War. It required the support of the American people. The decisions of leaders became national decisions as voters, Congress and the labor force willingly—nay, eagerly—accepted and implemented them. That eagerness was buoyed by the conviction that big military budgets meant jobs and prosperity generally. Called "defense spending," war economy became and remained popular.

By the 1950s a cross-society political consensus had developed around war economy. Businessmen, industrial workers, engineers, government employees, intellectuals all joined in the confident assessment that war economy on a sustained basis was not only viable but economically desirable. From the standpoint of national leaders, using military spending to ensure prosperity seemed like a politician's dreamboat: There is something here for everybody—or so it is made to appear. For example, Carl Vinson (Democrat, Virginia), chairman of the House Armed Services Committee, submitted a military public-works bill of about a billion dollars in 1958, saying to the House of Representatives, "My friends, there is something in this bill for every member." The spending proposals in the bill were portrayed for each state so that each member could see the benefits accruing to his constituents.[3]

In 1961 when John F. Kennedy sought to get the economy "moving again," one of his preferred instruments was enlargement of the military budget. In that choice he could count on solid backing from a population which, except for a dissenting handful, had faith in a set of political-economic beliefs that was linked to the basic idea that war spending brings prosperity.

This is no mere abstraction. It has supplied the political-economic marching orders from Truman to Kennedy and Johnson, from Nixon to Reagan. Since World War II, successive administrations have greatly enlarged the powers of the federal government on the basis of the self-assured estimates of strength of American industry, economy and society drawn from this assumption. The same idea has served as an underpinning for military forays abroad to establish a worldwide Pax Americana.

Money for the Pentagon has been lavished without stint. Here is the military-budget record, and projection to 1990.[4]

	Billions of Dollars
1950	13
1961	47
1972	80
1974	87
1976	97
1980	144
1982	217
1984	265
1986	322 (est.)
1988	411 (est.)
1990	488 (est.)

I underscore the fact that military budget plans for 1974 and 1975 showed no decline following the Vietnam agreements of early 1973. U.S. military planning is geared to wider perspectives within which Vietnam is one event in a continuing program.*

The belief that military spending is good for the economy has gained adherents from surprisingly diverse quarters across the political spectrum. On the political right, war economy has been supported as integral to the military confrontation with Communism. Among the liberals and those of the political center, war economy is supported as a solid application of Keynesian economic strategy which had not been given a real try by too timid policies of civilian economic intervention before 1939. Among radical critics of capitalism, war economy has been viewed mainly as an indispensable part of capitalism and therefore exempt from major restriction short of termination of capitalism itself. In sum, the belief that war brings prosperity has served as a powerful organizing idea for generating and cementing a cross-society political consensus for active or tacit support of big military spending as a sustaining feature of American public life.

However, an outward appearance of economic health can belie an underlying reality of economic decay. In the experience of many people during the thirty years after World War II, especially in the upper middle class and in the technical and administrative occupations, the expectation that war spending brings prosperity

* These are large numbers that are difficult to visualize in terms of daily experience. Imagine that a printing press was set up to print the $87 billions of new spending power given to the Pentagon in 1974. If the press printed dollar bills at the rate of one per second, then the printing of 87 billion bills would take 2,758 years, or until the year 4732.

was borne out. What went unrecognized was that war economy produces other, unforeseen, effects with long-term destructive consequences. These include the formation of a new state-managed economy, deterioration of the productive competence of many industries, and finally, inflation—the destruction of the dollar as a reliable store of value. These results were not visible to intellectuals and almost all others in the educated occupations. They assumed that increased money income (whatever the source) necessarily reflected more available wealth in the society. In fact, the $1,500 billion spent on the military since World War II produced no economically useful products for the society.

The confident believers in American war economy tacitly assumed that the four years of full U.S. concentration upon war production during World War II could be a satisfactory model for anticipating the results of thirty years of sustained high-level military-economy activity. This estimate failed to take into account crucial aspects of war economy in general and of the American World War II experience in particular.

From the economic standpoint the main characteristic of war economy is that its products do not yield ordinary economic use-value: usefulness for the level of living (consumer goods and services); or usefulness for further production (as in machinery or tools being used to make other articles).

The basic nonproductive nature of war economy was unseen by Americans during World War II because of several surrounding conditions. The government mobilized the 9,500,000 unemployed of 1939 and also brought millions of underemployed, women, youths and older people into the labor force on behalf of the war economy.[5] Further, they all worked long hours. The result was an industrial cornucopia, with increases in both military and consumer goods. The years of extended war economy following World War II did not permit a repeat performance of drastic enlargement of the labor force. That had been made possible in 1939 mainly by the existence of an immense "reserve army" of unemployed and underemployed numbering 18 million.*

Furthermore, full American participation in World War II lasted only four years. The major heavy capital goods of American society could endure even under high capacity use. That meant that the railroads, the power plants, the roads, the dwellings, the principal factories, all could be used through four years of wartime

* From 1939 to 1945, 7 million were added to the employed labor force and 11 million to the armed forces.

economy without basic replacement. But that is no model for a thirty-year-long war economy. During the extended period of war economy not only was major replacement required for things like power plants, communications systems, railroads and the like, it was also necessary to make substantial improvements in the technical quality of machinery and factories. A sustained input of technical brainpower and research facilities to produce new and more productive technology was required.

During the long period of the Cold War more than half of the research and development technical manpower of American society was drawn away from civilian industry and into work that was military-supporting, directly or indirectly. The concentration of labor, especially skilled labor, and capital over a long period to this nonproductive economic growth induced a set of deteriorations in American technology, economy and society that were not intended or anticipated by the prophets of prosperity through war production. An early analysis of the resultant industrial depletion was given in my book *Our Depleted Society* (1965).

A further consequence of the Cold War was a major transformation in the activity of the federal government, embodied in a new kind of institution that was set up to develop and manage America's expanding military system. At first the military system was simply part of a continuing "war economy"* which may be said to exist as military spending becomes a continuing, significant and legitimate end-purpose of economic activity.[6] As the activity continued through the 1950s it took the shape of a "military-industrial complex" and was then transformed under Kennedy-McNamara into a full-fledged centrally managed industrial system. In *Pentagon Capitalism* (1970) I outlined the main features of the new top-management control organization that was set up in the Pentagon from 1961 on to regulate the managers of about 20,000 principal firms that serve the Department of Defense (apart from about 100,000 subcontractors). This new organization represents a concentration of power hitherto unknown in American

---

* Within the war economy there are civilian and military economy sectors. The latter comprises the whole network of firms, research institutes and military bases whose primary function is designing, fabricating, storing and delivering military equipment and knowledge. In this formulation a few years of mobilization for a war would not qualify an economic system as a war economy; neither would military spending on the modest levels that prevailed in the U.S. just before World War II.

experience—industrially or politically. Only Soviet-type societies have had comparable centralization of top economic, political and military authority. In form the new state management is comparable to the central offices used to manage very large multidivision firms. *Pentagon Capitalism,* while diagnosing various features of war economy, focused on the corporatization of the federal government. It was particularly concerned with the dynamic factors underlying the functioning of the new corporate-type state-management institution in the Pentagon.

This book is directed to a broader problem: the nature of a new economic system, state capitalism, that operates a war economy. The new economy, erected at the side of and intertwined with the older business system, has firms that are a new economic breed. The textbooks and the literature of economics are based upon the interactions of model firms that minimize cost and maximize profit, doing that under more or less competitive conditions in the marketplaces where the action is centered. A new kind of enterprise has become characteristic of military industry. This firm *maximizes* cost and *maximizes* subsidies from the state management. In this universe, patterns of managerial decision-making rather than impersonal market interactions dominate the company scene.

The conventional façade of corporate outward appearances obscures the presence and the distinctive nature of the state-managed economy. This system concentrates on military economy. It can draw on the federal budget for virtually unlimited capital. It operates in an insulated, monopoly market that makes the state-capitalist firms, singly and jointly, impervious to inflation, to poor productivity performance, to poor product design and poor production managing. The subsidy pattern has made the state-capitalist firms failure-proof. That is the state-capitalist replacement for the classic self-correcting mechanisms of the competitive, cost-minimizing, profit-maximizing firm. The combination of cost and subsidy maximization, continuously operated, produces a range of consequences for economy and society that contrast sharply with the expectations of the ideological consensus on America's war economy.

I will show that the normal operation of the state-capitalist war economy has highly destructive effects on the rest of economy and society. It is important to recognize that these effects have been

unintended and unanticipated by the managers of war economy.
These men and their supporting echelons of specialists in management, law, the sciences and technology have been true believers in
prosperity through war economy. An appreciation of their faith
helps to unravel what is otherwise a mystery: how could the well-
educated platoons of "the best and the brightest" who served successive administrations formulate and implement systems of
economic policy with manifestly catastrophic results? Answer: by
constructing and operating a war system based upon articles of
faith rather than on empirically validated propositions about how
society in general and war economy in particular actually function.

The war economy of the United States is no mere extension of
private capitalism. Neither is it an undifferentiated state-capitalist
economy. Every capitalist country uses the state as an instrument
of economic control. In the United States, however, state capitalism has been given the particular form of a war economy. With
a duration extending for thirty years, and solid plans for more to
come, it is no editorial excess to understand it as a *permanent war
economy*. The dimensions of the war economy are basic data for
this discussion.

By every available measure the war economy of the United
States is a colossus. For 1974 President Nixon proposed that the
Department of Defense, the Atomic Energy Commission, the
space agencies, and related operations together be granted
$92,260,000,000 of new spending authority.[7] Let us translate this
sum into the number of man-years of work that this buys, assuming an average cost of $10,000 per man-year. On this conservative
basis 9,226,000 man-years of work in American society are to be
purchased through these military-serving agencies.

That is only the beginning. A dollar spent has indirect effects as
well, generating further economic activity. A "multiplier" effect of
one person indirectly affected for each person directly involved is
probably an understatement of this effect. By this reckoning,
18,450,000 man-years of economic activity are set in motion by the
new military money made available in 1974. The people involved
include not only the uniformed personnel of the various armed
forces but also the civilians employed by the Department of
Defense (about a million men and women in various bases,
headquarters and other installations), as well as the military-
industry people who are nominally employees of the several

military contracting firms. Thus, in five of the principal military-serving industries (ordnance, communications equipment, electronics, aircraft, shipbuilding) 2,029,000 men and women were employed full time in 1970.[8]

Another view of the scale of the U.S. war economy is obtained by comparing it with the gross national product of various countries. There are only eight countries in the world whose national product exceeds the $92-billion U.S. military-agency allocation for 1974 (U.S., U.S.S.R., Japan, West Germany, France, United Kingdom, China, Italy).[9]

In the allocation of federal expenditures, payment for past, current and future military operations has come to dominate the uses of tax dollars. Thus, by 1974 the payments for past, current and future military operations amount to $123 billion, or 62 percent of the total "federal funds" budget of the government, which accounts for all federal activity other than Social Security payments and the like.[10] The military bill of $123 billion exceeds 10 percent of the American gross national product. Within the federal budget the purchases of military goods and services dominate total federal purchases. The military element in 1971 was 73 percent of the $97 billion of total federal purchases for all uses.[11] As the purchases of military materiel and construction of fixed installations have accumulated, they reached a total money value of $214 billion by 1970. In that year the total assets of all U.S. manufacturing corporations was $554 billion.[12] Hence the assets of the U.S. military establishment were 38 percent as much as the assets of all U.S. industry.

Further, it is crucial to note that "since World War II we have spent $200 billion in research and development in the U.S. alone with 80 percent on defense, space, and the Atomic Energy Commission."[13] Year by year these sums for military research look like a minor part of national economic activity, less than 3 percent of the gross national product in any year. However, the relative importance of an activity is not necessarily mirrored in what it costs.

Sustained priority to military-related research produced payoffs and penalties. For example, as research in electronics was channeled into military and related applications a few industries, notably computers, gained from the government-sponsored research in their fields, but a host of consumer electronics industries like radio and television manufacturing, left to their own devices, have suffered massive depletion, closing of factories, transfer of work abroad and loss of employment opportunity in the United States. Such collateral effects are unsuspected and are rendered effectively "invisible" when the observer is guided by the conventional view that the money paid measures the worth of a thing, that military research boosts the economy generally, and that the amount of money involved (in military research) is a small part of the national product in any event. This effect on technical research is an important part of a larger process: a minority portion of the national product often shows decisive impact on the economy as a whole. A succession of major industries have been undermined for want of fresh technology, capital and the public attention that is sometimes needed to cope with problems that have no obvious solution.

These consequences were not only unintended, they were not even noticed by the proponents of war economy. Making weapons has been well-paid work for thirty years. Paying no attention to the fact that the product of all this activity was, economically speaking, nonproductive (not contributing to consumer goods and services or to further production), our economists counted all the money paid out for this work as part of the gross national product. A growing GNP seemed sufficient as a harbinger of economic health. Through the eyes of the conventional wisdom, the vast quantities of productive goods and services that were forgone for American society because of the sustained effort applied to war economy went unacknowledged. Unseen, for example, was the fact that while the stock of missiles was enlarged and renewed, the railroad rolling stock deteriorated without replacement.

The permanent war economy, far from solving problems of capital and labor surplus in American economy, as suggested by the conventional wisdom, will be shown to perform as a prime generator of uninvestable capital, unemployable labor, and industrial inefficiency. More than that, the permanent war economy will be shown to be a prime cause of the American inflation of the 1970s, a development that is inexplicable to those trained in contemporary economics that classifies military outlays as just another species of government spending.

Since war economy became institutionalized in American society[14] every suggestion for curtailing a military activity has produced a predictable outcry from Congressmen, Senators, managers, union officers and civic leaders that the particular operation must continue in order to prevent unemployment. By focusing on the size of the war-economy payroll and its locally stimulating effects on retail trade, real-estate values and the like, they render invisible the size and quality of what has been forgone for the wider society. Actually, the unintended effects of war economy have included wide-ranging deterioration of competence in many spheres of life. In 1965 (*Our Depleted Society*) I first tried to call attention to this process. But it was not yet visible to the wider public that had no direct involvement in industries and other activities that were beginning to suffer from deterioration. The possible relation of such developments to war economy was implausible to most people who adhered to the idea that America could have guns *and* butter. By the 1970s the depletion processes had gone far enough at least to shake popular faith in the idea of U.S. economic invincibility.

Against the background of a modern view of the limits of military power, it is possible to define very large sums, $25–50 billions and more, that are conceivably transferable from military to civilian economy. Once the money released from overblown military budgets reaches the annual sum of $25 billion and more, it becomes conceivable to start a process of economic reconstruction without centralism in the United States. Such perspectives are unrealizable so long as the ideological consensus that favors war economy is operative as a cross-society control system.

The idea that prosperity is linked to war is the base of this consensus. Before the election campaign of 1972 the veteran opinion analyst Samuel Lubell went on one of his national tours to sample the public pulse. Here are the words of a utility worker in Fredricksburg, Virginia, as reported by Lubell in the Washington *Evening Star*, August 14, 1972: "It's a helluva thing to say, but our economy needs a war. Defense spending should be increased to make jobs for people." One of the things that Lubell discovered on this multistate tour is, "In every community sample the argument rages: Do we need a war?"

The plan of this book is to first show how the military economy works on the inside and then to delineate the main effects of this system on the rest of the economy and society. Against this background of data and analysis, I will assess the validity of the main items of belief comprising the ideological consensus on war economy. Turning next to the military side of the justification for war economy, I will review and assess many conventional ideas in terms of the military experience of the last decades. The reader, I hope, will then be prepared to entertain some facts and proposals about how to go about converting from a military to a civilian economy. Against all this I will finally address head-on the issue that threads its way throughout the preceding analyses: Does American capitalism need a war economy?

Two

HOW THE MILITARY
ECONOMY WORKS: THE FIRM

A YOUNG ENGINEER was employed by an aerospace firm and assigned the task of preparing cost and price estimates for new products on which the firm would submit bids to the Department of Defense. In doing this work he was expressly prohibited from having any access to or communication with the accounting department. Neither was he permitted to read any of the firm's own internal accounting reports. Hence, he had no information available on the details of previous costs of similar work. On the face of it this is preposterous. How do you go about preparing cost and price estimates without access to cost data? In this case the management wanted no critical assessment of the components of total cost. A restriction of this kind would be unthinkable in any ordinary business firm. A management would ordinarily be interested in having its cost and price estimates prepared with the best available information in order to be well informed on costs as they relate to quantity of output and possible profit margins.

Our young engineer in this aerospace firm proceeded to prepare price estimates, using prices (not costs) of former products of his own firm, prices of aircraft products of other firms, and occasional information obtained informally from inside competing firms. This sort of job requirement proved to be unnerving to the engineer in question, because his training had instilled in him values about efficiency which he was unable to fulfill under the conditions imposed upon him. After a few years, he left this job in disgust.

He had been trained to apply techniques for engineering costing that required a critical assessment of every factor used in production. From his perspective he was not permitted to have access to basic data that are required for preparing proper engineering-cost estimates. These consist of the money value of each major input that is needed for making something in the desired quantity, including administration, engineering, production labor, machinery and factory structures, raw materials, marketing, and the cost of capital. The industrial engineer develops the cost of each element by considering not only the actual experience of the enterprise in making a similar product, as recorded by the accounting department, but possible alternative methods for each element of cost. Ordinarily, then, the task of engineering costing is to tell the management what something *should* cost, using the best available methods. Obviously, in the performance of this function the actual costs previously incurred (historical costs) are only a starting point. For the industrial engineer is charged with seeking out the minimum possible cost, not with simply repeating previous practices.

From about 1961, military-industry firms were required by the Department of Defense to use historical price information as a basis for future price estimates without necessarily diagnosing and evaluating the separate costs that build up to the price. Engineering costing is essential if one is trying to minimize costs. Historical costing, based upon past prices for price bidding, contains a built-in escalator for increasing costs and prices, because it does not provide for the possibility that future work might be performed at a lower cost than similar work done previously. In the absence of any regularly definable relationship between the costs of old and new products, the only rationale for using "historical costs" seems to be to afford a basis for justifying higher prices. As I will show below, this procedure is one example of a central characteristic in the functioning of military industry, namely the practice of *cost-maximization*.

Here is a second event, revealing another basic feature of the military economy. In June 1971, Secretary of the Treasury John Connally was queried by the Senate Committee on Banking on a proposed unprecedented loan guarantee to the Lockheed Corporation. He was challenged on the grounds that such a guarantee did not necessarily require the company to perform efficiently. Said Connally, "What do we care whether they perform?" He explained that he favored the loan so that Lockheed losses would be minimized and so that the firm could provide employment. "What do we care whether they perform?" is an unthinkable policy for the top management of an organization that is interested in minimization of costs or improvement in productivity as priority criteria for evaluation of its operations. Secretary Connally was reflecting here a second central characteristic of the military-industry system, and its top management in particular: they are oriented to the *maximization of subsidy payments* from the federal government to the military economy.

These two events demand explanation. From the personal accounts of "refugees" from military-industry firms, from former Pentagon staffers, from informants still engaged in military-industrial work, from the Pentagon's publications, and from data disclosed in Congressional hearings, I have found consistent evidence pointing to the inference that the primary internal economic dynamics of military industry are cost- and subsidy-maximization. What is there about the operation of the military economy that permits or encourages such behavior? Why does the military-serving firm avoid cost-minimizing practices? What role does the Pentagon management play in this mode of operating? Finally, how could such practices be widespread under the stewardship of men like Robert McNamara and his "whiz-kid" aides, renowned for their skills in management technique and for their commitment to "cost effectiveness"?

The history of arms production includes a record of substantial profit-taking that continued into the arms race of the nuclear era.[1] Once the Department of Defense decided to rely primarily on business enterprise rather than on government arsenals for research, development and production of weapons, the managers of such firms, old and new, lost no time in taking advantage of the opportunities for growth and profits that were afforded by escalating military budgets.[2]

Even the development of elaborate rules, procedures and Pentagon staffs for negotiating and monitoring military contracts did not abort the opportunity for attractive business gain at government expense. Instead, the government–business relationship developed into a loosely structured collaborative form called the military-industrial complex.

When Robert McNamara was installed as Secretary of Defense in 1961 all of this bilking of the public treasury by the military-industrial complex was supposed to change. Cadres of men trained in the techniques of statistical analysis and managerial control were recruited for top positions at the Pentagon for the purpose of designing and operating the largest industrial central office in the world.[3] The new Pentagon chiefs formalized control methods that were appropriate to the task of regulating more than twenty thousand subfirms. They emphasized the introduction of analytical methods and standardized computer routines. In combination, these control techniques were supposed to yield "cost effectiveness" in the military-industrial system.

From a statistical point of view, behavior is "under control" when it varies within predictable and acceptable magnitudes.[4] In this sense, the price of a new military product is "under control" when it appears to be within the range of known prices of similar or comparable products. In the world of military economy, however, "under control" has meant control around a rising average trend where the rising costs are incorporated as an inherent part of the price process. By accepting the record as a given condition, the Pentagon management perpetuated rising costs without determining whether the rising cost "history" is necessary—or why there is rising cost at all, especially since many technological-improvement options have tended to reduce costs. However, following their "control" reasoning, McNamara's staff developed techniques for calculating the trend of military product prices through time and for predicting in that way the likely and apparently reasonable price of future products.

In October 1965 the Air Force Systems Command formalized these methods by publishing a manual entitled *Cost Estimating Procedures*. In the section headed "Estimating Methodology," the following instruction is given for cost estimating on new products: "The estimating methods are based on projections from historical data. Historical data are used to project future costs." The manual stipulated that the industrial-engineering approach to cost estimating was prohibited.[5]

The historical-projection method

does not rely on a detailed description of the inputs to the system but rather considers system output characteristics such as speed, thrust, etc. Historical defense system cost experience is used to develop the relationship between such output characteristics and system costs. These empirical relationships are then used to project a portion or all of the costs of a new system.[6]

When these methods are used, the "planning estimate for the airframe for a new fighter plane often is derived from a cost–weight ratio of an earlier fighter that is considered to be roughly equal."[7] By means of such data, equations could be calculated and charts drawn showing the historical pattern of price development for major classes of weapons. Thereby, estimates of the cost and price of building the F-14 or the F-15 fighter plane are based on the experience of constructing the F-111. The F-111 is the famous swing-wing multipurpose plane whose final prices were about four times initial estimates. By such methods dramatic cost increases of one product become the baseline for estimating acceptable costs and prices of the next product.

This "control" practice preferred by the Pentagon was swiftly accepted and incorporated into the procedures of the military-industrial firms. They could present the cost and price record of a class of products as an acceptable baseline for formulating price bids on new products. However, these techniques of historical costing and pricing, while satisfying formal requirements of statistical control, do not necessarily afford a basis for cost efficiency or cost-minimization. In fact the historical costing techniques became centrally involved in pervasive cost and price increases in the military-industry system.

McNamara's preferred methods allowed the managements to incorporate whatever methods, including inefficiencies, had been part of making product A, B and C into the historical trend of costs and prices used for justifying yet further cost and price increases for product D. Hence, in the interplay between the analytically minded managerial controllers in the Pentagon and Pentagon-serving managers looking out for their own gain, there developed the pattern of cost and price increases called "overruns." This was the result of cost-maximization of local management, all made welcome by the Pentagon chiefs since the cost-maximizers complied with the formal rules that "controlled" the growing costs and prices.

For the military-industry enterprise, higher costs mean more activity, more facilities, more employees, more cash flow, and a larger cost base for calculating profits. For the military-industry top managers in the Pentagon, cost increases in the subfirms denote more activity under their control and are the basis for enlarged budget requests to the Congress. There is no built-in limitation on the cost-maximization process. The limits are external: the political acceptability of Pentagon budgets to the Congress and to the population as a whole.[8]

Also, from a national economic vantage point, the McNamara-type methods and their results were entirely justified by the standards of the ideological consensus as contributing to the disbursement of government funds, thereby creating job opportunities. In these ways the cost- and subsidy-maximizing aims of industrial firms and the goals of the Pentagon managers for enlarging their decision power became mutually complementary and mutually supporting.

Some people are bound to be skeptical of the assertion that the Pentagon top managers have committed themselves to a cost- and subsidy-maximizing system, for this state of affairs contrasts so sharply with the image of Robert McNamara and his aides as masters of managerial efficiency. As I demonstrated in *Pentagon Capitalism* (1970), these men were powerfully impelled by the managerial imperative to enlarge their own decision power. The available evidence tells us that McNamara clearly succeeded in systematizing and elaborating administrative procedures and in concentrating authority at the top of the Pentagon as never before.

We now know that these managerial successes were not achieved by the enlargement and integration of cost-saving and efficiency-maximizing enterprises and industrial systems. Instead, the McNamara stewardship (and those following) were marked by behavior that complied with both the ideological consensus of American war economy and the managerial imperative to enlarge decision power. In these terms alone we can explain what is otherwise a mystery: Why have the Pentagon chiefs applied such punitive measures against men whose offense was to try to introduce and practice well-known methods of cost-minimization in the military economy and who, as a last resort, spoke out publicly against the outrageous avarice of leading military-industry firms?

Principal names that come to mind here are Ernest Fitzgerald

(Air Force) and Gordon Rule (Navy). As senior civilian officials responsible for cost management, both were subjected to professional victimization for no other reason than their effort to restrain the cost-maximization process in military industry. In Fitzgerald's case President Nixon announced that he had himself passed on the decision to fire him. Ernest Fitzgerald's professional autobiography, *The High Priests of Waste* (Norton, 1972) is a unique account of the experience of trying to apply ordinary industrial criteria of efficiency in military industry.

By speaking out publicly against cost- and subsidy-maximizing (though not with these words), Fitzgerald and Rule were also challenging the competence and authority of the Pentagon top leadership. Intended or not, the effect of their action challenged the publicly held image of "cost-effective" managing with the reality of cost- and subsidy-maximization. That is why these men were swiftly demoted despite their high status and formal job tenure as veteran civil servants.

At this point a discerning reader, reflecting on what he once learned in Economics I, might recall that profit can be enlarged not only by raising price but also by reducing cost. Why don't the managers of military industry try for cost reduction, even while the Pentagon accepts price increases?

With respect to cost, price and profit, the conditions of business success are significantly different for the managers of military-serving as against civilian-product firms. For a businessman intent on increasing his profits, one of the available options is to raise the price of what he sells. Even if the rate of profit is constant, a higher price enables the businessman to earn a larger amount of profit. However, the managers of civilian-product firms are restricted in the use of this strategy. First, if competing firms choose not to raise their prices business can be lost to them. Second, customers may decide not to buy a product altogether, or to replace it with a substitute. That is why the managers of civilian-industry firms, striving for maximum profit, have given close attention to a second strategy: minimizing their costs, mainly costs of production. The businessman can enlarge his profit margin by reducing costs, or by offsetting increases in the cost of, say, labor or raw materials, through improvements in his internal efficiency. In fact, this mode of operation has been a continuing feature of private industrial capitalism from which gains were made by the society as a whole through the continued enlargement of the average productivity of the labor force.[9]

In the economy of military industry, these conventional business rules have been revised. Big contracts especially are arranged by negotiation with one selected supplier, so there is no competitor selling to the single buyer, the Pentagon. And the Pentagon, having ordered a product, usually wants it. Thus even if the price turns out to be as much as three to four times the originally negotiated amount, the Pentagon finds the money to pay for it. Under such conditions the managers of military-industry firms are under no external pressures to do all of the demanding work of problem-solving that is involved in trying to minimize costs through internal efficiencies. Why bother? If costs go up, so too can prices, and thereby profits. This, in a nutshell, is the logic of *cost-maximization*. Regardless of the formal technical diversity of Pentagon industrial contracts, this regular effect gives them the general characteristics of cost-plus arrangements.

On the Pentagon side, rising prices have ordinarily been paid by asking for and getting more money in the annual budgets appropriated by Congress. Again, the added money paid to the military-serving enterprises is justified as being good for the economy as a whole, making jobs and putting money into circulation. That is the logic of *subsidy-maximization*, the readiness of government to pay far more than the conceivable cost of given work if it were to be done under other than cost-maximizing conditions.

These, then, are the economic forces that made maximization of cost and maximization of subsidy into operating features of both the military-industrial firm and the state management at the Pentagon that controls them. By "firm" I mean both the separately identified enterprise and the military-serving divisions of larger civilian firms. There are no general instructions to these firms that read: Thou shalt maximize cost; thou shalt maximize subsidy. These features are built into the normal operating patterns that are both legally prescribed and otherwise accepted as the way of life in military industry.

The differences between military industry and civilian firms are not revealed in outward appearances. Names, titles of officers, annual reports, accounting statements, public announcements, job titles, securities offerings, all have the normal flavor and appearance associated with the familiar operation of American industrial corporations. Indeed, these firms even compete with each other, though in ways that provide us with a convenient point to indicate additional features which differentiate military from civilian industry.

The military-industrial firms compete with each other, but, in their race for fresh contract and capital grants from the Pentagon managers, they do not vie for who can achieve a lower product price and cost but rather who can compete best in terms of a display of "competence." Competence, in the jargon of the military-industry world, means the readiness and ability of the particular firm to satisfy the Pentagon's requirements in the judgment of its top management. It means its ability to collaborate with Pentagon-level administrators to turn out the sort of product that the Pentagon wants with regard to details of product designing, testing, producing and servicing. It includes, for example, the capability for coping with very large numbers of design changes once a product has been specified. It includes the expectation that the firm has the staff and the accompanying know-how for dealing with military managers and with the military user organizations on a continuing basis. It means knowing how to talk to the military, how to write the instructional and maintenance manuals needed for training people in the operation and maintenance of complex equipment.

Thus, while military-industry firms compete, often in much the same fashion as division managers under a central corporation, in their Pentagon-dominated world "competence," including political clout, is the coin of competition rather than the price–quantity contest that is more characteristic of civilian firms.

In response to readily available subsidies from the Pentagon, the internal decision processes of military-industry firms were molded into patterns of cost-maximization. This did not mean infinitely large growth. But it did support an array of operating practices that were, separately and in combination, lavish in the use of men, materials and money, to degrees that would be intolerable in civilian-product industries. Now, let us examine the main internal features and modes of operation of the military-industry firm.

Administrative costs are part of the necessary expense for operating any enterprise. In order to have production there must be decision-making. Someone must do the acceptable problem-solving, record-keeping and allied routines. In U.S. manufacturing industry as a whole by 1970, for every hundred production workers there were about thirty-six administrative, technical and clerical employees. In five military-serving industries (ordnance, aircraft, shipbuilding, communications equipment and electronics components) the average administrative overhead rate was 69.7 in 1970. The three highest management overhead rates were in ordnance (86), communications equipment (88) and aircraft (79).[10]

Obviously, administrative overhead ratios that are more than twice the average for manufacturing as a whole translate into heavy fixed costs in these enterprises. This is the result of more intensive managerial controls. Military-industry firms, for example, prepare more accounting reports in greater detail and with greater frequency than is usually acceptable in civilian firms. The cost constraints that limit the managements of nonmilitary product firms are simply not present here.

The records of American industry since the beginning of the twentieth century show steady growth in the cost of administration.[11] However, the top managers of the military-industry empire speeded and intensified the ordinary processes of extending the scope and intensity of internal controls. Here is how part of this process was seen by a physicist with long military-industry experience:

One point is the difference in *overhead rates* between defense and commercial-type business. Let me mention a few things that inevitably increase the cost of doing business with the government, and which in their totality can account for a very significant fraction, if not practically all of the overhead differences.

First, perhaps, are the ways in which competitive bidding is often carried out. I remember one case in which a $40,000 study contract generated 39 proposals from industry. The cost to each company of writing the proposal must have been between $2,000 and $10,000. All the companies were interested in getting it, as they felt that successful performance on this first contract would lead to more lucrative contracts later on, including the possibility of production of equipment. The successful bidder was a very large corporation, and one of the things that led to the award was the fact that the company would "cost share" so that the true cost of the work was perhaps $60,000 or $80,000. . . .

The cost of unsuccessful proposals has been fantastically high. It has led to the proliferation of wryly humorous signs seen in many offices, like "Proposals are our most important product," and so on. The government became concerned about this situation for several reasons. First, of course, the money must come from someplace; legal or not, a very substantial chunk of it was buried in increasing overhead. Make no mistake about it—in many cases this was necessary for mere survival. Secondly, government personnel charged with evaluating the rival proposals were simply swamped. Third, government people knew very well that fruitless proposal writing was a serious drain on scientific and technical manpower, which diminished the country's total capacity and weakened technical efforts on actual contracts. One of the expedients to ameliorate the situation was to make up bidder qualification lists for various areas; only companies on those lists would receive copies of the requests for proposals in time to be able to do anything about them. The result, of course, was that additional efforts had to be made to get on these lists, which meant additional marketing personnel to find out where, when and how one could get on them, expensive trips to talk to the technical people who decided who got on what list, and so on. While establishing these lists may have helped the government people, I suspect that it only added additional expense from industry's point of view. . . .

Much of defense work is classified, and this brings in the security system. This . . . is a very big and complex subject which would probably require a book for its adequate discussion. What I want to point out here is simply its high cost to industry. Inasmuch as such costs have no counterpart in commercial activity, they clearly must raise the cost of doing defense work. When I left government my DoD [Defense Department] clearance followed me in a matter of days to a few weeks. I also happened to need AEC clearance. This took nine months and had to be done twice because after the investigation was completed it was found that for one or two years during the war the investigation had been made by Army Intelligence instead of by the FBI, and AEC rules had been changed to require that everything be done by the FBI. So the whole business started all over again, doubling the time and expense and involving the FBI people going back to the same people they had talked to earlier and shamefacedly asking them the same questions. . . . I don't know what the costs are for DoD in general, but one can see what is involved with people making job changes, clearances having to be updated, the large number of people for whom clearances were required, the necessity for having security officers, staff, and records in every company doing defense work, the need, very often, for having new hires sit around for months before they can get to work on the jobs for which they were hired, the need for guards, safes, security check procedures, maintenance of classified libraries, and so on and so forth. I don't know what the total fraction of defense overhead ascribed to security is, but I think it must be a very large one.

Another factor in overhead is that the government generally insists (and with considerable justification, very often, one must admit) that the competent people whose biographies are included in proposals and who are thus "key men" actually be made available when the contract is awarded. Unfortunately, however, the government may take anywhere from three months to a year or more to make the award. Throughout this period one cannot tell whether the award will be made, one cannot have these people sitting around doing nothing during that time, particularly with the large numbers of unsuccessful proposals inherent in competitive bidding. Naturally they are doing something else when the contract comes in, so that one either is delayed in starting work on it or has to cripple something already going on. Obviously this is a source of "slippage" and inefficiency in defense industry and is inherently coupled to the way the government works. It is also the kind of thing that has led to "stockpiling" of technical people. . . .

Practices of this sort are unthinkable in most civilian firms, for the prices of most civilian products cannot absorb the costs of the administrative practices that have become normal in military-industry firms.

Giant-size administrative overheads in military industry seem to be an American specialty. The French designed and built the Mirage III with a total engineering staff of fifty design draftsmen. The Air Force's F-15 Program Office alone has a staff of over 240, just to monitor the people doing the work.[12]

Cost maximizing in administration was criticized on May 25, 1972, by Lieutenant General Otto J. Glasser, Deputy Chief of Staff for Research and Development of the U.S. Air Force. He said:

Let's look at another major difference between U.S. and European organizations. The European approach is characterized by very small, tightly integrated design teams manned by "top of their graduating class" engineers. Every man is an expert with considerable latitude for decision and very streamlined and abbreviated supervisory and management channels. Paperwork of all types is brief, concise, and limited in distribution. Contracts, directives and reports run to tens of pages rather than tens of volumes.

But what of the U.S. counterpart? We are literally suffocating from excess manning and excessive management—and I find it hard to

separate cause from effect. An additional management procedure requires additional people to carry it out. In turn, this expanded team
of managers comes up with proposed new economies and new
efficiencies which require more directives, more controls, more reports
and, in turn, more people—*ad nauseam*. I don't mean to discredit all
managers and all management, but when you have more monitors
than doers, the time has come to reverse the trend.

At this writing, there has been no reversal.

Research and product development are performed in the civilian-
oriented firm with the aim of designing products that are both
functionally *and* economically attractive. The latter is crucial in
civilian industry, for the most novel ideas have no interest for the
investor of capital if they cannot be translated into marketable
products. Therefore economic considerations weigh heavily in
civilian industrial research. Such constraints are virtually nonexis-
tent in the military realm. On a visit to a military post I found
some instrument materiel on display, smaller in size than a common soup can and clearly labeled "Low Cost Series—$10,500." At
that price the unit far exceeded its equivalent weight-in-gold
value. One of the consistent themes among product developers
inside military firms is "Who cares about the cost?" If the product
is more complex, it costs more and justifies a higher price; all this
is called "gold-plating" in the trade. In one major enterprise the
product-development staffs engaged in contests for designing the
most complex, Rube Goldberg types of devices. Why bother
putting brakes on such professional games as long as they can be
labeled "research," charged to "cost growth" and billed to the
Pentagon? Obviously, the military is penalized by receiving unreliable equipment—devices that are too complex, requiring hard-to-
find skilled maintenance talent and prone to malfunction. But that
is in the realm of unintended effects.

Engineers have been employed in military industry on a lavish
scale. Immense floor areas are devoted to engineers, often recruited in lots of hundreds and thousands even for single firms.
From ex-military engineers we learn about the deployment of
technical talent in ways that are unique to these industries. For
example, complexity in design of products is often pursued for its
own sake, as a sort of game, since, despite high costs, complexity
of product is often regarded as an indication of "competence." In
addition, work projects are often invented to fill in time when a

management wishes to stockpile engineers in the hope of receiving a future contract award for which their presence is required.

Division of labor into small details has become normal in military-industry firms. Engineers are apportioned minute parts of projects, making it difficult for the individual engineer to keep in view larger considerations of product function. How can any single person feel responsible for a larger outcome when his own part in it is miniscule on a technical level and when he has little or nothing to say about the larger design decisions?

Rapid turnover of engineers in military-industry firms has become normal, especially during periods of growth when military managements competed for the manpower needed to show "competence." Engineers and others job-hopped for fast promotions and pay increases. The inescapable result of employment instability is high cost of engineer recruiting and high costs entailed in breaking in new men into new organizations and tasks.

Wages to *production workers and labor costs* in military industry are generally higher than virtually all counterparts in civilian work. Especially for the more skilled blue-collar occupations, the growth of military industry became a bonanza of opportunities for wage increases and improvements in job grades. Labor's ease of bargaining was helped by the fact that the bill would of course be paid by the Department of Defense—a willing employer for whom "competence" of the military-industry firm was more important than holding cost down.

Veteran industrial engineers with diverse experience in military industry report that total work efficiency in these plants is low compared with the performance of civilian industry. When labor efficiency in major military-industry factories has been measured as the ratio of idle time to work time, or in terms of the work performed as against reasonable standards of work performable, the results show labor efficiencies of 50 percent or less. When the U.S. General Accounting Office did an audit of the operations of major Lockheed factories working on the C-5 airplane, they found that "about 8.6 percent of the production's assembly employees were idle" and that the whereabouts of a further 6.2 percent could not be determined from co-workers or supervisors.[13] Such inefficiency does not necessarily result from any concerted decision on the part of a work force, organized or not, to operate in this fashion. Rather, poor efficiency is the end result of a pervasive pattern of inefficient operation at all levels—managerial, technical and production.

Machinery used in military-industry work is ordinarily of two sorts. Much of the equipment is "general purpose." These are machines that perform similar functions to those required in many civilian-industry firms. Such equipment is standard, similar to that offered publicly by machinery-making firms. But military industry also requires much manufacturing equipment that is special in terms of such features as the materials, dimensions and precision required for the military product. Military-industry managers, with prodding from the Pentagon, not infrequently order equipment with "maximum capability" built in. This has resulted in the construction of machines with unique capabilities and high costs of operation to match, making them useless for most civilian operations.

A cutback in Pentagon orders led the management of a major military-industry firm to try to do subcontract work for commercial firms, making use of its large and varied stock of metalworking machinery. It soon discovered, however, that its costs and prices were far out of line with bids offered by experienced civilian-industry metalworking factories. I was informed that this inability to bid competitively was owing to a combination of factors. The military firm's machines were often more costly, hence requiring a larger fixed charge per hour. Its wage rates per hour were higher than those of civilian firms. Administrative overhead costs were higher. The result: it was hopelessly overpriced and could not penetrate a civilian market.

Production equipment and *factory structures* have been provided by the Pentagon to military contracting firms. This largesse has sometimes enabled such firms to make use of the Pentagon-provided equipment for civilian production operations at the same time. This has amounted to a virtual gift, at government expense, of manufacturing structures and machinery—while the full cost of this machinery was, of course, publicly borne.[14]

Raw materials with which products are fabricated are selected by military-industry firms in ways that are rather different from the methods used in civilian industry. The bias in military industry is toward materials capable of at least equaling and preferably exceeding the performance requirements expected of the military-industry buyer. Additional expense has been accepted and justified by both the firm and the Pentagon top management on grounds of giving improved "competence."

Capital, both fixed and working capital, is made available to military-industry firms in ways that are unthinkable for the civilian-industry enterprise. The Pentagon is empowered by law and its own regulations to supply not only buildings and equipment but also advance grants of funds, progress payments on work in process (but before delivery), and guarantees on loans that might be obtained by the military-industry firm from a private bank or similar institution. By these means the military-industry firm has access to quantities of capital under conditions that are not matched by a civilian-industry firm.

Consider the opportunity opened up for military-industry firms by the timing of progress payments from the Pentagon top management to its subordinate firms. Professor James W. Kuhn of Columbia University reports:

> During 1971, such progress payments averaged at any one time $8 or $9 billion. What the contractors designated as their current costs the government reimbursed promptly—every 11 days, on the average. But the firms themselves tended to hold on to the cash, delaying payment of their bills for up to 60 days. That same year, by holding the government's payments in their bank accounts before tardily paying their bills, defense contractors earned nearly half a billion dollars in interest from the banks. By not having to borrow short-term working capital from the banks in the first place, they saved about the same amount in interest charges as well. During production, then, defense contractors find the government simultaneously playing the roles of indulgent lender and eager customer for products undelivered.[15]

Ex-managers of military industry firms have confirmed this sort of practice. So military-industry managements are enabled to earn banking profits from the money which they hold before paying it out to suppliers and to others. Civilian firms are unable to obtain capital under conditions and on terms made possible for military-industry firms by virtue of government guarantees. That is one aspect of the famous Lockheed loan guarantee that was sponsored through the Congress by the President and the Pentagon top management during the summer of 1971. Such methods, of course, make military-industry firms failure-proof.

The ability of the Pentagon to do this does not rest on mere precedent and established usage. Under the terms of Public Law

85-804, as implemented through Executive Order 10789 issued under Eisenhower, the Department of Defense or any one of ten other federal executive departments is empowered to declare a firm "essential to the national defense." Once so designated, a firm can be given contracts or outright grants of money. From 1958 to 1973 the record shows 3,652 actions taken to rescue firms, involving $85.9 million. That, of course, does not include the largest grants and contract escalations of all to the Lockheed Corporation.[16]

The quality of *production management* in military industry and the *quality of its products* are for the most part a closed book, inaccessible to outsiders. Nevertheless, certain gross indicators and reported details on some major systems reflect performance in the military-industry sphere that would be unacceptable or would produce bankruptcy in civilian industry. In April 1972 the Joint Economic Committee of the Congress reported on a study of thirteen major aircraft and missile programs costing a total of $40 billion. Since 1955 "less than 40 percent produced systems of acceptable electronic performance . . . Two of the programs were cancelled after total program costs of $2 billion were paid . . . two programs costing $10 billion were phased out after three years for low reliability." The armed forces had spent a grand total of $4.1 billion on twenty-eight systems that had been abandoned before deployment, and $18.9 billion on fifteen more systems abandoned after they had been deployed, according to the Joint Economic Committee analysis.[17]

Industrial engineers have developed methods for comparing the cost-efficiency of factories with varied products. For each case the cost of a standardized unit of output is calculated. This refers to an average quantity of product judged to be producible by a worker who performs at an acceptable work pace. On page 44 are the results of such cost calculations for six military-serving firms, with the performance of a major civilian factory as a baseline. The original money data were changed to index numbers in order not to disclose the source.

This is what these numbers mean: Assume that a similar product is being made in several factories, say a television set costing $100 to make in the civilian industry. The same product would then cost $250, $478, and even $2,393 if produced in the series of firms whose costs per standardized unit of output are given here.

	Index	
Civilian industry	100	major metal-products firm (Midwest)
Military industry (sample of major firms)	250	armored-vehicle firm (*best performer*)
	478	missile firm
	590	missile firm
	644	missile firm
	1,184	electronics-avionics (typical)
	2,393 and up	electronics-avionics

This is a realistic and valid view of the results of cost-maximization in the military-industry universe.

The performance of the Lockheed Company, the largest military-industry firm, has been opened to partial public view, especially with respect to its work on the important C-5 airplane. These aircraft, originally designed to carry heavy equipment or large numbers of soldiers over intercontinental ranges, were supposed to cost about $29 million per plane and have wound up at prices of $62 million per plane and more. We are informed that

> C-5 suffers major technical breakdown once an hour during every hour of flight time. The unenviable pilot of the giant jet should anticipate, according to the General Accounting Office, that his landing gear alone will fail once every four hours. One of the planes already accepted by the Air Force and picked at random by the GAO auditors for inspection had 47 major and 149 minor deficiencies. Fourteen of the defects, the GAO reported to Congress, "impair the aircraft's capability to perform all or a portion of six missions" assigned to it.[18]

The Lockheed saga includes the experience of Henry Durham, a former production manager at Marietta, Georgia, who tried to bring to the attention of Lockheed top management what he discovered after being assigned as general manager for all production-control activities on the flight line. Durham has reported:

> "When planes arrive at the flight line of the assembly line they're supposed to be virtually complete except for a few engineering

changes and normal radar and electronic equipment installation, but I noticed these serious deficiencies. These weren't just minor deficiencies; these aircraft were missing thousands and thousands of parts when the Lockheed records showed the aircraft to be virtually complete.

"At first I thought it was an error in the papers. Then I initiated an audit. I found it was true. I was amazed. But I still thought there was some kind of mistake going on. Later I figured out what was happening was the company was consciously indicating through the inspection records that they had done the work so that they could receive credit payment from the Air Force when actually they weren't on schedule and hadn't done the work."

Durham also reported that, apart from the hazards to those flying such an aircraft, these practices accounted for much of the cost excess in the Lockheed record. Said Durham, "This resulted in exorbitant costs, overtime, reprocurement of parts that were lost, misplaced, never there in the first place or illegally removed."[19] The Durham story about production management and quality control at Lockheed also refers to the factory in Chattanooga, Tennessee. Durham reported that in the Chattanooga plant expensive tools and equipment were "rusting away in the backyard" while "procurement personnel consistently bought items at premium prices from outside suppliers even though the same item was stocked in the company's own warehouse in Marietta." He reported such matters to his superiors, only to discover that nothing was ever done about it.

Cost extravaganza in management, engineering and production have all been justified in the name of the need to "advance the state of the art," the "technical sophistication" and "extremely tight quality control" that supposedly characterize military-industry products. If this were so and if it was reflected in product performance to specifications, then a justification of unusually high cost could be publicly made and would probably be acceptable to all who support the military-political goals of the state-capitalist directorate. But the facts of the case go counter to such expectations. The largest military-industry operations, especially during the 1960s and 1970s, have been disaster-ridden, not only economically but also technically. The C-5A airplane program is a crucial demonstration of these results: the largest contract ever written, with the largest Pentagon supplier. Here are some highlights of the program that will cost more than $5 billion:

Initiated in 1965, the C-5 contract to the Lockheed Aircraft Company was supposed to deliver 120 aircraft to the U.S. Air Force, each with the capability of carrying a 265,000-pound payload over intercontinental ranges. The military would be able to speedily deploy armed forces, including heavy materiel, around the world. Furthermore, this contract was a showpiece of the McNamara "effectiveness" program. Under the "total package procurement" concept Lockheed was put in full charge of the project from the earliest design to the completion and maintenance support of the complex aircraft. The Lockheed performance, continuously monitored by the state management, includes the following.

Item: Major subcontracts were let by the Lockheed Company for parts of the aircraft before detailed wind-tunnel tests had been performed. Following such tests, major changes were required and subcontractors had to junk considerable work and start building to fresh design.

Item: Lockheed did not proceed by building a test model and then correcting deficiencies found through operation of such a model; rather, Lockheed went into production before full-scale testing was performed.

Item: After a jet engine had fallen off one of the C-5A planes during preparation for takeoff, a detailed examination of the engine pylon showed dangerous cracks owing to "improper fabrication" of these units by a subcontractor, the Rohr Corporation of California.

Item: The C-5A has the most intricate aircraft landing gear, designed to "kneel" the forward part of the plane so that heavy equipment could be driven aboard without the need of a separate ramp. Defects in the kneeling system have caused significant damage to the plane.

Item: Because of low reliability for its bad-weather flying instrumentation, the C-5A has been prohibited from operating with less than a mile visibility and a 1,000-foot ceiling.

Item: The Air Force banned the use of the automatic-pilot system until its problems were resolved. These mechanisms are designed to permit the plane to stay close to the ground on low-level missions.

Item: The Air Force has had to accommodate to the threat of structural failure by limiting the payload of the aircraft well below original requirement.

Item: Takeoff and landing procedures were modified to restrict stress on major aircraft parts.

Item: In April 1968, *Air Force Magazine* stated that the C-5A "can land and take off up to 130 times on primitive support air fields, with or without matting, before the strip has to be repaired. Actually the strip needs to be no firmer than the average lawn." Flight tests on unimproved runways have caused damage to jet engines, to the runways and to the aircraft. The C-5A has been restricted to hardened runways.[20]

Item: The designed service life of the C-5A is thirty thousand hours. The actual-use life will achieve this only with modifications to improve the fatigue life of the wing.

Item: The aircraft has been incapable of making radar landing approaches without ground aids. This restricts one of the originally desired features of the plane.

Item: The specifications for the C-5A included 75 percent operational readiness of the fleet as a whole. In 1972 the experienced readiness was 41 percent "because of unreliable aircraft components, and inadequate training and quantities of maintenance personnel."

Item: All C-5A aircraft have been delivered and accepted with a significant number of deficiencies. For example, between February and September 1971 delivered aircraft averaged 251 deficiencies per plane. By July 1972 this was down to 126 deficiencies.

Item: From 1965 to 1971 the cost per plane in the C-5 program rose from $28 million to $60 million. This may be contrasted with Boeing's 747 aircraft, once offered as a competitor to the C-5A and now widely used on the world's airways. It has similar dimensions to the C-5A and costs about $23 million per plane.

Item: The Air Force will have to spend $259 million beyond the purchase prices of the C-5A to repair defects in components—all this apart from the cost of wing rebuilding to extend the useful life of the plane, hopefully to original specifications.

Item: Said a Pentagon official, "We probably won't use the

airplane as much as we intended. After all, some football coaches
are used to saving their best players until they really need them."[21]

Obviously, in a civilian-market situation the result of such many-
sided incompetence would likely be the early bankruptcy of the
enterprises in question. What needs underscoring here is that the
incompetence that is revealed in the C-5A record has become an
institutional characteristic, built into the modes of job performance
of the employees of the firm.

From the vantage point of operating civilian-serving industry,
these accounts read like an industrial-management nightmare.
They could be used as case material on malpractice in courses on
industrial management, provided that the students are repeatedly
reminded that these materials come out of a military economy that
has operated as state capitalism and that these practices are
inappropriate in cost-minimizing industry.

While the C-5 case has received extensive treatment in the press,
comparable practices turn up in other major military programs. On
January 25, 1973, Senator Proxmire reported on the F-14, a new
swing-wing fighter plane being produced for the Navy by the
Grumman Corporation: "We already know that two of the first ten
prototypes have crashed, the second for reasons that are still unex-
plained. And an earlier series of F-14 tests conducted in late 1971
uncovered 43 major deficiencies and 75 other deficiencies listed as
minor." The Senator made these comments in connection with the
discovery by the Navy that the testing program of the F-14 had
been put into low gear. The Senator suggested that the contractors
might be "conducting a highly restricted test program designed to
cover up remaining problems." All this paralleled aggressive moves
by the management of the Grumman Corporation to obtain major
new Pentagon funding to cover very large cost increases on the F-
14 project.

Litton Industries came to public attention toward the end of the
McNamara administration of the Department of Defense when it
was awarded a major contract for producing a series of Navy
vessels in what was supposed to be a shipyard of the future.
Aerospace technology and management methods were to be applied to the production of naval vessels—the implication being
that naval shipbuilding would vastly benefit from the application
of methods that had been applied in the aerospace industries.

By late 1971–72, it was apparent that a major production disaster and a cost-maximization process was unfolding in the Litton Industries shipyards in Pascagoula, Mississippi.[22] Senator Proxmire's subcommittee of the Joint Economic Committee called attention to the audit report on the Litton operations by a team from the Naval Ships Systems Command and the United States Maritime Administration. The Senator indicated that the reports pinpointed poor workmanship, uncorrected defects, ineffective quality control, inadequate manpower, cumbersome methods of authorizing and keeping track of work, lack of adequate fire and storm protection, and low productivity.[23] After packing the new shipyards with many former aerospace executives, Litton top management decided that a primary requirement for turning out vessels that might be finally acceptable to the Navy was to replace these people.

From 1963 to 1972 the U.S. Army managed an almost nightmarish set of operations, purportedly in an effort to build a new supertank. Investigators of the House Appropriations Committee discovered that the Army had failed to build "a single operational tank in the program even though the program was started in 1963, as an ill-conceived American-German development with a schedule providing for the production of an operational tank by December, 1969." At the time of that report, 1972, it was indicated that there would be no result of the sort initially expected, at least until 1976. Apparently the required engine had been poorly conceived. The armament for the tank had been inadequately designed, developed and tested before being put into production for a series of tanks. Two hundred and forty-three tank turrets were produced, finally to be left in Army arsenals, unusable because allied equipment had yet to be prepared. Design changes were piled one upon another, and all the while the price of this supertank skyrocketed. The unit price of the M-60A1 tank during 1971 was $218,000; by 1972 it had leaped to $333,000; and for 1973 the price was estimated at $422,000 per tank. The end is probably not in sight.[24]

In an atmosphere that is characterized by the expectation of indefinitely large funds becoming available for military projects— good, bad or indifferent—it is no surprise that from time to time we learn about manipulations of accounting records in an effort to increase the net take to military-industry firms. A remarkable report on the effort to profit not by producing anything but by manipulating the books was published in the *Washington Post* on January 2, 1973, concerning the behavior of Roy Ash while he was a principal officer of the Hughes Aircraft Company. The *Washington Post* story details testimony from several court proceedings concerning "Ash's orders to over-credit inventory accounts, that is, to credit larger withdrawals of materials than actually had occurred. [James O.] White testified that the purpose was to enhance the appearance of authenticity of false affidavits supporting applications to the Air Force for payments for work completed." These practices and others were reviewed in a government audit of the firm, following which the Hughes Aircraft Company repaid the Air Force $43,400,000.[25] Former employees of aerospace-industry firms advise that "simulation" in accounting to the Pentagon is a recurring feature of management practice.

The conditions of *marketing* for the military-industry firm are worlds apart from those of civilian industry. First, the size of the market is defined by the one legally permitted buyer. The Pentagon buyer does rather more than just purchase the goods. This buyer also performs the functions of top management to the Pentagon-serving firms.[26] Furthermore, the strategies for selling in this market are rather different from those in civilian industry—a combination of diplomacy, politics, negotiation concerning "competence," and political pressures ranging from the intervention of trade unions and chambers of commerce to members of Congress playing a part in negotiations and assuring continuity of military-contract assignments to particular firms.

During the 1960s the Department of Defense gave up the general policy of producing test models of new weapons and working them through on a pilot-program basis before ordering large production runs. Instead, crash efforts were made to duplicate, compress and overlap research, development and manufacturing stages. The results included high costs that would not be endurable in virtually any other manufacturing endeavor. Until the 1960s the performance record in major military-industry projects included final prices that averaged 3.2 times initial estimates.[27] The data are not all in for the McNamara and subsequent periods. However, major programs in this era include the F-111, the C-5, the Main Battle Tank and the F-14, all of them characterized by large excesses of costs beyond initial estimates.

Cost-maximization as a central feature of the U.S. military economy stems from the patterned ways of behavior that we have just summarized. There is evidence of the generality of cost-maximizing processes. "As of June 1971, cost overruns on some 45 major weapons systems amounted to $35.2 billion—compared to $28.2 billion on the same systems a year earlier," according to an announcement by Senator Proxmire of the Joint Economic Committee.[28]

Two points need emphasis here. First, the very term "cost overrun" implies an exceptional condition. The fact is, however, that escalating levels of cost have resulted from the normal, approved, built-in operating characteristics of the military-industry enterprise system. Second, it is worth noting how much equivalent wealth is involved here. The $35 billions of cost excess by June 1971 was *not* the total cost of these weapons systems. It was the additional cost beyond the amount originally contracted for. Let us recall that $35 billion is a sum that exceeds by far the annual gross national product of most nations in the world.[29]

Military-industrial firms lack flexibility for conversion to civilian work. Habituation to cost-maximizing work habits has given the Pentagon-serving organizations a trained incapacity for operating in civilian economy. Repeatedly during the 1960s I was advised by senior officials of the Pentagon that there was "no problem" about the convertibility of military industry. As Robert McNamara once put it to me, the managements of the military-producing firms would be able to cope with this problem whenever it arose. They did cope—not by converting their organizations to commercial work but by dismissing their employees immediately upon notification of contract reduction or termination. One result has been the creation of concentrations of unemployment in certain military-industry areas without precedent since the Great Depression.*

From 1961 to 1970 I conducted a seminar on problems of conversion of industry from military to civilian economy at Columbia University. We sought out managers, engineers and others from military industry to tell us about various efforts by their firms to

* U.S. Department of Labor, *Area Trends in Employment and Unemployment*, October 1971, pp. 29–32. Here are a few of the cities that showed more than 10 percent unemployment rates in August 1971: Bridgeport, Conn., 10.5; New Britain, Conn., 13.6; Waterbury, Conn., 11.3; Gary-Hammond, Ind., 10.4; Lowell, Mass., 13.3; Muskegon, Mich., 12.3; Seattle, Wash., 13.9; Tacoma, Wash., 11.6.

enter civilian fields. The typical story was failure, traceable to one
or another style of operating that was just fine in the military economy but economically lethal in the civilian arena. The factors
involved ranged from product design to marketing methods. All
this is part of the larger issue of convertibility of military economy,
which I will discuss further in Chapter Nine.

The military-industrial firm is not autonomous. The ordinary
industrial firm is controlled by its management within limits prescribed by formal law and informal custom. The test of autonomy
is that a management makes final decision concerning the following agenda of matters: (1) obtaining capital for production, (2)
the product to be produced, (3) the quantity of output, (4) how
production should take place, (5) the price of the product, and
(6) distribution of the product. For the military-industrial firm,
final decision-making in each one of these spheres is retained by
the top management located in the Department of Defense. These
policy regulations set limits within which the military-industrial
firm management may operate. The pattern of relationship here is
comparable to the one that obtains between the central office and
the division management of a "decentralized" industrial firm. In
that scheme of things the central office decides on general policy
and the subordinate division managers decide how to implement
general policy in detail. Also, the central office polices the subordinate management for compliance with central policy. The
consequence of these patterns of decision-making and control is to
make the ordinary division management subordinate to the central
office even though the division management has a full complement
of managerial personnel and occupational titles that suggest all the
usual management functions.

No military-industry management may decide, on its own, on
weapons to be produced and on the quantity. Neither can such a
management decide autonomously on the price of the product or
on the selection of the customer. Where military materiel is sold to
customers other than the Department of Defense, this ordinarily
requires detailed approvals.

*The military-industrial firm is controlled by a state manage-
ment.* "State management" is a name I have given to the set of
organizations established in the Department of Defense under
Robert McNamara for the purpose of centralizing the management
of military industry. I gave considerable detail on this institution

in my book *Pentagon Capitalism*. Anyone interested in industrial organization will find *The Armed Services Procurement Regulations* fascinating reading. These are not, as the name seems to imply, a set of purchasing regulations. Rather, they are rules formulated by the state management for the guidance of the central-office staff itself and the guidance of division management.

Formal rules, elaborately indexed, are required to coordinate what is surely the largest industrial central office in the United States—probably in the entire world. With about 55,000 persons engaged in the work of allocating contracts and policing compliance in Washington and in regional and local offices, published regulations and detailed interpretive materials are essential. The extent of the control apparatus is indicated by the fact that in one important military-industry firm a staff of 210 Pentagon employees is in permanent residence, in addition to a group of ten military officers representing the armed-service branch primarily served by the firm in question.

There is no officially designated body in the Pentagon tables of organization that is termed "state management." This is, however, a functional designation for a set of organizations whose chiefs are the Assistant and Deputy Secretaries of Defense. These men, taken together, comprise a board of directors of the government-directed firm with about twenty thousand industrial divisions whose "president" is, functionally, the Secretary of Defense and whose "chairman of the Board" is, functionally, the President of the United States.

The prime relationship between the state management and the military-industry firm is control rather than ownership. While the state management has often made available land, buildings and machinery for the use of the subfirms, the main relationship of the state management to the managements of the subdivisions is that of control, while the formal ownership of most assets in the military-industry subfirms are nominally private in form.

The relationship between the large military-industry firm and the state management in the Pentagon has given rise to an important issue: *Who is the final decision-maker?* Who has the decisive control—the state management or the nominally private firms that are the chief military contractors? The issue is of special interest because of the fact that included among the hundred largest military-serving firms are the top industrial firms of the civilian economy as well. I wish to underscore the form of the question that I just formulated. I am not asking, Do the military-industry-firm managers attempt to influence the government? They certainly do. I am not asking, Are the managers of these firms able to affect government policy? There is a considerable weight of evidence that supports the view that they do. These firms know how to use money in political campaigns, to influence the votes of their employees in elections and to use their considerable skills as lobbyists in relation to public bodies. I view the managements of the top military-industry firms as important economic and political power-wielders in American economy and society. That, however, is not the question. Rather, the issue here is: As between the management of these major firms and the new government-based management with its unprecedented supplies of capital and decision-power, who controls, who is the final decision-maker?

Decisions on the total sum of public money to be devoted to military purposes are made by the state management through the Bureau of the Budget, finally confirmed by the Congress. Decisions on the allocation of military-industry work are made by the state management in the presence of considerable competitive pressures from the various military-industry managers.

While ideas and recommendations for military-industry technologies come from many sources, the decisions on which ones to concentrate on and to implement industrially are made by the state management's staffs. Similarly, the decision on termination of military-industrial programs is not made by any particular military-industry management but by the state management. The managerial details on which the state management can and does rule extend even to decisions on wage levels and acceptable industrial-relations patterns.[30]

While the state management is the final decision-maker, there exists a continuing symbiotic relationship between the military-industry firms and the state management in the Pentagon. They need and support each other. A collateral issue is the usefulness (or the indispensability) of military industry as a whole to the operation of the rest of capitalism. These are issues that I will deal with directly in the latter part of this book. At this point my purpose is to establish the existence of a network of firms whose operating characteristics are manifestly different in crucial ways from the operating characteristics of the cost-minimizing, profit-maximizing private firms of civilian industry.

Cost-maximizing requires a complementary process for paying the bill. That process is embedded in the central administrative office of the military-economy enterprise system. As noted earlier, the military-industrial firm is most accurately defined as a subsidy-maximizing rather than a profit-maximizing entity. In the ordinary business firm, "profit" is considered to be a reward for risk-taking. No one has even attempted to define what "risk" might be entailed for the Pentagon-serving subdivisions, other than the chance that a contract might be canceled or not repeated. But that is a different quality of chance-taking than the sort that is usually referred to as business risk. Nevertheless, the military-industry firms continue the formality of calculating profit-and-loss statements that show the customary residual line as "profit."

Net gain for the military firm thus appears not only in the form of the conventional "profit" line of the profit-and-loss statement. It also takes the form of new laboratories, new staffs, new production equipment, new land and new buildings acquired. Thus in the mature "subsidy-maximizing" firm, the management strives to maintain and deepen dependence on the government agency involved through pleas of serviceability to national defense, limitation of unemployment, and kindred well-appreciated social goals.

The concept of the subsidy-maximizing policy of the state management was set forth in a dramatic exchange between Senator William A. Proxmire and Secretary of the Treasury John B. Connally on June 8, 1971, as the Senate Banking Committee was considering the special legislation to guarantee a $250-million loan to the Lockheed Corporation.

> SENATOR PROXMIRE: . . . I would remind you in a subsidy program it is different, there is a *quid pro quo.* You make a payment to a railroad and in return they build trackage; you make a payment to an airline and they provide a certain amount of service for it.
>
> In welfare, of course, you make a payment and there is no return. In this case we have a guarantee and there is no requirement on the part of Lockheed to perform under that guarantee. A guarantee of $250 million and no benefit, no *quid pro quo.*
>
> SECRETARY CONNALLY: What do you mean, no benefit?
>
> SENATOR PROXMIRE: Well, they don't have to perform.

SECRETARY CONNALLY: What do we care whether they perform? We
are guaranteeing them basically a $250 million loan. What for?
Basically so they can hopefully minimize their losses, so they can
provide employment for 31,000 people throughout the country at a
time when we desperately need that type of employment. That is
basically the rationale and justification.[31]

The officers of a major military-industrial firm have given me
some details on how the "Department of Defense decides on the
money to be allowed to keep the firm going." The amount of
"profit" to be set aside is determined by arbitrary Department of
Defense decisions. These decisions are even affected by such
political calculations as an appropriate response to pressure from
members of Congress. In 1970, for example, the state management
controller for the firm in question decided to increase the formal
profit rate. He ordered the firm to limit expenditures on various
new facilities, thus enlarging the profit residue. Profits were regulated on another occasion by orders from the Pentagon to purchase
government-owned facilities which had previously been simply
made available to the firm on loan.

Such acts occur within a framework of ongoing decisions to
pump enough money into the major military-industrial firms to
keep them afloat, responding to the financial consequences of the
continuing cost-maximizing operation. One of the key "bailing out"
methods is known within military-industrial circles as the "golden
handshake," a private Pentagon commitment to subsidize the
financial losses generated by cost-maximizing.

The subsidy-maximizing side of the war economy serves a joint
purpose for the Pentagon's top managers. First, it enables them to
fulfill the professional-occupational-managerial imperative to enlarge their decision power. This is achieved by widening the scope
or the intensity of their decision-making, or both: hence more
people being controlled; more aspects of their work or lives being
regulated; control in greater detail; being checked with greater
frequency. A second goal attained through subsidy-maximizing is
fulfillment of the ideologically prescribed actions for sustaining
and improving the nation's industry and economy through war
spending. Thereby the chief operators of the subsidy-maximizing
system see themselves as national benefactors.

The state management has been highly innovative in its role as a
subsidy-maximizing agent. By the end of 1972 a new technique

was invented. The Navy purchased 17,414 shares of preferred stock in a relatively small firm, the Gap Instrument Corporation on Long Island. A Navy spokesman explained that this procedure was preferred by the Navy Contract Adjustment Board as against a loan which "would have been . . . saddling the guy. No one would invest with the company because there stands an albatross." Instead the Navy arranged to purchase the stock at par value at $1,741,000. The Admiral added that if the plan worked, the Navy might try it with other companies that were facing bankruptcy.[32]

In the presence of firms that maximize cost and maximize subsidies from a government-based top management, one of the principal efficiency-producing features of the private business firm is effectively terminated—namely, *the self-correcting mechanisms of the cost-minimizing firm.*

A civilian firm of proven incompetence is compelled to correct its position by changes in management and methods or face the penalty of bankruptcy. The military-industry firms, especially the larger ones, are shielded from these prospects.

A civilian firm with an unsalable product is required to either make the product salable or bear a financial penalty. The cost-maximizing firm has only to please the subsidy-maximizing top management.

When a civilian-product firm produces something that is technically unworkable, it faces the prospect of loss of market position to more competent firms. In the case of military-industry, the defective product may be reworked at the state management's expense or simply accepted, as has happened many times over despite crucial functional defects.

A civilian management that operates at too high a cost generates a penalty effect for the financial and other positions of the firm. Pressures on malfunctioning managers come from stockholders and, impersonally, from loss of market position owing to price noncompetitiveness. Military-industry firms operate in an environment in which the idea of an unduly large cost or price is undefined.

In the civilian cost-minimizing firm, engineers who produce designs that are economically extravagant, technically unwieldy, or uneconomic in terms of the raw materials that are specified are ordinarily subjected to corrective, if not penalty, action by the managements involved. This is not the case in military-industry firms, as I have learned from many hours of detailed interviewing on the professional experience of engineers in military industry.

Production methods that induce high costs or defective products are ordinarily viewed as unacceptable and as obvious targets for corrective procedures in civilian industry. Major military firms seem to operate with methods of this sort on a sustained basis.

Historically, the managers of civilian industry strive to minimize production costs by giving special attention to efficient utilization of capital and of the labor force. Where inefficiency of a gross sort is found, it is ordinarily the signal for replacement or retraining or revision of work standards. In military-industry firms, by contrast, experienced industrial engineers have found repeatedy that inefficient utilization of industrial equipment and worker man-hours are sustained as a normal feature of operation.

Buying or using machinery that is more elaborate than is needed for the work to be done is inappropriate in civilian industry, for that would impose a cost penalty on the product to be manufactured. Such practices are a signal for corrective action through review of company policies and evaluations of production-engineering personnel. In the land of military industry, cost excesses can be assigned to "cost growth."

None of this is to say that military-industry firms do not include some that practice cost-minimization. Many smaller firms that do part of their work for the military persist in workmanlike economizing. But there is little doubt about the main operating features of the military economy and its Pentagon directorate. These unique features have conferred special characteristics on the American economy as a whole.

Three

HOW THE MILITARY
ECONOMY WORKS:
THE SYSTEM

STATE CAPITALISM is a business economy whose top directorate is located in government. The state-capitalist part dominates the entire economy even though private business may still operate within it.* With respect to decision-making on production, the enterprises and the top management of state capitalism retain the essential characteristics of private-business capitalism. These features include separation of decision-making from producing; income linked to decision-making role; organization of decision-making on a hierarchical basis; a professional-occupational imperative among the decision-makers to extend their decision power individually and in competition with other management groups. These features continue under state capitalism even as the forms of control are different from private-business capitalism.[1]

In the classic business economy, the chiefs of the larger indus-

---

* Various writers refer to "mixed economy" as one that is only partly state capitalist, by various criteria—like percent of GNP coming from the "public sector." Rather than using taxonomic categories of "private" and "public sector" to differentiate economies, I prefer to focus on functional features of which mode of decision-making on production is central.

trial and financial units usually had substantial political influence. In state capitalism the chiefs of the economy are also the political chiefs of government. Hence, state capitalism joins peak political and economic decision power. This is visible in the mainly civilian-oriented state capitalism of Western Europe and Japan. In the United States and in the U.S.S.R., with their permanent war economies, military power is added to this concentration.

At the enterprise level, state capitalism involves substantial changes for the management of individual firms. Typically, the management of an enterprise cannot be autonomous as under private capitalism, where a business may be small but still independent, controlled by its managers or manager-owners. Owing to the location of the chiefs of state capitalism in government, political considerations are introduced into the relationships among local-enterprise managers. In dealing with higher authority they do not confront senior managers, as in private capitalism, but top managers who also wield political power.

Since the top management of state capitalism spans the whole economy in its sphere of control, its enterprise planning takes the effective form of national planning, even affecting enterprises that may be privately owned and controlled. At once this opens up opportunities for stability for the individual state-capitalist enterprise insofar as it is relieved of at least a part of the uncertainties stemming from dependence on unpredictable market behaviors. Thus a state-capitalist top management can, if it so wishes, guarantee the market for its subordinate firms. This is notably the case under the military form of state capitalism, where the government is the only legal purchaser of the product.

However, instability (as in unresolved class and race antagonisms, prices, production levels and relative value of national currency) remains a feature of state capitalism. The sustained competition for extension of managerial control among the submanagers, competition among the state managers of nations with state-capitalist economies, and the effects of the parasitic qualities of military economy all contribute to instability.

Under both private and state capitalism, access to capital is a crucial consideration. The state-capitalist enterprise manager (civilian-oriented) must compete for his share of capital by political-economic methods. The position is changed for the state-capitalist enterprise manager in military economy. He is assured of priority in capital allocation, since the military economy is given first place in the attention of government decision-makers.

In place of the self-correcting mechanisms of private capitalism, state-capitalist economy, especially in its military form, is more typically regulated by a system of subsidies. Such payments from government appear under private capitalism when government moves in to regulate parts of the economy. But subsidy systems flourish to their fullest under state capitalism, where the chiefs of the economy use their political decision power to enforce their economic priorities. Subsidies appear in civilian-oriented state capitalism, but they take on special characteristics where military economy is the priority state activity. In the latter case the subsidy is rendered on behalf of economically parasitic activity, thereby yielding no economic return to the society for the subsidy grant.

In the Marxist school of economics in particular, attention has been focused on inequality of income under capitalism, associated with occupational (class) position. From this standpoint, military economy introduces a new factor: relatively higher pay, job for job, in the military economy encourages loyalty to that system, thus blurring class and other interest-group conflicts. Thereby, state capitalism, in its military form, cuts through conflict of class versus class and introduces income inequality based upon type of industry and even geographical location, rather than upon occupation. Classic conditions of exploitation are thus revised in accordance with the military priorities of the state-capitalist rulers.

The military economy is more than a collection of enterprises and assorted research organizations that maximize costs and subsidies. On a macroeconomic or system level it is the core of a specifically American form of state capitalism.

The idea of the military economy as an economic subsystem within the larger economy is no theoretical abstraction, for that economy has been made into a deliberately managed industrial system. In *Pentagon Capitalism* (1970) I showed that there is a formal managerial organization, with detailed procedures for decision-making and for controlling the military-industrial and allied system. Further evidence on the system level of economic planning by the Pentagon comes from studies of the pattern of contract allocations, their location and their timing. For more than a decade military contracts have been awarded among major firms so that levels of activity could be sustained. As the work on one project was phasing out, a fresh contract was allocated to start a phasing-in process.[2] No pattern of this sort could endure over an extended period simply by chance or as the outcome of free-wheeling competition for the new money grants. The whole mode of operation has the characteristics of a production control system, unusual only for the large scale of operations.

As an entity the military economy has unique characteristics which affect the surrounding economy and society. A set of key characteristics is summarized here, without pretending completeness, in order to portray the range of consequences from the system as a whole. These are in four parts: first, aspects of the parasitic quality of military economy and its extension-of-control dynamic; second, the expansionist propensity of the managers of military economy; third, major impact on the civilian economy; fourth, the dominance of the military over the civilian economy in America's state capitalism.

The Parasitic Nature of Military Economy

The gross national product is composed of productive and parasitic growth. As usually measured and presented, GNP includes all of the money-valued output of goods and services—without differentiation in terms of major functional effect. To appreciate the nature and effects of a permanent war economy, a functional differentiation is essential. Productive growth means goods and services that either are part of the level of living or can be used for further production of whatever kind. Hence, they are by these tests *economically* useful.* Parasitic growth includes goods and services that are not economically useful either for the level of living or for further production.

Military goods and services are economically parasitic. This differentiation is fundamental. When it is applied it is possible to perceive and diagnose a series of consequences that flow from military economy. In the absence of the differentiation between productive and parasitic growth, the activity of military economy

---

* There are, of course, other kinds of usefulness: political, esthetic, military, religious. Here we are interested primarily in economic usefulness. Thus, the absence of economic usefulness does not preclude other effects.

appears as simply an extension or a part of the ordinary civilian economy. All money income, regardless of source, is then treated as contribution to wealth.

For most Americans, effects attributable to parasitic economic growth are not apparent. Such differentiations are virtually non-existent in textbooks of economics. Accordingly, the generations of Americans who have been instructed via the usual economics texts and courses are not equipped to see a part of the economy as parasitic. Instead, their appreciation of economy is dominated by theories about competitive market relations, the allocation of in-comes, and the role of government as a regulator of economy.

In a permanent war economy whole industries and regions that specialize in military economy are placed in a parasitic economic relationship to the civilian economy, from which they take their sustenance and to which they contribute (economically) little or nothing. This results in the operation of a system of "internal imperialism" among the states of the Union. This phenomenon shows up in the relation of federal tax payments by the individuals and businesses of a particular state to federal expenditures in particular states.

For example, in New York State from 1965 to 1967, $7.458 bil-lion was paid out in taxes to the federal government in excess of the federal expenditures in New York State. Similar relationships, though in lesser amounts, showed up for New Jersey, Pennsyl-vania, Illinois and Michigan. On the other hand, certain states enjoyed large net gains. During the same period, California re-ceived more than $2 billion yearly in expenditures from the federal government in excess of the total tax payments made from that state. Texas received $1 billion annually in excess of taxes paid out, and Virginia received $1.3 billion each year more than its tax payments.[3] Similar exploitative relations contribute to the indus-trial and general community deterioration in, for example, older New England and Midwestern civilian-industry areas as against the locales of military-industry concentration with their abundant evidence of good living and flashy "high-technology" work places.

The economic significance of parasitic economic growth is often rendered obscure by the apparently small magnitude of some of the spending involved. Money spent on military research and development reflects economically parasitic activity, but research and development costs are rarely a major item of expense in manufacturing industry. On the average, U.S. manufacturing firms spend about 3 or 4 percent of their net sales dollars for these purposes. In the nation's gross national product about one and a half percent has been spent on military research. But the significance of this activity cannot be measured by its proportionately small cost. Thus, when research and development is not properly done on behalf of civilian industry, results like poor product design or poor production methods can have disastrous effects on the economic position of the industry. When as little as one and a half percent of U.S. national product is diverted to military research it seems little enough, but that accounts for more than half of the national research and development effort and has left many U.S. civilian-products industries at a competitive disadvantage due to faltering product designs and insufficient improvement in industrial-production efficiency.

The Propensity to Expand

A second basic feature of state capitalism is the relentless thrust for enlargement of decision power that is normal to management. Under state capitalism this conventional occupational imperative is given unprecedented capability in terms of the resources that can be applied to these goals. In turn, the state managers have enlarged their goals in keeping with their ability to draw larger resources from the national income for their purposes. By 1965 the state management of the Pentagon actually advertised for advice on how to "maintain world hegemony."

The Army Research Office announced a public request for bids for a wide-ranging study on methods of achieving a Pax Americana. Here is the exact announcement as it appeared in the U.S. Department of Commerce *Daily Bulletin* asking for bids for government work:

Service and materials to perform a RESEARCH STUDY ENTITLED "PAX AMERICANA" consisting of a phased study of the following: (a) elements of National Power; (b) ability of selected nations to apply the elements of National Power; (c) a variety of world power configurations to be used as a basis for the U.S. to maintain world hegemony in the future. Quotations and applicable specifications will be available upon request at the Army Research Office, 3845 Columbia Pike, Arlington, Va., until 1 May 1965.[4]

With goals of such dimensions, we may begin to understand why there has been a sustained growth of the budgets of the Department of Defense throughout the 1960s and even the further planned growth from 1973 through 1980.

The military-industry system operates under the assumption that indefinitely large capital funds are available for the military and related plans of the state management. In this understanding the state management is strongly supported by key members of Congress, as, for example, by Congressman F. Edward Hébert. (Democrat, Louisiana), chairman of the House Armed Services Committee. Said Congressman Hébert in 1972, "I intend to build the strongest military we can get. Money's no question."[5]

As the military economy endured, its enterprises looked like reasonable investment opportunities. With the enlargement of assets, private and government-provided, these, in turn, became part of the scope of decision-making to be conserved by the Pentagon's top managers.*

In 1964, Senator George McGovern and thirty other members of the Senate, paralleled by similar efforts in the House, offered legislation for setting up a National Economic Conversion Commission. The bills were killed by decisive pressure from the White House and senior officers of the Pentagon.[6] Thereby, these men saw to it that there was no ordered capability in the United States for moving from a military economy to a civilian economy. Job dependence on the Pentagon was maintained. The Council of Economic Advisers in 1969 defined an agenda of productive economic replacements for military spending (which I will discuss in Chapter Eight). Its work was ignored and never followed up. The military-industry firms and the state management that directs them have avoided or opposed steps to prepare for a peace economy, apparently on the assumption that to do that would remove a major justification for the continued high level of military budgets.

---

* At the same time the employees and communities involved in the military economy became, for obvious self-interest, protagonists of the larger policies that sustained a permanent war economy. When Ernest Fitzgerald appeared at the gate of an aerospace firm in California for a meeting on the war in Vietnam, supporters of the war policy distributed lapel stickers with the motto "Don't Knock the War that Feeds You."

The Impact on Civilian Economy

The economic consequences of a permanent war economy for the host society are a compound of civilian goods and services forgone and major damage inflicted on the economically productive economy. The full cost to a society of parasitic economic growth exceeds the money value of the materials, man-hours and machinery used up for military products. Equivalent inputs turned to economically productive uses yield their direct output many times over. Beyond that, the outputs include improvements in the quality of labor and capital.

The operation of a permanent war economy entails a large cost for American society, measured in terms of what has been forgone in order to build and operate an immense military system. From 1946 to 1975 the combined budgets of the Department of Defense were more than $1,500 billion. This exceeds the value of all commercial and residential structures in the United States.[7] Thus by putting this much effort into the military system what was forgone was an opportunity to reconstruct physically whatever has gone into disrepair in America's towns and cities. Here is another view of opportunity forgone: I once estimated that $22 billion a year would spur economic development—worldwide; about a third of America's military economy bill for 1946–75 would have funded such a worldwide effort for twenty years.[8]

Calculating the cost of the Vietnam War to the U.S. economy will doubtless engage the attention of economists and others for many years. For a start, Tom Riddell estimates the cost at $676 billion, including not only the direct military outlays but also the military assistance to client governments, interest on national debt and payments for veterans which will endure for a long time.[9]

How have the U.S. military outlays actually affected other kinds of spending within the American economy? After all, the same dollar can't be spent on different things at the same time. What exactly have we not purchased by buying a permanent war economy?

Professor Bruce Russett at Yale has researched this problem by means of statistical analyses of the main parts of the U.S. national-income accounts. These data, appropriately diagnosed, can answer the question: For each dollar spent on the military, what did we buy less of? Russett has shown that, on the average, over the period 1939–68 each U.S. dollar spent for military purposes was associated with $.163 less expenditure for durable consumer goods, $.110 less for producers' durable goods, and $.114 less for homes—among other decreases.[10] "Guns" take away from "butter" even in the United States, with a gross national product valued annually at over $1,000 billion.

Actual U.S. investments in machinery and nonresidential buildings was $1,481 billion from 1946 to 1973. At the same time, because of heavy military spending, the U.S. economy missed out on major new capital investment. The value of the production equipment and buildings that were forgone in U.S. economy from 1946 to 1973 because of military spending was at least $660 billion, or 45 percent as much as was actually invested. If one includes a further allowance for a compounding effect in such calculations—i.e., machines producing other machines in addition to final products—then the total capital outlays forgone in the United States from 1946 to 1973 because of the preemption of capital for the military exceeds $1,900 billion, or 135 percent of actual investment. However conservative the mode of estimation, one result is clear: the relatively poor condition of plant and equipment in many U.S. industries is no mystery. U.S. policy traded off renewal of the main productive assets of the economy for the operation of the military system.[11]

Ordinarily a civilian economy can look forward to making substantial advances in its total productivity because of the gains that can be made in the efficiency of machinery and in the efficiency of labor. Thus as new machinery is designed and used in production there is more output per unit of labor time, and very often even more output per unit of capital invested. The increments of additional output per unit of capital continue as long as the new machinery is used. However, if new machinery, however efficient, is installed for producing military materiel, then what emerges is military materiel which no factory can use for any further production. The result is that the normally available addition to production capability which stems from installing new production equipment is forgone for the whole society. That is also the reason why investment in military industry, while adding to the flow of money, does not serve as a competent offset to declining investment in new productive machinery.

Similar reasoning applies to the productivity of labor. Economists have been giving increasing attention to improvement in the quality of "human capital," meaning especially the better work capability that is the consequence of good physical and intellectual upbringing. For individuals, that capability leads to improvement in real income. The same is true for societies. The cost of education to the individual or to the community can be viewed as an "investment" that yields a net return to the individual and the community in the form of increases in actual earnings, due to a greater work capability. Such an annual increase can be calculated as a percent of the "investment" to show an estimated "rate of return." Thus high-school education has been associated with yearly improvements in earnings that amount to 28 percent of the cost of the education. For college graduates the average gain in earnings has been at the rate of 15 percent yearly on their educational "investment."[12]

When the investment in fresh educational competence, at whatever level, is subsequently applied to nonproductive economic activity, then the community loses the potential economic gain from human competence that ordinarily accrues to it when that capability is applied to productive work.

A second major form of impact of the military on the civilian economy is a process of industrial deterioration that generates uninvestable capital and unemployable labor. An unprecedented phenomenon has appeared in the United States: the formation of a large network of depleted industries and a flight of capital from the country. (Chapter Four will give details on "depleted" industries: those that have lost capability for serving all or part of their domestic markets and have been replaced by foreign producers because of a combination of technical, managerial and economic deterioration.)

Many theorists of capitalist economy, especially those in the Marxist tradition, have sought to explain recurring problems of capitalism as a result of the tendency of a business-based economy to generate surpluses of capital and surpluses of labor. Uninvestable capital and unemployable labor were certainly fundamental features of what happened in the United States during the Great Depression, 1929–39. The World War II economy soaked up surpluses of capital and of labor. In the chapters that follow, I will provide evidence to demonstrate that the U.S. permanent war economy, through depletion of industry and the flight of capital, has been a prime generator of uninvestable capital and a prime generator of unemployable labor.

The sustained normal operation of a large cost- and subsidy-maximizing economic system produces a major unintended effect in the transfer of inefficiency into the civilian economy. Insofar as the cost-maximizing style of operation is carried with them by managers, engineers or workers as they move individually from military to civilian employment, the civilian economy becomes infected with the standards and practices that these men and women learned in the military sphere. For civilian industry, the introduction of such practices is definitely counterproductive. To be sure, this need not apply to all individuals in the same degree. But to the extent that professional-occupational patterns are transferred, the transfer of inefficiency is "impersonal"—i.e., it operates independently of particular features of individual personality.

The U.S. civilian economy has also suffered from domestic inflation and a decline in the value of the dollar—both effects strongly impelled by the permanent war economy, and accelerated by the disastrous war in Vietnam.

In 1950 the Treasury of the United States had $24 billion in gold reserve.[13] This declined to $9–10 billion by 1973. This dissipation of the U.S. gold reserve has been due substantially to a massive net accumulation of dollars in the hands of foreigners as a consequence of foreign military spending by the U.S. government. With large military forces overseas since the end of World War II, U.S. bases in thirty countries, and fighting the Korean and Vietnam Wars, U.S. armed forces have spent dollars heavily abroad. Dollars were accepted in payment for goods and services rendered and the relative value of the dollar was maintained until 1971, when the dollar holdings abroad exceeded three times the U.S. Treasury's gold reserve. Around the world doubts arose about the Treasury's ability to redeem these dollars in gold. The unreadiness of foreigners to buy American goods at existing market prices combined with the glut of dollars to generate a crisis in the value of the U.S. currency, culminating in the financial debacle of August 15, 1971. The U.S. government suspended redemption of dollars held abroad for gold, and the relative value of the dollar dropped. The full financial and political consequences of this process have yet to be seen.

Economically parasitic output contributes to price inflation. While price inflation has diverse causes, there is no escaping the fact that war-making in the United States since 1945 has occasioned sharp price increases. This was especially true for the period 1965–73. Having the ideological consensus faith that the U.S. economy is indefinitely productive and able to turn out guns *and* butter as desired, the Johnson administration proceeded to heat up the war in Indochina. But there was no "reserve army" of unemployed and underemployed skilled workers around as in 1939, so the swift pile-up of war-serving economic demands from 1965 on fueled a fast price inflation.

After all, parasitic economic growth involves payment for work whose product immediately leaves the marketplace. The materials, power and equipment that are used up for making military products, and the goods consumed by the military-industry labor force must be supplied by the civilian labor force, which receives nothing that is economically productive from the military economy. This is not to say that harsh political control measures might not restrain such a process; but that would imply a rather more controlled society than has been acceptable to Americans. Significantly, the military economy suffers little or no hardship from inflation or decline in the relative value of the dollar. For the military top management receives a fresh levy of capital each year as a proportion of the national income. Rising prices at home or abroad have not deterred maintenance or enlargement of the military economy.

The Dominance of the Military Economy over the Civilian

How important is the state-capitalist controlled military economy in relation to the traditional civilian economy? Which economy in the United States is the more powerful one? I propose three tests of importance: (1) control over capital; (2) control over research and development; and (3) control over means of production of new technical personnel.

The name of the economy is capitalism, and control of capital is a decisive feature of the system. Capital, in conventional usage, means the accumulated funds of a size that makes them useful for investing purposes. Thereby a million dollars is not only a million

times greater than one dollar; for the latter can be used primarily
to get consumer goods, while the former can be used to buy
machinery and buildings and to engage workers to do the bidding
of a management. It is therefore vital to know what is the relative
position of the managers of the state-capitalist military economy as
controllers of capital, as against the private economy. Profits
retained by corporations and the sums set aside for capital consumption (machinery and buildings "used up") are a measure of
the fresh capital available to private U.S. management for investment. In 1939, for every dollar of this private corporate capital, the
War and Navy Departments received thirty-five cents from the
federal government. By 1971, for every dollar of this private
corporate capital the budget of the Department of Defense alone
received $1.06. That means that by 1971 the government-based
managers of the U.S. military system had superseded the private
firms of the American economy in control over capital.[14]

The main military department of the federal government could
deploy for its purposes more than the maximum capital fund that
remained (after tax levies) for the managers of all U.S. industrial
and commercial corporations. That the federal government as a
whole, not to say one section of it, should have such economic
power reflects a substantial change in the institutional location of
economic decision power, from the private corporation to the
federal government's state management.

Americans who have been critical of concentration of economic
power have focused on the corporate giants of U.S. industry. The
new state-capitalist power, however, dwarfing the big firms in
physical assets and scale of operations, was erected and sustained
in the name of defense, and has been bolstered by an ideological
consensus that strongly justifies its operation as a fine pillar of the
economy. However, no Presidential budget message—from Truman to Nixon—ever declared the desirability of making the
federal government into the top management of a state-capitalist
economy. People would be dismayed at the very idea.

The second criterion is control over research and development.
Its importance is indicated by the fact that this function determines control over new technology for products, materials and
production methods. This is a key element in the operation of any
technology-dependent society. In this respect the dominance of the
federal government and of its military agencies has been over-

whelming. More than half of the research and development brains
of the United States has been applied to military and related
research activities during the decades 1950–70. The military and
related agencies of the federal government have accounted for 80
percent of the federally sponsored research money, which has
dominated the field.[15]

The third criterion is control over means of production of new
technical talent. During the 1950s and 1960s the federal government and its military-serving agencies in particular played a
dominant part in enlarging funds for research and for graduate-
student support and in opening up new job opportunities for
young engineers and scientists. One of the main effects of these
initiatives was to induce the deans and faculties of American engineering schools to revise their curricula and research orientations
to emphasize knowledge and training best capable of servicing the
expanding requirement of the new military economy. Owing to the
new emphasis on where the action was (money, jobs), there was a
relative deemphasis of manpower, attention and money in the
universities and technical schools from training men and women
for civilian-industry technologies. "Sophisticated technology," the
code word for military-sponsored work, became the obvious
center of attention for bright young people who were set on
"making it" in the universities and the "nonprofit" think tanks that
were speedily established in response to the money proferred from
the Pentagon. In the engineering schools of the country the period
1950–70 saw the flowering of "engineering science," with highest
prestige accorded to no-application, pure research, flashy new
facilities and lots of support for graduate students, especially in
fields like electronics—with direct or indirect military or space-
agency interest. At the same time, curricula and technical research
in classic fields of civilian-engineering responsibility, like power
engineering, were accorded lesser priorities.*

* In universities, commitments to programs and to faculty, once made, can
be long-enduring. I therefore remember the comment of a senior electronics
engineer, saying that during the 1950s and 1960s those who went into power
engineering were "the dregs" of the profession. With this "I'm all right, Jack"
outlook, this man's main concern was to justify the priority accorded his brand
of work, and never mind these awkward problems about energy supply and
utilization. By implication such problems can be left to "the dregs." In a
similar vein a bright undergraduate in a leading engineering school assured
me that there was little point in his school's curriculum being cluttered up

By these tests of decision power the new state-capitalist economy has become the dominant one as against the private-capitalist economy in the United States. I do not imply that the corporate managements of private capitalism have withdrawn from the scene or have ceased to utilize their position to affect government policies that are favorable to their interests. However, the new condition of economy and society means that the chiefs of the state-capitalist economy dominate the scene and utilize their peak authority over economy, politics and the military to direct domestic and foreign policy to their purposes. This has introduced new capability for systemwide policy flexibility, made visible by the moves toward detente with the U.S.S.R. and China, coupled with impressive budget increases for the military core of the state-capitalist economy at home. This ability to maneuver at will nevertheless does not denote indefinite policy rationality and control. For the successes of state capitalism, in its own terms, bring about a range of effects, mainly unintended, that are crisis-producing in the wider economy and society.

---

with instruction bearing on how things are made, since the school was not really interested in training engineers so much as in training "leaders."

Four

UNFORESEEN EFFECTS: DECLINE OF INDUSTRIAL EFFICIENCY

WHILE PRESIDENT NIXON was hailing the manned lunar landing in August 1969 as "the greatest week since the Creation," a rather different technological drama was enacted in America's largest city. Millions of New Yorkers were suffering the effects of breakdowns in basic industrial services. Firms that could no longer be reached by phone placed ads in the newspapers to announce that they were still in business. The telephone service, normally taken for granted, seemed to be falling apart as ordinary local and long-distance calling became annoyingly difficult. At the same time the gradually deteriorating commuter railroads into New York City reached a new low in unacceptable performance, with collisions, casualties, train cancellations and delays.

Even more disastrous for normal functioning in modern urban life were the successive breakdowns in electric-power-generating plants of Consolidated Edison during the August heat waves, leaving buildings without air conditioning, elevator service or proper illumination.

Economists and engineers commonly agree that competent power supplies, transportation and communication comprise the infrastructure of a modern industrial system. That is to say, in the presence of these services, competently performed, it is readily possible to design all manner of modern industry. In the absence of such services a country is understood to be "underdeveloped." And so it came to pass by the summer of 1969 that the conditions of economic underdevelopment manifested themselves in New York City.

The same conditions now are repeated in other metropolitan areas and—with respect to the telephone service and power shortages—threaten to become epidemic in the whole United States.

Only a few years ago a technological debacle of this kind would have been unthinkable in the United States. For as long as any person can remember, Americans have regarded the state of their industrial technology as one aspect of American society and economy that was beyond criticism. Here, beyond any doubt, were the world's greatest achievements in applying mass production on a large scale. American industry, its management, research, production methods and product design had been held up as a model to all the world. However, the events of August 1969 in New York City are but one fragment of a larger process of deterioration of American industrial efficiency that casts serious doubts about the belief in U.S. industrial superiority. The deterioration is in some respects absolute, and in others it is a relative decline compared with other countries. In order to show the scope of what is involved, here are two additional examples of unprecedented events occurring in the early 1970s, each illustrating major aspects of a crisis of industrial efficiency in the United States.

In July 1971 an unusual development was noticed in the American automobile industry. Here is the report from Detroit:

> While this is the best auto sales year in the nation's history, with sales expected to approach 10 million cars, unemployment in Michigan is approaching 10% of the work force and is at 16% in Detroit. Never before has there been a combination of a strong auto year and a high unemployment in the nation's leading automobile production state. One major reason is that one of 7 new cars sold comes from Europe or Japan, while another 700,000 are being imported this year from Canada for sale in the United States.[1]

Here is an unprecedented combination of financial success for the major automobile firms and high unemployment rates in their industrial home base. Apparently it has become increasingly profitable for the major American auto producers to invest fresh capital abroad and import foreign-made products under their own label into the United States. Similarly, they have been investing in shares of foreign automobile producers and contracting for the importation of automobile parts which they then assemble in "American-made" vehicles. Until recently this pattern was of minor importance in the auto industry. The larger firms had long had subsidiaries abroad. However, they also exported from their American factories. Their foreign-made cars were produced mainly for the foreign market. The new condition in the automobile industry combines an extensive exporting of capital, and thereby jobs, to overseas locations by American firms, together with growing importing of foreign production for the U.S. market.

This development in the automobile industry is linked to the inability of U.S. manufacturers to design products that are at once attractive and producible at low enough price to be salable abroad. This turn of events in the automobile industry is but one piece of a larger pattern which I will deal with below.

Event number three: In 1971, for the first time since 1893 the United States as a nation had a negative balance of trade in relation to the rest of the world. This meant that more goods and services were bought abroad by Americans than were purchased by foreigners from the United States. Indeed, the U.S. surplus of exports over imports had long reflected the country's industrial competence in designing and producing both capital goods and consumer goods. The surplus in exports was a major source of strength to the American dollar on a worldwide basis. From 1965 to 1970 the surplus dropped from $5.3 billion to $2.7 billion, and by 1971 a deficit of $2 billion was registered. This multiplied threefold to a trade deficit of $6.4 billion by 1972.[2]

The failures of the underpinnings of industrialism in big cities, trade deficits and the Detroit unemployment of 1971 are the bitter fruit of a permanent war economy. From the time when the United States became an industrial economy, manufacturing managements in this country paid higher wages per hour than employers in other parts of the world. American industry could produce goods that were competitive in the domestic market and acceptable abroad. Industrialists were able to offset the high hourly wage of American workers by combined efforts in good managing, capital investment, research and development, product design, mechanization and organization of work. By these means, the productivity of American workers outpaced that of the Europeans. The result was that the unit labor cost of U.S. products could be held low and the final selling price made competitive.

There is nothing really mysterious about the process that makes it possible to pay a high wage to workers and managers, offsetting this high wage with such efficient use of all resources that excellent products can be produced at stable and even diminishing prices. Probably the classic example of this phenomenon is the case of electric power. From 1905 to 1960 the price of kilowatt hours to industrial users in the United States declined year by year. Furthermore, these are prices in current dollars without adjustment for changes in the purchasing power of the dollar. This spectacular performance in reducing the price of electric power over more than half a century was made possible by increased efficiency in the conversion processes, in their control, and in power distribution. Yet, through that same period every one of the major input factors in the electric-power industry increased in price.

Indeed, the history of American industry has been a history of such success stories. The main strategy that produced American industrial preeminence, and also the factors whose absence has produced the declining competence of the 1970s are laid out in the following excerpt from an article which appeared in the December 1924 issue of *Factory, The Magazine of Management*. The headline reads "Manufacturing Policies that have Offset Europe's Cheap Labor," in an article announcing: "Though the American manufacturer cannot pay his workers the low wages that prevail in foreign countries, he can repel foreign invasion of American markets with his own weapons—better equipment and more effective management."

Requirements for Industrial Efficiency

The capability for offsetting a high wage rate requires a combined set of inputs. On the *management* side, it must include cost-minimizing as an important goal. Managements have been impelled in the direction of cost-minimization by the operation of self-correcting competitive mechanisms. If a management becomes incompetent to offset the wage rate, it is penalized by being forced to have a lesser part of the market, or by being forced into bankruptcy. Under such pressures, managements are compelled to revise industrial methods and bring in men who are competent to operate in a cost-minimizing fashion.

There is also, of course, reward for those managements who function competently. They earn the profits which they can then translate into further investments, thereby enlarging the decision power of the management group concerned.

Recent conventional wisdom in American management emphasizes a stagnationist prognosis for the American economy. Investors want to be able to take their money out in three years after an investment is made.[3] This behavior leads to a bias toward short planning periods. The emphasis in schools of business is on making money, not necessarily on making good products. In the words of one major corporate management to its own employees: "We are not here to make machines, we are here to make money." Everywhere one hears it denied that it is feasible to use appropriate technology to make production in the United States competitive once again. An astonishing example of this attitude was offered in a recent business text which instructed the student readers: "By 1971, . . . there seemed to be no indication that the United States would gain further comparative advantages from technological or agricultural breakthroughs, nor could it limit price increases any more successfully than its major competitors."[4] Neither these writers nor others of their persuasion offer any evidence whatever in support of such conclusions. The prevailing gospel, as in the business text cited, rests on a static and unhistorical view of technological options and their potential.

The more traditional American view, based upon solid engineering experience, is that with appropriate technology it is possible to offset U.S.–foreign wage differentials. This has been strongly reaffirmed in some major industrial-management journals. In September 1972 the magazine *Business Week* tried to dramatize the idea of productivity as the nation's "biggest underdeveloped resource" (September 9, 1972). The case of the Black and Decker Manufacturing Company, the world's largest maker of power hand tools, was cited as a success story in industrial productivity. B and D's least expensive quarter-inch drill "was introduced in 1946 at $16.95 and has been steadily cut in price since; after the most recent 10 percent cut earlier this year, it now sells for $7.99." By 1972 another success story in American industrial productivity was made visible by the rapid appearance of very small electronic calculators at modest prices. Swift strides in the design and utilization of integrated circuits made it possible to produce such machines so simply that "the finished product can be assembled by a high school student in less than an hour. Suddenly, the assembly cost of the calculator is less than the 5% import duty on such Japanese products into the United States."[5]

A second requirement for industrial efficiency in the United States is the *productive use of capital*. U.S. competence in this respect has been severely limited by two principal developments: first, the proportion of available capital assigned to the military; second, the export of capital from the United States. For 1967–69 we know that for every dollar of gross domestic fixed investment (all investment in factories, equipment, buildings and homes) the United States spent fifty-two cents for the military. In Germany fourteen cents was spent for the military, while in Japan the figure was two cents.[6] The economic consequences of such large differences in the functional use of capital are independent of the ideologies or intentions of governments and leaders.

Another source of depletion of the capital supply for U.S. productive investment is the remarkable scale of U.S. direct foreign investment during the 1960s. "Direct foreign investment" means money directly utilized for starting or operating enterprises. Therefore, this excludes money sent abroad to banks or for purchase of securities or the like. Until 1960 the accumulated total U.S. direct investments abroad amounted to $31 billion. By 1970 this direct investment had risen to a total of $78 billion. This increase represents a hemorrhage in the supply of capital in the United States without historical precedent.[7] In this way, added to the direct military drain, the supply of capital invested in the United States was sharply reduced.

In every industrial country it is well appreciated that the scale and quality of technical *research and development* has a major effect on the productivity of the industrial system as a whole. When knowledge is applied to improve product design and to raise efficiency in production for economically useful goods, then the research involved has an immense multiplier effect. Economically useful goods enhance the productive competence of the whole society by improving the level of living, or by raising the productivity of labor and capital. None of this can be said for research that improves the firepower of weapons or speeds up their production. Therefore, the amount of money that a country spends on research is not a sufficient indicator of its technological competence. That depends on the degree to which the research effort is applied to productive economic growth. By this test the massive size of U.S. research budgets gives a misleading impression of its efforts toward productive competence. The largest part of U.S. research and development work has been in the service of the military economy.

Let us examine the quality and the scale of U.S technical research. We know from independent studies that in U.S. industry from 1957 to 1963 research and development averaged 4.05 percent of the net-sales dollar. Of this amount 1.74 percent was money provided by the firm itself, while 2.31 percent came from the federal government.[8] The federal government, in turn, has been dominated by military and military-related (read: economically nonproductive) research. Thus, the National Science Foundation advises: "Two-thirds of the federal R&D monies in industry were provided by the Department of Defense in 1969. The National Aeronautics and Space Administration (NASA) contracted an additional 22%."[9]

From 1950 to 1970 the sharply increased demand by the government's military-space operations, coupled with generous funding, resulted in a swift rise in the salaries of government-supported engineers and scientists. There was a notable rise in starting-salary ranking of engineers from 1953 to 1960. At the same time an estimated "20 to 30 percent of the increased activity supported by the federal government was made possible by a transfer of people from industrially supported projects. The remaining increase was accomplished by absorbing the supply of new technical people."[10]

There is no escaping the fact that much of the research-and-development component of what is required for civilian industrial competence in the United States has been missing owing to direction of this effort in the service of the military economy. The people researching military-rocket motors are unavailable for developing efficient motors for civilian vehicles. The designers of naval vessels are unavailable for making an economically proficient merchant marine. One of the major casualties of this military emphasis has been the potential effort forgone in the design of new productive equipment, and the innovation of technologies for fabricating the means of production themselves.

The *price of machinery* has an important effect in either spurring or limiting investment in new industrial equipment. In the eyes of industrial managers, machinery is ordinarily seen as a trade-off against manual labor. This is plainly the case in mechanical manufacturing (in the chemical industries the economic trade-off is in the form of machinery as against the prices of raw materials). This means that managements trying to calculate the least-cost way of doing given work can design production operations with varying mixes of machinery and labor. Thus if labor is relatively inexpensive as compared to machinery, then a least-cost mix will include a lot of labor and a little machinery. However, when the cost of labor per hour is high and machinery is relatively inexpensive, then it is attractive to industrial management to buy more machinery and to install it in manufacturing processes. The result of the latter preference, of course, is to increase the average productivity of the man-hours used in production.

The crucial element here is the relative price of machinery compared to labor. In the United States, as in other industrial countries, industrial development over a long period of time has included the tendency of the wages of labor to increase more rapidly than the prices of machinery. The result has been, from management's perspective, an increasingly attractive trade-off favoring the use of machinery in place of labor. This process proceeds as long as managements are forced by worker pressure on wages to consider alternatives—namely, relatively inexpensive machinery. The reason why the prices of machinery can increase less rapidly than the hourly wages of workers is that the productivity of machinery production itself can be improved. The result is that the rise in the prices of machinery need not be as great as the increase in the wages of the workers who make the machines. The continuity of this process is a core element in promoting industrial productivity.[11]

From this vantage point it is crucial that from 1965 to 1969 there was a sharp drop in productivity improvement within the crucial machine-tool industry. These are the firms that supply the drills, lathes, milling machines, etc., that are the basic machinery of an industrial system. Output per man-hour in the machine-tool industry changed by less than one percent. In parts of that industry there was even a decline in productivity. As new machinery looks less cost-attractive as a replacement for old equipment, managers make do with their older machines. For each firm this is economically sensible. For the U.S. economy as a production system the result is damaging.

In the United States during the 1950s and 1960s the relative attractiveness of machinery prices to labor costs ceased in many key industrial areas. From the wholesale-price information that is regularly gathered by the U.S. Bureau of Labor Statistics, I have identified fifty-four machines of various types whose prices from 1957 to 1970 increased as much as or more than the average wages per hour of industrial workers (see Appendix 1). This rise in machinery prices has a countermechanization effect. It means that industrial managements find it unattractive to discard their existing equipment as trade-off for more machines as the wages of their workers increase. The net effect of the failure to buy new machinery is, necessarily, to slow down the growth of industrial productivity in the economy as a whole.

A direct effect of the process producing a high cost of machinery relative to labor was to accumulate an aging stock of production equipment in many key U.S. industries. By 1968, 64 percent of the metalworking machinery in use in American factories was ten years old or over. This figure contrasted sharply with the newer metalworking equipment in West Germany, the U.S.S.R. and Japan. The combination of unattractive machinery prices for civilian investments and slower general economic growth made for a low level of productive investment in the United States compared with other countries.*

_____

* At five-year intervals the McGraw-Hill Company counts the machine tools in U.S. industry. In October 29, 1973, *American Machinist* (p. 143) summarized the 1973 inventory: "The number of young (less than ten-year-old) machines declined slightly, as shown by the fact that only 33 percent of the present total is less than ten years old. This is the lowest level that has been recorded for the young machines since 1940, just before World War II, when—after ten years of depression—the level was 30 percent." In the same issue (p. 162) the editors report that the important "population of numerical control equipment in metalworking has doubled in five years, is now nearing 1.0 percent of machine tool total." A further indicator of the trend in the productionally vital machine tool industry is the presence of 14 Japanese firms as advertisers in the same issue of *American Machinist*.

By 1969 sharp differences appeared between the United States, West Germany and Japan in the proportion of gross national product invested in fixed assets (durable equipment and nonresidential business structures). In the United States for 1969 the percentage of GNP invested in fixed assets was 10.7, in West Germany 19.1 and in Japan 29.6.[12] By 1969 the United States reached the lowest recorded level during this century in productivity growth in manufacturing industry. In that year the percent gain in output per worker man-hour in manufacturing was 0.4. This contrasts with annual productivity gains ranging from 3 to 5 percent per year over a long period of time.[13]

The condition of the principal factors required for industrial efficiency has resulted in a depleting effect on the *productivity* of U.S. industry. When the Secretary of Commerce had to explain the 1971 trade-deficit debacle to the House of Representatives, he included the following summary statement on industrial productivity in the United States:

> Historically, U.S. productivity and productivity growth far outpaced other countries mainly because of large scale import of capital and foreign technology, immigration of skilled adult manpower, growth in markets, high wages which induced labor-saving devices, innovative spirit, lack of rigid traditions and comparatively low war losses. From 1870–1950 the U.S. rate of productivity growth exceeded Europe by 60% and Japan by 70%. Starting in 1950, the situation was reversed, and U.S. productivity growth now lags well behind Europe and Japan.
>
> From 1950–1965 our productivity growth rate trailed Europe by 35% and Japan by 60%. The trend since 1965 shows an even more rapid relative decline: U.S. rates trailed Europe by 60% and Japan by 84%. These differentials in rates result both from unprecedented levels of productivity growth in Europe and especially in Japan, and from declines in U.S. productivity growth (1965–1969) which was only 1.7% compared with 4.5% in Europe and 10.6% in Japan.[14]

As the withdrawal of the conditions of industrial efficiency became epidemic in American industry, that gave rise to an altogether unforeseen development. A network of industries appeared with the common quality of lacking in the technical and economic capability to serve all or part of domestic or foreign markets, or both. For each industry so depleted it is possible to construct ad

hoc explanations in terms of its particular history, firms and
personalities. What they share in common is the relative absence
of capital and technical talent that had been made abundant in
military economy, and the linked absence of managerial and technical methods that would be essential for industrial efficiency and
economic competence.

Consequences of Industrial Inefficiency

Up to this point I have illustrated the defective condition of
primary factors needed for industrial efficiency. I will now show
that industrial inefficiency has become commonplace in a wide
array of important industries. For this I have concentrated on
those industrial areas that are obviously critical in the functioning
of any modern industrial society. These data supply the reader
with a solid base for understanding, first, the decline of competitiveness of U.S. industry in the world marketplace and, second,
why surplus capital was exported from the United States in search
of better investment prospects, with the effect of creating labor
surplus in the domestic economy.

I opened this chapter with an account of the failure of the
industrial "infrastructure" in New York City. Those conditions of
communication, power supply and rail transportation were not
unique to one week in that one city.

In 1970 the Federal Communications Commission, making its
first national survey of telephone service, compiled voluminous
evidence that while the New York City phone system was judged
to be the worst in the country, and getting worse, the condition
there was not unique. Reports from twenty large cities serviced by
the Bell Telephone System indicated that failure to satisfy the
industry's own service standards was the rule, not the exception, in
principal metropolitan centers of the United States.[15]

By 1971 a national energy crisis was clearly in evidence, showing
signs of being durable and likely to become rather more intensive.[16] The same problems of crisis extend to fuel supply, in the
form of natural gas. Optimistic assumptions about the availability
of natural gas, which surely lay behind the construction of inter-
state gas lines and the conversion of gas-using units to natural gas,
were unreasonable estimates based on faulty knowledge.[17]

In the electric-power-generating industry, knowledgeable men report that by 1972 there had developed a "critical shortage of engineers qualified to design the new power plants so urgently needed . . . throughout the nation."[18]

After decades of neglect of public rail transportation within and among cities, attempts were made in the late 1960s to start systems like the BART network in San Francisco. In order to do the work, however, it was necessary to investigate foreign-developed rail technology on a large scale, since no recent domestic models were available. It emerged that the most interesting developments in railroad transportation, utilizing wheelless, linear-electric-powered, air-cushioned vehicles at 250 miles per hour have been developed in France. And there is nothing in sight on the American scene to compare with the Japanese high-speed railroad lines.[19] Also, when the civil-engineering work for the Bay Area Rapid Transit System was put out for bids it ran into an unexpected snag, for "the management had confidently expected that many noted domestic and overseas contractors would submit bids." The BART management, however, had not "reckoned with the fact that many of these firms were committed up to their eyeballs on construction work in Vietnam and were not eager to take on additional work."[20] Contracts for the construction were finally let, but only after some delay and without the clear assurance that the most competent and experienced firms would actually be involved.

By late 1971 the BART System for San Francisco was in trouble. Prototype models had been built for a system that was scheduled to be in operation by 1968. The prototypes crashed late in 1971. The price of the system zoomed from $792 million to $1.4 billion.[21] This is a type of "cost growth" which is ordinary in military economy. It is surely not accidental that the prime contractor for the system was the Rohr Company, which made its reputation in the aerospace and related industries. (The Rohr Company, we may note, was also the subcontractor to Lockheed for the engine pylons which cracked on the giant C-5A transport.)

During 1969 new railroad equipment was delivered to the Long Island Rail Road and to the Penn Central. Here is part of what happened:

The Long Island Railroad accepts 94 new cars and finds mechanical defects in all 94. . . . Because of breakdowns, it takes a standby

fleet of 10 replacement cars to keep an average of 18 cars moving on
the New York to Washington Metroliner. Two of the new Metroliner
cars must be scrapped for spare parts. Twenty additional cars are
delivered more than 6 months behind schedule and they also have
serious defects.

According to one railroad executive, "It seems nobody knows how
to make a passenger car anymore."[22]

Dr. Robert Nelson, chief of the federal government Office of
High Speed Ground Transportation, said of the rail supply industry: "The industry simply does not have the massive manpower
and technical resources that, for example, the aerospace industry
has. The profits in railway supply equipment have been depressed
for some years and bright young engineers have not been going
into it."[23]

The U.S. performance in railroad transportation contrasts with
that of other countries. By June 20, 1971, we learned from Reuters
that Japanese railroad officials were pressing plans for a high-
speed, magnetically powered train to run above the tracks on an
air cushion at 310 miles per hour. Development of public transit
systems along such lines is also proceeding in Germany and in
France. Indeed, in France, a monorail system, based on a linear
induction motor, was designed by a French engineer (a graduate
of MIT, incidentally), and a working prototype was erected and
put into operation for further development and sales purposes.

Defects in the industries that comprise the "infrastructure" of
the U.S. industrial system are paralleled by technological and
allied deficiencies in a host of industries ranging from steel and
autos to consumer electronics. The diminishing U.S. position in the
so-called "high-technology" industries is especially important for
its impact on the U.S. world-trade position.

The steel industry of the United States has become a major
center of industrial depletion, with about 18 percent of the domestic market being serviced from abroad.[24] In January 1971 we were
advised that negotiations were under way with the steel industry
of Japan involving an understanding on limitation on the further
rate of penetration by the Japanese industry into the U.S. market.
The crucial question is: Why is there an inability of the steel industry to compete against the steel industry in Japan?

About 80 percent of the Japanese steel industry makes use of the
basic oxygen process, whereas only about 50 percent of the U.S.

industry is so equipped. The U.S. industry's managements have failed to do research and development on a scale necessary to offset cost differentials between U.S. and foreign countries. The consequence is that costs in the U.S. steel industry have risen to a level making imported steel salable at from $20 to $40 per ton less than domestic steel.

Profit margins are also a factor. The non–U.S. steel-makers have been prepared to operate at substantially lower than American profit rates. A report by the Iron and Steel Institute shows profit differentials between the U.S. steel industry and a series of identified Japanese firms. Thus, in 1968 net income as a percent of revenues averaged 5.3 percent in the U.S. steel industry. The related figures for the identified firms in Japan are: Yawata, 3.0 percent; Fuji, 3.3; Kawasaki, 2.8. Similar comparisons obtain for the relation of U.S. steel-firm profits to those of Belgium, France, West Germany and Italy.[25] The higher U.S. profit applied to U.S. costs has meant a substantially higher price and hence noncompetitiveness. These are important elements in explaining how it happened that the steel structure of the World Trade Center, constructed at the foot of Manhattan, was shipped to Manhattan Island from Japan and not from any U.S. steel source.

The U.S. auto industry has been, without question, the home base of modern mass-production technology, where ideas of standardization, the assembly line and mass production as conventionally understood were initiated and put into wide practice. During the 1960s, car models and options proliferated such that in the case of one of the Big Three, the Chrysler Corporation, the number of parts in use rose from 12,000 to 23,000 within the decade.[26] This is a tribute to the multiplication of design complexity, the failure to apply standardization technique and modular design, and the elaboration of model change for stylistic or allied merchandising purposes. In 1972 I counted forty-three models in the "low-cost" line of one large firm. The result of such multiplication of parts obviously increases unit cost and price. The U.S. auto industry became by the 1960s a classic example of failure to utilize many aspects of modern production engineering.

The case of civilian electronics is perhaps the most striking example of industrial depletion in the United States. For example, the design and manufacture of small radio receivers and most TV sets has dropped sharply in the U.S., as any reader can verify by a visit to his nearest hi-fi store. Civilian electronics is close to the burgeoning military-space electronics field with its cost- and subsidy-maximizing practices. That kinship has helped to spread the cost-maximizing traditions of the military-serving parts into the civilian area. Civilian electronics firms have managed to avoid technological options that could help make U.S.-based production economically viable once again.

On September 19, 1971, Robert A. Schieber, vice-president of operations for the RCA Corporation's consumer electronics division, called attention to a new circuit module for television sets developed by RCA printed on ceramic wafers. Barton Kreuzer, an executive vice-president of RCA, predicted that if the adaptation of the devices went as smoothly as he hoped, "it could make us competitive once again to the point where we could bring back at least a good part of the industry to the United States." He further said that by the end of 1971, through the use of ceramic modules, "we should be competitive with Oriental costs and next year we ought to be able to beat them."27

In order to realize this potential, it would be necessary, however, to implement a major process of standardization in circuit design for television sets. Only then would it become economic to design and operate the manufacturing facilities needed to mass-produce the ceramic base modules. These modules have the further capability of being readily manipulated by mechanical means, even for assembly in many arrangements. However, the American firms have refused thus far to undertake the standardization process. The result is that this technology potential cannot be carried out.

By contrast, the Japanese manufacturers have been developing standardized integrated circuits for industry-wide application. The consequence of this pattern has been the comparative cost incompetence of U.S. civilian electronics plants.

After the Second World War, industry in the United States developed strong leads in certain "high-technology" fields. These industries included computers, commercial jet aircraft, nuclear power and the design of semiconductors. These classes of products benefited directly from the force-feeding of areas of U.S. technology that were of special interest to the military. Indeed, the U.S. lead in these fields led to fears in Western Europe and elsewhere of a "technology gap" between the United States and Western

Europe. This fear did not endure very long, as European and Japanese industrialists began to reap the benefit of their sustained concentration on civilian research. Thus:

> Foreign steelmakers . . . were . . . installing new processes, such as the basic oxygen furnace, on a wider scale than American steelmen. And even in the early 1960's, U.S. heavy machinery builders such as the makers of turbine generators were running into intense foreign competition on design as well as on price. . . . These days some of Europe's older high-technology industries such as chemicals and electrical equipment, are selling more and more of their products and licensing more and more of their technology to U.S. companies. . . . Extra high voltage transmission, a more efficient way of conducting electric power for long distances, was pioneered in the U.S. by ASEA, the Swedish electrical equipment maker. When Colt industries sought to rescue its faltering program for developing big diesel engines, it had to turn to Austrian consultants for help. . . . Some U.S. shipbuilders are finally adopting cost-cutting methods that were developed in Sweden. The American construction industry is just beginning to use "systems building" techniques that are already widely applied in Europe.
>
> The aircraft industry is a notable example of the new international competition. In France and in Japan airframe and aircraft engine builders are developing designs that are sharply competitive with U.S.–made products. Mr. Alan E. Puckett, Executive Vice-President of Hughes Aircraft Company, says, "Our R&D money just isn't keeping pace."[28]

The DC-3 was one of the most successful commercial aircraft of all time. Its special operating characteristics of slow landing speed, short takeoff requirement and rugged operating characteristics continued to be valued more than thirty-five years after the plane was initially introduced. In the mid-1960s the Federal Aviation Agency announced a contest for the design of a successor plane to the DC-3. I reported on this in my book *Our Depleted Society* (1965). No American aircraft producer entered the design contest—not even the Douglas firm, which had been the designer and fabricator of the DC-3. However, at the international air show in Hanover, Germany, a few years later, the Soviet aviation industry presented a short-haul passenger jet that aspired to the workhorse virtues of the venerable DC-3. This plane was three-engined, seating thirty-four passengers, and was offered at the obvious bargain price of $770,000 per plane, or about one-third the price of a small airliner made in the West.[29]

The design and manufacture of electrical generating plants has long been a field in which U.S. firms excelled. For some years the United States had two main factories, those of General Electric and Westinghouse, manufacturing large turbines and generators. There is to be a third manufacturing facility in this country, to be located in Virginia, resulting from an investment by the Brown-Boveri Corporation of Switzerland. This investment, announced on April 14, 1971, reflects the success of Brown-Boveri in addition to other European and Japanese firms in cutting heavily into the U.S. domestic market for heavy power equipment, to the point where that firm finds it appropriate to move some production into the U.S.

It should not be assumed that the only prospective U.S. competitors in major-technology fields will continue to be West European and Japanese. Recent evidence indicates that Soviet enterprises are pressing hard to be admitted as bidders on large generators to be constructed at the federal government's Grand Coulee Dam.[30] The Kaiser Aluminum and Chemical Corporation has indicated that it is one of a growing stream of American firms licensing metallurgical technology from the U.S.S.R. This is obviously a payoff to the Soviets from a long research concentration in that field.[31]

Finally, to round off this sketch of depletion, especially in industrial technology, there are the recent developments in the U.S. machine-tool industry. Since this industry supplies the basic metalworking equipment that is used in all manufacturing, it plays a fundamental part in the productivity of any modern industrial system. In 1959 I did studies of machine-tool production in the United States, Western Europe and the U.S.S.R., issuing a formal report on that industry in Western Europe.[32] At that time, U.S. machine-tool builders regarded forecasts of the possible technological noncompetitiveness of their industry as so outlandish as to be unworthy of notice.

By 1970 a different tune was being sung. The leading firms of the industry had arranged during the previous decade to invest heavily in foreign machine-tool plant facilities. One of the principal managers of the industry, Henry Sharpe, president of Brown and Sharpe, reported that imported machines have been selling at between 25 and 30 percent less than U.S. prices for comparable equipment. By 1969, the effective foreign penetration of the U.S. machine-tool market had reached about 20 percent. The above percentages are stated in dollar terms. When the market penetration by foreign products is stated in terms of machine units, then in 1969 it reached 39 percent. Sharpe's prognosis is for a continuation of this development, owing to the noncompetitiveness of U.S. production in this basic industry.[33] A major government study of the machine-tool industry, unpublished at this writing, has found that by 1972 the U.S. industry had lost world leadership, being outpaced in production by West Germany and the U.S.S.R., with the Japanese moving up fast. Foreign sales to the United States were deemed likely to grow. Crucially, the edge in technology design, a feature of the U.S. industry, appeared to be slipping rapidly.

These developments in the vital machine-tool industry confirm a prediction about the link between kinds of industrial research and industrial efficiency. Various studies of research in industry have independently concluded that, in the words of one investigator, the cost to the United States "of defense-space R&D were lower productivity, higher costs, and poorer products in the civilian sector."[34]

Noncompetitiveness in World Trade

By 1971 the federal government was alarmed by the appearance of a massive trade deficit for the United States. Senior men in the executive branch started listening to economists like Michael Boretsky of the Commerce Department who had long been predicting these trends. Boretsky analyzed the deterioration of the U.S. trade position, judging that this was likely to continue given the following developments:

1. A gradually growing deficit in trade with minerals, fuels, and the like (e.g., from $1.7 billion in 1957 to $3.3 billion in 1969).

2. A dramatically growing deficit in trade with non-technology-intensive manufactured products (from a surplus of about $1.1 billion in 1957 to a deficit of $5.6 billion in 1969).

3. A rapidly deteriorating trade situation in the technology-intensive manufactured products, the only commodity groups still yielding size-

able surpluses, with imports persistently growing at a rate about 2.5 times as fast as exports and about 3.2 times as fast as the growth of the GNP (in current prices).

4. A rapidly deteriorating trade situation with nearly all the developed world and a dramatic deterioration with Japan and Canada.

The principal causes of this deterioration have been

1. The gradual loss of industrial and technological superiority by U.S. industry (narrowing of the gap).
2. Weak international price competitiveness of U.S. industry.
3. Inadequate natural resources in the United States relative to the economy's needs.[35]

In response to the deterioration in the U.S. world-trade position, a White House study by Peter G. Peterson disclosed that in a range of industrial products imports accounted for significant parts of the total U.S. consumption of these goods. By 1970 the percentage of imports in U.S. consumption of steel was 15, of leather shoes 30, of sewing machines 49, of radios 70, and of magnetic tape recorders 96. (See Appendix 1.)

With respect to the U.S. trade position it is crucial that the main area of U.S. industrial capability, namely the "high-technology" goods, have been showing the sharpest signs of international competitive failure. This is revealed in the following summary of U.S. imports of major classes of high-technology goods from 1960 to 1970. In these four industries, chemicals, nonelectrical machinery, electrical apparatus and transport equipment, U.S. manufacturers have until recently been preeminent on the world industrial scene. What has developed during the 1960s is a sixfold increase in U.S. imports of these classes of goods. It is notable that

U.S. IMPORTS OF "HIGH-TECHNOLOGY" GOODS, 1960–82

	MILLIONS OF DOLLARS		
	1960	1982	Percent Increase
Chemicals	807	9,493	1,076
Nonelectrical machinery	438	9,620	2,096
Electrical apparatus	286	16,122	5,537
Transport equipment	742	33,635	4,433

SOURCE: U.S. Department of Commerce, *Statistical Abstract of the United States, 1971*, Washington, D.C., 1971, pp. 777–78; *ibid.*, *1984*, p. 840.

"electrical apparatus" of all classes show the largest (absolute) increase of all.

By 1973 the United States was turning to French suppliers for modern railroad equipment. Amtrak imported the first of a series of French-built turbo trains.

> Why did the United States have to turn to France for a turbo train? Mr. Day [Amtrak official] explained that the American and Canadian turbos built by United Aircraft have had so many mechanical difficulties that the New York–Boston turbo run is no longer an extra-fare charge. And the French trains, costing about $2.7 million, are cheaper, he said. But Amtrak hopes to stir up further competition among builders.
>
> One of the main difficulties is the condition of American tracks. Jean Fleche, chief test engineer for the research department of the French National Railways, said that he had operated the RTGs at better than 160 miles an hour. But one official noted that 70 is the top allowable speed now between Chicago and St. Louis.[36]

In industry after industry requiring quality engineering there has been a manifest falling off of the U.S. position. Miniature ball bearings are an important component of many precision devices; by 1971 over half of the U.S. requirements of miniature ball bearings was supplied by imports, mainly from Japan.[37]

Until 1971 federal officials were confident about the competitive economic position of American industry. They believed that, come what may, American strength in the "high-technology" industries would more than overcome noncompetitiveness in traditionally "labor-intensive" industries. Therefore when a weakening position showed up in the areas of presumed strength, alarm bells sounded in the federal establishment. The scale and quality of U.S. industrial research was reviewed on July 27, 1971, by Maurice H. Stans, the Secretary of Commerce, when he appeared before the House Committee on Science and Astronautics:

> Though the U.S. still maintains a much higher level of R&D expenditures than any individual country in the world, it is becoming evident that other countries, notably Western Germany and Japan, are placing a much higher relative emphasis on civilian R&D. In 1968, the U.S. spent $13 billion for civilian R&D. Equivalent figures for Japan and West Germany amount to $3 and $4 billion, respectively. These individual expenditures represented 1.5% of U.S. GNP, versus 2.6% of German GNP and 2.0% of Japan's. If the capitalized value of purchased foreign technology is computed and added to these figures,

the U.S. level stays the same but both German and Japanese levels jump to $5 billion annually.

While the dollar level of our R&D exceeds the sum of West German and Japanese expenditures, there are two factors that qualify this apparent conclusion. One is that wage costs in those countries are much lower, with the result that they can purchase more R&D per dollar invested. Secondly, and perhaps more importantly, it takes a greater R&D effort, at much greater cost, for the leading country to find innovations to stay ahead.[38]

The relative size of the U.S. research and development effort is qualified by the uses to which it is put.

For 1982, the National Science Board, of the federal government's National Science Foundation, has shown the ways that the U.S., (West) German, and Japanese governments allocate their R&D spending. Three classes of R&D uses show crucial differences: defense and aerospace; civilian technology; and health and basic research, such as basic research in universities for general advance in knowledge.

PERCENT DISTRIBUTION OF GOVERNMENT SUPPORT OF
RESEARCH AND DEVELOPMENT, BY NATIONAL OBJECTIVE

	Defense and Aerospace	Civilian Technology	Health and Basic Research
United States	63.7	17.2	18.2
West Germany	24.4	46.2	29.5
Japan	16.8	72.0	15.3

SOURCE: National Science Board, *Science Indicators*, 1982, p. 199.

The contrasting uses of R&D shown here are dramatic. The United States, with by far the largest R&D budget, has concentrated this nation's technical innovation talents in the areas of defense and aerospace, while Germany and especially Japan have focused on civilian technology targets. There is no mystery whatever about the results of these differing priorities. You can see them on display in the automobile showrooms that feature the German cars that claim an important part of the higher priced and sport market, and in the shops laden with ingenious Japanese-made electronics and optics. West European and Japanese products now account for important parts of markets for traditionally American specialty items: from electrical household appliances to computer-controlled machine tools to earth-moving equipment.

Federal budgets of the 1980s show a heavier priority to defense and aerospace. President Reagan's "star wars" project accounted for the largest single block of R&D funds in the government's budget projections for 1986 and after.

The immense funds allocated to military and allied technology development contrast with the tight-fisted handling of money for certain obviously important civilian technologies. The generation of power is obviously a matter of sustaining importance to a major industrial society, especially as fuel and power shortages have become a characteristic pattern in the United States—not only of certain large cities, but of entire regions. These considerations would seem to give great importance to the development of fusion-power capability—that is, the controlled hydrogen-bomb process being turned to account for the generation of energy. However, in 1971 the Atomic Energy Commission found only $31 million for sponsoring the development of fusion-power technology. Failing rapid and imaginative development of new energy sources, the United States is confronted with the prospect of rapidly escalating costs of energy that will run up costs throughout the economy, in production and in consumption.

Noncompetitiveness of U.S. industry in the world marketplace is linked to swift U.S. price inflation. But market price is not autonomously produced. While "supply-versus-demand" relationships surely exert some effect, it remains that price is ordinarily based upon cost (plus profit). Therefore it is only prudent to examine the underpinnings of price.

The inflation of the 1960s was bound up with technological depletion. The engine that had long generated improvement in productivity (output per man-hour) in the American economy was damaged by limited capital for civilian productive investment, and by the absence of necessary civilian research and development and public attention. Virtually all Americans had come to assume that growth in the productiveness of U.S. industry was an automatic process and could be taken for granted. This process of productivity growth was what held U.S. products price-competitive by offsetting high wages and salaries with parallel productivity increases, thereby producing a stable or only moderately increasing unit labor cost.* But wage and salary increases in key

* Usually "unit labor cost" refers to the pay of production and allied workers per unit of product. In this discussion the payment to workers and all other employees are included.

parts of the U.S. economy during the 1960s were not matched by equal degrees of improvement in productivity. The result was that the employee cost per unit of output increased, leading to a higher cost per product sold. Of course, price is also affected by profit-taking and by conditions of supply in relation to actual market demand. In the latter respect it is noteworthy that in U.S. manufacturing industry there was at least 10 percent of unused capacity, on the average, during the 1960s. Hence, apart from industries especially caught by sharp increases in demand owing to the Vietnam War, there was extra, unused capacity still at hand during the period.

From basic data on U.S. wages and productivity in manufacturing industry we can gauge the deficit in productivity during the 1960s which contributed to an increase in the unit labor cost.[40]

From 1960 to 1965 U.S. productivity in manufacturing increased more rapidly than hourly compensation to employees. Any price increases during that period were *not* due to higher unit labor cost. After 1965 unit labor cost rose sharply because productivity did not increase enough to offset the rise in hourly pay. Here are the actual increases in productivity for 1966 to 1971:

1966	1.22%
1967	.10%
1968	4.70%
1969	1.43%
1970	1.51%
1971	3.43%

The following are the productivity increases *that did not occur and that would have been additionally necessary* to offset the increases in hourly pay.

1966	3.16%
1967	4.83%
1968	2.50%
1969	5.01%
1970	5.06%
1971	2.74%

This productivity growth that was forgone was a price that this country paid for assigning to the military economy the technology resources that were essential for achieving the additional productivity. For this crucial period the total U.S. productivity gap was 28 percent. Actually, the productivity changes that would have been required year by year to achieve a stable unit labor cost (the sum of the two figures for each year) are well within the range of performance of other economies during the same period. The nations of Western Europe showed yearly productivity increases of 5.5 to 7.5 percent from 1966 to 1971, and in Japan the productivity growth was 7 to 16 percent per year.

Insofar as cost pressures played a role in the U.S. inflation and noncompetitiveness of the 1960s there is little doubt that in the manufacturing industries this was a byproduct of the new technological incapacity owing to the permanent war economy.

Creation of Surplus Capital and Labor

By the 1960s the American war economy had come full circle: from being welcomed as a solution to problems of capital and labor surplus to becoming a prime generator of surplus capital and surplus labor. The long concentration of talent and money on nonproductive economic growth had made the growth prospects for American civilian industry look plainly unattractive. Technically and economically, American firms became less competitive and hence uninviting to investors. But holders of investment capital in the United States, unimpressed with the growth of domestic opportunity, had attractive options abroad, especially in Western Europe and Canada. The capital made surplus by conditions "at home" was swiftly converted into profitable investments abroad.

The scale of the movement of capital abroad during the 1960s alone is unprecedented in American experience and, indeed, in the experience of any nation on earth. In the ten years $47 billion was moved abroad mainly by U.S. industrial corporations.[41] This was one and a half times the total foreign investments made by U.S. firms until 1960. Never before had there been such a vote of no confidence by American industrial and financial managers in the economic viability of investment in the United States.

In Western Europe and Canada, compared with the United States, capital, research and skilled manpower were directed with preference to civilian productive work. This created rapid economic growth rates that made these countries look attractive as environments for investments.[42] That is why Western Europe and Canada became the priority areas for new investment from the United States; and that is why the new surge of U.S. direct investment abroad has been primarily concentrated not in the more traditional extractive fields but overwhelmingly in the manufacturing and related industries.

Most analysts of the balance of payments have noted with approval that in association with fresh direct investments abroad there has been a pattern of profits recouped and returned to the United States. In the conventional accounting, these are entered into the balance-of-payments calculation. Hence, it has been argued that the net effect of extensive investments abroad is good for the U.S. economy on the grounds that it yields at least an equal, if not an excess, return to the U.S. economy as a whole in terms of profits returned here. Ignored in this calculation is the diminished opportunity for productive employment in the United States that has become the major consequence of starting or relocating production operations abroad.

There is actually no direct count, as by an industrial census, of the number of jobs terminated in this country owing to the closing of factories and their relocation abroad. Neither is there a full count of the number of jobs created abroad by the direct investment of U.S. capital that represent employment opportunities forgone in the United States. However, it is possible to make useful estimates. First, there are published and privately assembled reports of factory closings and jobs terminated, followed by reestablishment of production facilities in foreign countries. Second, there are estimates of the number of jobs represented by the surplus of imports that have moved into the United States, as in 1972; there are estimates of the number of jobs created by U.S. firms abroad; and, finally, we can gauge the maximum job-creating prospects from the export of capital that has taken place.

On March 6, 1973, a representative of the AFL–CIO gave the Senate Committee on Finance the following examples of export of jobs, caused by the export of capital.

More than 1,000 steelworkers' jobs were exported from the Meriden-Wallingford, Connecticut, area to Taiwan by Insilco [International Silver] by 1971. The stainless-steel flatware formerly made in Connecticut now is imported by Insilco. This is just one example of the export of jobs of steelworkers by multinational firms which have sent thousands of jobs in ball bearings, roller chain and other steel products out of the U.S.

Six hundred machinists' jobs in Elmira, New York, were exported from the United States when the Remington Rand typewriter plant, which once employed over six thousand, closed in 1972. High costs and imports were some of the many factors blamed by local managers for the shutdown. Some production was moved to Canada. But this year the local union reported that some of the machinery was sent to Brazil, where Sperry Rand, the multinational owner of Remington Rand, also has an interest. Typewriters made under license to Remington Rand specifications in Japan have been imported. The Elmira machinists joined an estimated thirty thousand other typewriter employees in Missouri, Connecticut and other states whose jobs were exported in the five years before 1972.

One hundred eighty ladies' garment workers' jobs in San Francisco were exported by American Hospital Supply to Juarez, Mexico, in 1972 where the paper garments they made could be shipped to the U.S. market from an area just south of the U.S. border. Along that strip another fifty thousand jobs in toys, electronics, apparel, replace the jobs of American workers from Indiana to Los Angeles, from Pennsylvania to Wisconsin, as the giants of American industry joined small employers to export assembly jobs from the nation's cities and towns to Mexico, where goods for the U.S. markets are produced.

Two thousand machinists in the GE plant in Utica, New York, had their jobs exported to Singapore between 1966 and 1972, when GE made its last radio in the U.S.

Two thousand auto workers' jobs were lost in Los Angeles when Chrysler shut down. From Japan Chrysler-Mitsubishi began to send the compact Colt to the West Coast of the United States in 1971.

Sixteen hundred workers' jobs in Philadelphia Ford-Philco were affected in 1972 by the latest of a long history of job exports and relocations that has persisted in that city since 1963, when Ford-Philco began to make its worldwide shifts in electronics. Ford-Philco is one of the major exporters from Taiwan to the United States, now that Taiwan has become the largest supplier of black and white TV sets to this country. "The jump in imports from Taiwan is attributable partly to the Japanese, but the bulk comes from a continued transfer of output from U.S. to Taiwan by Admiral, Motorola, Philco Ford, RCA and Zenith. (*Consumer Electronics,* "Television Digest," February 5, 1973.) Henry Ford reportedly told the Mayor of Philadelphia that he did not expect to build any U.S. plants in the foreseeable future. Five hundred glass workers lost their jobs in a Libby-Owens Ford sheet glass plant in Shreveport, Louisiana. Pittsburgh Plate imports sheet glass from abroad.

The service jobs in America's ships have been exported until the U.S. home fleet carries only about five percent of the foreign trade volume, and U.S. employment in shipping and shipyard work is low.

Nineteen thousand shoe workers in Massachusetts alone lost their jobs in the 1960s as American shoe manufacturers faced foreign competition and followed the policy of "If you can't lick them, join them." Large conglomerate multinationals like Interco and Genesco produce shoes in France, Canada, Belgium, England, Italy and South America. A Milwaukee shoe firm announced five years ago that it would make shoes in Ireland, exclusively for the U.S. market.[43]

A number of individual trade unions have detailed the impact of plant closings in favor of imports from abroad in their industries. The United Textile Workers say: "In our organization we have lost over 235,000 jobs." At a 1972 trade-union meeting, the following was heard.

> DELEGATE RICHARD LIVINGSTON, CARPENTERS: We have over three thousand men out of work in Washington and Oregon. The timber being cut on government lands is being shipped to Japan. This lumber is processed into plywood paneling and shipped back to this country.
>
> DELEGATE LESTER NULL, POTTERY WORKERS: The pottery industry is dead. In the next four years your industry can be dead. Let's stop talking and let's start acting.
>
> DELEGATE GEORGE KNALY, ELECTRICAL WORKERS: We are vitally affected in our manufacturing division by runaway plants. Our members have lost eighty thousand jobs over the past three years in these plants. In the Chicago area, we have a large local with approximately thirty thousand people which had dropped to fifteen thousand over the last year.[44]

Unions in the textile and apparel industries claimed in 1970: "A hundred thousand of our jobs vanished this year. We think a lot of those jobs went overseas. The victims of low-wage textile imports."[45]

Thanks to the investigative reporting of CBS on November 14, 1971, we have the following details concerning the closing of American factories in the electronics field.

Ford-Philco recently dropped 1,300 workers in Philadelphia—and switched its TV production to Taiwan and Japan. IBM gets its computer components from this new factory in Taiwan. General Instruments shut down a plant in Massachusetts and another in Rhode Island. They hired over 7,000 workers in Taiwan to produce TV tuners, recorders and other components. Admiral, Zenith and RCA also have color sets made in Taiwan. Sylvania makes some of its TV sets in Hong Kong, where Motorola buys its TV components. Because of this industrial exodus, about 100,000 jobs in America have disappeared; one out of every five in consumer electronics . . . One American company, Westinghouse, doesn't make consumer electronic components at all anymore in the United States. You can be sure, if it's Westinghouse and electronic, it comes from overseas. . . .[46]

The decline in the technical and economic competence of U.S. industries produces a curious effect from the standpoint of the U.S. economy as a whole. Japan has become a heavy importer of raw materials from the United States—grain, coal, timber, iron ore—and an exporter of mass-produced high-technology products to the United States. This is, of course, one of the classic relationships of industrialized to colonial economies.

The electrical workers' unions estimate that the closing of U.S. factories in their industry and the opening of exported plants have cost them more than 120,000 lost jobs. In Appendix 3 I have given details, company by company and plant by plant, of cutbacks in U.S. employment and production, and transfers of factories abroad, on specified consumer electronics products.

The large and influential trade group, the Electronics Industries Association, has developed a split interest in consumer electronics: firms still producing in the United States retain some orientation toward cost-minimizing technology; those heavily invested in foreign production (most of the industry) are now interested in conserving their new investments. At the 1973 annual meetings of the Institute of Electronic and Electrical Engineers there was no reference to problems of domestic production, though one session did promise helpful pointers on setting up operations abroad.

By 1972, 24 percent of U.S. automobile industry sales were accounted for by foreign imports, including imported components.[47] This was equivalent to 256,000 jobs in the U.S. industry. Profitability of major U.S. firms, together with high unemployment in Detroit and other industrial centers, can thereby be combined.

The Chrysler Corporation has arranged with the Mitsubishi Company for production of the Colt, a small car marketed by Dodge. The General Motors Corporation has purchased a 34 per-cent interest in Isuzu Motors Ltd. Ford has been negotiating a major Japanese investment.

The plans of U.S. automobile companies are for an increasing proportion of U.S.-assembled cars composed of foreign-made com-ponents. Ford's small car, the Pinto, has its 80-horsepower engine and transmission made in England and its 100-horsepower engine made in Germany. The four-speed transmission for the Vega of General Motors has been made in France.[48]

The Ford Motor Company's arrangements for foreign part pro-duction include car-cooler compressors from Diesel-Kiki (an affili-ate of Isuzu Motors), automobile pumps from Nippon-Denso, auto condensers from the Matsushita Electrical Industrial Com-pany, bearings from the Koyo-Seiko Company and alternator diodes from the Tokyo Shibaura Electric Company. At the same time a series of smaller American-based firms have been entering the Japanese industrial-investment field.[49]

Diversity has been the rule in foreign industrial arrangements.[50] Nevertheless a definable substitution process has been set in motion. This was outlined for one of my seminars at Columbia University by the research director of the United Electrical Workers, Nathan Spero, on November 23, 1971. Mr. Spero sum-marized the matter as follows.

> Following investment made abroad by the U.S. firm, the first effect of setting up a foreign subsidiary is to substitute for the export from the United States to the foreign country. The second step . . . is where a U.S. company that has been exporting from the U.S. to a third country has its foreign subsidiary take over that export now serving the third country. The result is, then, two sources of displacement. The third effect is that the foreign subsidiary begins to take over the U.S. domestic market of the multinational company.

Officers of the AFL–CIO estimate that during the period 1966–69 the growth of imports to the United States compared with exports represented a net loss of approximately 500,000 American job opportunities in that period.[51]

Another way to reckon employment forgone in the United States is the job equivalent represented by import surpluses. For example, in 1972 the surplus of imports to the United States over exports amounted to $6.4 billion. Allowing for an average year of labor as costing $8,000 to a U.S. employer, then the import surplus alone represents the equivalent of about 800,000 man-years of labor.

A more comprehensive way of gauging the employment forgone in the United States is the number of jobs created abroad by the direct investments of U.S. firms. The U.S. Tariff Commission has concluded that by 1970 U.S. firms employed about 5 million persons abroad. Of these, 3.5 million were in manufacturing enterprises.[52]

Finally, it is worth estimating the surplus-labor effects of U.S. direct foreign investments in terms of the jobs represented by that much investment. I have excluded the U.S. investment in foreign mining and petroleum on the assumption that there is no U.S. domestic option. From this vantage point the increase in U.S. direct foreign investment in manufacturing and other industries during the period 1960–70 amounted to $31.376 billion. We know that for manufacturing industry in the United States the average net investment in property, plant and equipment per employee amounted to $7,794 in 1965. So the $31 billion invested abroad during the 1960s was equivalent to the investment required for 4 million American industrial employees.[53] This estimate of employment forgone represents manufacturing and other industries as compared to the Tariff Commission estimate of 3.5 million for manufacturing alone.[54]

I judge that it is entirely reasonable to understand that the export of $31 billion in capital during the 1960s resulted in not fewer than 3 million and as many as 4 million job opportunities forgone in the United States. (At the same time, 4 million Americans were registered as unemployed during 1970.) Unmistakably, surplus capital and surplus labor have become primary products of the permanent war economy.

In American industry competent technology and industrial efficiency have become casualties of the war economy. This is revealed by the epidemic deterioration of research and production capability in major industries, by the progressive inability of many firms to hold even the domestic market against foreign competitors, and by the consequent formation of capital and labor surpluses. Though probably unintended, these results were unavoidable in the presence of the relentless drive by the war-economy directorate to enlarge its decision power in the name of national security. But the cost of this "protection" has come very high, not only in industry but in other areas of life where failures have been the price of successful preemption of capital and talent for the priority goals of the war economy.

Five

UNFORESEEN EFFECTS: SOCIETAL FAILURES FROM WAR-ECONOMY SUCCESSES

IF THERE HAS BEEN a single defining feature of United States policy during the long Cold War, it has been the relentless effort to hold a position of military and economic dominance in the world. Americans will therefore be unprepared for the idea that by 1982, or sooner, the economic output per person in the Japanese economy will exceed that in the United States.[1] This forecast assumes nothing more dramatic than a continuation in each country of the trend of economic performance between 1960 and 1970. This unexpected turn of events fits neither with the ideological consensus about the U.S. economy nor with the urgency for being Number One that pervades American culture. To Americans, the idea of being Number One means not merely having unsurpassed military and industrial power, but also a high and rising level of material well-being for the population as a whole. Being superior in both guns and butter has been part of the American self-image.

For two centuries, the people of the United States were able to draw upon a cornucopia of natural wealth, agricultural and mineral, readily available from the vast lands of this country. As the labor of millions of immigrants (and, for a time, slaves) was applied to this natural hoard, spurred by self-interest or driven by economic necessity, the resulting accumulation of means of production and consumer goods was unprecedented in human history. There was so much to go around that while the Morgans and Rockefellers could take their piles, an increasing proportion of the working and middle classes could believe in the prospects of better living for themselves and their children. So pervasive was this self-perception that even many educated Americans were caught by surprise at the appearances of books which described an "Other America" than the land of growing middle-class affluence. The growth of material wealth was paralleled by improvement in the quality of "human capital." Especially after World War II, higher education received an immense spur, giving the U.S. an unequaled population of scientists, engineers and technologists and the means of producing more of them.

By contrast, the people of Japan have had little of the natural-resource base available to the United States. The Japanese must buy in and haul in their main raw materials. They live on a string of islands with none of the advantages that inhere in having a large land mass. Only a quarter century ago much of their productive capacity lay in ruins as a result of American bombardment. That a people so situated could, in little more than a quarter century, rise to the point of equaling and surpassing the productiveness of Americans is a historically startling achievement.

Flip explanations about Oriental inscrutability, manual dexterity and diligence, the "work ethic" or the operation of a "Japan, Inc.," do not account for Japan's success. In modern industry, productivity growth is achieved by mechanization, by organization of work and by stable operation of the means of production by a work force of growing competence. When all of this is applied in high concentration to productive economic growth, the resulting multiplication of effect can result in just the sort of economy-wide growth rate in Japan that has surprised the whole world. That surprise, however, would be of most use if it were turned around and converted into the question: What is the essential feature of the use of resources that made the Japanese achievement possible?

The Japanese attended to productive economic growth while the United States built and operated a permanent war economy. As a result, American society has become incapable of utilizing its immense technological and other economic resources to assure a high-quality productive future for the American people. *The fundamental fact is that the directorate of the state capitalism which dominates American economy by controlling the major decisions on the use of production resources has no institutional or ideological commitment to ensure a productive future for American society.*

Ideologically, the state managers are committed to "national security" as their main responsibility. Translated, that has meant utilizing military and economic methods for expanding and maintaining the scope of Pax Americana throughout the world. Institutionally, the state managers are dedicated to maintaining and enlarging their decision power. Principal strategies toward this end have included sustained emphasis on nonproductive economic growth at home and strong encouragement to the export of capital from the United States to other countries. In the ideologies of the state-capitalist directorate there is no place for consideration of long-term consequences of current strategies. The shortsightedness of American state capitalism is illustrated by the response of the state managers to two major events which, in their own understanding, were appreciated as genuine crises requiring their intervention. These were, first, the appearance of a major U.S. foreign-trade deficit and, second, the collapse of the value of the dollar in relation to other currencies.

When, in 1971—for the first time since 1893—a deficit appeared in U.S. trade with other nations, federal officials became alarmed at the manifest noncompetitiveness of U.S. industry in the world marketplace, and by the predictions of more to come. The government announced a series of moves toward improving civilian technology. William Magruder was moved from NASA, where he was in charge of the supersonic-transport program, to the White House and asked to plan civilian-technology programs. A task force from the President's Office of Science and Technology was set up to encourage the transfer of federally generated technology to state and local governments. Research and development pooling among smaller companies was to be promoted, and patent policies were to be altered in order to encourage private use of government-owned patents. Furthermore, the government indicated that it was planning to make money available to start new high-technology enterprises, and a bill was submitted to the Congress in 1972 for this purpose. Also, a series of investigations was started to discover ways of inducing business firms and others to develop and utilize new technology. All of this was oriented to the agreed requirement that productivity in U.S. industry has to be accelerated.

Every reader could draw up quite a list of new technologies or product changes that would improve the quality of life and that are not in process. These include the design of housing, materials and devices that are used in the household, vehicles for public transportation, facilities for health care, etc. Consider a mundane matter like the design of school buses which are used to transport 19 million pupils daily in the United States. The National Highway Safety Bureau investigated the safety factors in school-bus design, and a host of grave defects were found, ranging from unsafe bus bodies and seats to poorly designed vehicles for high-speed travel. The National Transportation Safety Board concluded that the six principal manufacturers building 25,000 school-bus bodies each year could not, on their own, afford the engineering needed to design safer buses.[2] Civilian-oriented engineers could, without difficulty, draw up agendas of product and production method improvements that would yield significant upgrading of U.S. industries, their products and their productivity.

By March 1973 this entire orientation had been terminated. In the words of one official, "It seems to be a subject that no one in the administration wants to talk about anymore. The White House doesn't want to stir up more debate about multinational companies at a time when it is trying to get labor unions to drop their support of protectionist legislation."[3] This explanation from inside the administration hardly begins to explain what had taken place.

During 1972 administration officials seemed to recover from the panic which had seized them in 1971 upon observing the growing imbalance of trade. They had begun to seek out alternatives for making large sales overseas which they, the state managers themselves, could initiate and operate. They soon discovered major opportunities. First, the Department of Defense came through with a major plan for enlarging world sales of armaments from the United States, increasing such exports from $925 million in 1970 to $3.8 billion per year in 1973.[4] Negotiations were undertaken with the U.S.S.R. for large sales of agricultural produce, and the administration proceeded to deal vigorously with the Japanese to slow down the rate of Japanese penetration into U.S. markets and accelerate the export of U.S. goods to Japan. At the same time, the administration hoped for an across-the-board stimulus to U.S. exports as a result of devaluing the dollar in relation to other currencies.

With this orientation it seemed unnecessary to initiate industrial-technology programs that would involve varying degrees of government intervention into the affairs of U.S. industrial operations. For example, it is conceivable that if the average efficiency of industrial plants were raised to the productivity level that is attained by the group of most efficient plants, industry by industry, then the average performance would be appreciably improved. But before a payoff could be expected, this would require a very considerable effort, extending over at least five or ten years, on the part of government, the managements of firms, engineers and workers—including major new capital investments in the United States and a national productivity campaign. The strategy for improving the competitiveness of U.S. industry by raising productivity was put aside and the work required was forgone by orienting to the state managers' own strategy. In this context the appearance of familiar incantations about government-ought-not-interfere-with-free-enterprise has the quality of ideology to justify the selective preference of the state managers for solving problems with methods that are serviceable for maintaining and enlarging their own authority. That is exactly what they proceeded to do.

The enlargement of armaments sales abroad is the largest single effort that the state management devised for restoring a favorable balance of trade to the United States. This effort will ensure high-capacity utilization of many military-industry facilities in the United States, with all the depleting consequences that are to be expected from that work. To be sure, that result is not anticipated by the military-economy managers, because their world view does not include deterioration of civilian production as an effect that is related to the successful performance of their military-industry work.

The federal government's managers concentrate on their industry (the "public sector") for which research and development money and man-hours are assigned in abundance, while the rest of technology gets a hand-me-down treatment. Spin-off from military technology is predicted, but nothing is ever demonstrated as worth 80 percent of all government research spending. American state capitalism shows no capacity whatever for thoughtful attention to the great array of technological issues whose neglect or constructive resolution will make an immense difference to the quality of life in this country ten and twenty years hence. The military-oriented single-mindedness that has dominated decisions on U.S. technology for more than a quarter century has little or no place for the idea of a productive future that deserves or requires deliberate attention. Instead, the productivity growth of American society is taken for granted as a "given" condition—in relation to which the cost of the military economy is to be accepted as a reasonable service charge.

In the relation of the United States to other countries, the collapse in the value of the dollar formally declared in August 1971 was traceable to the sustained U.S. military expenditures around the world. The cost of operating 340 major military bases in more than thirty-six countries, together with the military spending occasioned by the Korean and Vietnam Wars, produced net U.S. military spending abroad, from 1947 to 1969, totaling $52 billion ("net" means after subtracting income to the military from the sale of armaments around the world). By August 1971, central banks of Western Europe in particular found themselves holding tens of billions of dollars which were not needed by their own economies for purchases in the United States.

Then a remarkable drama unfolded. During the two weeks preceding August 15, 1971, many U.S. firms, anticipating a reduction in the value of the dollar relative to Western European currencies, moved large (dollar) cash holdings abroad and purchased Western European currencies with their dollars. This, and allied money speculation, had the quality of a "self-fulfilling prophecy," for it weakened the readiness of the European bankers and governments to hold U.S. dollars (equivalent to IOU's on U.S. economy) indefinitely. As Europeans tried to cash in their dollar holdings for U.S. Treasury gold, President Nixon declared, on August 15, that U.S. dollars held abroad were no longer convertible to gold on demand. Had gold convertibility been retained, the U.S. Treasury's gold reserve could have been wiped out. The sustained increase in foreign dollar holdings, paralleled by gradual erosion of the federal Treasury's gold stock, are portrayed in the accompanying chart prepared by the First National Bank of Chicago.[5]

Immediately, the value of the dollar relative to other currencies

U.S. Gold Stock and Foreign Liquid Dollar Holdings

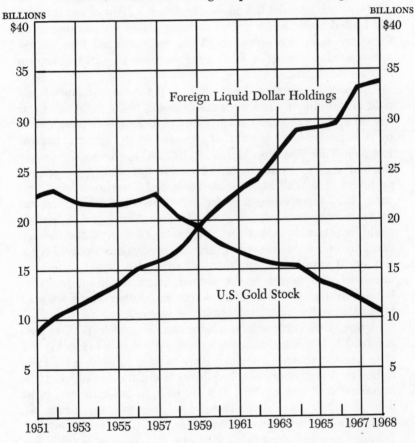

began to fall. This meant that U.S. man-hours were now salable to Europeans at a lower price in European currency. Stated differently, Americans would henceforth pay higher prices in dollars for European and virtually all other foreign goods and services. Thus the debacle of August 15, 1971, in the hitherto preeminent position of the U.S. dollar was directly traceable to the long-sustained military outlay by the U.S. abroad and to the flight of capital from the United States seeking advantageous places for investment. In these processes the operation of the multinational firm is best appreciated as being a facilitating instrument rather than an autonomous factor.

One way of gauging the decline in the relative financial and political position of the United States owing to the flight of capital abroad and the new nonconvertibility of U.S. dollars is suggested by an unprecedented report that appeared on the financial page of *The New York Times* on March 13, 1972. Alan Greenspan, former chief of staff to President Nixon in the 1968 election and then president of a Wall Street firm, Townsend-Greenspan and Company, Inc., reported in a letter to clients that foreign central (government) banks holding a $53-billion hoard of U.S. dollars could conceivably use these dollars to take over the foreign divisions or subsidiaries of American corporations established in Europe. It wasn't long ago that any such idea would have been dismissed everywhere in the United States as an unthinkable, farfetched speculation, let alone worth publication on the financial page of the nation's most influential newspaper.[6]

As foreigners became increasingly unwilling, after 1971, to simply hold U.S. dollars as assets (as though they were gold) the state managers were compelled to try to offer something for them to buy at attractive prices. The pile-up of dollars abroad had to be at least slowed and a return flow induced. In order for this to be done the dollar was made cheaper relative to other currencies. This lowered the prices of American goods—in terms of, say, Japanese yen and West German marks. But patterns of trade had already developed based upon the relative undesirability of many classes of U.S.-manufactured goods.

As American manufactured goods became less attractive to foreign buyers the range of salable American goods has tended to narrow down, with greater emphasis on raw materials and agricultural products. The result has been that during the late 1960s and early 1970s Japanese purchases from the United States had accented the purchase of wheat, meat, logs for wood and similar products. Large-scale purchases of American wood, reaching about 10 percent of the American output in 1973, contributed to a real shortage in lumber available in the United States for construction and other work. The result has been sharp increases in the price of lumber and lumber products, with resulting increases in prices of new homes built largely of wood.

Increased export of U.S.-produced grains to Japan, Western Europe and the U.S.S.R., all pressed by the government as major moves for soaking up dollars held abroad, led to sharp reductions in American stocks and dramatic price increases in grains and in grain-dependent products for the domestic markets. Thus the prices of all grades of meat products in the United States increased dramatically during 1972–73 as a response to the increased cost of feeding and fattening cattle. The export of grain was pressed by the federal government to bring back dollars and to stave off further loss of confidence in the dollar abroad and further loss of its value in relation to other currencies. Hence, in order to "defend" the international value of the dollar, the grain exports on a large scale and their consequences had to be borne. The consequences included not only higher prices of meat to American consumers but increased exports of U.S. meats, especially prime cuts, to Japan. In Japan prices of meat and meat products have been higher than in the United States, and American meat prices were made more attractive in terms of Japanese yen as the dollar became worth about 20 percent less. One result has been that prime cuts of meat became unavailable to American buyers in many parts of the country.

Consider the range of consequences from the large-scale exportation of wood and meat. Wood for housing and high-grade foodstuffs were both made far more expensive and therefore less available to Americans. Necessarily, it produced a drop in the level of living for the tens of millions of families who were compelled during the winter of 1973, for example, to shift their eating habits in response to higher meat prices. Millions had no out but to heed the advice that flowed from Washington: eat chicken! eat fish! eat cheese! eat vegetables! and, finally, eat less! The effect of the dollar devaluation did not stop there.

The rising prices of foodstuffs and lumber products had been part of across-the-board sharp price increases that were spurred by the military economy. From 1965 to 1973 wholesale prices in the U.S. rose 37.4 percent. In Chapter Four I showed how the failure to increase productivity helped to induce price increases owing to the pressure of cost. The present discussion adds another factor to the inflationary process: increase in price owing to physical shortage of goods in relation to market demand. In these ways American state capitalism has finally generated the combination of upward pressure on prices from higher costs ("cost push") and upward pressure on prices from inadequate supplies to waiting purchasers ("demand pull").

Inflation has a further effect on the quality of life, reaching far beyond price inflation at the supermarket counter. As larger parts of available wage and salary incomes must be spent on necessities of life under the pressure of, for example, rising food costs, less is available for the whole range of things that are part of a good life style. Furthermore, across-the-board price inflation diminishes the purchasing power of money that has been put aside as insurance against economic insecurity. This includes reduced purchasing power of savings, pension funds and income to be received from fixed-return investments like government bonds. Thereby the 36 percent increase in the cost of living from 1968 to 1974 alone has the corresponding effect of destroying the value of every kind of saving by the same percent.

Starting with the decline in the international value of the dollar owing to economic noncompetitiveness of U.S. industry and military expenditures at home and abroad, an economic mechanism is set in motion that finally takes away current income and savings from every citizen. This process diminishes the economic capability of every institution in American society except for the directorate of American state capitalism. That group draws fresh capital funds as a percent of the taxes that are extracted from the income of the entire nation. From the standpoint of the state management, price inflation is easily offset by simply increasing the budgeted funds for its operations.

One consequence of the decline of the value of the American dollar is its considerable impact on American business. Ordinary business planning of every kind is made very difficult by highly unstable prices and wages. At the same time, there is increased opportunity for selling American-produced goods abroad because of their more attractive price as the value of foreign currencies rises in comparison to the dollar. However, the impact of a devalued dollar, newly regarded as an unstable currency—and hence as an uncertain store of economic value—extends to long term structural changes in the operations of many U.S. firms. From a businessman acquaintance I have obtained a personal account of the impact of the declining value of the dollar and the declining acceptability of the dollar on the operations of his firm. The essential facts are given here, leaving out, however, the identity of the firm.

About three years ago [1970] an American corporation, engaged in doing business throughout the world, acquired a Swiss office and formed a wholly owned legitimate Swiss subsidiary in order to be able to do more business with European customers. As a result, it now had the same merchandise warehoused both in New York and Europe. The purpose was for both corporations to be able to act independently, each having its own capital.

This new corporation, being wholly subject to Swiss law, employs only Swiss citizens and has its own directors and officers (a majority of whom must be Swiss), its own accountants and attorneys (who must be Swiss). The American corporation has members on the board, and in order to conform with both American and Swiss law, the subsidiary is completely autonomous and legally does as it pleases. It has the legal right to employ any people and services it wishes and pay whatever it wishes for these employees and services. It can create its own prices, even if they be different than those charged by the American parent firm, and can negotiate its own contracts for merchandise.

This plan has developed several interesting conditions. On the one hand, it acts as the savior of the business. On the other hand, it seriously prejudices the business activities of the parent corporation (as against its financial interest).

Originally, both corporations were entering into similar contracts with writers, paper manufacturers, printers, etc., and sharing the publications that resulted. The only difference was that the parent corporation paid in dollars and sold in the United States, Canada, and Mexico for dollars, while the sub sold in Europe and was paid in Swiss francs or French francs, which were readily convertible to Swiss francs. The important thing to remember is that almost all the writers, printers, etc., worked in France or other European nations.

Over the last two years [1971–72] more and more of the producers of the component parts have formed Swiss, West German, or Japanese corporations, even though they are located physically in

France, and almost all of the writers are now demanding payment in either Swiss or West German currency. In short, the parent firm is finding it more difficult to produce in its own name, as it must pay its bills abroad in the currency of those countries. Convertibility of dollars is becoming a problem, and it is increasingly expensive to change dollars into foreign currency (exchange fees, arbitrage, devaluation). We also are unable to raise prices in the United States in dollars to overcome the results of European inflation and American devaluation.

As a result, it is becoming apparent that, as time goes on, the American parent will more and more be unable to act as a producer until finally it will simply be a sales agent for its Swiss subsidiary. Fortunately, being a legal entity in Switzerland, the subsidiary is not subject to several Swiss laws that would further hamper, if not destroy, the American operation. (1) It is not subject to the ban which exists from time to time on American dollars being sent into Switzerland for exchange into Swiss francs, and (2) it is not subject to the 8 percent per annum tax on American monies sent into Switzerland. This allows the U.S. parent firm to purchase from its Swiss subsidiary and pay in dollars to them, but does not allow the parent firm to directly obtain Swiss francs in Switzerland without penalty. If the U.S. corporation cannot obtain the Swiss francs without penalty, or eventually perhaps at all, then it will have no way of paying the writers, etc., in the francs they demand for their services and products.

With the cost of doing business in this field being very high, further compounded by extremely high overhead in the United States, it is only a matter of time, with a few more roadblocks placed by either the producers, the United States government currency regulations, or foreign government regulations, that it will become impossible for the parent corporation to continue to do business in the United States. It will then be in a most peculiar position: the American corporation will be unable to continue in business in the United States; the Swiss subsidiary will do business in Europe *and the United States* and employ only European personnel, writers, and suppliers; and at the same time be totally subject to Swiss law and the business judgments made on its behalf by its Swiss directors.*

There are several lessons from this example of an American firm that invested in a foreign-based subsidiary: due to growing weakness of the dollar, foreign governments restrict the use of dollars; the parent American firm gradually loses authority over the operations of its wholly owned foreign-registered subsidiary; owing to

* At some future date a restriction might be placed by the Swiss government on the payment of profits by the Swiss firm to the American parent firm.

its easier access to preferred European hard currencies, the subsidiary is in a gradually improving position to do the business originally shared with the parent firm in the United States; the U.S. parent firm, if this trend continues, will become mainly a sales outlet for the activity controlled by the separately managed foreign subsidiary; finally, the parent firm in the United States can continue to profit from the subsidiary's operations as long as the government that registers the subsidiary permits the free transfer of profits to the United States.

Hence, within the framework of relationships of this sort, the declining value of the dollar carries the promise of less work for the American parts of multinational firms, less authority for the American parent firm, and the unspoken threat to profit-taking from foreign subsidiaries. As such dramas unfold they vitiate a part of the strategy of the directorate of America's state capitalism which has strongly encouraged foreign investment and operations by U.S. firms as part of a larger strategy of locking-in the foreign economies involved with the economy of the United States. Ironically, the U.S. state managers, with their arrogant military preoccupations, caused the debacle in the value of the dollar and the consequent undermining of their own economic thrust for world hegemony.[7]

Every year since 1961 the Secretary of Defense has presented to the Congress a report on the military-security position of the United States. The content of these reports has been wide-ranging, from military-technology subjects and the balance of payments to various efforts by the Pentagon to participate in the War on Poverty. In none of these elaborate statements is there so much as a hint that the Pentagon's enterprise might have a negative effect on the domestic security of the American people due to the drain on capital, manpower and the preemption of social attention. There is also a year-round effort by the military and civilian officers of the Pentagon to justify the operation of the military directorate as an all-around boon to American economy and society. Finally, however, even the biggest propaganda barrage cannot cover up the cumulative effects of nonproductive economic growth. The dollars that pay for the operation of the military system finally represent something forgone from other aspects of life, especially those parts that are also dependent on financing from the community's public budgets.

1974 FEDERAL BUDGET

Civilian-Economy Cuts	($ million)	($ million)	Military-Economy Increases
CUT in grants for basic water and sewer facilities under HUD Community Development Program	7.3	6.9	INCREASE for MK 48 torpedo
CUT in construction loans and grants for higher education	18.0	15.3	INCREASE for E-3A airborne warning and control system
CUT in education for the handicapped under HEW Office of Education	23.9	22.9	INCREASE for SAM-D missile
CUT in library resources under HEW Office of Education	33.9	29.0	INCREASE for B-1 bomber
CUT in federally supported hospital and health-facility construction	36.0	39.5	INCREASE for manned-space-flight research and development under NASA
CUT in operations, research, and facilities of the Environmental Protection Agency	75.4	73.9	INCREASE for NASA
CUT in Indian programs under Minority Assistance Programs (to broaden opportunities for economic participation and self-determination)	82.2	94.3	INCREASE for A-X tactical attack aircraft
CUT in federally aided health training and education	86.0	92.0	INCREASE in Air Force research, development, test and evaluation

CUT in child nutrition for elementary and secondary education	200.0	194.2	REQUEST for SAM-D missile
CUT in manpower revenue-sharing under Labor Department Manpower Administration	252.0	239.9	INCREASE for F-15 tactical fighter aircraft (77 planes)
CUT in emergency employment assistance under Manpower Administration	519.7	546.3	REQUEST for S-3A Viking anti-submarine-warfare aircraft
CUT in elementary and secondary education	1,500.0	1,200.0	REQUEST for one Trident submarine

NOTE: The civilian-military trade-offs illustrated above have become a continuing feature of federal budgetry. The idea that the U.S. can have both guns and butter in unlimited amounts, and continuously, is not borne out by the development of federal budgets through 1986. For 1986 the trade-off problem became acute, as the administration's budget plan proposed a $32 billion reduction in civilian obligations in order to achieve a $32 billion increase in military spending. This latter development is mirrored in the trade-off pattern shown on pages 200-202.—S.M.

119

Public expenditure trade-offs form a major connection between war economy and quality of life, and the link is visible in a set of choices made by the Nixon administration for 1974. Note the preceding list of proposed cuts in civilian items contrasted with increased money recommended by the administration for particular military and related matters.

In making these contrasts I do not imply that if the tax money were not spent on the military that it would necessarily be applied to the indicated civilian uses. Rather, I wish to underscore that within a given level of public spending (there are limits to the taxes that people will bear), such trade-offs are being made in effect, though rarely stated openly. The existence of a tradeoff is denied by the operators and apologists for war economy on the grounds that the money spent on the military does as much for the economy as money spent on civilian activities. Nevertheless, there are economic consequences from their actions apart from the justifications that are offered.

The cumulative effects of such choices are highly visible in the principal cities of the United States. In April 1971 the mayors of seventeen large cities gathered in New York City, and after they had seen some of New York's most depressing sights—the abandoned and devastated blocks of the Brownsville section of Brooklyn—the general comment of the visiting mayors was that it reminded them of home. "It's just a difference of degree—we've got the same problem," was the comment of the mayor of New Orleans. And the mayor of Boston responded to the Brownsville vista by saying, "This may be the first tangible sign of the collapse of our civilization." The mayor of New Orleans made known his judgment that his city "was going down the drain." And the mayor of Detroit spoke of his "disaster plan" budget.[8]

A national survey by The New York Times disclosed that not only amenities that make life more pleasurable but also basic services are being cut back in the principal cities of the United States. Education appears to be the hardest hit of all the public services, but various amenities that raise the level of living are also being cut back. Here are some examples: In Detroit, some park toilets have been closed to save money, and a third of the city museum has been closed daily for the same reason. In Atlanta, a proffered gift of $27,000 worth of trees to grace the downtown area was rejected because the city could not afford to keep them watered. In Portland, Maine, a $3,000 donation by the city to the city symphony was dropped, along with $2,000 for a children's theater. In Toledo, Ohio, the budget squeeze has forced a reduction in the hours that the city's swimming pools are kept open.[9]

The deterioration of American big cities is linked to the failure to carry out an economic-development process for the American underclasses who have been increasingly crowded into the central cities. Economic development is the name of the many-sided process by which a person becomes more capable, and hence more productive. This result is obtained by simultaneous improvement in education, health care, housing, training in work skills and work habits and greater competence in the host of capabilities that go into knowing how to live in a highly productive as against a poor society.

In 1966 I calculated the all-inclusive cost of economic development for the 30 million Americans who needed it. The estimate was about $50,000 per family of four. This included an allowance for new capital investment needed to provide job opportunities. All told, I found that about $375 billion worth of effort, extended over a ten-year period, would be required to make the leap forward that is called economic development. But sums of this magnitude were never available through the so-called War on Poverty, which was, at most, a token effort from the start. From 1965 to 1970 the real war in Vietnam and the paper "war" on poverty used up, together, $115 billion. Vietnam took 91.7 percent and the "war" on poverty 8.3 percent.[10] The estimate I have given here on the cost of serious economic development in the United States does not include the sums necessary for physical reconstruction of so much of America's big cities that are, in the understanding of their own mayors, major distressed and disaster areas.

American society pays for this economic underdevelopment in the form of economic output that is forgone by the unemployed, the underemployed, and those whose work capability is a fraction of what it could be. Conservatively, this output forgone is not less than $50 billion per year. To this must be added, of course, the special social cost (police, fire, jails, courts, welfare) of maintaining deteriorating cities and degraded populations there and in the countryside. The additional social costs of sustaining an impoverished population is probably about equal to the estimate of the value of output forgone. All told, then, the cost to American society of maintaining economic underdevelopment is not less than $100 billion per year.[11]

On grounds of "economic rationality," in the form of a social cost–benefit analysis, it seems irrational to continue a pattern of this kind. Rationality would dictate an effort to make a social investment whose return would take the form of increased economic output and reduced social cost. But calculations of this kind elude the policy-makers, the Congressmen, the intellectuals and others whose scale of what is important has been informed by the ideological consensus of American state capitalism. In the conventional wisdom it is fashionable to calculate many economic conditions in terms of national averages. This has the direct effect of concealing variations, permitting the privileged high performers to mask the presence of sizable "hidden" populations whose economic lot is underdevelopment.[12]

The extent of economic deterioration in the cities of the U.S. would be a mystery forever if we had no way of explaining the unique consequences of nonproductive economic activity. After all, the decay of America's cities occurred during a period of economic growth in the United States. From 1950 to 1970 the yearly economic product per person rose from $2,342 to $3,516 (measured in 1958 dollars of "constant" value).[13] At the same time the additional taxes generated by the new income were being preempted for the military. This involved not only the direct removal of money and men for military work but also the cumulative effect of productive output forgone.

Professor Bruce Russett has shown that in American experience from 1939 to 1968, one dollar of expenditure for military purposes resulted in $.29 less fixed investments in the United States (among other reductions). This finding is of special interest because of its effects on the quality of the American economy into a far future. Russett points out:

> Since future production is dependent upon current investment, the economy's *future* resources and power base are thus much more severely damaged by the decision to build or employ current military power than is current indulgence. According to some rough estimates . . . an additional dollar of investment in any single year will produce 20–25¢ of annual additional production in perpetuity. Hence, if an extra billion dollars of defense in one year reduced investment by $292 million, thenceforth the level of output in the economy would

be *permanently* diminished by a figure on the order of $65 million per year.[14]

During the late 1950s and early 1960s, one of the articles of faith among many American policy-makers and their supporting intellectuals was the idea that U.S. military spending gives the United States not only a military advantage but also a lead in an economic contest. The assumption was that the United States, but not the U.S.S.R., is rich enough to run a fast pace in an arms race. Therefore by forcing the Russians to compete, the United States would be wearing down the other side. The purveyors of this shrewd idea never allowed themselves to admit the possibility that the American war economy could also devour the civilian economy of the United States.

The assumption that sustained war economy brings economic and allied well-being encounters a cruel contrast in the shape of what is forgone in the United States in health care, housing, education and minimum nutrition. These are all recognized areas of public responsibility partly because the consequences of deficiencies in these realms have blighting effects on the entire society.

For this book I cannot attempt a rounded portrait of the effects on the quality of life that are owing to long deterioration of productive economic investments. I will only sample the scene. Perhaps the best place to start is to call attention to the condition of life in the South Bronx, an area of New York City that has become one of the concentration points of human and physical deterioration of every kind. Four articles appearing in *The New York Times* January 15–18, 1973, portray a nightmare of human misery, deterioration and decay in this benighted community. Let the first four paragraphs of Martin Tolchin's reporting speak for themselves.

The fire hydrants are open, even in this biting cold weather—town pumps that provide the sole water supply for drinking, washing and sanitation for thousands of tenants in 20 percent of the housing in the area. When one hydrant freezes over, the residents pry open another.

Packs of wild dogs pick through the rubble and roam the streets, sometimes attacking residents. As protection, many mailmen, health workers and deliverers carry dog repellent.

A drug pusher is murdered by a youth gang acting on a $30 contract from a rival pusher. A youngster is nearly stomped to death outside a school in an argument over a soda bottle. Merchants close their stores at sunset even though many are armed and some conduct business inside their stores behind bullet-proof glass.

This is the South Bronx today—violent, drugged, burned out, graffiti-splattered and abandoned. Forty percent of the 400,000 residents are on welfare, and 30 percent of the employables are unemployed.[15]

The idea that quality of life could be a public responsibility gained support from a sizable minority in the United States during the 1960s. However, political leaders, many intellectuals and the general populace did not concur. The quality of life was to remain mainly a personal and private responsibility, while grudgingly subsidized from the public purse. The rule here was subsidy-minimization. The ideological consensus obscured the actual connection between priority to military economy and deficient health care, decay of the central cities, and the general failure to carry out economic and social development for the unindustrialized parts of American society. Guns took away from butter.

Item: From 1970 on, the federal government undertook across-the-board reduction in sponsoring scientific research of every sort. In particular, major reductions or total elimination was ordered for educational support of new biologists, chemists, physicists, and every other science. Thereby the directorate of war economy withdrew investment in the future of the United States as a productive society.[16]

Item: By 1970 the actual demand for new doctors in the United States was 50 percent greater than the 8,500 new M.D.s receiving their degree in that year.[17]

Item: In New York City the municipal hospitals had 4,480 nurses on their staffs, but needed 1,400 more to meet reasonable standards.[18]

Item: The National Academy of Sciences in September 1972 found that emergency medical services represented "one of the weakest links in delivery of health care in the nation," and that thousands of lives are lost through lack of systematic application of established principles of emergency care.[19]

Item: The American population as a whole is described as a nation of "nutritional illiterates," and among the poor one out of four have been found to be anemic to the degree requiring medical care. Among children of migrant workers malnutrition is found as severe as that once seen in Biafra during the civil war and siege of the 1960s.[20]

Item: California, the capital state of military industry, has been importing 70 percent of its physicians, 75 percent of its registered nurses and 60 percent of its pharmacists, thereby draining the medical resources of the donor states.[21]

Item: In 1970, studies of adult literacy showed that "half the nation's adults may lack the literacy necessary to master such day-to-day reading matter as driving manuals, newspapers and job applications."[22]

Item: From 1970 to 1973 there was an epidemic of reductions in school budgets, teaching personnel and educational programs throughout the country. The length of the school year was reduced in a series of large cities.[23]

Item: Meanwhile the elite military academies of the Pentagon operate on a business-as-usual basis, costing as much as $30,000 per student-year.[24]

Item: To maintain Pax Americana, dictatorships are supported, including the ones in Southeast Asia, which sponsor a hard drug traffic toward the United States. The dreadful human effects of mass addiction are apparently acceptable to the directorate of military economy, and their supporters, as part of the price of sustaining these client governments.[25]

The war in Vietnam and the other military, political and economic policies of the United States during the Cold War are all justified by the political directorate of the war economy as essential for the security of the United States even though the proximate effects of aggressive military adventurism include profound deterioration within the United States as represented by mass drug addiction and the breakdown of minimal requirements for human community.

Societal failures from successes in American military economy are transmitted, tragically, to many of the developing countries of the world. More often than not the new elites of these countries feel strongly impelled to emulate the U.S. example of how the government of an industrial society behaves. A young professor in an African university once put it to me that, "after all, the young and developing countries of the world must look to a model of what constitutes an industrial, fully developed country in order that they may have an example to emulate." In the present case, for developing countries to follow the American example is to slow their economic development—even to the extent of helping to widen the productivity gap between themselves and the developed nations.

From an authoritative report of the United Nations we learn:

> Although military spending in developing countries is very low in relation to that of the advanced countries, it is significant that in the decade of the sixties the rate of growth of military expenditures was appreciably faster in the developing countries than the world average —in contrast to what has happened in the six nations which are the major military spenders. Against a world rise of about 3 to 4 per cent a year, military spending in the developing countries has been increasing at a rate of some 7 per cent a year. When the needs of economic development are so pressing, it is a disturbing thought that these countries should have found it necessary to increase their military spending so speedily, particularly when their *per capita* income is so low. To the citizen of a developing country, with a *per capita* income of about $200 a year, even the diversion of a few dollars for military purposes may rob him of one of the necessities of life.[26]

During 1973 the United States alone was responsible for $10.7 billion worth of military assistance of diverse sorts, mainly to less developed countries. In that year, sixty-four countries received U.S. military assistance, twenty-seven of them being governments that permit no political opposition.[27]

In the developing countries, by 1970, military expenditures from their own budgets (not including gifts, grants, etc.) totaled $28 billion. By contrast, their entire spending on urgently needed health and education was $25 billion.[28]

Priority to military development in the developing countries, strongly encouraged by the United States and the Soviet Union,[29] has the parallel effect of holding back economic development in most of the world. From 1960 to 1970 the total per-capita output of the developed countries of the world increased by 43 percent. But in the poorest part of the world, the per-capita increase in that decade was only 27 percent.[30] There is no question but that the consequence, intended or not, of the permanent war economy in the United States (and its Soviet counterpart) has been to help maintain the depressed condition of the poorest people of the world.

From the standpoint of the ideological consensus, this was not supposed to happen. In that view of the world, guns are supposed to help make butter. That viewpoint is one of the core contradictions between war-economy ideology and reality.

Six

REALITY CONTRADICTS IDEOLOGY

THE LONG TENURE of the American war economy has afforded ample time and incentive for elaborating a wide-ranging system of beliefs around the core idea that war brings prosperity. But that belief system is now in crisis because it is contradicted at many points by the actual shape of economic events. That crisis is no mere abstraction, involving as it does the world view (identity) of many millions of Americans. Moreover, there are substantial grounds for supposing that the collision of ideology and reality will not simply "go away," since so many of the economic realities are, in fact, the consequences of the war economy itself.

War Economy Beliefs versus Reality

Belief: Military spending contributes to economic activity as much as does any other public or private spending.

Reality: From an economic standpoint spending on the military differs from other spending in that the goods and services it generates do not, in any traceable way, contribute to the level of living or to further production. Military spending does put money into circulation by taking tax dollars from the whole community and distributing them to the military-serving parts. In return, the people of the military economy deliver goods and services which have no economic utility to anyone. However, their work is paid for with generous claims on the civilian goods and services produced by the rest of the society. This is highly visible in the good living that abounds in the major military-economy centers (San Francisco Peninsula, Dallas–Fort Worth, Los Angeles suburbs, Route 128 at Boston, etc.). The military economy makes disproportionate claims on the society's stock of consumer and producers' goods and services.

The absence of economic functional usefulness is the reason why expenditures on even the most intricate equipment in military economy don't replace investment in civilian productive equipment. When you invest in civilian productive equipment, fresh output can be produced year by year. With the military product, however technologically sophisticated, there can be no productivity of capital, because there is no further production. Therefore with spending on a military technology what is forgone is not only the immediate economic use of the product but also the incremental "productivity of capital," which is forgone forever. This basic functional difference is shielded by the assignment of money values to military as well as civilian equipment, implying merely different magnitudes of the same thing and helping to obscure difference of kind.

Belief: The United States economy can produce both "guns" and "butter" in indefinitely large amounts.

Professor Walter Heller, onetime chairman of the President's Council of Economic Advisers, has said: "Economists can serve as angel's advocate [in putting at the President's disposal] the resources needed to achieve great societies at home and grand designs abroad . . . [and by providing] the wherewithal for foreign aid and defense efforts and for financing Vietnam on a both-guns-and-butter basis."[1] In a comparison of two recent American wars, the "war" on poverty and the real war in Vietnam, Professor Nathan Glazer, spokesman for political conservatives, concluded: "Throughout the [Vietnam] war the United States has hardly stinted on butter to pay for guns; in fact, we have spent ever increasing amounts to cover both."[2]

Reality: The American economy is large and wealthy, but there are limits to its wealth. There is a trade-off between military and civilian production, as I show in Chapters Three through Five. By massive diversion of human and physical capital from economically productive to nonproductive military use, the government has been using up the "seed corn" capital that is a prime source of future productivity. In this way a policy of "no future" was followed for American society.

The record of money spent on the war in Vietnam and on the ersatz "war" on poverty show that although the government spent more than before on poverty programs, the latter got only 8 percent of the combined total of government spending on these two wars (Chapter Five), with the result that there was a clear failure to perform major economic development for the millions that needed it in the United States.

Belief: Money spent on the military makes jobs and bolsters the economy.

Spiro Agnew, then Vice-President, claimed in a speech during the 1972 Presidential campaign:

> While he [Senator George McGovern] has gone around the country deploring present rates of unemployment, he is apparently oblivious to the fact that his defense proposals would throw an estimated *1.8 million* Americans out of work. But I'm sure the people of St. Louis and the employees of McDonnell-Douglas are not unaware of that fact, especially since the Senator has specifically stated that he would cancel the F-15 as part of his defense cutbacks.[3]

Reality: An increase in military spending certainly helps employment in military industry, and certainly enhances the sales of those firms. Also, military products are counted in the money-valued gross national product for that year, thus swelling the figure. However, these calculations do not take into account the inexorable trade-off process by which civilian parts of national income are reduced by military spending. War economy also induces reductions in the productivity of capital, which holds down productivity and hence job growth for the civilian economy as a whole into a far future. That is not "bolstering" in any sense. When Agnew threatened job loss for the employees of McDonnell-Douglas in St. Louis he was speaking as a surrogate for President Nixon, the top manager of the military economy, reaffirming the unwillingness of that management to initiate other than military-economy employment. Senator George McGovern, the defeated candidate, was committed to major civilian-job initiatives by the federal government.

Belief: War economy solves problems of surplus capital and surplus labor.

Reality: The unique American experience during the few years of World War II showed how war economy gets fast results in making jobs and consuming capital. However, the data and analyses given here show that a permanent war economy, by diminishing resources available for productive work, has the traceable effect of *generating* uninvestable capital and unemployable labor, even though the immediately visible consequence of military spending is employing people to do that sort of work.

Belief: Spending on the military has something for everybody.

Sidney Lens, a veteran trade-unionist and peace activist, enunciated a typical view from the American left when he wrote:

> No one, of course, planned the Cold War as an antipoverty program. Nonetheless it has been one, despite the fact that the most ardent cold warriors in Congress have consistently opposed welfare measures. . . . It is conceivable . . . that had defense spending remained at the picayune billion-dollar-a-year level of prewar, unemployment might have been almost as ominous a specter as in the gloomy 1930's. . . . Supported, however, by a trillion dollars of postwar military expenditures, the economy faltered only four times in the quarter of a century after the war and unemployment never reached more than a 7 per cent figure. In fact the word "depression" all but passed out of the language and economic downturns were referred to by the milder term "recession."[4]

A lot more happened after World War II besides the spending of more than a trillion dollars on the military. The U.S. economy, the only big industrial system left intact after the destruction of that war, became a world source of machinery, durable consumer goods, and even foodstuffs. A lot of purchasing power, deferred by wartime forced savings, fueled a seller's market in the United States for every kind of consumer goods after the war. All this, in turn, justified major new investments in production facilities. By contrast, the military economy, beyond its immediate spending impact, constrained productive investment and job opportunities and played a major role in exporting investments and new jobs from the United States.

Sustained operation of the military economy has produced a major concentration of income flows in certain industries, occupations and regions. Thus the newly expanding military industries received major allocations of capital; their employees received exceptionally high pay and rapid promotions; and the geographic regions in which all this occurred underwent unusual "economic growth." However, as I will show, all this was paid for by the taxes drained off from states and regions which were oriented toward civilian economy. Unseen was the quiet but sustained using up of capital plant in important parts of civilian industry and in many public facilities. The decay of American cities is a central part of this deterioration. Also, the poor of American society were essentially left in their condition of underdevelopment.

Belief: As long as the gross national product grows, that means added wealth for the nation, and it doesn't matter what the money is spent on.

Reality: The enlargement of the gross national product may or may not mean additional wealth for the nation. That depends entirely on what sorts of goods and services have been produced. By "wealth" I mean economically useful products—hence, useful for the level of living or for further production. Additions to the GNP that consist of nonproductive growth add no wealth and even detract from wealth—as in the immense quantity of capital productivity that is forgone.

Belief: The dollar is as good as gold and will be so accepted everywhere.

President Lyndon Johnson announced, early in 1965, that "the soundness of our dollar is unquestioned." A month later he said, "The dollar is and will remain as good as gold, freely convertible at $35 an ounce."[5]

Reality: Until it happened, the characteristic judgment of American economists, officers of the government's Federal Reserve banks and others was that a decline in the value of the dollar was unthinkable and that a drain on the U.S. Treasury's gold reserve owing to a loss of confidence in holding dollars by central banks of

Europe was "out of the question." The latter judgment was based on the estimate that "the Europeans are too dependent on the United States" to venture a financially upsetting claim on the U.S. Treasury's gold reserve. By August 1971, of course, precisely those events took place owing to the cumulative effects of war economy as exacerbated by Vietnam. American multinational corporations greatly contributed to the fall of the dollar by profiting from early purchases of European currency which could then be traded back for more dollars than they had before.

Belief: The military contractors are similar to civilian corporations and operate as extensions of the civilian corporate economy.

Reality: The military-industry firms are quite different in their internal operation from the conventional business capitalist firm. As we have stressed earlier, the military firm maximizes cost and subsidies; it sells to one customer which also constitutes the top management to which the firm is responsible. While many of the formal modes of record-keeping and reporting of the military-industry firm seem to be similar to that of the business firm (e.g., the presentation of profit-and-loss statements), the meaning of the categories and magnitudes are quite different in the military case. Inasmuch as the market is guaranteed, "profit," for example, cannot represent a reward for risk-taking in the military-economy firm.

Belief: Defense-supported research and weapons development contribute to civilian technology and to the nation's economic growth.

David Packard, industrialist and onetime Assistant Secretary of Defense, believes that "defense supported research over the past 25 years has been a decisive factor in both this country's military capability and its economic growth."[6] Congressman Mendel Rivers, a former chairman of the House Armed Services Committee, once announced, "The industrial know-how that supports our military forces provides a vital national resource which can help in all types of problems ranging from education to housing, water and air pollution and transportation."[7] Presidential (Nixon) assistant Caspar Weinberger expressed the belief that "a $30 billion reduction in the Department of Defense budget would be a 'reckless attack on the economy's technological base' and would mean a 'massive reduction' in jobs for skilled workers."[8] J. J. Clark, a professor of economics and specialist in business economics, banking and finance, found that "military research is of significance for the civilian economy . . . military equipment incorporates myriad devices, processes and designs of potential importance for the civilian economy."[9]

Reality: The ideologues of war economy started from the notion that the United States can produce both guns and butter, and they soon supplemented this with a really original concept: guns produce butter. This contention is simply not proven. Specialists in the Commerce Department have told me that, in their judgment, there may be a five percent transfer of knowledge from military to civilian technology.

Not surprisingly, military research produces military technology. From time to time where basic new knowledge is discovered, some aspects of it may be applicable elsewhere. However, the extravagant claims of the military-research advocates for extensive civilian spillover are not matched by confidence in reverse spillover: hence supporting priority to civilian R&D, on the grounds that there would be appropriately massive spillover for military technology.

A major reduction in nonproductive use of the country's technology manpower is a precondition for restoring competence to civilian technology in a wide number of American industries.

Belief: Centralized government control is the efficient way to get things done in a big country.

Reality: This idea has been an article of faith in and around the Department of Defense, especially since the long stewardship of Robert McNamara. His reorganization certainly did centralize decision power in the largest department of government. However, the performance of the centrally controlled military-industry firms during his tenure cast doubt on the assumption that greater efficiency was produced by the centralization of control. Thus, the technical reliability of major military systems produced in the 1960s was lower than comparable systems in the 1950s when there was less centralized control. Also, the patterns of management practice that yield cost- and subsidy-maximization were formalized during the McNamara era.

Belief: For American capitalism war economy is indispensable for solving problems of economic stagnation.

Jerome Wiesner, as science adviser to Presidents Kennedy and Johnson judged that "the armaments industry has provided a sort of an automatic stabilizer for the whole economy."[10] On this subject J. J. Clark, in his *New Economics of National Defense,* estimates:

> Capital expenditure items within the military budget, which are particularly consumptive of labor, tend dually to counteract cyclical unemployment and to stimulate those basic industries that frequently receive the initial and most severe impact of economic recession. In this manner, the allocation of resources to the military should become less disruptive of the civilian economy. Along with other similarly designed programs, they are able to assist in placing a floor under the economy so as to cushion cyclical declines in employment and production.[11]

Herbert Gintis, professor of economics and a frequent contributor to *The Review of Radical Political Economics,* noted in an evaluation of American Keynesianism: "The military-industrial complex has eliminated the spectre of secular stagnation."[12] By 1950 the editors of *U.S. News and World Report* maintained: "Business won't go to pot so long as war is a threat, so long as every alarm can step up spending-lending for defense at home and aid abroad. Cold War is almost a guarantee against a bad depression."[13]

Reality: While in an immediate view military spending puts purchasing power into an economic system and enriches the recipients of that purchasing power, the sustained performance of that act and the sustained production of parasitic economic growth have manifestly depleting effects in industry and economy generally. There is no theory of economy or society which would characterize sustained price inflation, industrial noncompetitiveness, the creation of capital and labor surpluses, the flight of capital, sustained unemployment and underdevelopment, and collapse in the value of the dollar as other than stagnation.

Belief: Politically there is no workable substitute for war economy. Spending on the military is the only thing that can get

SUPPORT FOR GOVERNMENT SPENDING ON MAJOR PROBLEMS

*Composite Scores**

Combating crime	88
Helping the elderly	87
Coping with the drug problem	86
Reducing water pollution	81
Reducing air pollution	80
Improving education of low-income children	80
Improving medical and health care	80
Expanding Medicaid for low-income families	74
Providing college education for the poor	72
Rebuilding rundown sections of cities	69
Providing better mass transportation	66
Building more parks and recreation areas	66
Providing better housing	64
Building better roads	63
Providing low-rent public housing	62
Improving situation of black Americans	57
Spending for defense forces	32
Maintaining U.S. forces in Europe	29
Spending for space	25
Providing economic aid to foreign countries	24
Providing military aid to foreign countries	21

* Scale for composite scores: 100 = increased federal spending
                                                     50 = maintaining present level
                                                       0 = reducing or ending altogether
SOURCE: "Split Views on America" *Time*, Dec. 25, 1972, p. 13.

overwhelming popular and Congressional support in the United States.

Reality: For all those who accept the previous eleven propositions on war economy as valid, the above proposition is a natural outcome. The other ideas serve as a self-fulfilling prophecy to make this one valid. Once there is agreement and implementation on war economy as preferred economic policy, then in the absence of other ideas and plans there is no available, workable substitute for war economy. Under such conditions the military-spending plans secure popular and Congressional support.

Some people have alleged that civilian economic "substitutes for war" would be inadequate in filling the role played by military economy because a substitute program would be too cheap and would not use up enough resources. I have shown, above, a variety of civilian economic agendas that are not cheap and are essential for repairing the economic damage done in the United States by the permanent war economy.

At the close of 1972 the editors of *Time* undertook to find out what kinds of spending by government would get major public support—or opposition. A nationwide cross section of Americans were asked whether they favored increased, maintained or reduced federal spending for specified purposes. Here are the results. Clearly, "spending for defense forces" had become unpopular.

Ideological Spinoff: Further Beliefs About Military Economy

During the long tenure of the permanent war economy there has been ample time, opportunity and encouragement for the development of ideas that are supportive or collateral to the mainstream ideological consensus. I have collected the following principal items of ideological spinoff, with brief comments on each one.

Belief: War economy has always been a major factor in U.S. economy.

Reality: From 1900 to 1930, apart from the two years of World War I, less than one percent of the country's gross national product was used on the average for military purposes. From 1931 to 1939, 1.3 percent of the country's gross national product was used for military purposes. During the decade of the 1960s that percentage ranged from 7 to 10 percent. The present importance of military economy has no sustained precedent in American society.[14]

Belief: The defense budget does not dominate public spending.

Reality: In the federal budget for 1974 the funds allocated to the Department of Defense and other payments for past, present and future military operations amounted together to $123 billion of the total federal budget of $199 billion on a "federal funds" basis.[15] (The federal-funds basis of the budget includes the money currently appropriated by the Congress. It does not include the insurance funds administered by the federal government, like the Railroad Retirement Fund and Social Security payments.)

Hence, when one includes only the funds that are regularly recommended by the Office of Management and Budget and controlled by the Congress, defense-related expenditure amounted to 60 percent of this budget. In "defense-related" expenditure I include, besides the Department of Defense budget itself, funds allotted to the Atomic Energy Commission, appropriate parts of the space research budget, veterans' benefits, three fourths of the interest on the national debt (i.e., the ongoing costs of past wars), certain collateral programs like ocean shipping, and impacted-school-area aid associated with military activity. The Joint Economic Committee pointed out in its 1972 report that these expenditures added up to $109 billion; the Department of Defense alone accounted for $75 billion. For the next fiscal year the comparable figures were $119 billion and $81 billion as reported by the committee.

There is no doubt that military and related budgeting does dominate the federal budget.

Belief: The defense budget is declining.

Reality: For civilian incomes it is often feasible to calculate the impact of price changes and thereby know whether or not an increase in money income is "real" or just more money that is offset by price rises for the goods and services that are bought. While the Department of Defense has alleged such a case for itself, neither it nor anyone else has produced the required price index of military goods and services which is the indispensable tool for such analyses. In its absence it is prudent to give more attention to the mounting billions of military funding and less to the unsupported special pleading of the war-economy directorate.

In current-year dollars the Pentagon's budgets have been growing. The defense budget in a given year includes items like starting money to initiate new weapons programs. These current commitments do not necessarily anticipate the sums that will be allotted to these programs in years to come. Thus, in 1971 it was noted that funds for new hardware in weapons programs under development implied aggregate costs of $142 billion (no estimate for cost growth included). Furthermore, we can't yet foresee the full effects of increasing emphasis on equipment to reduce U.S. combat casualties and the full costs of increasing reliance on foreign manpower. Meanwhile, senior Pentagon planners are looking ahead to a budget of $112 billion by 1980.[16]

However, the federal government has been successful in broadcasting the idea that its military spending is a constantly declining part of the federal budget. Thus, a sympathetic columnist like the economist Milton Friedman reported to the readers of *Newsweek* (April 2, 1973) that for 1974 "only 35 percent of the $269 billion [total federal planned spending] is for national defense plus veterans' benefits . . ." The Nixon administration claim of a trend toward proportionate decline in military spending is ambiguous. For example, the more comprehensive estimate of military spending for past, current and future wars as prepared by the Joint Economic Committee produced the estimate of 60 percent of the federal budget (on a federal-funds basis) being used for national security.

Belief: The Department of Defense was fundamentally reorganized for the better by Robert McNamara, who introduced efficiency and modern management methods into the Pentagon.

Reality: McNamara continued the previous patterns but intensified the concentration of control in the directorate of the Department of Defense and intensified controls over the subordinate industrial firms. During McNamara's tenure very much was made by the public-relations apparatus of his "Department of Defense Cost-Reduction Program."[17] Many particular cost reductions were achieved by limited application of methods that are familiar in industrial practice: standardization; redefining requirements; long-range contracting; incentive contracting. The fact is, however, that the savings achieved by such methods were overwhelmed by the systemwide policies of cost-maximization and price increases.

By 1970 a Presidential commission reviewed the organization and internal operation of the Pentagon. In a summary statement the chairman of the commission, Gilbert W. Fitzhugh, chairman of the board of the Metropolitan Life Insurance Company, stated of the Department of Defense, "Everybody is somewhat responsible for everything, and nobody is completely responsible for anything. So there's no way of assigning authority, responsibility and accountability . . . They spend their time coordinating with each other and shuffling paper back and forth . . . Nobody can do anything without checking with seven other people."[18]

Belief: Military cost overruns are really cost growths to be expected for high-technology products.

Reality: The good-quality consumer electronics and optical equipment from Japan are high-technology products. The small calculators based upon integrated circuit technology are high-technology products. Their production, whether in Japan or the United States, is not characterized by cost overrun and cost growth. If it were, their production and mass sale would be unfeasible. The cost and price growth in U.S. military industry are not necessary aspects of high-technology products, but of the cost-maximization criteria and practices that prevail in the military-industry economy.

Belief: Why single out military economy for criticism of inefficiency without mentioning such nonmilitary industries as the railroads and the building trades? The cost overrun on the Rayburn Building in Washington was 100 percent, on the John F. Kennedy Center 150 percent, and on the Sydney, Australia, Opera House 210 percent.

Reality: In military economy, cost- and subsidy-maximization have been institutionalized, hence made into sustaining, normal features of that activity. To the extent that subsidy-maximizing has been encouraged or permitted elsewhere, then cost-increasing pressures are to be expected. The military system is by all odds the most important piece of the U.S. economy where cost-maximizing is both practiced and applauded. Furthermore, it is so important a part of the total economy as to strongly affect much of the rest.

Belief: Military contractors do not make exorbitant profits.

Reality: Profits have characteristically been understood as a payment for risk (especially the risk of investing capital). No one has ever explained the nature of the risk facing a defense contractor whose market is guaranteed by contract, who undertakes to produce quantities specified by contract, at a minimum price set by contract. One of my colleagues reminded me that there is a residual risk: the contract might be lost and not renewed. I submit

that this is a different order of risk from that traditionally prescribed by economists as the justification for profit, any profit. The
calculated size of military-industry profits is heavily affected by
the accounting rules and assumptions that are used in the calculations: in a given case profit as percent of sales can be low, while
profit as percent of investment is high because little private and
much government capital is used in many military-industry operations. Owing to these considerations, as well as the paucity of
independently audited company data, the subject of the profitability of military industry was not resolved by the Logistics Management Institute (a research arm of the Department of Defense),
which found that during the 1950s military business was more
profitable than civilian sales (by the same firms) and that the
reverse was true in the 1960s. However, there was no ambiguity in
the data from the federal government's Renegotiation Board,
whose 1972 activity disclosed 131 firms whose after-refund profits
exceeded 50 percent of net worth; of these, ninety-four earned
between 50 and 100 percent, forty-nine earned between 100 and
200 percent, twenty-two earned between 200 and 500 percent,
and four exceeded 500 percent. Senator William A. Proxmire
commented, upon announcing these data, that "the average profits
on stockholders' equity for all manufacturing firms ranges from 18
to 20 percent annually."[19]

Belief: Military spending does not compete with private
markets.

Reality: The researches of Bruce Russett have shown that for
the whole economy there is a definite reduction in consumer-goods
and capital-goods spending as the accompanying consequence of
additional military spending. In that way military spending, by
reducing spending in all civilian economic categories, is directly
competitive with civilian markets (See Chapter 4).

Belief: If U.S. firms do less producing it is because we are
becoming a service economy.

According to G. W. Miller, President of Textron, "We're a
producing company . . . and we're looking at a trend where the
U.S. is less and less a producing country. It's a service country. So
in a sense we have some skills that are not really going to be
required in the major growth pattern in the U.S."[20]

Reality: One of the ideological accommodations among economists and others to the declining production competence of U.S.
industry is the formulation that the United States can function in
relation to the rest of the world as a "service economy." These
ideologists proclaim that the United States through providing
capital, banking, management and allied services for American-
owned and other firms around the world would thereby yield
enough net income to the American economy as a whole to offset
the employment forgone owing to the transfer of production activities abroad. This is not proven. There is no evidence that the
millions of jobs forgone for the United States as a result of the
exodus of capital have been offset by either money received here
or new jobs created here. Profits returned from foreign investments are controlled by corporate managements and shared by
recipients of corporate profits. Hence the primary benefits from the
foreign investing of U.S. firms are concentrated among a small
high-income population.

Other parts of the "service economy" ideology hold that the
conduct of production in the United States on a price-competitive
basis with other countries is becoming less feasible and that conceivable technology and other production conditions for doing this
are essentially unavailable. In fact the loss of price competitiveness
of many U.S. industries is not due to some mysterious factor like
being a mature economy (whatever that may mean), but is rather
a traceable result of a definable process of economic deterioration.
Similarly, on the technology side there is no condition intrinsic to
technology that perpetuates technological inadequacy of many
industries. The cause is to be found instead in the concentration of
engineering talent and money in the military economy.

Belief: If the export of American capital and technology and the
import of foreign-made goods were all restricted by law, then the
deteriorating competitive position of U.S. industry could be re-
versed and jobs for American workers could be increased.[21]

Reality: Insofar as the export of capital and technology have
been made central parts of the "world hegemony" thrust that
powers the directorate of the war economy, it is reasonable to
expect that these policies are not separable from the very existence
and operation of the war economy. The trade-union chiefs whose
membership base is eroded by the loss of job opportunities in the

United States are caught in a contradiction in their attempt to respond to these conditions. Many labor leaders, notably the chiefs of the AFL-CIO, have been advocates of military economy for combined political and economic reasons. As adherents of the political and ideological consensus of the Cold War, they are hard put to respond to the unintended effects of the permanent war economy which bear down upon them—without embarking on a criticism of the war economy itself. Accordingly, they are compelled to address some of the consequences of war economy while avoiding any address to the root cause of the painful problems of American workers owing to the decline of U.S. industrial efficiency (See Chapter 5 and Appendixes).

Belief: If the military-industry system were nationalized it could be made more efficient.
Reality: From the standpoint of control it is effectively "nationalized." Indeed, the Pentagon already owns important parts of the fixed assets (land, buildings, machinery) used by the larger military-industry firms. For example, the Lockheed-Marietta factory in Georgia that has been responsible for the C-5 is owned by the federal government. There are no grounds here for proposing that federal ownership necessarily endows that or similar operations with cost-minimizing instead of cost-maximizing characteristics. Formal nationalization of the military-industry firms might very well provide civil-service status for many of their employees, thereby locking them into place for the indefinite future on government payrolls.

Belief: Japan and Germany were countries that have been protected by the United States and spared the cost of defense forces.
Reality: The U.S. strategic forces are designed to deter Soviet attack on the United States and conceivably to "prevail" in an all-out nuclear exchange with the Soviets. Insofar as the deterring result is operative for Western Europe or Japan, that is a tag-along effect: it makes little difference to the basic design or cost of the U.S. strategic forces.

The main military deterrents mounted by the U.S. against potential Soviet attack on Western Europe or Japan are the nuclear weapons, ranging from land mines and artillery along borders to medium- and intercontinental-range missiles and air-craft. While a contingent of U.S. general-purpose forces is em-placed in both Western Europe and Japan, there is no way to separate their "conventional" tactical mission from the nuclear arms. The latter are an integral part of the array of weapons for ensuring military superiority. Escalation into the nuclear range is to be expected as the generals of two superpowers confront each other, each with instructions to win.

The strategic nuclear armed forces designed to deter major Soviet military incursions cost about 25 percent or less of the U.S. military budget for 1974. The intercontinental delivery systems that are the core of these forces are designed to combat the Soviet strategic forces, not to shield Germany or Japan, or the United States as such. The U.S. general-purpose forces emplaced in Western Europe and Japan are there on behalf of U.S. political objectives and not primarily for the military defense of these lands.

Belief: If military spending were reduced, that would mean less military security for the United States.

Reality: Apart from the patterns of waste and extravagance that have come to characterize the U.S. military establishment, the heart of the issue posed by this belief lies in the main functional design of U.S. armed forces. By 1971 U.S. military spending was traced to three major objectives: first, nuclear deterrence against external attack on the United States (and principal allies); second, operation of the worldwide military system (and bases) for en-forcing Pax Americana; third, the Vietnam War. The $74.5 billion that the Pentagon was spending in 1971 broke down as follows:[22]

Nuclear deterrent for defense	$16.3 billion (22%)
Pax Americana	44.0 billion (59%)
Vietnam War	14.2 billion (19%)

Plainly, the forces that are explicitly designed to prevent military attack on the United States comprise a small part of the Pentagon budget, which is dominated by the spending on behalf of U.S. world hegemony.

Belief: It's no use being critical about military economy and its effects, since that is largely determined by the inexorable tide of technological progress, which, like it or not, has a momentum and direction of its own.

Reality: No technology creates itself. No materials are self-programmed to take technological form. All technology, from can opener to oil refinery, is man-made and represents the directed application of knowledge of nature to serve particular social requirements. Accordingly, motor vehicles could be cleaner, safer, less fuel-using and more durable. But the business requirements of sales-maximization and profits are the priority criteria that engineers are directed to use. That determines the design of the product and its characteristics for the user. Change the social criteria and you change the product. American military technology is therefore the specific outcome of government orders to create instruments of destruction under cost-maximizing conditions in a nation with vast accumulated wealth.

None of this is to say that technologies, once created, do not have substantial impact on society. They do. But that is quite different from the assumption that man is the powerless creature of technologies which have a life of their own apart from man's preferences. The latter belief, while untrue, is serviceable for rationalizing compliance with the economic and political status quo in the name of accepting "the machine" as it is.

Belief: The reason why Japanese and West German industry is doing so well economically is that the United States gave these countries massive help for economic reconstruction after World War II.

Reality: The Marshall Plan gave political-economic support that shored up the economies and regimes of Western Europe after World War II. Among its varied effects, the Marshall Plan also expanded markets for U.S. producers of capital goods. Nevertheless, the size of this effort was small compared with the self-powered economic expansion of West Germany and Japan.

From 1948 to 1971 Japan received $21.8 million all told in economic assistance from the United States.[23] West Germany received $1.6 billion of economic aid. By way of comparison: during the period 1967–69 the average annual new capital investment within the West German economy was $35.6 billion and in Japan $51.2 billion.[24] While the economic assistance directed to West Germany during the Marshall Plan period was probably meaningful at the time, the total money value of this activity has obviously been a minor part of the West German national product, which, by 1970, was $186 billion per year.[25]

How Ideology Is Maintained

A reader who has gone this far may wonder why the conventional beliefs about America's war economy have endured so long in the face of events that contradict them. We can identify at least three factors that probably determine this result: first, the need to rely on experts; second, the "cultural lag" that is evident in the teaching and research on economics; third, the ideological controls that are operated by the guardians of conventional beliefs and policies.

People depend on specialists with expert knowledge for the formulation of ideas on complicated matters. The nonspecialist assimilates the conclusions, or acts according to expert advice. Most people cannot derive explanations from their own experience as to why U.S. industrial goods are not competitive or why the value of the dollar is reduced or why the price of wheat and other foods goes up. In the case of economics, the public is dependent on the economists' analyses and predictions.

Fortunately, such dependence has limits. It should be no surprise if many ordinary people, nonspecialists in economics or kindred fields, develop serious doubts about parts of the prevailing ideology. This can happen when economic developments having a painful effect on the individual simply overwhelm him and either are in conflict with particular parts of the economic ideology or lead to distrust in the competence of the public authorities, or both. Relentless price inflation, which reduces the level of living and destroys the value of savings, has such potential effects. Similar consequences may be expected among the people who are discharged from U.S. factories that move abroad or that close down because they are noncompetitive with foreign producers. But it is one thing to develop doubts or cynicism about particular elements or ideology and quite a different matter to abandon a world view or allegiance to leaders who are its spokesmen. The latter is constrained not only by the systems of available ideas but also by social controls whereby the guardians of the conventional wisdom limit criticism of the status-quo supporting ideology or access to alternative ways of understanding economy and society.

One way to gauge the quality of economic ideas available to the educated American public is by examining the principal textbooks used in the recent past for the first courses in economics in American universities. After all, the graduates of colleges become the writers, teachers, journalists, etc., who interpret the meaning of events to the wider public. What economic tools have these people been given to make sense of the operation and consequences of America's war economy?

The Peaceful World of Economics I

Introductory courses in economics, as reflected in principal textbooks used in American colleges and universities, usually do not recognize the existence of the military-industrial firm or of a war economy. In these texts the magnitude and the characteristics of military-economy activity in the United States since the Second World War either are not mentioned at all or are dealt with in a few sentences or paragraphs.[26] From the standpoint of understanding how the American ideological consensus on war economy is justified and reinforced, these textbooks are most revealing.

The world of Economics I is an orderly civilian world, making and exchanging goods and services. In this world individual consumers and private profit-making firms dominate the field, although there is a "public sector," and government "regulates" industry and the levels of economic activity. Military industry, by implication, is one industry among others, and is not differentiated in quality, in terms of control, or in effects on the rest of the economy. The corporation serving the Pentagon is not distinct from other corporations.

Economic growth, employment levels and the diagnosis of national income are subjects of considerable importance in textbooks, but none attempts to differentiate economic growth or employment in terms of productive or nonproductive economic effect. Money-valued goods and services are lumped together. No textbook, for all the discussion about economic utility, recognizes that military goods and services, whatever their worth other than economic, yield no economic utility in the ordinary sense of contributing to consumer goods or services, or to capability for further production.

The depletion of important parts of American industry is nowhere referred to; the idea is unknown. The implication is that thirty years of military priority have no particular depleting effects, that there is no relation between the technical and economic decline of many civilian industries and the priority assignment of technical manpower and fresh public capital to aerospace and related work. In no text is any link defined, or question raised, concerning the possible connection between priority in our engineering schools to the development of military technology, and the manifest deterioration of many formerly competent U.S. industries.

The idea that many such industries, including those at the base of the "infrastructure," are unable to supply existing markets is not expressed in any of the textbooks that I have examined. I found no attempt to formulate or cope with the question, Why is it that the technical and economic capability of many U.S. firms for offsetting high wages and producing goods at a low unit-labor cost was abridged during the Cold War?

No textbook I examined contains a trace of data or analysis concerning the growth of state management—that is, state capitalism—over military and allied industry in the United States. The development of centralized control along managerial lines in the Department of Defense during the 1960s under John F. Kennedy and Robert McNamara is nowhere recognized as having had any special economic effect. Accordingly, there is no attempt to diagnose a shift from private-civilian to government-military control over capital in the United States.

No textbook I have examined for this analysis includes any reference to the growth of a new type of industrial firm, rather different from the model business enterprise that is autonomous, cost-minimizing and profit-maximizing. There is no suggestion that the collection of wholly military firms and military divisions of civilian firms, organized under the state management, constitutes a new economic decision-making entity that is competent to fundamentally affect the economy as a whole in many ways.

The size of this military economy and its central control constitute a new economic and technical factor in American economy and society. No textbook in economics includes data on or analyses of these characteristics and their consequences. Instead, the existence of the military-industrial empire, a sustained war economy, is subsumed under a discussion of government and the "public sector."

In seven textbooks widely used as the basis for instruction in Economics I until 1972, I found no reference in the texts or the indices to defense, the military, disarmament, Vietnam, or war. In the remaining textbooks examined, these subjects typically are treated in one to three paragraphs.

The most numerous references to war economy and its consequences appeared in Paul Samuelson's *Economics* (eighth edition, 1970), the most widely used textbook of all. Peace, the text says, would enable increased economic growth to take place (page 804), but there is no indication of why military spending does not produce such growth. No distinction is drawn between productive and nonproductive economic growth except for an unelaborated comment that military spending "differs completely from" nonmilitary spending (page 150). Samuelson is critical of the conventionally optimistic assumption about civilian spinoff from military technology (page 804). A connection between government spending abroad and international deficits is mentioned (page 804). Says Samuelson: "The so-called 'military-industrial' complex must not be allowed to call the tune" (page 94), but the complex is not described or diagnosed. What tune does it call? This text has numerous references to Vietnam War expenditures and their inflationary role. However, there is no discussion of military spending and military economic organization having special economic qualities that would particularly account for inflationary and industrial depletion processes over a long period.*

The inability or refusal of military-industrial firms to plan or execute conversion to a civilian economy receives no more than passing mention in the textbooks of Economics I. They do not take up such questions as: What sorts of entrepreneurs are these who can serve only one market? What sorts of firms are these whose

---

* By 1972–73, revised editions of standard textbooks and new texts appeared in which the writers gave serious treatment to aspects of war economy. Included among these books were C. McConnell, *Economics, Principles, Problems and Policies*, 5th ed., McGraw-Hill, 1972; R. Heilbroner, *The Economic Problem*, 3rd ed., Prentice-Hall, 1972; K. Lancaster, *Modern Economics*, Rand-McNally, 1973; E. K. Hunt and H. J. Sherman, *Economics: an Introduction to Traditional and Radical Views*, Harper and Row, 1972; H. Sherman, *Radical Political Economy*, Basic Books, 1972.

managements have no options? If these are not ordinary profit-making firms, what are they?

Nor do they consider the significance of the military-industrial firm, both as a unit and as a superfirm group under the state management for the character and control of capital and production resources, and for pricing. What does all this mean for concentration of control? Is it still sensible to appreciate the old centers of industrial and financial control as dominating the capital markets? Have the financial centers of private capitalism been displaced by the state management? Has state capitalism in its Pentagon form become the dominant form of American industrial capitalism? These problems are typically not mentioned, let alone discussed, in the Peaceful World of Economics I.

The principal textbooks of Economics I give a purported portrait of the economic system in the small and in the large. By largely omitting the military-industrial system, they accordingly obscure its development, its central characteristics and its effects. Students of economics are given no means for evaluating military industry and its controllers, who thereby are shielded from critical appraisal.

The ideas of the Peaceful World of Economics I are reflected in the functioning of the President's Council of Economic Advisers, which diagnoses the state of the national economy and makes policy and legislative recommendations to the President and the Congress. The Council members are an elite group of economists and can draw upon all the resources of their profession. Their reports, combining diagnosis and policy, have unique importance. A review of their annual reports from 1961 to 1974 shows them to be permeated with the ideas of the war-economy consensus, as are the greatest number of textbooks of Economics I. Under Kennedy, Johnson and Nixon there was no deviation from the ideology of war economy even as the Council acknowledged the existence of serious problems. Even though the Council assigned major responsibility for 1965 price inflation to the Vietnam War, it failed to note any connection between that result in 1965–66 and the massive buildups in military spending that began under Kennedy in 1961.[27]

The Council's discussion of the U.S. balance-of-payments problem did not identify the crucial role of foreign military spending as a prime causal factor. Productivity is recognized as a very important aspect of the economy, but the economically damaging effects of military preemption of capital and talent and the export of capital are not dealt with in relation to productivity. Economic growth is a sustaining topic, but nonproductive growth is unrecognized. In the world of the President's Council of Economic Advisers there is no war economy.

The Maintenance of Ideology

An incident out of my own experience will help to illuminate the process by which the ideological consensus has been consolidated and maintained. In 1962 I prepared a forty-page article for submission to the editors of a journal, who were publishing a special issue on economic and other aspects of the arms race and disarmament. They declined to publish what I offered them. On the face of it there is nothing noteworthy about this (except perhaps the fact that I was the invited editor of the special issue). Not everything that is written deserves publication. Editors have a duty to publish only what is appropriate for their journals. They must also cope with limitations of space, balance of subject matter, etc. However, considerations of the latter sort were not at issue. What happened to my article in 1962 is of interest because of the political-intellectual character of the referees who reviewed my paper.

In that article I set forth data and analysis on the following six points:

1. The machinery-producing industries of the United States were undergoing technical deterioration. This was traceable to emphasis on military rather than on civilian productive investment in the United States.
2. The value of the dollar was in jeopardy owing to sustained imbalance of payments for the United States, and the decline in the Treasury's gold reserve; these effects, in turn, were traceable to large military expenditures by the United States abroad.
3. Thirty-eight million Americans were living in poverty, and there was no foreseeable hope for rescuing them from that condition.
4. The military-industry system was giving rise to a new

phenomenon in American political life: forms of bureaucratic statism.

5. The combined international and domestic policies of the United States had the strong prospect of leading to political defeats despite vast military power.

6. Instead of an arms race (with its effects 1–5) as a central method of U.S. international relations, the United States had the theoretical capability of launching a peace race, a worldwide move for industrialization powered by unused industrial capacity in the United States.

The article containing these ideas was circulated among referees for the journal, among them eminent men in economics and political science. Their unanimous opinion was that the article should not be published. Their opinions included no challenge either to particular data or to the inferences that were drawn from them. One referee noted that the facts and analyses concerning trends in certain basic industries were not relevant evidence for inference about the industrial system; that the analyses were inconsistent with the evidence of economic growth that was visible by 1962. Another referee argued that the point about danger to the value of the dollar was not warranted, since the Kennedy administration had just appointed a committee on this problem. By implication, the situation was therefore well in hand.

After the editor of the journal told me of these referees' opinions, I urged him to override their recommendation and publish the article on the ground that their comments included no question of the validity of either particular facts or inferences drawn from them. The editor replied that while he sympathized and even agreed with my view, he was nevertheless in the position of having to run a journal. As an editor, he needed the cooperation and editorial help of academics like the men involved in this case. If he did not act on their judgment, he would no longer have them as helpers. Therefore, the argument ran, in the interest of maintaining this institution (the journal) he had to accept the judgment of these readers independently of his own views on a particular matter.

The conclusion that I drew from this and similar experiences was that, at least for some years (after 1962), I should give up on trying to publish in the principal scholarly journals in economics, since the economic theories and value preferences of the leading men in the field were well represented by the group of readers who rejected the article in question. I therefore oriented myself to writing mainly book-length materials on such subjects, or publishing under conditions where the editorial controls of such men could be bypassed.

This incident affords a good example of how a group of men committed to a particular set of theories about economy and political preferences for society acted as guardians of the prevailing ideology. By preventing the publication of material that would challenge some of the main consensually held ideas on economic and political issues, they helped to protect the war-economy ideology. In my own case their censorship was only partially effective, since I could find other channels for publishing and otherwise communicating to wide publics. Consider, however, the position of students and younger faculty who are subject to these men's judgments of what is acceptable research in economics or political science. There is no appeal from the decisions of their teachers, who determine acceptable course grades and hence the granting of academic degrees which are tantamount to professional licenses, and professional placement. By such means research oriented to disproving beliefs in the ideological consensus is discouraged.

I underscore that the issue in this case was formally one of permitting publication, not of endorsing my analyses. However, as advisory editors, these men evidently felt that if they permitted this article to appear, then, by implication, they could be regarded by their fellows as partially responsible for its publication. More than intellectual responsibility for the validity of ideas was involved here. This group of men included advisers to government during the Kennedy period; the article at issue challenged a series of important administration policies and assumptions. Permitting such a publication to appear would not have been what was expected from loyal members of the team.

The consensus ideas on war economy delineated above have held sway as defining ideas in our time. These ideas have been serviceable to the directorate of American state capitalism, for the ideas have been accepted as sensible and in the public interest. To say that they have been serviceable does not necessarily mean that the beliefs were created by the ruling groups. I prefer to leave the discussion of who formulated these ideas to students of the history of ideas. For this analysis the functions served by the ideological consensus on war economy and the relation of the ideology to reality are the important matters.

Like other ideologies, the statements of ideological consensus on war economy combine beliefs about how social systems can and should work. Of greatest interest is the social function fulfilled by these ideas. One might argue that an idea, after all, is not an action. However, people act in accordance with their understanding of social reality and propriety as explained by the historically prevailing ideology. Social behavior is not random. It is therefore worth taking ideas seriously, inasmuch as they not only specify but also limit possible action. By defining what is possible, ideology helps to set a boundary to what may conceivably happen. One of the central features of the economic ideology we have been reviewing here is its role in setting limits to what the American people understand to be either appropriate or possible economic policies to support.

These ideas are not merely statements that purport to describe how the world works. They also include prescriptions, norms about how things should be. Therefore these ideas have also served the vital political role of defining and justifying economic policies of American governments since World War II. Insofar as the ideological consensus served such functions, it is not surprising that the men involved in formulating, interpreting and implementing these ideas have held to them with some tenacity. Through these ideologies, these men justified their professional behavior to themselves and to their colleagues. Formulators and interpreters of these ideas have been accorded seats next to the pinnacles of power in the federal government.

The durability of the ideological consensus is linked to the personal and professional stake that the ideologues had developed in their idea systems. As against such powerful considerations, the mere facts of the case in the performance of economy and society are often insufficient to compel a reassessment of ideas. Among intellectuals mere validity has been put aside, repeatedly, in favor of usefulness to government policy as a decisive test of the acceptability of ideas about economy and society.

Noam Chomsky notes that "one mark of a culture in the firm

grip of ideological controls is that what must be believed to justify state policy will be believed, regardless of the facts."[28] In the realm of economics, ideological controls range widely. At one end there are formal decisions like the publication decision that I recounted above and publisher pressures on textbook writers to adhere to conventional (sales-maximizing) wisdom. However, decisions of this sort do not approach in importance the conditioning effect of the weight of already existing literature, courses of instruction, and the domination of the field by the men whose status is determined by this work. These factors define the boundaries of economics as a field of inquiry and as a problem-solving technique that is supportive, directly or indirectly, of the ideological consensus on war economy.

Apart from the pattern of institutional controls described above, there are the limits on inquiry owing to the conventional structure of ideas in the field of economics. By using the conventional model of the business firm, as do most economists, the military-industry enterprise is undifferentiated and hence invisible. Emphasis on normal exchange relations and markets obscures the unique conditions of decision-making in war economy. If the economists' categories of undifferentiated growth are used as a basic unit of analysis, then the special effects of military economy are blotted from view. Conventionally, the economic and technical decline of many U.S. industries either is not treated at all or is treated as though it were an ordinary feature of the recurring birth and death of industries and products. Economic literature includes virtually no analysis of the reasons why U.S. industries have become less capable of serving the U.S. market, nor are the requirements for reversing that condition discussed. Economists have tacitly assumed that the occupational performance of people in military industry and kindred organizations (bases, research institutes) is characterized by the same regularities as occupations in civilian economy or civilian government departments. Hence, the economics profession can believe that conversion from military to civilian economy is a simple matter to which little attention need be given. For in their understanding the problems of change would be mainly those of individual adjustment to new jobs, new communities, etc.

The selection of economic problems for inquiry involves value choices, stated or tacit. But it is one thing to make the choice—I prefer not to study war economy—and quite a different thing to imply that it isn't there. The values of many American economists include, however tacitly, assumptions not only about the desirability of capitalist economy, but also about the durability and continuity of capitalism as an economic system, even to the extent that they often fail to acknowledge manifest changes from private to state capitalism. As the propositions of the ideological consensus on war economy pervade economic thinking, so do the social values that are embodied in these propositions. In these ways, the economic thinking of our time has become permeated with ideology that supports war economy.

The very idea of a durable war economy is supported by innovations in language. For example, during the late 1960s discussions of government policy and practice began to include the words "private sector" and "public sector" in connection with American economy. "Public sector" is, of course, a euphemism for military economy, since that is the activity that dominates the operations of the federal government.

Economists ordinarily believe that their tools, theories and procedures afford them a mode of analysis that is objective in the sense of being value-free. As the present discussion shows, that is not quite the case. In my judgment a more sophisticated handling of the relation between social values and social research would be facilitated by a more relativist view of the connections between values and the subject matter and methodologies of economics. Therefore, apart from being responsible for complying with requirements for validity of ideas, economists (and other social scientists) have the further intellectual responsibility of specifying their value preferences as part of the explanation of their work. Such explanation of values has been in short supply where the ideas of the war-economy consensus are discussed.

It is a responsibility of intellectuals to tell how the world works, to formulate alternatives for society and to define their consequences. When that work proceeds and yields fresh options for economic organizations, then economic and other social options are extended beyond what is deemed possible by existing ideology. It would be foolhardy, however, to underestimate the sort of historical assessment given by Marx that "in every epoch the ruling ideas have been the ideas of the ruling class."[29] Sidney Hook, in his incisive explication of Marx's ideas, aptly states:

It does not follow that ideological indoctrination is always deliberate or that those who embrace a doctrine can themselves distinguish between what is true in their belief and what is merely helpful in achieving their political purpose. In every system the deepest and most pervasive kinds of cultural conditioning are never the results of a mechanical inculcation. In the course of his life-career the individual imbibes the values and attitudes which are accepted as natural by those who surround him. A system of checks and approvals controls conduct at every step—not only on those rare occasions when an individual rises from one social level to another but even within his own class. The tone and model of behavior, the very objects of ambition, are set by those who wield power or who serve those that wield it.[30]

After full allowance is made for the effectiveness of social training and control, it remains that the power of leaders is conditional upon the willingness of populations to accept their authority. Ideology plays an essential part in producing that willingness by justifying and thereby legitimizing the policies of governments.

The ideological consensus on war economy prevails because, overwhelmingly, intellectuals propagate these ideas, identify with them, use allegiance to these ideas as a test of professional competence, interpret these ideas to the government and to news media, proclaim them as the whole truth, and almost never concede that many of the ideas propounded are not checked by empirical inquiry but are based upon theoretical assumptions that are weighted with ideological preferences.

Seven

LIMITS OF MILITARY POWER

AT THE CLOSE of the Second World War the men of the American Establishment saw themselves as chiefs of the preeminent military and economic power in the world. This confidence was based on the visible evidence of massive destruction in other principal industrial areas of the world as contrasted with the intact population base and industrial machine of the United States. It was assumed that with American scientific and technical know-how, a monopoly in nuclear power and the availability of almost unlimited funds, the United States could surely hold position as Number One military power, using that power for worldwide political control.

By the 1960s under President Kennedy, military-political plans for the United States were aimed at being prepared for fighting "two and a half" wars at one time. Apart from a nuclear war, these were to include a conventional European war with the U.S.S.R., a Southeast Asian war and a lesser military engagement in Latin America (hence the one half). (Under President Nixon these goals were revised downward to "one and a half" wars, in addition to a nuclear exchange.) That was the military expression of the U.S. national policy goals that reached out for Pax Americana and "world hegemony."

These confident estimates were shaken twenty-five years later by the failure to score a clear military win against the guerrillas and

158

the armed forces of impoverished countries in Indochina. One of the major byproducts of the U.S. war in Vietnam was a greater readiness among many Americans to question the idea that unlimited military power was purchasable at will by the government of the United States.

Everyone knows that modern weapons have capability for vast destruction. Nuclear weapons could conceivably destroy all of mankind, and even the nonnuclear weapons have tremendous destructive capacity. In discussions of military affairs so much emphasis has been given to the destructiveness of nuclear weapons that the idea that military power can have limits has been characteristically bypassed. An understanding of what can be done with military power requires a parallel assessment of what cannot be done. This latter approach has not been encouraged by American military institutions or by the committees of Congress that formally oversee them.

During the long Cold War period the Armed Services Committees of the Congress have filled thousands of pages of hearings with statements and discussions on various "threats" and how to respond to them with military power, proposals for particular weapons "superiority," and ways of making possible "flexible response" to myriad situations in which military power could conceivably be applied. These committees of Congress took their cue from the annual military-posture statements of the Secretary of Defense and from the teams of Pentagon witnesses who gave expert testimony on what was needed in money, manpower and materiel to offset "threats," achieve and hold "superiority," and operate a "mix" of forces to make possible selective use and escalation of armed force. The sustaining theme of these assessments of U.S. military power has been military capability. Obviously, the idea of limits of military power does not fit in with promises to counter diverse threats, deliver weapons superiority across the board and afford an array of military options to political decisionmakers. Neither is the idea of limits appropriate to securing ever larger appropriations for weapons, bases, military pay and military research—all operated on a worldwide basis.

The name of the principal military agency of the U.S. government is the Department of Defense. Can that department defend the United States? If not, and the evidence points in that direction, then, on grounds of elemental honesty in public affairs, isn't that a limit that should be known, discussed and taken into account as a population is marshaled to support escalating military budgets in the name of defense that cannot be delivered? The ideologists of military power and of the economic necessity of war economy have had virtually clear sailing in their continuing program of justifying their expropriations of public wealth. However, the U.S. government's military, political and economic operations in Vietnam have been part of a very expensive lesson, paid for mainly by the benighted people of Vietnam, that military power, even U.S. military power, has limits.

In order to set the stage for a discussion of limits of military power I will first summarize the capabilities of the armed forces of large, mainly nuclear-armed nations:

1. The nuclear (and nonnuclear) forces can be used to threaten other states and populations with destruction.
2. The nonnuclear armed forces of major states can be used to assault smaller, nonnuclear states, except as that would lead to military confrontation between nuclear powers—for example, the United States versus the U.S.S.R. in Cuba, 1962.
3. Armed forces of major countries can be used to occupy the territories of other countries, mainly under conditions that involve formal agreements between governments, as for military bases.[1]
4. Smaller states can use military power for limited periods of time for assaulting other small states—for example, the Six Day War in the Middle East, 1967.
5. Large and small governments can use armed forces for internal police operations to maintain the rule of a particular government.

This enumeration of the present functions of armed forces, especially of major states, appears to omit a traditional part of the purposes of armed forces—that is, for shielding a country from external attack and winning wars that subdue the armed forces of lesser states. This omission reflects one of the main characteristics of the new limits on military power that have developed during the nuclear era. Let us examine these limits systematically.

Limit: The governments of the world no longer permit armed conflict among nation-states to proceed to military solution.

Since the end of the Second World War there have been a great number of armed conflicts between the military forces of national states. It is a unique feature of this long period that in no case was such a conflict permitted to operate to a military conclusion. In each instance other nations intervened, singly or through concerted action—as through the United Nations—to bring military operations to a halt well before one national power was able to overwhelm the other side militarily, compel surrender and use that fact to dictate political terms.

The large number of lives lost in the procession of smaller wars after 1946 rules out the possibility that a new concern for human life was the operating factor. Rather, this new development was a result of the well-founded and pervasive fear of the consequences from extension and escalation of what began, in each case, as limited national conflict. Extension means involving other countries. Escalation means greater intensity of violence. The feared end result of military extension and escalation has been confrontation between superpowers leading to nuclear war. It is widely appreciated that this outcome cannot be excluded, since the generals of each side are indoctrinated to win and because each major nuclear state wields nuclear weapons in abundance.

In the relations of the nuclear superpowers, the consequences from use of conventional forces are not separable from nuclear forces. Each state trains and operates armed forces to apply successive levels of force as required to prevail militarily. Recourse to nuclear weapons must therefore be expected.

Similar reasoning applies to armed conflict among nonnuclear states where there is a prospect of extending the boundaries of conflict to include the nuclear powers. Owing to the long Cold War and its worldwide scope, there has hardly been a case of conflict between two smaller states that has not involved the possibility of the major powers taking sides. The result has been a new development in the relation of states: unwillingness to risk the prospect of escalation to nuclear war and the deservedly feared consequences of such an escalation.

Limit: There is no definable shield, no defense, against nuclear weapons.

The idea of literally shielding the United States against external attack is, I am told, no longer discussed among the senior military officers of the United States.

The nature of nuclear weapons and their availability in large quantity have transformed the possible characteristics of warfare among the nations so equipped. An overwhelming advantage has been given to the offensive in military operations, for nuclear warheads can be delivered in diverse sizes and by varied delivery systems. Against the number, diversity and explosive power contained in substantial numbers of nuclear warheads, defense is essentially unfeasible. It is this condition which underlies the oft repeated judgment from Presidents and Secretaries of Defense in the nuclear era that it is no longer feasible to prevent nuclear-armed opponents from delivering a destructive blow to each other, regardless of which one moves first.

Military technology, now and in the foreseeable future, can deliver great destructive power for operating a threat system. But military technology cannot deliver a physical shield—that is, defense—in nuclear war.

Limit: Deterrence is a threat system, not a shield.

In place of the now unworkable function of defense as a true physical shield, military strategists have developed the concept of "deterrence." This is a threat system whose theory is that if an opponent is confronted with a believable threat of sufficient magnitude, then well-founded fear will freeze him into immobility. Plainly, this is a psychological calculation that neglects ordinary knowledge of human behavior: that many men respond to threat not by frozen immobility but rather by amplified rage and aggression. There is no science from which to predict that political and military leaders are more prone than others to being deterred. Neither are there grounds for excluding the possibility that two governments wielding nuclear weapons could each assume that the other side is rationally deterred—leaving it free, in each case, to act, and thereby producing the fateful nuclear collision.

Limit: People cannot be killed more than once. Overkill, once achieved, defines a limit to enlargement of military power.

Prior to the invention of nuclear explosives and their delivery systems, large armed forces stockpiled bullets, shells and various forms of explosives which, on a one-to-one basis, even exceeded in number the military personnel *and* the populations of possible enemy countries. Nevertheless, there were no efficient means by which these bullets, shells, etc., could be brought to bear on an opposing force or an enemy population with sufficient concentration to destroy all or virtually all of them. It is this critical element of concentration in time and place that was contributed by nuclear weapons. The destruction of Dresden was performed by hundreds of planes dropping thousands of explosives over many hours.[2] The destruction of Hiroshima and Nagasaki was done in each instance by one explosive carried by one plane, and was accomplished in a few seconds. This concentration of energy release now possible with nuclear explosives is well in excess of the amount required to destroy entire communities. This excess of destructive capability, new in human experience, required the invention of a new word, "overkill." That invention implied that strategic military technology had become absurd. Weapons have been developed in kind and quantity to exceed any plausible estimate of requirement for destruction of armed forces and populations.

The chart summarizes the number of nuclear warheads deliverable by American and Soviet strategic delivery systems. For the United States the chart is surely an understatement of the intercontinental systems on hand. For example, the aircraft of the fifteen carrier task forces operated by the United States Navy are not counted there. I estimate that the long-range planes of these carriers alone could deliver not fewer than 2,700 additional warheads. Despite the understatement of U.S. nuclear delivery capability, the chart shows in stark fashion the meaning of the overkill factors. Since the early 1960s the United States's major nuclear weapons alone were equivalent to more than six tons of TNT per person on earth.

Limit: A city or country cannot be destroyed more than once.

By 1970 the Soviet Union had about 219 cities of population 100,000 or more and in the United States there were 156 cities of this size and larger. One way of understanding the idea of deterrence is that a government of either the United States or the Soviet Union would be effectively constrained in the face of a threat to destroy that many of its population-industrial centers: a government that is not deterred by such a threat would be composed of men too insane to be deterred by anything. Therefore, one way of defining an outer limit of requirement for staying the military hand of a major nuclear power is the capability of destroying this many city centers. Since each of the nuclear warheads counted in the chart is a city-destroyer, it is relevant to compare the number of deliverable warheads (by 1972) with the number of sizable population-industrial centers of each society. By this conservative form of reckoning, the United States could conceivably overkill the population-industrial system of the U.S.S.R. twenty-six times, and the Soviets could destroy the United States's counterpart fifteen times over.

The human, military and scientific absurdity of the overkill development is revealed in the question: Who is ahead, the Soviet Union or the United States, with respect to nuclear military power? Nuclear warheads of considerable size (the 20,000-ton-TNT-equivalent Hiroshima warhead is now considered small) can be delivered by planes, missiles, torpedoes, mines, cannon, mortars and suitcases of diverse size. In the mid-1960s the Secretary of Defense informed us that the United States possessed "tens of thousands" of nuclear warheads. Considering the American and Soviet plans for weapons construction until 1977, these governments will then have, respectively, 10,213 and 3,869 nuclear explosives deliverable by intercontinental systems (missiles, planes, submarine-launched missiles). This will give the U.S. government overkill capability of at least forty-six times on the U.S.S.R., and the Soviets will have twenty-four times overkill on the population-industrial centers of the United States.[3] All of this may be contrasted with an assessment given in 1968 by Secretary of Defense Robert McNamara that from two hundred to four hundred one-megaton nuclear warheads would be an adequate U.S. deterrent force (capable of swiftly destroying 52–74 million Soviet people and 72–76 percent of Soviet industrial capacity).[4] Obviously, U.S. forces have gone far beyond that kind of recommendation, as the chart of nuclear-warhead growth shows.

In both the U.S. and the U.S.S.R. the development of nuclear weapons has proceeded into a realm of military make-believe. The ongoing multiplication of nuclear warheads is explicable only as the result of internal forces of each society that press for ever larger armament systems, regardless of limitations on the military or human meaning of adding to overkill capacity.

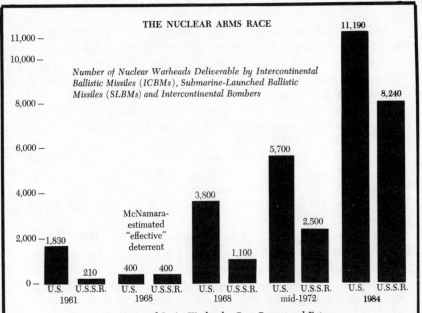

THE NUCLEAR ARMS RACE

Number of Nuclear Warheads Deliverable by Intercontinental Ballistic Missiles (ICBMs), Submarine-Launched Ballistic Missiles (SLBMs) and Intercontinental Bombers

McNamara-estimated "effective" deterrent

	1961		1968		1968		mid-1972		1984	
	U.S.	U.S.S.R.	U.S.	U.S.S.R.	U.S.	U.S.S.R.	U.S.	U.S.S.R.	U.S.	U.S.S.R.
Warheads	1,830	210	400	400	3,800	1,100	5,700	2,500	11,190	8,240

American and Soviet Warheads—Past, Present and Future

Method of Delivery	1961		1968		MID-1972		1984	
	U.S.	U.S.S.R.	U.S.	U.S.S.R.	U.S.	U.S.S.R.	U.S.	U.S.S.R.
ICBMs	circa 50	c. 50	1,054	900	c. 1,900	1,550	2,100	5,800
SLBMs	c. 80	c. 10	656	45	c. 1,650	810	5,540	2,100
Bombers	c. 1,700	c. 150	2,144	150	c. 2,150	140	3,550	340
Total Number of Warheads (approx.)	1,830	210	3,800	1,100	5,700	2,500	11,190	8,240

SOURCES: Compiled by SANE, from: Secretary of Defense Melvin R. Laird, *Fiscal Year 1972-76 Defense Program and the 1972 Defense Budget*, March 9, 1971, and *FY 1973 Statement*; Ralph Lapp, *Kill and Overkill* and *The Weapons Culture*; Stockholm International Peace Research Institute, *SIPRI Yearbook of World Armaments and Disarmament, 1968/69* and *1969/70*; the Center for Defense Information, *The Defense Monitor*, Vol. 13, No. 6, 1984.

Former Secretary of Defense Robert McNamara has contended that it is the number of nuclear warheads that is significant in assessing strategic power. In a speech before the UPI Editors and Publishers in San Francisco on September 18, 1967, he said: "For the most meaningful and realistic measurement of nuclear capability is neither gross megatonnage, nor the number of available missile launchers, but rather the number of separate warheads that are capable of being *delivered* with accuracy on individual high-priority targets with sufficient power to destroy them."

Less than a year later, in February, 1968, in Congressional testimony on an adequate nuclear deterrent for the United States, McNamara stated that: "In the case of the Soviet Union, I would judge that a capability on our part to destroy, say, one-fifth to one-fourth of her population and one-half of her industrial capacity would serve as an effective deterrent. Such a level of destruction would certainly represent intolerable punishment to any 20th-Century industrial nation." McNamara went on to present data suggesting that such a capability could be accomplished by a force of from 200 to 400 one-megaton nuclear warheads. He estimated that such a nuclear force is capable of destroying from 52 to 74 million Soviet people (21 to 30% of the population) and from 72 to 76% of Soviet industrial capacity.

Limit: Once nuclear arms are available in quantity, more weapons or firepower do not necessarily add to military power.

American society has been asking military technologists to produce something which, on the evidence, cannot be delivered: a workable shield against nuclear destruction from without, and military superiority in both nuclear and conventional warfare. Despite the known technological limits in these spheres, military technologists and military officers present themselves to the Congress and to the public at large recommending the expenditure of large public funds for their activities, each of which is, implicitly or explicitly, presumed to contribute to a plausible military defense of the United States or to superiority of American armed forces.

An accumulating body of evidence suggests that the effort to enlarge and intensify nuclear-threat systems tends to invite reciprocal acts, with the net result of diminishing the military security of all parties. For example, the effort to secure advantage by locating nuclear weapons close to Soviet borders has encouraged the Soviets to do the same in relation to the United States, achieving that effect with oceangoing submarines.

The escalation of nuclear threat (deterrence) produces inevitable hazards. The Senate Foreign Relations Committee has cautioned that the American policy of surrounding the Soviet Union and Communist China with atomic weapons could very well provoke nuclear-war crises should either of those countries seek to "break out of the nuclear ring" by deploying their nuclear weapons overseas. In that case, the committee warned in a 1970 report, "we could face an international crisis comparable to that of the Cuban Missile Crisis of 1962." The committee underscored that:

> The United States went to the brink of nuclear war when faced with the possibility that the Soviet Union was putting missiles in a country 90 miles from the United States. We must assume that the Soviets, as they view our placement of tactical nuclear weapons in countries far closer to their borders than Cuba is to ours, will seek to break out of the nuclear ring that has been drawn around them.[5]

Limit: Among nuclear powers it is probably impossible to carry out a surprise attack that so overwhelms the victim as to preclude a return nuclear strike.

Governments have understood this problem and have devised

nuclear systems that make it unfeasible for an attacker to wholly destroy nuclear-delivery capability. This has been accomplished not only by numerical increase but also by mounting nuclear warheads on elusive submarines, in massively shielded fixed silos, and in bombers that can release missiles several hundred miles from a target. Nevertheless, the older military mentality prevails, and uncounted billions of dollars have been expended on endless cycles of weapons systems to fulfill the artilleryman's dream: successful "counter-battery fire" that destroys the enemy's artillery and thereby leaves his forces naked and open to systematic destruction. Essentially, this is the model for the theory of a nuclear "first strike," especially of a "counterforce" sort: destroy the enemy's nuclear weapons and he will then be compelled (rationally, that is) to submit to the will of the attacker. The probability of such a response is not one of the topics on which the thinkers on nuclear strategy have much to say.

A plethora of problems is provoked by any attempt to plan nuclear wars. For example, is it rational to respond with nuclear weapons when a society has already been attacked and destroyed? Such problems are not susceptible to "solution," because they are cast in the humanly alien perspective of planning for the end, not of some people's lives, but of the life of entire societies, of the human race itself. The realism that is developed on behalf of such objectives is deservedly termed, after C. Wright Mills, crackpot realism.

From a more limited military standpoint, however, the heart of the matter is this: The power of nuclear weapons, combined with the diversity of delivery systems and allied strategies, no longer permits either side so equipped to attain a decisive military superiority. Once overkill capability has been attained on two sides, then refinement of the details of weaponry becomes militarily and politically irrelevant. Numerical military advantage cannot be wielded for political ends.

Limit: In nuclear war if you apparently win you very likely stand to lose.

If this statement seems like a play on words it is because of the changed meaning of words like "win," "military advantage" and "lose" in the nuclear era.

The number of nuclear warheads that can be launched by each

superpower is so great that a "successful" nuclear "first strike," destroying all or most of the nuclear-response capability of an opponent, could also release so much radiation into the atmosphere as to produce a self-destroying backlash on the aggressor society.[6] There is no science from which to predict that a major nuclear attacker scoring a perfect first-strike knockout would thereby remain unscathed from massive release of radioactive materials and other damage to the earth's atmosphere.

The ambition to achieve a nuclear-surprise blow characteristically does not take into account the nature of the opponent's options in responding to such suspected capability. An opponent can conceivably respond in kind with similar technology, for the laws of nature cannot be patented. He can develop diverse nuclear-carrying delivery options, including: nuclear warheads in orbiting satellites; nuclear warheads placed underwater so that their detonation would shower deadly fallout over a vast area; submarine-mounted nuclear warheads that are unreachable by attacking missiles, however accurate their potential guidance.

The simplest response option of all could take the form of a change in nuclear strategy: from nuclear response to a received attack, to nuclear "launch on warning." Thus, a nation fearing attack could so instrument its nuclear systems that missiles or other devices are launched not after an enemy's missiles (or other vehicles) have been thoroughly identified and their impact has been felt, but once an attack has been identified as being en route. In such circumstances, assuming an attack by missiles, the "first-striking" superaccurately guided warheads would be delivered to empty missile silos. Under these conditions of U.S.–Soviet confrontation, the security of the United States would become hostage to the accuracy of Soviet radars and Soviet data-interpretation systems, and to the reliability and rationality of Soviet command-post personnel.

Limit: Among nuclear powers military superiority is no longer definable or achievable.

The conditions that make this so have already been identified. Nevertheless a quest for superiority continues, with consequences that were probably not intended.

The very effort on the part of one power to find advantage against another has been used, repeatedly, as the justification on the other side for proceeding in a similar fashion, to outdo the competitor. By this process, best described as "antagonistic co-operation," the managers of military economy in the U.S. and the U.S.S.R. support each other. The relentless pressure of each military directorate to be "first" promotes an arms race that has no definable termination or condition of "winning." But one result is assured: the militarist extremists of the United States assure larger military budgets for their counterparts in the U.S.S.R., and vice versa.

Limit: The spread of nuclear weapons cannot be readily halted.

The importance given to nuclear-weapons systems by the United States and the U.S.S.R. had encouraged other nations to acquire similar weapons. This, of course, diminishes much of the "advantage" that may have been held by a few states when they alone possessed weapons systems of this kind. For a few years after the Second World War the United States alone had nuclear weapons. Swiftly thereafter the U.S.S.R. and the United Kingdom acquired the means of production for nuclear weapons. These were followed by France, and finally in the 1960s by China. By the 1970s an array of other states ranging from India to Israel have been judged as potential nuclear-weapons builders.[7]

Limit: As a result of the diversity of technological options that have been developed for weaponry, as in biological warfare, military dominance is not assured even by overwhelming military expenditures.

The United States and other great powers have made major efforts since World War I to develop chemical and biological-warfare agents.[8] One of the controlling features affecting the possibility of biological-warfare applications is the wide diffusion of relevant knowledge. As one biologist put it to me, a biological-warfare laboratory is "a hospital turned upside down." The implication is that the men and women trained in disease control have in their hands relevant knowledge for disease propagation. Since this refers to the very large number of medical men, biologists and technicians, it is reasonable to understand that the final limitation on utilization of such weapons must reside in the values that people live by, on the acts thay they regard as thinkable as against those that are unthinkable.

Limit: Conventional military forces wielding superior firepower cannot necessarily subdue a military opponent organized along guerrilla lines.

Guerrilla warfare involves special military-technology innovations of an organizational sort. These do not consist primarily of particular weapons. This organizational innovation sets limits on conventional military power and hence on the meaning of many military-technology developments.

The essence of guerrilla warfare involves military-political operations under the following conditions: (a) a group of men sufficiently committed to a common purpose to risk their lives for the end in view; (b) support from the surrounding population (and/ or part of a government) for the guerrilla fighting group; (c) capability by the guerrillas for taking on appearances similar to that of the surrounding population.

Whenever these three conditions have been fulfilled, it has become very difficult for conventional armed forces to overcome the group of men so operating. During the last decades, major armed forces have been repeatedly frustrated by guerrilla-type operations that fulfill the three conditions noted above. This was starkly revealed in the frustration of the German Army during the Second World War against the Yugoslav guerrillas, and was further demonstrated by the frustration of American armed forces in their relation to the guerrilla organization of the National Liberation Front in Vietnam.

There is no question that in every department of weapons technology, American armed forces in Vietnam, and those supported by them, enjoyed overwhelming superiority. The guerrilla opponent in Vietnam demonstrated military staying power despite the fact that he possessed few heavy weapons, no navy, no air force, and nothing like the technically elaborate military and industrial infrastructure that supports American and allied armed forces. During the 1960s American armed forces did not stint on research and development for counterguerrilla operations.[9] The array of new-weapons development to facilitate the counterguerrilla operations in Vietnam ranged from new lightweight weapons, footgear and protective clothing to devices to "smell" a possible opponent concealed in a jungle, and antipersonnel bombs of diverse sorts with highly destructive effect. The inability of the most elaborately equipped armed force in the world, backed by the world's largest military-technology research and development network, to overcome the guerrilla forces of a small, poor country helps to define a limit on the capabilities of military technology.[10]

This is not to say that guerrilla operations cannot be overcome. They can, if one or more of the three conditions listed above are altered: if the surrounding population is destroyed, then there is no "sea" in which the guerrillas can "swim." In Vietnam the United States finally turned to removing or destroying the populations in areas under guerrilla control. The breakthrough to a new level of frightfulness in the pursuit of power in Vietnam is illustrated by the destruction of the countryside by bombardment and chemical defoliation and the concentration of Vietnamese peasants into towns and cities where they could be more readily controlled.[11]

Limit: Small nations cannot compete in the arms race on an across-the-board basis. But nuclear and other weapons have an "equalizing" effect in the military relations of large and small nations.

One of the characteristics of many new technologies is that they tend to become less costly as more is known about them. Design and fabrication can often be simplified if that is desired. This general feature has also been characteristic of the nuclear-warhead material and nuclear weapons: they have become smaller and, it is said, cheaper. An important military consequence flows from the accessibility of smaller states to this technology. When smaller states have nuclear power, the overwhelming concentration of destructive military power in the hands of the superstates is at least partially checkmated. However "small" such weapons and their numbers, the nature of nuclear weapons and the possibility of delivering them by alternative means opens up the nightmarish possibilities of military-political confrontations in which major powers find themselves threatened by small nations wielding nuclear "equalizers."

Limit: Possession of very large air forces does not necessarily ensure victory in the use of air power against a determined opponent.

The swift development of airborne weaponry since World War I has led many people to expect that air power automatically yields military supremacy. The U.S. war in Indochina included an unprecedented saturation of many areas by aerial bombardment. Entire regions of Vietnam, Laos and Cambodia were made to look like moonscapes as a result of the dropping of more explosives on that land than were used by the U.S. Air Force in all of World War II.[12] Not even this unprecedented destruction sufficed to subdue the National Liberation Front and the People's Revolutionary Government of North Vietnam. During the entire period of the U.S. government's war against the Vietnamese, the preponderance of firepower in favor of the U.S. and U.S.-supported forces was overwhelming.

A very important limit on air power was disclosed by the American experience in bombing Hanoi and Haiphong during December 1972. In those operations the loss rate of the big B-52 bombers rose to a level that threatened the destruction of a significant part of the U.S. Air Force's strategic air fleet.

About two hundred of the B-52 aircraft were used in the bombing of North Vietnam during December 1972. During a period of eleven days the loss rate of these aircraft amounted to 7.5 percent. If this rate had been sustained for thirty days about forty-five of these aircraft would have been lost. That would have amounted to somewhat more than one in ten of the total B-52 fleet available to the U.S. Air Force. It has been noted that for aircraft "a 2 percent loss rate is supportable for years of warfare, as World War II showed, as long as replacements for bombers and crew are available."[13] The B-52 loss rate was three and a half times that. Moreover, B-52s were not being currently produced, since they were intended for either a nuclear-deterrence function or for strategic-warfare application. Also their crews are a very valuable military asset in terms of long and costly training and experience. If such aircraft were put into current production they would probably cost not less than $25 million each. Hence, the opportunity cost of fifteen of these aircraft is probably not less than $375 million (one indication of the materiel cost of the eleven-day bombing blitz against the Hanoi-Haiphong area).

By the end of December 1972 the bombardment of Vietnam had ceased to be a "milk run" for the B-52 air crews. The war turned grim for these men as they were shaken by the intensity and effectiveness of the Vietnamese defensive antiaircraft fire. The high B-52 attrition rates probably played a part in the Nixon decision to call a halt to the U.S. bombardment in North Vietnam.[14]

Limit: Military systems as a whole can no longer be improved by improving parts.

Suboptimization is the strategy for improving a system as a whole through improvement of the parts. In military-technical form, this has meant a rifle with more firepower, more lethal bullets, faster airplanes, infrared devices for sighting small arms at night, an improved tire, an improved bandage, an improved uniform, more accurate radar, an improved guidance system, an improved missile fuel—each of these being pursued on the assumption that from the sum of the unit technical improvements there will emerge, necessarily, an improvement in a system as a whole.

A military officer's view of unit improvements desirable during the 1970s was given by Brigadier (Ret.) Kenneth Hunt in a paper on "The Requirements of Military Technology in the 1970's." Hunt wrote, in 1967:

> The soldier is interested in infra-red or laser sighting devices to enable him to see and aim at night or in fog; light-weight radar or sensory aids to detect enemy approach; weapon-locating radars to pinpoint enemy guns or mortars by calculating the path taken by the shells they fire; the location of enemy concentrations and particularly nuclear artillery, with sufficient accuracy and speed to enable them to be hit before they move or fire; the engagement of high-speed attacking aircraft, preferably before they release their weapons. The sailor must find the enemy submarine, surface ship or aircraft, which is no doubt moving, and engage these fleeting targets before they engage him. The airman has his target to strike, fixed, moving, pre-determined or opportunity; the enemy interceptor, bomber or missile to engage; the enemy defences to counter.[15]

The suboptimization strategy of military-technology improvement is constrained by two of the limits on military power discussed above: nuclear overkill and guerrilla warfare. Improvement in overkill is nonoperational and hence militarily, humanly and scientifically meaningless. Ever greater firepower for destroying an opponent under conditions of guerrilla warfare is meaningless insofar as the opponent cannot even be identified. (Note that once an entire population is identified as the opponent this constraint is bypassed, as was done by U.S. forces in Vietnam.[16])

In weapons development, technological improvement has typically taken the form of attempts at superiority in destructive power, accuracy, speed, range and reliability. Consider Brigadier Hunt's shopping list of technological improvements in terms of these factors. Each of these developments might very well produce some particular military gain under Second World War conditions, provided it is not checkmated by a counterdevice: radar can be "confused" by various countermeasures, weapons can be shielded from observation, nuclear artillery is not necessarily distinguished from other heavy artillery, etc. Once nuclear weapons are introduced in quantity, however, the military meaningfulness of particular weapons gains is vitiated.

Limit: In military (and other) technology, complexity can generate unreliability so as to overwhelm improvements in the quality of single components.

Due to the way error is generated by complex systems, it is possible that the quality of individual parts can undergo substantial improvement at the same time that the reliability of the mechanism that uses more and more of them actually declines. This may occur owing to the fact that the error of a mechanism as a whole is not a sum of the errors of the linked parts; instead, it is the product of the errors of the components. Therefore, if a mechanism is made more and more complicated and the number of components is greatly enlarged it becomes possible for the reliability of the mechanism to diminish even while the reliability of many of the parts has been individually improved. This probably accounts for the notorious unreliability of new-generation complex aircraft like the F-111 and the C-5A, and the difference in military electronics systems between the 1950s and the 1960s. In the latter period the reliability of military electronics systems showed a decline. This decline occurred even though a massive technical effort had been made to improve the quality of individual electronic components.[17]

Limit: Faster response in military systems can reduce reliability of control over these systems.

One of the assumptions made by weapons technologists, and by those who have willingly voted them unlimited funds, is that faster response in military systems, as in communication, transportation, speed of weapon delivery, etc., corresponds to an improvement in military capability. Professor Herbert F. York, physicist and Director of Defense Research and Engineering under President Eisenhower, has pointed out the contradictory effects due to efforts to design a "hair trigger" for fast response and a "stiff trigger" for safety factors into the same mechanisms or systems. The "hair trigger" design is to get greater speed for military advantage. The "stiff trigger" design is to achieve deliberate control. The two effects are in contradiction with each other. Such contradictions pervade the nuclear strategic mechanisms and systems.[18]

On May 2, 1974, *The New York Times* carried this remarkable dispatch from *Reuters* in Washington.

> Israel, Egypt and Syria all shot down large numbers of their own planes with surface-to-air missiles during last October's war, United States military experts said today.
>
> Syria on a single day downed nearly 20 Soviet-built MIG fighters that had been supplied to her by Iraq, the sources said. Israel shot down a large number of her Mirages with both SAMs and air-to-air missiles from other Israeli fighters, they added.
>
> Dr. Malcolm R. Currie, Director of Defense Research at the Pentagon, said at a conference in San Diego, that a major problem with the missiles was coordinating their use with interceptor aircraft in the defense against enemy air raids. . . .
>
> Dr. Currie said that the United States could not be confident it would be able to operate its own missiles much better and that builders of tactical missiles must give priority to consideration of this problem.

Limit: More accurate weapons are not necessarily better.

As nuclear warheads of about a million tons of TNT equivalent can destroy brick structures within a six-mile radius, the conceivable meaning of improvements in accuracy is not immediately understandable. Nevertheless, we are told that the advanced thinkers in the Pentagon have been moving ahead with their yearly $9-billion research-and-development budgets to improve the accuracy and explosive force of U.S. nuclear warheads. The following is an account of some contemplated changes in accuracy and explosive force of U.S. nuclear weapons.

> ACCURACY—Each Minuteman warhead is designed to land within one-quarter mile of its target, or within about 1,300 feet. It is technically possible, weapons specialists say, to improve guidance to come within a few hundred feet of the target, thus increasing the chance of

destruction and decreasing the chance of destroying population centers in the vicinity.

The multiple warheads on Poseidon missiles aboard Polaris submarines are less accurate, but with deployment of a so-called stellar inertial guidance system, can be made as accurate as land-based ICBM's, Pentagon planners say. This system would correct errors in the warhead's trajectory during flight.

MORE POTENT WARHEADS—At present the Minuteman-3 carries three warheads of about 160 kilotons each; the Poseidon, 10 to 14 warheads of about 40 kilotons each. A kiloton is equal to the explosive force of 1,000 tons of TNT.

Pentagon officials say that the explosive force of these warheads can be increased by a factor of four or more.

For comparison, the big Soviet SS-9 missile can reportedly impact only about one-half mile from its target. Some are equipped with three warheads of 5 megatons each, others with a single warhead of 25 megatons. A megaton is equivalent to one million tons of TNT.

An improved larger version of the SS-9, built but not yet test-fired, is potentially able to carry 20 warheads of one half to one megaton each, intelligence sources say.[19]

It is worth contemplating some aspects of these projected developments. They are incredibly expensive, using up vast quantities of labor, power, machinery and raw materials. The entire enterprise has a science-fiction quality: guidance is to be "improved" to "within a few hundred feet" for explosions equivalent, on the low end of size, to tens of thousands of tons of TNT. Entire laboratories are devoted to solving intricate problems of detail that absorb the talents and energies of highly trained technologists. All the while no one is supposed to ask whether the whole project makes any sense, other than as a job-sustaining program. Note the last paragraphs of the news article above. They contain the required admonition about what "they" are doing; this is the operation of the "antagonistic-cooperation" mechanism.

Inertial-guidance systems (self-contained devices that tell the vehicle where it is) went through successive refinements, so that single warheads in missiles could be directed with ever smaller scatter to the desired targets. Further, guidance systems were developed to permit a single missile to carry multiple warheads, with each warhead being separately targeted—thus MIRV, the Multiple Independently Targeted Reentry Vehicle program. More recently, we learn of the Advanced Ballistic Reentry System

(ABRES) program, which involves warheads capable of identifying and maneuvering toward their own targets. This latter development is said to make possible the targeting of individual nuclear warheads with unprecedented accuracy, to the known positions of enemy ICBMs and other military installations. Still, under no conceivable conditions could the United States escape destruction even if a U.S. nuclear first strike could destroy all Soviet missiles in fixed positions. Their submarines could respond with devastating force.

Limit: Human and machine errors, failures, misjudgments, miscalculations or misperceptions in the use of modern weapons can have catastrophic effects.

The Poseidon missile represents the most technically advanced intercontinental missile launched from American nuclear submarines. That missile carries multiple warheads which are separately targeted and guided. Thereby each missile may be able to deliver as many as ten city-destroying nuclear explosives. The following was reported in May, 1973.

A Poseidon missile fired from a submerged submarine whipped violently out of control last evening, blew apart and hit the Atlantic Ocean in full view of a Russian spy ship and 200 guests of the United States Navy.

One section of the errant missile plunged straight down, trailing a bright yellow flame, and splashed into the sea only four or five miles from this tracking ship crowded with spectators. A second piece cartwheeled into the ocean several seconds later. . . .

The Poseidon, key to the Navy's nuclear deterrent force, was launched on what was to be a routine test flight from the U.S.S. *Henry L. Stimson* about 30 miles east of Cape Kennedy. . . .

The 34-foot Poseidon, carrying a dummy warhead, popped out of one of the *Stimson's* 16 submerged launching tubes, ignited normally and roared into the cloudy sky toward an Atlantic target area more than 1,500 miles to the southeast.

But after about 15 to 20 seconds of flight, the stubby black and white rocket wheeled off course. It appeared to recover, gained altitude and then began fishtailing wildly, its brilliant exhaust spewing from side to side.

Range safety officers at Cape Kennedy allowed the rocket to perform in this fashion for about a half-minute as it gained altitude and distance from the Range Sentinel and the Soviet vessel. Then, 57 seconds after launching, a radio signal was sent to the missile, which detonated an emergency explosive charge and severed the rocket.[20]

Consider the possible effects of a misdirected missile of this type. It normally carries ten separate warheads. Each warhead is equivalent to about forty thousand tons TNT (roughly twice the power of the nuclear warhead that destroyed Hiroshima). Human or machine failures in an instrument with these powers open up the possibility of multiple catastrophic effects.

Similar consequences, though not of the same physical magnitude, are linked to errors in the use of conventional weapons. The B-52 bombers with "conventional" high explosives that were used to bombard Vietnam carried in each plane twenty-four tons (48,000 pounds) of high explosives. Three such planes devastate one and a half square miles. I once tried to convey the meaning of this statement to some of my students by suggesting that the New York City area bounded by 110th and 125th Streets, Riverside Drive and Amsterdam Avenue is one and a half square miles; and that area includes Columbia University and a series of other major educational and religious institutions as well as thousands of residents in multistoried dwellings. The entire United Nations complex and the Wall Street financial district are, in each case, less than one and a half square miles in area.

The great power of present-day conventional and nuclear weapons opens up destructive capacities that were never before conceivable. Full prevention of unintended destructive effects is restricted not only by imperfections in mechanisms and individuals, but also because of the cumulative effect of concentrated decision power in the operations of modern governments. A recurring feature of these organizations has been their errors of judgment about the intentions of opponents. Thus, the whole history of the Cold War lends itself to restatement in terms of the multiple and diverse meanings assigned to single events by each side in that contest. The sequence of operations leading up to the Cuban Missile Crisis of October 1962 is a classic example of the enactment of this process.

Limit: Military command and control procedures are not error-proof.

A good illustration of the combined operation of human and equipment error was afforded by a dramatic incident in 1971.

Even though the operation of nuclear military systems is cloaked in massive secrecy, from time to time events occur which cannot be held secret and which demonstrate such dangers. On February 20, 1971, the National Emergency Warning Center, located in the North American Air Defense Command (NORAD) headquarters at Cheyenne Mountain, Colorado, issued a national teletyped warning to all radio and television stations at 9:33 A.M. ordering them to go off the air and operate only under the elaborately preplanned conditions for communicating to a population in the event of nuclear war. This message was supposed to be sent only when the President had declared a national emergency.

Investigation soon disclosed that the wrong tape had been fed into the teletype transmitting machine. Said the operator, who had worked at the center for fifteen years, "I can't imagine how the hell I did it." The warning center was not equipped with readily available procedures for canceling this error, and so forty minutes elapsed between the false transmission and the sending of a cancellation signal. The experience of radio stations throughout the country varied during this incident. Some did not receive the emergency message or act on it, the reasons varying from delay in reading the printed tapes as they came from the station ticker to the jamming of paper in news ticker receivers. This incident, with its nonfatal consequences, served as a spontaneous test of the warning system. It demonstrated the built-in potential for mechanical and human malfunction that inhere in highly complex systems designed to perform at high speed and under conditions where allowances for deliberate verification procedures are not made in the interest of minimizing the time for getting the military result.[21]

Another problem in the quality of military control is illustrated by the problem of restricting the spread of nuclear explosives.

A worldwide problem involving control of atomic-bomb raw material has been created by the rapidly expanding quantity of "material flowing through nuclear industries that could be used directly in nuclear explosive devices." These "will reach thousands of kilograms in several countries by 1980 and will continue to increase rapidly thereafter for the foreseeable future." So stated a key part of a report to the American Nuclear Society and the Atomic Industrial Forum in 1972. Professor Mason Willrich, chairman of an international group on the problem of control of nuclear material to prevent "the building of home-made atomic bombs by mentally disturbed people, ambitious small nations or gangsters," indicated that uranium and plutonium "were valued at $3,000 to $10,000 a kilogram, roughly the price of heroin."[22] Attention to this problem, begun early in the nuclear era, continues to the present. By 1968, Dr. Theodore Taylor, a nuclear physicist who was once chief of the Defense Department's bomb design and testing program, stated: "I've been worried about how easy it is to build bombs ever since I built my first one." His concern reflected the view of increasing numbers of scientists, including the members of a panel formed by the Atomic Energy Commission to advise the commission on ways of safeguarding against the development of a black market in nuclear materials.[23] The report to the Atomic Energy Commission by the Ad Hoc Advisory Panel on Safeguarding Special Nuclear Material recommended steps to tighten control and enlarge penalties for unauthorized diversions of special nuclear materials.[24] AEC Chairman Dr. Glenn Seaborg conceded that "it is possible" that a black market in nuclear material could develop.[25]

Limit: Higher price does not necessarily denote higher quality in the realm of military hardware.

The F-14 swing-wing fighter-bomber produced for the Navy by Grumman has been priced at $16–20 million per plane. Its operating characteristics are rather similar to the proven F-4 (Phantom) that is sold by McDonnell-Douglas to the Navy and the Air Force at about $4 million per plane. It has been estimated that "on the average, costs for the heavier, more complex class of combat aircraft have increased by a factor of 10 about every 18 years."[26] Also, the full-system costs (spares, training, auxiliary equipment, etc.) of new-generation weapons have characteristically far exceeded degrees of improvements in operating performance as set forth by the military services.[27]

For the billions paid out to military industry it would seem reasonable to expect delivery of high-quality—even if expensive military materiel. However, the quality of much materiel has been affected by poor design, incompetence in production, and such atrocious neglect of stipulated quality as to almost exceed the imagination. The C-5A aircraft, the largest quantity-produced aircraft in the world, designed and produced by the leading military-industry firm, underwent a price increase from $28 million to $61 million per plane. The resulting aircraft, however, has also displayed a remarkable array of failures and limits on capability. The wing has shown serious fatigue failure; engines have fallen off. In order to lessen strain on the plane it is to be operated at only 80 percent of its designed load and will be used only on modern concrete runways—not on the unimproved landing fields for which it was designed. This aircraft is to operate at only 75 percent of its original scheduled time per month. The landing gear is the most complex of any aircraft in the world (apparently reflecting the Rube Goldberg tradition of industrial design) and suffers repeated failure. Many of the electronics, or avionics, in the C-5A have shown repeated defect. Bad-weather flying instruments have been found to be unreliable. The use of the automatic-pilot system has been restricted. The inertial-navigation system has been failing at between eighty and a hundred hours instead of at the planned thousand hours of use. A "stall" warning system had to be replaced. Low reliability was discovered in the system designed to detect problems in other systems. Thus the C-5A's malfunction detection analysis and recording system has been listed among ten other systems as having the highest failure rate.[28]

This kind of performance doesn't just happen. It takes systematic, continued, institutionalized practices to produce these results. Owing to the defection of Henry Durham, a former production manager on the C-5A assembly line in the Lockheed Corporation, we have details of many aspects of Lockheed's production practices, including the observation that literally thousands of parts were omitted from the C-5A's when the planes were actually delivered to the Air Force. In 1971 Durham responded to an interviewer:

> Did you tell the management that the safety of the C-5A might be endangered by those missing parts and management procedures?
> Yes. In the letter I wrote to Daniel Haughton, Chairman of Lockheed, I said I was concerned that the plane might crash because we'd find missing parts shortly before one was scheduled to fly, on a test flight, for example . . .
> What types of parts are these—in terms of the functional capacity of the plane?
> They are all types. Everything from tiny parts to something as big as a door. A wide range of parts. Relatively inexpensive parts to very expensive parts . . .[29]

In the largest program of the largest military-industry firm, quality in design and in production has not necessarily accompanied high price. It is important to understand the order of magnitude of what is at stake here. Thus, the "Department of Defense estimates that it will cost more than $153 billion to acquire the 116 weapons systems currently under development. Some $89 billion of that amount is yet to be appropriated by the Congress."[30] The cost estimate of $153 billion is not, of course, the final price to be paid. That represents a current estimate prepared by the General Accounting Office and cannot take into account further price increase under the impetus of the cost-maximization process. On August 3, 1972, Senator Proxmire reported that the estimated costs of forty-five selected major weapons systems had increased by $36.5 billion over the original planning estimates for those weapons.[31]

Limit: Access to the laws of nature cannot be monopolized.

This straightforward statement simply means that the idea of really secret weapons, exclusively held military technology and superiority based upon special knowledge of nature and its application reflects an unrealistic expectation. Once several large nation-states are determined to develop military technology, able men and women are found everywhere who can perform this task. Again and again during the last quarter century the United States has taken a lead in one or another military technology only to discover that other countries were able to be close runners-up.

Limit: Military power cannot necessarily ensure economic or political stability.

Within the United States the largest accumulation of military power in world history has in fact been a source of economic instability, as I have shown in Chapters Four and Five. Massive application of U.S. military power to Vietnam has certainly not yielded political stability despite success in temporarily shoring up U.S.-preferred rulers in South Vietnam.

In U.S. foreign policy, words like "stability" have become code words for regimes or social structures preferred by the government of the United States. Where such regimes are established with major doses of U.S. military power in countries with large populations in rebellion against their governments or ruling classes or both, time has been bought during which an attempt could be made to regulate domestic and international relations of the subject country in a fashion preferred by the U.S. government. Such arrangements, however, do not terminate the operation of local forces of a nationalist or economic revolutionary nature. When such groups are driven underground and resort to guerrilla methods under the required conditions discussed above, the way is opened for sustained struggle. In that sense, there is a limit on the maximum "stability" purchasable with armed force.

Limit: Economic health does not depend on having superior military power.

The productive economic strength of Japan and Germany since the Second World War is a striking demonstration of the consequences for economic health owing to moderation or minimization of national investment in military power. The pattern for the United States and the Soviet Union, however, shows economic weakness along with great military power in each case. The data for the United States are contained in the earlier chapters above.

In the Soviet Union there is evidence of constraint on economic development that is surely traceable to the long priority given to military industry and military technology. For example, in dispatches from Moscow one reads that citizens are mobilized to help bring in the yearly harvest of truck produce around the Soviet capital, because the mechanization and organization of agriculture has not proceeded to the point where newspapers need not exhort Moscovites with headlines proclaiming "Decisive Days," "Every Hour Counts," and "The Capital Awaits its Potatoes."[32]

In an official summary of the "Draft Directives of the 24th CPSU Congress for the New Five-Year Plan" one finds that "it is planned to raise labor productivity in industry by 36–40 percent over the five-year period, securing thereby 87–90 percent of the total increment in output." Labor productivity is, of course, a centrally important economic matter for the Soviet Union. From the standpoint of industrial productivity, attaining the stated goal depends on intensive mechanization of existing plants and construction of new, highly productive industrial facilities. This result is unlikely without a substantial transfer of Soviet technical talent from military and space activities to productive economic work.

I find it significant that despite considerable differences in political-economic conditions, problems of economic depletion or limited economic growth in the United States and the Soviet Union involve a common factor: long concentration of technical talent and capital on parasitic economic growth.

Limit: Excessive armed forces can endanger the very civil liberties in whose name they were justified.

Military organizations are the most authoritarian of known social structures. To the degree that such organizations acquire more decision power in society, that fact automatically weakens institutions of personal and political freedom. Free speech, free press and organized political opposition are unthinkable within the framework of conventional military organizations.

Numerical superiority in nuclear military power vis-à-vis the Soviet Union does not ensure the character of domestic American institutions. That is necessarily determined by conditions of society inside the United States. Neither does superior military power as against the Vietnamese strengthen institutions of personal and political freedom within the United States. The contrary is probably the case. For as resources, manpower and prestige are accorded to authoritarian military and quasi-military organizations there is no final barrier to growing decision power by these organizations within the United States. An important part of the background of the Watergate scandal was the readiness of the White House to utilize the Department of Defense and the Central Intelligence Agency (limited by law to foreign operations) for affecting political institutions within the United States.

Limit: The military competence of large armed forces is dependent on the popularity of their mission among the population that supports them.

Firm commitment to military-political goals by the top leadership of a large and elaborately equipped military force is not sufficient in itself to ensure the planned functioning of that organization. The further requirement is willing acceptance and implementation of those goals among all ranks, as well as general compliance with the intricate network of military rules and standards which ensure planned performance of a military machine.

The latter element is lacking when the population base from which armies are drawn opposes the military mission. This was a crucial aspect of the American war in Vietnam. Volunteers and draftees were drawn from a population that had a higher education level and that was therefore less manipulable than ever before. Its material level of living had been rising, and fast, worldwide communications, as on TV, limited the ability of leaders to deceive that population at will. The statements of leaders often contrasted with the war scenes on the daily TV programs. There were reported instances where people watching TV in their homes saw relatives wounded in military actions.

The contrast between official ideology and Vietnamese reality produced massive disillusionment with the authority of the war leaders. It even compelled the political retirement of Lyndon Johnson, whose overwhelming political victory in the election of 1964 followed a campaign in which, at one moment, he stood in the back of an open car and shouted through a bullhorn, "Do something for Molly and the kids. Vote for peace."

As the Vietnam War was being desperately pressed, even without military success and with increasing disenchantment among American soldiers, an epidemic of drug addiction broke out in U.S. armed forces which could be finally limited only by the withdrawal of these soldiers from Vietnam. This was paralleled by resignations of key officer groups, racial tensions, and large-scale graft and looting of military supplies. Obviously, hard-drug addiction undermines human capacity for work, including the performance of military work.[33] The Secretary of the Navy announced that 6,700 men were discharged in 1970 from the Navy and the Marine Corps alone due to drug abuse, while drug abuse in the Army, especially in Vietnam, reached epidemic dimensions.[34]

Fighting a war whose performance was in growing contradiction to its avowed purposes encouraged race confrontation inside U.S. armed forces.[35] The morale crises in the military extended to the elite academies that prepare cadres of future military leaders. It was a blow to Army leaders when thirty-three of their most promising young officers, all of them teachers at West Point, left the Army within eighteen months during 1971–72.[36] A team of *Washington Post* reporters investigating American military bases in the United States, Germany, Italy and Vietnam found an Army torn by internal conflicts and tensions, including racial tension and disorientation that is symptomatic of the absence of shared purposes.[37]

The contradictions between actual limits of military power and the make-believe of U.S. military practice wants an explanation. Is all this simply the behavior of men so stubbornly committed to what they want that actual conditions cannot be allowed to stand in the way of their quest, however unattainable the goal? I doubt it. While stubbornness and the "denial" of the unpleasant are well-known parts of human capacity, the explanation of apparent official disregard of limits of military power requires institutional rather than individual psychological explanation. Two factors dominate the scene: first, the momentum of institutions; second, the economic functions served by these activities.

When research organizations, for example, reach the limits of their potential contribution to a given technology, as is the case with most military-research institutions, how can one account for the perpetuation of such organizations? The answer must be sought in an understanding of the social dynamics of organizations. A well-esteemed large organization that has high status, large budgets, a technically qualified staff and a network of interrelationships with important institutions in society has a large stake in perpetuating itself. Military-research establishments draw upon past successes to sustain their operations, with the promise of military-technology "improvement" always in prospect. Indeed, improvement in detail can generally be delivered even though the larger avowed purposes that must presumably be served by military technology get lost from view.[38]

Once it was established, the American war economy proceeded to function in accordance with the dynamics that were built into it from the start. This includes the managerial imperative to maintain and enlarge decision power, now given unprecedented scope by access to the wealth of the whole society as a source of capital and by the gradual formulation of goals that finally attained planning for "world hegemony." Such a war economy with its supportive ideologies is powerfully motivated to keep moving, keep trying. The chiefs of the U.S. war economy have been doing just that.

But there are limits, even to their most earnest efforts. Military superiority vis-à-vis the Soviet Union (or other major nuclear powers) became unattainable once such countries had developed extensively along nuclear military lines. The most persistent application of U.S. military power since World War II, in the Indochina War, produced a "no-win" result for the United States. While large and sustained military budgets have yielded an impressive war economy for the United States, the unintended effects within American society have included economic and other weakening.

Powerfully impelled, the make-believe continues. The Congress was told by the Secretary of Defense in his statement in support of the 1974 budget that "U.S. strategic offensive forces have long been designed to carry out retaliatory options appropriate to the nature and level of provocation as well as to maintain an assured destruction capability," and, further, that the general-purpose and mobility forces "must be capable of rapid worldwide deployment to meet a wide range of military contingencies."[39] The announcement that nuclear forces are prepared not only for deterrence but also for varied "retaliatory options" is new, and means that the military plans to operate nuclear wars of varied size and intensity. This is madness. And there is promise of misery for untold millions and unchecked moral and material decay for American society in the "worldwide" use of general-purpose forces for a "wide range of military contingencies." This is the harbinger of future wars of intervention.

These military preparations give solid assurance of capability for one result: the destruction of human society, if not of the human race.

The efforts to exceed the limits of military power have not succeeded. If the trends we have defined here continue, the U.S. military investment since the Second World War will come to be judged, on military grounds, as a trillion-dollar miscalculation.

Eight

ECONOMIC RECONSTRUCTION WITHOUT CENTRALISM

THERE WILL BE a chance for a new opening in American public life if the belief system that supports the war economy is sufficiently eroded and if people who are trusted by wide publics seek out and proclaim new orientations in economy and society. But new public policies do not spring from the earth spontaneously. Given the characteristic human distrust of unfamiliar economic and social forms, one task for intellectuals is to formulate proposals for political-economic change that have some roots in American experience and that will thus have a chance of being accepted. Alternative political-economic ideas must be at once practical solutions to the serious problems created by the war economy and also culturally congenial to a majority of the population.

Moreover, new ideas for policy have little chance of implementation without a major alteration in the composition of the Congress. Since the executive branch of the federal government has an immense stake in perpetuating the military economy as the main base of its own power and authority, there is little hope that it would risk reduction of its power by initiating a shift to civilian economy. Instead, given a change in popular beliefs, it is more feasible to send representatives to Congress who would reflect a nonmilitarist orientation.

During the long Cold War, there was a mutually reinforcing relationship between the militarist emphasis in public policy and the sustained thrust for centralization of economic power in the Pentagon. After all, there is nothing that compares with modern hierarchical military organization for intensity of centralized, authoritarian decision-making. It is clearly unequaled as an instrument for extending the scope and intensity of centralized controls and for keeping them intact. With the support of the "national-defense" ideology, the growth of a military form of organization was generally accepted during the Cold War.

One of the real dangers to the prospects of political freedom and economic competence in the United States is the degree to which the Pentagon style of organization and operation has become accepted as an indispensable model for American economic life. A national turn away from war economy will require not only new economic orientations in the form of new national priorities, but also new ways of organizing to get productive civilian work done. Centralized forms are the organizational aspect of militarist policies. A determination to change fundamental policy therefore requires accompanying alteration in mode of organization. The main aim of this chapter is to show that plausible ideas for economic reconstruction can be defined and that alternatives to centralist forms of organization can be devised for carrying out new productive work on a large scale.

Economic reconstruction needs a program of work, an estimate of cost, ideas on where the money should come from, and plausible ways to organize the work. As we have discovered, the scale of economic and other deterioration and neglect in American life is enormous. Hence the relevant efforts to repair this damage must be large and costly. Therefore I will begin with some ideas on where large sums could be found for new productive work. The main place is the swollen military system and economy.

I judge that there are three primary areas in which the United States's military budget could be substantially reduced. First, most of the nuclear strategic forces could be retired, inasmuch as these represent unnecessary overkill. Second, armed forces designed to achieve "world hegemony" through Vietnam-type interventions could be terminated. Third, by giving recognition to the limits of military power, a curtailment of the futile and costly arms race can be undertaken. As against the Nixon administration's military budget of $87 billion for 1974, I estimate that armed forces that would afford the American people an adequate measure of military security could be operated at an annual cost of not more than $29 billion. Redesigned and reorganized armed forces could have a solid capability for discouraging (deterring) armed attacks on the United States and on states whose security is judged to be vital to the United States (Western Europe, Japan), for guarding the United States and for participating in international peacekeeping with other states.* To illustrate the possibilities for major military-cost reductions I have made available in Appendix 4 an analysis by Lieutenant Colonel Edward L. King (Ret.) on military manpower that was given to the Senate Armed Services Committee.

For the present discussion, what is crucial is the prospect of having $58 billion a year, or more, of public money that could be turned to productive uses. Who should control the application of these resources for economic reconstruction that is sorely needed? That issue compels attention to the problem of centralism in government and economy. I judge that the application of such sums mainly to reduce taxes would, by dispersing the money, short-circuit opportunity to make the major new capital investments. Tax reduction could be sensible after, say, ten years of new productive activity.

The present discussion, as well as that in the remaining chapters, rests upon the following assumptions. When and if there is widespread interest in dismantling important parts of the military economy, it will be useful to have in hand even rough blueprints of the economic activity that could replace it. Moreover, the very existence of such plans would encourage a realistic view of the feasibility of alternatives to war economy, thereby defusing at least some of the fears associated with long dependence on the military dollar. One item of the ideological consensus on war economy is the idea that there is no real economic alternative to it because (1) there is no other undertaking that needs resources on a similar scale, and (2) even if there were such a vast enterprise which needed doing, there would be no chance of undertaking it, because an economic effort of a civilian sort would necessarily

* In my *Pentagon Capitalism*, Appendix C, I gave the main outline of the security policies and design of forces to serve these functions.

involve the government in economic competition with private corporations who would then use their power to stop it. We shall evaluate these views below as we consider various proposals for economic reconstruction.

During the last decade, a number of economic alternatives to war economy in the form of programs for civilian investments on a large scale to repair neglected areas in American life have been formulated by governmental and private groups and individuals. The emphasis is on work that is usually accepted as government responsibility. Four ways of viewing economic needs are summarized here: first, via comprehensive national programs; second, through the cost of economic development for underdeveloped families; third, by the economic needs of major cities; and, fourth, by viewing alternatives to military economy from a sampling of civilian–military trade-offs.

The single most important national economic program was prepared by the Cabinet Coordinating Committee on Economic Planning for the End of Vietnam Hostilities under President Lyndon Johnson. It was published as one of the last acts of that administration in the *Economic Report of the President* for 1969. The report included a series of illustrative new programs, or expansions of existing federal civilian programs, proposed for the fiscal year 1972.[1] As the table on pages 192–93 shows, here was an agenda for new work in education, health, nutrition, jobs and manpower, area economic development, problems of crime, delinquency, quality of environment, etc. The prospective new spending covers many of the neglected areas in American life, adding up to $39.7 billion of new work to be done each year for an indefinite future. Because of price changes, the money value of this program would be about $50 billion per year in 1974.

We know two things about this program of work that add to its significance. First, it was drawn up on the basis of plans that had been prepared by various government departments in response to the War on Poverty legislation of the Johnson administration. A considerable amount of in-house planning was done that was never funded because both money and political energy were increasingly concentrated on the shooting war in Vietnam. Second, all the estimates were understated. The money judged to be productively spendable for each item was reduced to form this recommended program.[2]

ILLUSTRATIVE NEW PROGRAMS OR MAJOR EXPANSIONS OF EXISTING FEDERAL CIVILIAN PROGRAMS, FISCAL YEAR 1972 (DERIVED FROM PROPOSALS OF TASK FORCES AND STUDY GROUPS)

Program	*Hypothetical expenditures (billions of dollars)*
Total expenditures	39.7
Education	7.0
Preschool	1.0
Elementary and secondary	2.5
Higher	3.0
Vocational	.5
Health	3.8
Kiddie-care	.5
Medicare for disabled	1.8
Comprehensive health centers	1.0
Hospital construction and modernization	.5
Nutrition	1.0
Community service programs	.8
Jobs and manpower	2.5
Public jobs	1.8
Manpower Development Training Act	.5
Employment service	.2
Social security and income support	9.5
Unemployment insurance	2.0
Public assistance	4.0
Social security improvements	3.5
Veterans	.3
Economic, area, and other special development programs	2.2
Entrepreneurial aid	.5
Area redevelopment	.5
Rural development	1.0
Indian assistance	.2
Crime, delinquency, and riots	1.0
Violence and riot prevention	.1
Safe streets programs	.3
Rehabilitation of offenders and delinquents	.3
Prevention of delinquency and crime by special measures for delinquency-prone youth	.3
Quality of environment	1.7

Program	Hypothetical expenditures (billions of dollars)
Air pollution prevention and control	.1
Public water supply construction programs	.3
Water pollution control and sewage treatment	1.0
Solid waste disposal	.1
Natural beautification, environmental protection, and recreational development	.2
Natural resource development and utilization	1.4
Land and forest conservation	.2
Water resources and related programs	.5
Mineral and energy (excluding hydroelectric) development	.2
Natural environmental development	.5
Urban development	5.5
New cities	.5
Land acquisition and financial planning (suburban)	.5
Urban mass transportation	.5
Model cities	2.0
Other urban facilities and renewal	2.0
Transportation	1.0
Airway and airport modernization	.4
Rapid interurban ground transit	.1
Modernization of merchant marine	.2
Motor vehicle and transportation safety research and safety grants	.3
Science and space exploration	1.0
Post-Apollo space program	.5
Scientific research in oceanography communications, social and behavioral sciences, and natural sciences	.5
Foreign economic aid	1.0

SOURCE: "Report to the President" from the Cabinet Coordinating Committee on Economic Planning for the End of Vietnam Hostilities, in *Economic Report of the President,* transmitted to the Congress January 1969. The Report includes an explanation of the content of the program categories.

Finally, it should be noted that such an economic program could have major consequences for employment, mainly in the varied industries that would provide contracted equipment, buildings, construction, etc.

Assuming an average outlay of $10,000 per man-year to perform the diverse work involved, direct employment of 5 million—not counting any employment side effects—would be generated by an effort along these lines.

A second agenda for national economic development was published in my book *Our Depleted Society* in 1965. There I outlined a considerable array of new productive activities to be done, again focusing on depleted areas in American life. The performance of that economic agenda would have required outlays of $56-72 billion a year. Allowing for price changes since 1965, that agenda under 1974 conditions would require spending $78-100 billion per year.

Another sort of agenda of new productive economic activity was outlined by the Joint Economic Committee of the Congress in December 1966.[3] This one lists only the cost of construction for an array of public facilities listed in the table on page 195. The public facilities include water-supply systems, sewage-treatment systems, various transportation facilities, schools, health facilities, recreational and cultural facilities, and miscellaneous public buildings. This agenda of new capital investment for construction work alone adds up to $40.5 billion a year. Even if changes were made in some of the categories listed by the Joint Economic Committee (like reducing the oversize items for highways and moving the money into mass transit and railroads), there is no escaping the main implication of this program. It tells us that the United States needs a very large infusion of productive capital to make up for the quarter century of concentration on military economy.

In July 1962 the U.S. government's Arms Control and Disarmament Agency responded to a query from the Secretary General of the United Nations on the economic and social consequences of disarmament.[4] The agency's assessment of civilian alternatives to arms spending included a considerable array of new work to be done, again in the familiar list of neglected areas of American life requiring major outlays from public budgets.

New agendas for national economic development have come from business sources as well. *Fortune* magazine of March 1969 titled an article "We Can Afford a Better America."[5] It listed and priced work to be done that is well appreciated as public responsibility—in pollution control, mass transit, removing eyesores (meaning things that cause eyesores), suburban sprawl and inner-

PUBLIC FACILITY NEEDS
Projected Capital Outlays of State and Local Public Agencies

	DOLLARS IN MILLIONS	
	1965 Actual	1975 Estimated to Meet Needs

Basic Community Facilities

Regional and river basin water supply systems	$ 2	$ 30
Public water supply systems	1,040	2,250
Rural-agriculture water supply systems	*	140
Sanitary sewer collection systems	385	1,090
Storm sewer systems	417	1,820
Water waste treatment plants	625	1,240
Solid wastes collection and disposal facilities	130	270
Electric power	766	1,350
Gas distribution systems	44	70
Subtotal, basic community facilities	$ 3,409	$ 8,260

Transportation Facilities

Highways, roads, and streets	7,782	15,330
Toll bridges, tunnels, and turnpikes	388	500
Offstreet parking facilities	102	300
Urban mass transit facilities	242	960
Airport facilities	261	530
Marine port facilities	159	50
Subtotal, transportation	$ 8,934	$17,670

Education Facilities

Public elementary and secondary schools	3,650	4,480
Area vocational school facilities	†	790
Academic facilities for higher education	915	1,750
College housing and related service facilities	301	720
Educational television	5	30
Subtotal, education facilities	$ 4,871	$ 7,770

Health Facilities

Hospitals	⎫	480
Clinics and other outpatient facilities	⎬ 494	100
Long-term care facilities		130
Community mental health centers	⎭	220
Facilities for the mentally retarded	34	130

PUBLIC FACILITY NEEDS (*Cont.*)

	DOLLARS IN MILLIONS	
	1965 Actual	1975 Estimated to Meet Needs
Health research facilities	°	240
Medical and other health schools	°	360
Subtotal, health facilities	$ 528	$ 1,660
Recreational and Cultural Facilities		
State and Federal outdoor recreation facilities	313	530
Urban local outdoor recreation facilities	360	2,200
Arenas, auditoriums, exhibition halls	600	910
Theaters and community art centers	°	460
Museums	14	40
Public libraries	103	240
Subtotal, recreation and cultural	$ 1,390	$ 4,380
Other Public Buildings		
Residential group care facilities for children	°	70
Armories	1	15
Jails and prisons	°	120
Fire stations	191	170
Public office and court buildings	218	400
Other	214	°
Subtotal, other public buildings	$ 410	$ 775
Total	$19,542	$40,515

° Not available.

† Included in public elementary and secondary schools.

SOURCE: *State and Local Public Facility Needs and Financing*, Joint Economic Committee of the Congress, December 1966, Vol. 1, pp. 24–25.

cities disrepair, crime control, welfare reforms, medical care and education. The annual bill for *Fortune*'s better America was $57 billion a year.

Finally, private groups like the Urban Coalition and the Brookings Institution prepare periodic recommendations for major new public expenditures, of which the Urban Coalition's *Counterbudget* has been the most widely discussed.[6]

In sum, from diverse sources, ranging from economic advisers of the President to private institutions and individuals, there is agreement that the United States needs new civilian work of very large dimension. The scale of what is required equals or exceeds in annual money cost the sums that might be freed from any conceivable near-future reduction in military-type spending. Now let us refer back to the ideological objection that this work would not be of sufficient scope and/or would be competitive with private industry. The money value of what has been listed here is obviously large. An examination of the listed items shows that they are all, or almost all, of a sort that have come to be well-accepted aspects of government budgets. Therefore the funding of such work by a government need not be competitive with private firms, which generally do not make capital investments in such areas as water-supply systems, urban transit and the like. Private firms would play the role of suppliers of equipment and contractors.

We may also approach economic reconstruction as an economic-development problem. Everywhere in the world, economists understand that economic underdevelopment means a combined set of human conditions: high infant-mortality rate, limited life span, limited education, low income, a high incidence of disease, and low productivity. These are the conditions of life for roughly 7 million American families, the number varying according to arbitrarily set boundaries of years of life, income levels, etc., that are set to define underdevelopment.

What would it cost to do economic development for these people? The economic-development agenda must include capital for creating a job (averaged for U.S. industry), money for vocational-occupational training, medical care, compensatory education and social services, allowances for improvement in housing and community facilities, and support for changing location of residence. When such many-sided efforts to effect economic development are calculated on an average per-family basis, they amount to an investment of about $60,000 per family unit. If a comprehensive effort were organized for 7 million families, a capital outlay of about $420 billion would be required at 1974 prices.

The use of a "family" as a unit of measurement here does not imply that the economic-development transformation is an issue which alternatively could be left to individuals. Without organized intervention for economic development that breaks the self-reinforcing circle of sustained poverty, there can be no exit. The exit from poverty is done most effectively as a social movement so that people can learn by example and can give mutual support to help make the changes in life style that are part of economic development. Since such an effort must be carried out over an extended period, to be brought to fruition in, say, ten years, then the required expenditure is $42 billion per year.

Yet another way of viewing the prospects for new civilian economic investment in the United States is by gauging the requirements of particular communities. Specifically, what are the needs of the people for basics like housing, medical facilities, education budgets? Such estimates have been prepared for the principal cities of Michigan.[7] The thrust of this 1972 analysis is that Michigan, more than any other state, has subsidized the wars and allied programs of the Pentagon by receiving no visible return to the state from 50 percent on every tax dollar going to Washington. That is the highest percentage for any state in the Union. Michigan has suffered a net loss of more than $1.9 billion each year to finance America's war economy.

For example, the citizens and businesses of Detroit before 1972 paid about $3.1 billion to the federal government in corporate and personal income taxes, Social Security and excise taxes. The city of Detroit and its citizens received from the federal government payments for Social Security, military contracts and salaries, school aid, urban renewal and other purposes, of $1.5 billion; hence there was a net annual drain on Detroit of $1.6 billion per year. What does Detroit need that these drained funds could replenish if they were available? A partial shopping list of unfunded projects includes: 31,600 new housing units; 3,600 more teachers in the public schools to achieve a student–teacher ratio of twenty-two to one; capital improvements to these schools worth $400 million; 800 more M.D.s and 400 more dentists; 700 new hospital beds and 3,900 to be modernized; public-parks improvement costing $160 million annually; and sewerage construction worth $101 million per year. The public-budget shopping list for reconstruction of Detroit adds up to an agenda of about $870 million per year, which if spent for these purposes would generate somewhat more than 80,000 new jobs per year.

By applying similar reasoning to other cities of Michigan—Ann Arbor, Bay City, Flint, Grand Rapids, Jackson, Kalamazoo, Lansing, Muskegan and Saginaw—it becomes evident that from their vantage point the federal government regularly appropriates large sums that become unavailable for the productive needs of the state and its communities.

The same approach may be taken with respect to the city of New York. With 7,800,000 inhabitants, this city needs, first of all, major capital investments in elemental power, communications and transportation services to be a well-functioning city. Beyond that, the city needs reasonable housing, streets in good repair, modernized waste-disposal facilities, industrial-park facilities to attract industry, and new educational plant for training a skilled labor force appropriate to the needs of a national metropolis and world business center. In all of these respects, New York City has been suffering deterioration, and the investments required in all these aspects of life are immense.

For example, the city needs 66,000 new apartments a year to keep balance with new family formation and the deterioriation or abandonment of existing housing. What New York City has actually been getting from all sources, private and public, is 19,000 new housing units per year. So there is a constantly worsening deficit condition in required housing. The city is in desperate need of modern transit facilities. The latest thing in big-city transportation is not two steel wheels on steel rails. Other places in the world have done rather better than that. The city needs very large new water-supply, waste-disposal and street-cleaning facilities. Health-care facilities on a large scale are urgently needed, especially in parts of the community which have been suffering an exodus of doctors during the last twenty-five years.

Where could the money to restore New York City's needed public facilities come from?

A substantial reduction in the U.S. military budget could have a decisive effect on tax funds available to the citizens and firms of the city. I estimate that by 1973 the people of New York City were paying $642 per person each year for the support of the Pentagon. As a first approximation, I will assume a military budget of $54.8 billion, as proposed by Senator McGovern in 1972, which accounts for only 55 percent of the reduction that I suggested as prudent on military grounds. With this lesser military-budget reduction, the reduction in tax burden on the people of New York City would average $231 per person. If they could share in the benefits of such reduction in a proportionate manner, then for 7.8 million people of the city there would be a total federal tax saving of $1.8 billion.

Assuming further that this sum could be directed and applied to the new facilities required in the city, it would more than double the capital funds available to the city government and would employ, directly, more than 180,000 people. With similar reasoning: if the Pentagon budget were dropped to a total of $29 billion, the savings to the taxpayers of New York City would be $3.3 billion. Again: if such a sum were applied to productive work it would afford at least 330,000 direct jobs. New work on this scale could continue until the end of this century without exhausting the more obvious public-works requirements of New York City.

Finally, there is yet another way of viewing options for economic reconstruction in this country, and that is via a set of "trade-offs." The list in the accompanying table is a sampling of military

SOME CIVILIAN–MILITARY TRADE-OFFS

460 meals for the homeless in Grand Central Terminal	= $439	= One 155-mm. (conventional) high-explosive shell
The Senate Republicans' 1986 budget proposal for freezing the cost-of-living adjustments in Social Security and similar pension payments, which would push 420,000 people into poverty, plus suggested cuts in farm-income subsidies as well as in Federal funds for housing	= $25 billion	= The MX Peacekeeper missile program
Proposed cut in funds for mass-transit systems	= $2.8 billion	= Navy (EA6B) airplane program for surveillance and communications jamming
Proposed 1986 cuts in guaranteed student loans and in campus-based financial aid for students	= $2.3 billion	= 1986 budget for the M-1 Abrams heavy tank
Proposed 1986 cuts in funds for veterans' medical care and housing	= $336 million	= 220 Phoenix air-to-air missiles
Proposed 1986-87 cuts in Federal funding for	= $8.7 million	= 800 Army multiple-launch rockets

subsidized lunches for New York City school-children		
Proposed 1986 cut in Medicare services	= $4 billion	= Proposed low-altitude anti-satellite weapons system
Proposed cuts in small-business loans and Job Corps services	= $1.1 billion	= The Department of Defense's Latin American programs for 1986
Proposed Federal cuts in housing for the elderly and handicapped, and the cut in energy assistance for poor people	= $1.5 billion	= One projected (LHD-1) Marine amphibious assault ship
1982-86 cuts in Federal job training and in funds for public-service employment in New York City	= $1.2 billion	= 18 Navy F-14 jet fighters in 1986
The proposed 1986 cut in Amtrak and in modernization of the Northeastern railway corridor	= $741 million	= 26 Navy air-cushion landing craft
Proposed 1986 cuts in natural-resource and in environmental controls, and in recreational facilities	= $1.4 billion	= The Army's 1986 funding for chemical-bacteriological weapons and research, and for rebuilding 48 (CH-47) heavy-lift helicopters
Proposed elimination of the Federal share of a 15-year national plan for sewage treatment to meet minimum Clean Water Act standards	= $30 billion	= The Navy's Aegis (CG-47) cruiser program
Proposed 1986 cut in Acquired Immune Deficiency Syndrome (AIDS) research and control activities	= $10 million	= 5 air-launched cruise missiles
Mayor Koch's 10-year plan for repairing New York City's infrastructure	= $40.6 billion	= The Stealth radar evading bomber program
Federal funds needed by Connecticut for rebuilding bridges and roads	= $3.7 billion	= 1986 planned research and development for the Strategic Defense Initiative ("Star Wars") program

Annual additional funding needed to abate deterioration in Federal, state and local public facilities	= $18 billion	= 3 nuclear-powered aircraft carriers with their planes and support ships, plus the Navy's antisubmarine-airplane (P-3C) program
Annual additional funds needed to restore acceptable maintenance of New York City's public schools	= $440 million	= 2 B-1B intercontinental bombers
Governor Cuomo's plan for new low-income housing in New York City	= $4 billion	= Half of the 1986 funding for additions to the United States' stock of 37,000 nuclear warheads
Estimated cost of cleaning up 10,000 toxic-waste dumps that contaminate the nation's soil and water	= $100 billion	= The Navy's Trident II submarine and F-18 jet fighter programs
Proposed 1986-88 cut in New York City Medicaid funding, reducing medical services to the poor	= $1.2 billion	= Half of the Air Force's 1986 heavy-transport (C-5B) airplane budget
1982-85 cuts in Federal income and nutrition programs that left 20 million people hungry among the 35.3 million living in poverty	= $12.2 billion	= The Army's Patriot ground-to-air missile system
Estimated cost of renovating an average five-room medium-income Manhattan West Side apartment	= $42,287	= One (F-16 jet fighter) antenna pulley puller tool; one antenna clamp alignment tool; one antenna puller height gauge; one antenna hexagon wrench
What is needed to abate the growth of hunger: a one-third increase in funding for the Federal school-lunch program, food-stamp program, and Women, Infants and Children (WIC) program	= $5.3 billion	= The Army's single-channel ground and airborne radio system

These data also appeared in *The New York Times*, April 22, 1985.

items matched against particular civilian goods or services of equivalent cost. (A more extensive list, with details of data sources, is in Appendix 5.) I am providing this list as a way of concretizing the meaning of both the military and the civilian sides of these trade-offs. When the scale of the civilian items is reduced from the aggregated level of billions of dollars, they can be more readily visualized (e.g., a school instead of U.S. education). Then, too, the economic significance of particular weapons is more visible when compared with what has been forgone. In this listing of trade-offs, particular attention should be given to the quality of many of the military items. For example, the nuclear aircraft carrier is at once very expensive and highly vulnerable, so much so that military specialists estimate that about 63 percent of the aircraft it carries are assigned to the defense of the carrier itself. Furthermore, its military function is primarily to serve as a mobile air base in Vietnam-type interventions. Another prominent new item, the B-1 bomber program, is the last gasp of the General Curtis Le May school of military technology. It would do what the later-series B-52s are already able to do—deliver nuclear warheads over intercontinental distances while standing off several hundred miles from their targets. But the B-1 would do all this faster and at a cost for the whole system that could reach $75 billion.

Whenever enough Americans decide to abandon the illusions and burdens of a war economy, they will be confronted not only with the problems of what else to do—and in what order—but also with the issue of how to organize the new work. What in fact is the range of options for coping with industrial and other aspects of economic reconstruction?

Industrial Reconstruction

The reconstruction of depleted industries would be a major part of any attempt at economic reconstruction from the effects of a permanent war economy. If economically incompetent firms were few in number and scattered randomly among industries, then within the framework of a largely competitive capitalist economy a case of sorts could be advanced for relying on the ordinary processes of business failure and reconstitution of viable enterprises by more competent entrepreneurs. These, however, are not the latter-day conditions of American industrial depletion. The economic and technical deterioration is concentrated in a group of industries (as shown in Chapter Four) which have core importance for any modern industrial system. Moreover, the resulting economic weakness of these firms and industries has mixed origins: in part it is due to conditions outside the control of these industries, like limitations on technical talent and fresh capital; another part of the weakness is due to internal conditions of decision-making, including a weakening of cost-minimizing traditions and increasing reliance on short-term planning and rapid returns on capital.

For these reasons a national economic effort to restore the viability of depleted industries cannot rely on the "unseen hand" of bankruptcy and competitive replacement. Replacement of depleted industries has indeed been going on, very importantly by American investments outside the United States. Insofar as American-based multinational firms have been part of the replacement-from-the-outside process, there is financial advantage to such firms even while the production competence of the American community is diminished, as I showed in Chapter Four. From the standpoint of conventional business criteria, there is nothing wrong with making a profit on goods that are imported and which once had originated in, or are producible in factories located in, the United States. However, in this way, the financial advantage, growth and other well-being of American firms can be served while the productive competence of American society is diminished. The use of the term "depletion" in this entire analysis refers not so much to the financial condition of single firms or entire industries as to their production competence. This differentiation is central to the analysis of this book, for many American firms show financial success while their American-based production declines either absolutely or as a proportion of their total activity.

Until now there has been no program of economic reconstruction in any country that had to cope with a similar kind of problem of industrial competence. The various efforts in Western Europe, Japan and elsewhere to spur industrial productivity had to contend with industrial conditions that were different from the American industrial depletion. I know of only two places in the world where civilian industry has been damaged or had its growth restrained, as a result of long priority in money and talent to a permanent war economy. These economies are the United States and the Soviet Union. Since the operating details of the Soviet economy are probably different in many respects from the American pattern and are, in any event, unavailable to us, there is no prospect of being able to test the Soviet experience for possibly useful ideas. We can, however, review a set of options that are available in Western economic experience. These options include: the self-correcting mechanisms of the cost-minimizing firm; government loans or guaranteed loans; government subsidies; nationalization of industry; and, finally, industrial reorganization and change of management criteria.

The self-correcting mechanisms of the cost-minimizing firm cannot be relied upon, since they have been substantially short-circuited in the depleted industries. Indeed, that fact is a defining feature of the managerial side of the depletion process.

There is a strong tradition in the United States for granting government loans or loan guarantees as a device for shoring up firms through a period of economic transition or temporary financial difficulties (like shortage of working capital). The Reconstruction Finance Corporation, established by President Hoover and continued through the administrations of Roosevelt and Truman, was used to give financial support, especially to larger enterprises whose financial viability was deemed important to capitalism as a whole. But such a system of loans does not necessarily affect the cost- and subsidy-maximizing criteria of decision-making that are employed within these firms. Moreover, there is no evidence that further use of this loan-support method would necessarily produce changes in these criteria. For example, the government-guaranteed loans to the Lockheed Corporation in 1971 did not require a reversal of the cost- and subsidy-maximizing practices of that firm. Therefore, insofar as institutionalized operating characteristics of firms are a major source of incompetence, they cannot be repaired by making capital available to finance operations in the same incompetent pattern.

For these same reasons, a program of government subsidies does not afford a hopeful way for achieving reconstruction of depleted industry. Subsidies that are used to make up for high costs due to technical and managerial incompetence only ensure a continuation of the conditions that generate depletion. Despite these drawbacks, subsidies might be used if they only had to be applied to minor parts of the economy. In the present condition, however, major sections of U.S. industry would be candidates for continual subsidies, and the cost of such treatment would be so great as to probably be unbearable for political-economic reasons.

Similar reasoning applies to nationalization. Where depleted enterprises (like the Penn-Central Railroad and the Lockheed Corporation) continue to be operated by similar managements, utilizing similar criteria of decision-making, then the change of ownership to government would be only a "cover" for guaranteeing indefinite subsidies for the continuation of the depleted enterprises.

All of these considerations strongly suggest that necessary steps for erasing industrial depletion and restoring economic viability must include changes in management's decision-making criteria and economic and technical practices. I know of one effort in the Western world to achieve related objectives—the Industrial Reorganisation Corporation in Great Britain from 1967 to 1971.[8] This imaginative attempt at industrial reorganization bears close examination for our purposes.

The Labour government under Harold Wilson allocated £250 million to a semiautonomous corporation whose directors (reporting annually to the Treasury) were empowered to use this capital fund to induce mergers and reorganizations of firms and industries in order to improve their economic competence. The directors of this corporation were a group of industrial managers and financiers whose marching orders included not only restoration of managerial and enterprise competence but also making the economy of the United Kingdom less dependent on imported goods. The latter is important, for it defines a major change in criteria of business decision-making. Financial success and allied growth were thereby defined as unacceptable, by themselves, as criteria for enterprise competence. In effect, the IRC was empowered to change the criteria of decision-making by major industrial firms to include serviceability to the productive competence of England's economy as a whole.

The directors of the IRC used their money and their professional influence to cause mergers, changes in top management and policies, and internal reorganization of industries and firms. The subject firms were then required to continue as autonomous entities while the IRC interest (and holdings of shares) were withdrawn. The partial record that is available from the annual reports of the IRC indicates that it had achieved substantial results in a number of important industries, including ball and roller bearings and electrical machinery.

As might be suspected, this activity produced real fright among many old-line, traditional managers, who saw their own positions potentially threatened. When Prime Minister Heath's Conservative government came to office in 1970, one of its first moves was to order the dismantling of the IRC.

I believe that the experience of the IRC deserves close study. In 1972 I discovered that even sophisticated financial writers in the United States had little knowledge of this British institution and its record of operation. In my judgment what is unique about the IRC effort is the inclusion of fundamental change in decision-making criteria and enterprise objectives as part of a formal public program of industrial reconstruction. The experience in other countries with public economic responsibility (Japan, the Scandinavian countries and France, for example) should also be examined to learn about institutional innovations that might be applicable to the American economy. I emphasize, however, that there are major aspects of the American problem which will require thoughtful innovation.

In American experience, one of the major barriers to technological reequipment of existing enterprises has been the fear among middle management and workers that their jobs would be disrupted or ended, leaving them individually to bear a burden of change that was advantageous to the top management and the stockholders. There is little precedent in American experience for institutionalized ways of cushioning a work force through a period of job change. On the side of management there is often reluctance to go through what it fears would be an endless hassle with unions over job standards and job definitions in relation to new industrial equipment. On their side, unions do their best to hold on to rights and work practices that were extracted through long years of struggle. The combined effect of such management and union positions is to make industrial reconstruction very hard to achieve. Accordingly, institutional inventions are required to cope with well-justified fears and to offset what would otherwise be major barriers to restoring economic viability. It will surely be necessary to review the experience of other countries for relevant information, as, for example, the operation of Swedish law and administration for cushioning "technological displacement" of workers in industry.

The Problem of Centralism

A key item of the ideological consensus deriving from the experience of the Great Depression and the subsequent World War II economy is the belief that major problems of economy and society are best solved by centralized federal-governmental institutions.

Centralism became one of the main forms of American economic and political development since the Second World War. In response to all manner of economic and social problems, men of ideas have mainly preferred dependence on centrally administered plans in the federal government. The consequence of this reliance is visible in the expanding size of federal expenditures in relation to the gross national product. The 1950 federal expenditures of 14 percent of the national product rose by 50 percent to become 21 percent of the national product by 1971.[9]

At the bottom of the Great Depression, in 1932–33, there was agreement throughout American society that the "unseen hand" of business competition could no longer be relied upon to restore economic prosperity. City, county and state governments were financially prostrate, and it was unthinkable that they could be a source of initiatives to raise the general level of economic activity. These governments could not even feed the hungry, and many were unable to pay their own employees. The government body of last resort was the federal government, and it was swiftly made into an active agent for economic regulation and decision-making. By the 1970s the issue with respect to government's role in many spheres of economic life is no longer government versus no government. Rather, the issue is: What kind of government and what means shall be used for implementing its social responsibility? The assumption that centralism is synonymous with government responsibility lends support to ever more concentration of control.

The main model of a centralized government operation since the 1960s has been the organization and functioning of the Pentagon. If the central office of the Pentagon were used as a model for government administration, then the perspective for American society would include the establishment of central offices to cope with problems of transportation, water supply, waste disposal, environmental controls, restoration of industrial competence, education, housing, urban redevelopment, etc. In that perspective, apart from the limits of centralism as a mode of efficient decision-making and administration, reliance on a central office to control nationwide operations in each of these spheres would lead to a central-office society in the fashion of *1984* that would surely endanger all democratic processes.

The commitment of American intellectuals to one or another version of state capitalism has created an ideological barrier to questioning the web of rationalization that has surrounded war economy. On the political right, state capitalism has been supported in the name of its serviceability for "defense" and for the operations of the Cold War. The liberal center has backed growing decision power in the federal government in the name of an avowed hope that social welfare would thereby be advanced. On the left, support for centralism has derived from a critique of capitalism which defined the wielding of government power—in new hands, of course—as the main alternative to the dominance of businessmen.

However, an important part of the scientific-academic community in the United States has become, by the 1970s, disenchanted with certain of the main enterprises that emerged from the cult of centralism in government: the ever-growing military establishment; the Vietnam war; the space agency. At the same time there is a widely felt need for more research and applied science on the whole array of civilian needs that have been left in disrepair owing to the massive priority to military-space in the last quarter century. Among the very persons so minded, however, there has been a reluctance to consider new ways of organizing and effecting civilian-oriented research and application. The most common response to the need for new areas of research and development is to think of setting up "NASA-type" agencies responsible for new activities. There is an apparent commitment to centralism in organization and control rather than to a meaningful change in the uses of science.

Yet reliance on centralism has a number of drawbacks. In the first place, it leads to an emphasis on those problems which appear most amenable to handling by central government. Thus, the relations of the nation as a whole to the rest of the world on a political-military level has always been appreciated as being necessarily the responsibility of central government. But the general readiness to rely on central government has facilitated a concentration of tax power. This made immense sums available for operating military-political foreign policies of the United States that are selectively preferred to further enlarge the decision power of the central administrative authorities and their big-businessmen compatriots. Furthermore, centralism has given rise to alienation in the population, as people feel physically and socially remote from those who make decisions affecting their lives. The consequence is a withdrawal of identification and support from those decision-makers. Effects of this kind, though sometimes acknowledged, are generally written off as a necessary cost of centralized operation which is regarded as inherently efficient, therefore justifying occasional unsatisfactory byproducts. It is assumed that central administration is effective in its own right and that this mode of control has the further result of inducing efficiency in the controlled units.

Is central (federal) control of social programs an inherently more efficient system? Fortunately, there need be no mystery about the validity of this belief, for we have data about the intensity of managerial control as it relates to industrial efficiency: first, the relationship of the growth of administrative and other white-collar occupations to productivity; second, the relation between the costs of managing and efficiency in industry; third, the causes of increasing costs of managing; and, fourth, the evidence of efficiency of operations in the Department of Defense, which has become a prototype of concentration of managerial control.

Some decision-making activity must accompany all production, since there can be no production without decision-making. But that is not to say that the managerial mode of decision-making is the only conceivable kind, or that increased complexity of decision-making (like more frequent checking on more aspects of a given activity) necessarily yields more quantity or quality of the product that is finally desired. Thus the frequency and detail of accounting reports can be continuously increased without necessarily affecting production operations in the least degree. Some accounting is necessary for the planning that is directly useful for production. But the largest part of administrative work in managerially controlled enterprises is not traceably linked to production. In the United States during the period 1950–70, while the labor force as a whole grew by 31 percent, the white-collar part of the labor force enlarged by 70 percent.[10] The second half of this period saw a

concentration of industrial deterioration, finally reflected in unprecedented low levels of productivity growth and industrial
noncompetitiveness.

Various studies that I have done on the growth of managerial
control in manufacturing industry do not support the assumption
of a link between efficiency in production and centralism. The cost
of administration can be large or small, according to the style of
decision-making. Also, the cost of administration is not necessarily
proportional to productivity or efficiency, however measured. Generally, increases in the cost of administration result from increases
in the scope and intensity of decision-making. Thus, more kinds of
accounting (scope) and more frequent reports for ever smaller
units (intensity) cost more.[11] Such changes in industry have been
made without necessarily resulting in greater efficiency.

In government operations a similar pattern has appeared, for
example, in the operation of programs like Medicare and Medi-
caid. Participating hospitals were required to greatly enlarge their
business-office staffs to handle the paperwork that has been imposed upon them by the regulations formulated by the federal
central offices. Similar effects have been noted in other institutions
that were subjected to centralized managerial-control systems. At
the University of Washington, responding to enlarged governmental reporting requirements, a 50 percent increase in business-
office staffs was recorded in a few years. Investigation by a House
of Representatives Public Works Subcommittee in 1971 disclosed
that certain federal offices had developed remarkably elaborate
forms and reporting requirements. In one instance a single form
described as "the size of a small tablecloth" contained 8,800 small
squares for listing information on "environmental impact" of proposed projects. In another agency, paperwork once required for a
particular request grew from thirty to 250 pages during a few
years' time. A state official has reported that half the man-hours
devoted to "control of water pollution in his state are consumed by
federal paperwork."[12]

The cause of such developments, whether in industry or nonprofit organizations, has been similar. Whenever a managerial-
hierarchical mode of decision-making is operative, there is a
sustained pressure among administrators to enlarge their decision
power. Toward this end managers act to complicate the control
routines that they administer. This process has been operative in

every aspect of administrative work in industry and in government and has been strongly supported by an ideological consensus that affirms that there is a strong connection between centralized control, intensified control and efficiency of operations. The evidence of formal studies does not support the conventional ideology.[13]

If there were any solid foundation for the belief that links centralism and efficiency, certainly one of the places to find it would be in the operations of the Pentagon. Especially since the regime of Robert McNamara (1960–67), the Department of Defense has been regarded as an ideal type of centrally managed government organization. This view was energetically propagated by an imposing public-relations machine, reinforced by the books and learned papers produced by intellectuals who were employed as administrators of the Department of Defense. It was given a further boost by the insistence of Lyndon Johnson that other government departments should emulate the main control techniques introduced by McNamara. In fact, as we have shown in earlier chapters, the long regime of Robert McNamara was notable for both a powerful thrust toward central managing and cost excesses of unprecedented magnitudes.

During his tenure as Secretary of Defense, the F-111 whose final price was three times the initial estimates per plane, the C-5A transport which generated a $2-billion cost excess, the Deep Submerging Rescue Vehicle estimated as costing $463 million per six craft as against a $36-million initial estimate for twelve craft, and other performances of a similar sort were all undertaken. All told, by December 30, 1969, the General Accounting Office, in a report that spanned the McNamara period, stated that major weapons systems were costing at least $20 billion more than original estimates, and that the condition of record-keeping and control in the Department of Defense was such that no person knew "the total number of systems required or their cost."[14] Whatever else, this performance would not ordinarily be called "efficient." Nevertheless, editors, blinded to the facts of the case by ideology, have repeatedly written such nonsense as "the mistakes that Mr. McNamara made . . . qualify but do not offset his many brilliant successes in managing the huge Pentagon establishment and increasing its effectiveness by these same managerial methods."[15] Of course, the major undertaking of the Department of Defense under McNamara was the Vietnam War; that enterprise is not ordinarily characterized as a "brilliant success" or a demonstration of "effectiveness." This sort of editorial usage reflects a cult of personality and a readiness to justify centralized managerialism under almost any conditions, rather than a matter-of-fact estimate of performance.

Parts of the Pentagon record are grimly humorous. For example, the following account is given of the technical defects and cost excesses in connection with a new Army truck, the Gamma Goat, designed to go through water as well as over land.

> Representative Otis G. Pike (Democrat, Riverhead), Chairman of the Armed Services Subcommittee created to investigate the six-wheel-drive Gamma Goat truck, said the manufacturer, Consolidated Diesel Electric Company, was asked to look into the complaints that the vehicle sometimes sank. Pike said the company concluded that no such problem existed. "This assurance may have satisfied the project manager," Pike said, . . . "but it did nothing to keep the Goat afloat. In field tests it continued to sink."
>
> Major General Vincent H. Ellis, Army deputy for matériel acquisition, acknowledged that he could not disagree with Pike's indictment of the vehicle's mechanical problem and a 300-percent increase on the original estimate of a cost of $5,000 per unit, but he praised the truck in most of his lengthy testimony submitted to the Committee, saying the Army considered the Gamma a success.[16]

Under the Pentagon regime that promoted centralism as never before, management "success" and effectiveness were also manifested in major economic-organizational and personnel policies like the production capacity of the aerospace industry and the ratio of command and staff to fighting men in the armed forces. The aerospace industry was long encouraged (by Pentagon readiness to pay the cost) to maintain far more production capacity than was conceivably required. The cost of superfluous facilities and staff ordinarily appears as part of the overhead cost excesses of military industry. By 1972 some senior military men were appalled at the way this was eating into budgeted money. One officer, Lieutenant General Otto J. Glasser, Air Force Deputy Chief of Staff for Research and Development, accused the U.S. aerospace industry of being "overbuilt, overmanned, and overmanaged." Glasser charged that "not only are there too many companies, but collectively they have more production capacity than we have any conceivable need for." Glasser asked in a speech to the Aviation Space Writers Association in New York City, "Well, what about the inefficiency of unused aerospace facilities? . . . Who pays for these inefficiencies? We both know the answer to that. These costs appear in the next contract or the next subcontract, driving up the costs so that quantities are even further reduced."[17] This pattern of maintaining production facilities regardless of cost is consistent, however, with the diagnosis of the centralized military-industry chiefs as a state management driving to maintain and enlarge their industrial and other decision power.

In the military, as in industry, the thrust for enlarging managerial control has led to increasing ratios of controlling as against operating employees. In the military, the pressures for enlarging power were expressed, among other ways, in rapid growth of officer and command staffs in relation to combat personnel. At the peak of the Vietnam War in 1969 the military had 18,277 colonels/captains (Navy) in armed forces of 3.5 million. In 1945, with a 12-million-man armed force, there were only 14,898 colonels/captains on duty. In December 1969 there was one officer or noncommissioned officer to supervise "every two lower-rank enlisted men."[18]

From analyses prepared by Lieutenant Colonel King we learn that in an infantry division of 16,200 soldiers, fewer than 7,500 have direct combat assignments. For 1973 the Army's planned strength was 841,000 men, of whom 233,000 were assigned to thirteen divisions and five brigades; the others, 608,000 men, had no combat-unit assignment. They are service and support troops (supplies, medical, training) and the staffs of the multilayered military command and headquarters bureaucracies. Behind these numbers is a gradual process of inflation of command levels and paperwork routines that has resulted in military pay amounting to about 56 percent of the military budget.

The above record of operation of centralism in its showplace institution has not deterred persistent advocates of centralist solutions, even as a response to the very problems that were created by central control in the first place. The implied assumption has been that there is no plausible alternative way of organizing public activity. Economists, for example, have proposed formal nationalization of large military-industry firms as a response to the host of problems that have resulted from the centralist control of the last decade.[19] The Executive Council of the AFL–CIO, desirous of more capital investment for civilian purposes, has proposed "an office of public investment coordination" in the executive branch of the federal government,[20] disregarding the evidence that investment coordination has been going on all the time—on behalf of the military economy.

Sustained reliance on a centralist approach has been justified on the grounds that state and city governments are inherently incompetent to cope with problems requiring public investment initiatives and that the federal government is "where the action is." The potentiality of city and state government deserves to be appreciated in a fresh light. It has been charged that city and state governments are inherently graft-ridden and easy prey for special interests seeking their private gain. The amount of municipal incompetence, however, including the cost of graft in large cities and states, cannot conceivably approach the scale of the cost excesses recorded in major weapons systems by the Department of Defense. For example, in June 1972 investigative reporters of *The New York Times* disclosed graft in the construction industries of New York City on an order of magnitude of $25 million in illegal payments each year. That amount is a drop in the bucket when compared to the immense social cost of the institutionalized incompetence and greed that produce the "cost overruns" in the tens of billions of dollars in the aerospace and related industries. Furthermore, whatever negative features may be charged against city, county and state governments of the United States, the plain fact is that by law and by custom these government bodies are prohibited from making military treaties with foreign countries and from initiating military adventures abroad.

But all these considerations are secondary to the main one which continues to compel attention to the federal government and its centralized agencies as a primary means for attempting national problem-solving. The heart of the matter is the control of very large taxing power in the federal government. The immense funds that are gathered there and controlled in one budget are at the core of the federal power.

In order to get perspective, it is worth recalling that before the Second World War the federal budget was of miniscule size compared to what we have become accustomed to in the latter part of this century. The first full year of Franklin Roosevelt's administra-

tion, 1934, showed the federal government with total receipts of
$3.5 billion. This increased to $6.7 billion by 1939, after six years of
New Deal development.

By 1946, the first year after the Second World War, the receipts
of the federal government totaled $39.1 billion. The tax intake
increased by $156.3 billion to a total of $195.4 billion in 1970.
Meanwhile the annual receipts of all state and local governments
rose by $119.5 billion, from $12.9 billion to $132.4 billion. At the
same time federal decision power over state and local government
multiplied through grants-in-aid from the federal budget. These
grants to state and local governments rose by $23.3 billion, from
$1.1 billion in 1946 to $24.4 billion in 1970. This signaled more
than a twentyfold increase in centralized federal control over
funds available to state and local government.[21] Nelson A. Rockefeller, no foe of centralism, felt compelled as governor of the state
of New York to call sharp attention in 1971 to the concentration of
taxing power in the federal government and the consequences that
this had in diminishing the competence of state and local government. He pointed out that the federal government collected 91
percent of all income taxes, which is two thirds of all taxes collected in the United States.[22] While federal decision power has
been growing as a result of concentration of tax power, state and
city governments have become increasingly wary of the system of
federal grants and federal cost-sharing programs. State officials
have noted, to their dismay, that federal programs are sometimes
launched with the promise of attractive supplementary federal
grants for proposed new local expenditures, but that thereafter the
federal government has exercised its powers to withdraw these
promised funds or diminish the federally committed proportion—
thereby leaving the local government holding the bag.[23]

One of the justifications given by liberal pro-centralist Americans is that a large federal tax revenue is needed so that this
money may be redistributed to states and cities that have less
income and therefore less taxing power than the wealthier ones.
From this standpoint, one would expect that federal expenditures
would be allocated with emphasis to those states whose inhabitants have the lowest per-capita income. In 1968–69 the following
states had average per-capita incomes of under $2,500: Alabama,
Arkansas, Mississippi, South Carolina and West Virginia. During
the preceding period, however, the lion's share of federal expendi-

tures was not in those states but rather in high-income-per-capita states that were also concentration points of military industry and military bases. During the period 1965–67, for which detailed data are available owing to an inquiry by a committee of Congress, three states were notable beneficiaries of federal expenditure. These were California, Texas and Virginia. California received an average of $2 billion a year more than was paid in taxes by its citizens and firms. The state of Virginia received $1,300 million a year over and above tax payments. And Texas received an average of $1 billion a year, net.[24] By contrast, the five poorest states showed a combined net intake from the federal treasury of $1 billion per year during the same period.

Alternatives to Centralism in Government

The American people need ideas on how to organize and operate the growing realm of public-responsibility functions in a large society. The importance of this issue is understood as soon as one considers the technical limitations and political consequences of trying to administer the public affairs of more than 200 million people out of one headquarters. The diversity of industry, climate, culture, living conditions, all put constraints on centrally regulated controls on a standardized basis over such a vast population. Even the availability of large-capacity information machines like the newer computers does not resolve the limits of efficiency on central controls.[25] Of course, if what is desired most of all is a centrally managed society along authoritarian lines, then efficiency limitations are no hindrance, since these may be regarded as part of the price that is worth paying for the main end-in-view. However, if an authoritarian result is not desired, then it is worth exploring an array of possible options to centralism-unlimited.

There is something to be learned from the experience of American industry with centralism that bears on these issues in government.

The organizers of the largest American industrial firms were characteristically men who applied themselves to a drive for power with immense energy. They had the capacity to control farflung operations "out of their vest pocket" while holding tightly to the reins of power. The history of these firms repeatedly discloses this pattern: when the great entrepreneur-organizer had gone, it no longer seemed sensible to try to operate in the same fashion. Typically, a replacement for the Old Man either was not desired or could not be found, or both. Also, his successors discovered that it was unwieldy to try to manage from one headquarters the myriad details of large enterprises with many subunits and widely dispersed operations.

During the 1930s, an organizational invention was increasingly applied to large American firms. It was called "decentralization." More exactly, this involved a change in the style as well as the location of decision-making. In the "centralized firm" detailed, particularized decisions for the operation of factories and subfirms were typically concentrated in the head office. The chiefs of local units in the "centralized" firm were typically "production superintendents" or similar functionaries whose tasks were primarily to oversee the production operations while final decisions on buying, selling, design and selection of products and investment were made by the head office. Under the organizational form called "decentralization" a central office staff was set up to formulate general policies which became the guide for managers of subdivisions who exercised detailed control over the affairs of their divisions, effectively making them subfirms. The new allocation of decision-making was: policy-making (and checking for compliance) at the central office; particularized, detailed decision-making by the local management. Thus, the central office decides on the class of products assigned to a division, and the managers of the division select particular products—research, design, produce—and sell them. Under these conditions, the local management includes the whole spectrum of managerial functions and exercises discretion over details, within the policy limits defined at the center. The local managers report to the central office on the conduct of operations. In this pattern each subdivision becomes, functionally, a quasi-autonomous enterprise.

In many major firms "decentralization" permitted and encouraged considerable initiative by the subdivisions. The managers in each case had incentive and opportunity to initiate changes and extensions of operations. From the standpoint of the business objective of extension of economic power, "decentralization" has proved effective. This is not to say that this organizational style is a universal solvent for all problems. "Decentralization" has involved, for example, an unresolved tension between central office and local management. This arises from the professional-occupational code of managerialism, with its imperative to seek ever more decision power. The point here is that within the framework of the business firm there is a large body of experience that is meaningful for the issue of centralism and alternatives thereto in government. It has been possible to combine centralization of policy with decentralization of implementation and detailed control.

What could this combination of organizational forms mean for alternatives in national policy? Let us assume that there is a national policy decision to eliminate substandard dwellings within a stated period. A centralist approach would include detailed design specifications for the dwellings to be constructed, either centrally formulated or locally designed but reviewed in detail at a national headquarters. Federally supported housing has heretofore included years of "lead time" to allow for micro-review of details of design and construction at the headquarters offices in Washington. A decentralized approach would involve national formulation of housing standards with accompanying performance standards—like internal temperatures and load-bearing capacity of floors. Thereafter, the details of design and construction would be left to the people in particular locales, who would vary building materials and style of construction in accordance with local climate, costs and tastes.

The strong tradition for centralizing and concentrating decision power has been given fresh capability by the invention of the computer, which makes it possible to store and manipulate very large quantities of data. For the centralists in industry and in government, there has been no greater boon. Computer capability for recording and collating millions of facts has vastly expanded accounting capability of every kind; national chains of department stores, or national networks of factories, can produce daily reports on the national status of inventories and sales. But this data-handling technology does not resolve the details of production problems. For example, it cannot organize the kind of cooperation in production which yields optimum productivity in industrial facilities, large or small.

With the aid of fast computers, communications and transportation, centralized concentration of control can be made technically workable, especially for keeping track of money transaction. However, decentralization and local control are especially suited for coping with problems of production and other operations for which flexibility, innovation and the cooperation of the people on the spot are the crucial requirements. Politically, centralism is the preferred instrument for authoritarian rule. Decentralized organization enables people on the spot to get into the decision-making act.

Without pretending to "solve" the problems engendered by centralism in government, I would like to call attention to some of the policies and practices that can be utilized as alternatives to centralism in government. First, national standards can be formulated for a great variety of purposes, ranging from minimum-performance characteristics of consumer goods to minimum standards for new housing construction. These standards could encompass facets of life that the community believes should be vested with public obligation. A few examples will suggest the range of possibilities: strength of buildings; quality of foods; rating of tires; strength of vehicles; purity of air; drinking water; educational achievement standards; minimum incomes. Formulating and enforcing national standards could substantially improve the quality of life in the whole population and remove many sources of gross inequity among American citizens. A national performance standard opens the way for diversity of implementation, varying ways of meeting the requirements of the standard. For example, a standard for functional characteristics and durability in a passenger-automobile tire leaves the selection of materials, the construction of the tire and the methods of manufacture to diverse solutions. A standard for minimum heating in housing can again be left to diverse solutions in accordance with conditions of climate, preferences in building material, and alternative ways of insulating homes and maintaining desirable temperature. A national standard for quality of drinking water or minimum achievement in education can be combined with diversity of locally controlled methods of implementation.

A regional approach to problem-solving offers another kind of organization for public economic activity. Initiative by a central government may be essential where cross-regional interests are involved, as, for example, in initiating the design and construction of the Tennessee Valley Authority facilities and similar river basin developments. In such cases, however, even where there is central initiative, implementation can very well be in the hands, as in the TVA case, of regionally located and regionally responsible controlling organizations. The workability of regional patterns of organization was spurred by the formation during the 1960s of more than 140 "councils of government." These are voluntary organizations of states, municipalities and counties designed to cross over the traditional jurisdictional lines for the purpose of implementing operations in which a number of government entities have a common interest. These councils came into being in order to cope with public needs ranging from sewage-treatment plants to anti-poverty programs. As a consequence of this experience the competence of local-government bodies has increased.

A parallel idea, relating especially to the larger metropolitan centers, was developed by John V. Lindsay when he was mayor of the city of New York. He suggested the establishment of "national cities." In his words, "That would be a new metropolitan federalism—with a national-regional and neighborhood government."[26] Sol M. Linowitz, chairman of the National Urban Coalition, has proposed the formation of metropolitan-development authorities in each of the great cities. In his words:

> The Metropolitan Development Agency should have virtually total authority to organize and act in an efficient manner. This would include:
> The power to acquire land, through eminent domain or otherwise, and the power to lease, develop and rehabilitate improvement.
> The power to pre-empt local zoning and building regulations under appropriate circumstances.
> The resources for social services which are often the key to the successful operation of physical developments.
> The power to tap private capital by issuing special-purpose indebtedness backed by federal guarantees . . .[27]

In the absence of democratic participation and control, town, city and state governments offer no obviously desirable alternative to centralism. These governments have often been controlled by local elites who turned them to the service of their private interests. This condition has generated much support for relying on federal agencies with their formal bureaucratic styles to administer social services hopefully in a standardized, impartial manner. Nevertheless, organizational forms are neither the autonomous cause of inequality and misrule nor the sufficient basis for ensuring disinterested public service. The power structure and the value system of any society strongly determine the quality of performance by public organization. Therefore an alteration in the character of local (and federal) governments awaits substantial value changes in the population and the determination of a majority to participate in and make government perform to its will.

The choice of methods of disposing of military-base areas and facilities affords a good example of the centralist-versus-local-control options. The Department of Defense operates about six hundred major military bases in the United States. Some of these cover tens of thousands of acres and are favorably situated as potential sites of new cities or new industrial areas in the neighborhood of existing cities. Planning for civilian use of present military-base areas on a large scale could afford some fresh starts in city planning and city construction. This, however, requires a fundamental policy decision by the federal government as well as capability on a regional basis to cope with such undertakings.

An indispensable requirement for the reversal of the centralist tendency in American government is a relative reduction in the tax receipts of the federal government and an increase in the taxing powers of state, city and other local governments. There is no law of nature that endows funds disbursed by federal agencies with special productiveness as against money spent by city and state governments. A reversal of the process of centralism in tax power could start with the federal grant-in-aid fund, which by 1970 totaled $24.4 billion. For a start, half of such funds could be released as taxing power that could then be drawn upon by the cities and the states. The other half could be allocated afresh from the federal government by the principle of size of aid in inverse proportion to the economic competence of the area making the request. Thereafter, reductions in the federal budget, notably in the swollen military funds, could be converted mainly into reductions in taxing power of the federal government, thereby opening new opportunities for the cities and the states. A city like New York City has its own income-tax mechanism and is fully competent to draw upon tax power that has been released by the federal government. (Indeed, such a development would have the further effect of relieving taxpayers of additional federal-tax burdens, since the taxes locally collected become the basis for a claim of tax deduction on the basis of existing law.) I do not imply that under such conditions every locality would make equally efficient use of newly available tax power. But there would be some incentive to improve the efficiency of local tax-gathering and local administration. Furthermore, if improved local taxing power were accompanied by a program of national standards for many public-responsibility activities, every locality would be under obligation to perform according to minimum standards; that would bring improvement to many communities. For example, compliance with public-health standards for fresh-water supply would mean an improvement in water supply for about a third of the population.

Improvement in the competence of local communities for economic planning and administration is a vital element for building up the viability of decentralized economic forms in the United States. It is worth recalling at this point that one of the important events that made centralism an "obvious" approach in the United States was the Great Depression with its demonstration of collapse and incompetence of local governments. Thereafter the main course of public policy built up the resources and status of the federal government—until Vietnam. The popular revulsion against that war and the federal authorities who operated it probably did much to cause many Americans, especially among the young, to seek local-community alternatives for influencing conditions of life. Interest in community-based organization was spurred by aspects of the War on Poverty activity. The Office for Economic Opportunity funded small but significant units like the Center for Community Economic Development, in Cambridge, Massachusetts. Such units have attempted to define competent methods of organization by which communities can sponsor economically efficient enterprises by applying local responsibility and authority, operating through democratic procedures and controls. In my opinion, a movement for the development of theory and practice of local-community control over economic and other activities would play a vital part in giving confidence in the viability of decentralized options for economic reconstruction.

For some time to come, economic development will be a major problem in several regions of the United States. In order to carry on such work at a reasonable tempo, it would make sense to channel funds from the more prosperous parts of the country to states, counties and towns that are candidates for economic development.

One possible way of doing this is via support from federal government to state, city and other local governments by a rule that allocates federal funds in inverse proportion to income per capita. Thus, by such a rule, federal support for an array of economic-improvement activity would be ten cents on the dollar in Westchester County in New York State but ninety cents on the dollar in almost all of Arkansas. In this way, federally gathered tax funds would become a true instrument for promoting economic development for the areas of the country that need it most.

If serious efforts were made to decentralize many types of public functions, the federal government would continue to remain a point of initiative for certain activities that are vested with a national interest and which benefit from either a degree of central coordination or central funding, or both.

Certain scientific research (e.g., high-energy physics) requires equipment so costly as to require a degree of centralized decision-making. There is a national interest in certain kinds of basic and applied research, as, for example, the development of the fusion reaction as a source of energy. In such cases it is sensible to have centralized establishments that partly initiate and certainly coordinate research and development in such spheres. However, this is a far cry from the Manhattan Project of World War II that produced the atomic bomb, or the NASA operations that yielded the manned lunar landing, which serve as the centralists' model for the operation of research in science and technology.

Scientific research has become such an important public activity that having alternative ways of sponsoring it is a matter of great importance. U.S. science policy has combined primary reliance on the federal government for research and development money, together with particularized, individual control over projects and persons by national headquarters. This has given immense power to federal agencies and to their committees of selected scientists who make the decisions on what research proposals are worthwhile and deserve support.

The United States could learn something from Great Britain, where a significant portion of the government funds available to the universities are allocated to institutions rather than to individuals. If this method of the British University Grants Committee were applied in the United States, the universities and similar institutions would confront new internal problems of how to allocate available research funds. Considerable social innovation would be required to devise rules and procedures for this purpose. At the same time, there is something to be said for retaining a measure of individual allocation from centralized sources—in order to limit the possibility of worthwhile projects going unattended for considerations other than of merit (local-university politics, rivalries, etc.).

I am not optimistic about the likelihood of readily overcoming the weight of ideology and administrative vested interest in centralism in government and in industry. So much energy has been poured into ways of concentrating power and so little has been done to fashion ideas for new institutions of local control. But these gaps can also be seen as constructive opportunities for all who are willing to break with the ideologies of centralism-at-all-costs and participate in some innovative thinking for defining the limits of centralism, and the characteristics of alternative ways of organizing, wielding and controlling economic and political power.

Nine

WHAT IS CONVERTIBLE AND NONCONVERTIBLE IN WAR ECONOMY?

THERE IS LITTLE REASON to suppose that the availability of civilian economic opportunity would suffice to attract managers, engineers and workers away from military economy. People do not usually regard organizational upheavals or the uncertainties and difficulties of job changes as attractive prospects. Also, for many who work in military industry or on military bases, there is nothing available in civilian economy that matches their present positions in terms of income, profits, status or the protection of civil-service tenure of base employees. It will take a major political and cultural push, a revulsion against war economy in the whole society, to move the military-serving population into civilian work. The prospects and limits of making that change an orderly one is what this chapter is about.[1]

Conversion of major parts of the American war economy to civilian work would be an undertaking without precedent. In no other country has there been a military economy that is comparable to the American one in size and longevity. Having endured for thirty years, it has occupied the occupational lifetime of millions of workers, technicians, managers and soldiers. Never before in American experience has the military establishment utilized so many industrial and other facilities, employing millions of people, constructed specifically for military requirements.

Following the two World Wars, the larger part of military-serving industry could reconvert to the civilian tasks that previously occupied these factories and their employees. But there is no reconversion prospect for the largest number of military-industry people serving the Pentagon during the 1970s, for the factories and bases where they work have no previous civilian experience. This means that in such establishments there is no institutional tradition of serving a civilian market or of meeting other civilian requirements.

By 1971 at least 6 million Americans were directly employed either by the Pentagon itself (3.8 million) or in military-serving private employment (2.2 million).[2] Military-related employment probably exceeds this because these numbers do not necessarily include the work going into the increasing levels of military assistance to other countries, much of which is not traceable in the Pentagon budget and which amounted to more than $10 billion in 1973 (equivalent to one million man-years of work at $10,000 per man-year). Neither do these millions of U.S. employees account for the private armies of the CIA in Indochina and elsewhere. The direct employment of course has indirect economic effects. Assuming an understated multiplier effect of one, then the indirect employment generated is not less than 6 million, for a total of at least 12 million. This amounts to 14 percent of the total American labor force (87 million). Moreover, for a large but unknown proportion of those dependent for their livelihood on the military dollar this has been their primary work experience.

Long experience with the functioning of military industry and of varied industrial attempts to adapt to civilian work indicates that, to be nationally significant, a conversion process requires a national political and economic movement toward this goal. Trusted leaders must proclaim conversion to civilian work as a vital national objective. The organization for such an effort has to be pervasive, encompassing industry organizations, unions and professional societies, as well as activity at the state and community level. Paralleling a political mobilization for conversion, a second requirement is the formulation of a program of new economic investment along the lines suggested by the various agendas for economic reconstruction that I presented in Chapter Eight. These new investment programs translate into new market opportunities for existing civilian or converting firms and new jobs to perform the necessary work. Only against the background of concrete market opportunities can the planning for institutional or occupational conversion be carried forward with confidence and with plausible expectation of success.*

What needs to be converted? The core of the conversion problem is in military industry and the military-base system. Apart from the armed forces themselves, these are the concentration points of the military-serving population. Though qualitatively very important, the technical research done for the military outside of industry accounts for only a fraction of those employed in industry and directly by the Pentagon.[3]

Any society that embarks on a significant effort to convert half to two thirds of its military establishment to civilian economy would also find it necessary to convert major parts of the armed forces, their headquarters, as in the Pentagon and other locations, and the military-serving research and development establishment. Furthermore, a serious conversion process would necessarily involve a major alteration in the function of members of the Congress who have become involved in a complex agent–client relationship vis-à-vis communities and firms in their districts and the Department of Defense. In the discussion that follows I will present the main outlines of requirements for conversion of each sector of the economy and also the factors that militate against conversion and for a continuation of the war economy.

For all the institutions and occupations engaged in the military economy, there is a common factor that presses strongly for retaining the status quo. Most members of the work force, from top managers down, have a stake in maintaining the status quo of their occupations, livelihood, community, and circle of social con-

* In the absence of these preconditions and collateral political support for economic conversion, the primary response of military-industry managers to reduction in Pentagon orders has been rapid discharge of employees. Here are some of the headlines: "Hard-Hit Seattle Closely Watching President's Moves"; "Down and Out Along Route 128"; "Where Defense Cuts Hurt Most"; "Job Losses at Grumman Send Shivers Through Long Island"; "Connecticut Seeks a Way Out of Mire of Unemployment"; "Aerospace Cuts Cause Job Crises"; "Slowdown on Route 128." These are from *The New York Times*, Aug. 24, 1971, Nov. 1, 1970; *U.S. News and World Report*, Oct. 5, 1970; *The New York Times*, Oct. 21, 1971, Jan. 14, 1971, Dec. 20, 1970, Oct. 11, 1970.

tacts that is linked to their work and community. For this reason, it is not realistic to expect any initiative for conversion to civilian economy to come from inside those occupations whose livelihoods and social status are tied to the war system. At the same time, however, it is reasonable to expect that these people will participate in a conversion process when two requirements are met: first, when the wider community indicates without ambiguity that this is what it wants; second, when economic and social supports for making an occupational and community adjustment to civilian-serving work are provided for in the conversion process, so that the burden of change does not fall unfairly on the people whose presence in the military economy has been, in part at least, due to the bidding of the wider society.[4]

For the military-serving enterprise, the starting point of conversion planning is the selection of new civilian products. These must be both producible and salable by a converting enterprise. Apart from inventions in goods and services that do not correspond to anything now available, the salability of potential products can be defined through two routes that have already been identified in this book. The list of depleted industries provides one route. This represents goods that are being bought by Americans from suppliers who are increasingly located outside the country. A second clue to salable products is given in the lists of new investments in economic reconstruction. The latter is of special importance for the potentially converting military-industry enterprises, since the agenda of new capital investment would represent major new market opportunities toward which a converting firm could orient itself.

Research on the potential-new-product problem for converting industries has thrown up a considerable list of opportunities for principal military-industry enterprises. Here, for example, is a list of new-product opportunities for military electronic enterprises, each of which has a definable market potential:

Office automation
Automatic distribution
Automation of process industries
Automation for piece-parts manufacturing
Electronic controls for road traffic
Electronic controls of railroads

Aviation support equipment
Communications equipment
Electronic self-instruction devices
Electronic library
Medical electronics (diagnostics, hospital design, prosthetics)[5]

The enterprises of the airframe industry (a section of the aerospace industry) are specialists in lightweight, high-strength design and fabrication. They have demonstrated considerable capability for using lightweight alloys for the fabrication of aircraft and other flight structures that require great strength. Apart from the production of civilian aircraft, the technology of lightweight high-strength structures can be applied to the following classes of products.

Prefabricated house sections
Prefabricated commercial-building sections
Railroad cars
Passenger cars for railroad use
Monorail transportation systems
Electric road vehicles
Hydrofoil and surface—effect boats

The shipbuilding industry, overwhelmingly occupied with naval construction, could conceivably be converted to the construction of commercial vessels on an international price-competitive basis. Only a small minority part of the freight that is shipped to and from the United States is carried in American-made or American-operated vessels. This has been owing to the depletion of the civilian shipbuilding competence under the impact of long naval subsidy experience. This would require a major overhaul in the product design and manufacturing methods of the industry in favor of introducing new technology in the design of vessels and modern production engineering methods for their fabrication. Also, the shipbuilding industry could conceivably undertake the design and construction of fishing vessels to reconstitute the competence of the American fishing industry, now well along in a process of technical and economic deterioration.[6]

If the government commits itself to continued expenditures in public-responsibility fields from transportation and water pollution to housing, these prospective expenditures translate into markets for which aerospace firms could conceivably offer bids. For example, it is virtually certain that the next half century will see an increasing requirement for electric-powered transportation within, around and among cities. Aerospace firms have considerable technical capability in design and fabrication of lightweight, high-strength structures. These are major elements of the stationary and moving parts of electric transportation systems.

For all potential industrial conversion operations, the common requirement is the performance of a full redesign of the military-serving enterprise with the expectation that this must include major retraining and reorganization of occupations, as well as explicit changes in the decision criteria that pervade the enterprise. Cost-maximization must be dropped and a reorientation must be made to cost-minimization within the constraints of commercially viable products.

When the people of any military-serving enterprise contemplate some of the product lists given here, they may very well shy away from the whole affair on the grounds that this means entering fields where old firms are often established and operating. In many cases, however, notably those of the depleted industries, the old firms have become less than competent to innovate product design and to reach out for new market opportunities. I have a vivid recollection of an experience in 1966 while serving as a member of Mayor Lindsay's Task Force on Air Pollution. When we called in a representative of a major manufacturer to brief the group on electric transportation, his central point was that there is no foreseeable way to improve on steel wheels riding twin steel rails. Not long after, it became clear that while his firm was stuck with steel wheels on steel rails, European firms were making major advances with electric-powered monorail designs utilizing lightweight, high-strength units for fast, cost-competitive transportation. In a word, old established firms are not necessarily bearers of unbeatable competence.

Once new products and markets have been defined, industrial-conversion planning requires reconstituting the management, the technical occupations, the tasks of blue-collar workers, and the physical plant and equipment itself. Let us try to see the conversion problem as it appears in "Universal Aerospace," a composite firm that actually combines many major features of its industry.

The Case of "Universal Aerospace" (UA)

UA has 125,000 employees, factories on the East and West Coasts and a solid reputation as a major aerospace firm. It started as a small aircraft builder before the Second World War and zoomed to importance when the United States wanted fighter planes by the thousands to win World War II. There was an interregnum from 1946 to 1950 during which the fortunes of the firm looked chancy. The bottom fell out of the military market, and various ventures into civilian production by UA after World War II never really caught fire. From Korea on, however, the situation changed, and, while there was variation of as much as 20 percent in the level of activity, the Department of Defense and NASA together managed to phase in new programs at just about the time when particular contracts were being completed. One result is that the managers and employees of UA are joined in the solid understanding that UA is here to stay as a provider of valued aerospace products for American military and space purposes.

Over all these years, the federal government became more than just a good customer. The relationship became closer all the time, and the federal agency even provided land, buildings and production equipment, so that 50 percent of UA's fixed assets are really not the property of the firm but are government-owned, though intermixed with the other half of strictly company property. This is, of course, a formal mystery whose details are known only to some accountants and auditors. To the people who work in the place, these fine differentiations have no practical meaning.

Actually, UA isn't all military and space. Over the years, by accumulating part of the profits earned, the management bought up controlling interests in various enterprises engaged in unconnected but all profitable activities: motels, car-rental agencies, bakery products, hospital supplies, computer software and oil-field-equipment specialties. UA then became a conglomerate as well as an aerospace firm with something more than half of its annual sales to the federal government. The diversification into other industries means a lot to the top management and to stockholders. This is their assurance of the continuity of UA, come what may in the government market.

Over the years, UA engineers and middle managers developed occasional ambitions to move parts of the aerospace capability into civilian-product ventures. Various things were tried, ranging from aluminum canoes and houseboats to specialized medical instruments. The main record of these ventures was catastrophic. They just didn't come off. It turned out that the UA staff didn't have the design, production and marketing know-how for operating with civilian consumers. UA couldn't make it in terms of an acceptable civilian product at a low enough cost and price. Finally, the top management made a rule: whenever something came up that looked like a feasible civilian product, it was either sold to another firm or, in a few cases, made the basis for new enterprises that were sponsored by UA top management, but set up and operated, in each case, as autonomous firms with separate names, locations and top managers. The idea was to prevent the spread of aerospace ideas and traditions into these new enterprises. Therefore, UA is a diversified firm with its main base still in aerospace.

UA has lots of the hallmarks of a private firm, but who ever heard of a real private firm with ten senior military officers and two hundred federal civilian staffers in permanent residence at one of its divisions? These people, politely called "the government liaison staff," have the job of checking out many aspects of UA's operation. UA's managers have to live by The Book called *The Armed Services Procurement Regulations* and the library of auxiliary rules and interpretations. Since the main customer is also the top management in the Pentagon to which this liaison staff reports, UA finds it essential to maintain its own representatives in Washington, close to the main management center. UA's links to government also include about fifty former generals and admirals in UA executive posts and close ties to the Senators and Congressmen in UA's districts and states.

In 1971 I visited with one of the executive vice-presidents of UA and asked him his views on the prospects of the firm in a conversion to civilian economy. His comment was, "As an institution, UA has poor prospects for conversion; the people of the firm, however, could learn new jobs and, if necessary, change jobs." He went on to say that the senior officers of UA are patriotic in the sense that they believe in the importance of trying to be Number One militarily and that the government should and will have a similar interest in the future. Their view of their firm and of the chief "customer" does not include a turn to civilian work.

Underlying the judgment about the nonconvertibility of UA as an institution is the whole style of operation in the service of the Pentagon, whose principal representative at UA has stated over and over again, "Our prime concern is to protect our industrial base." Since this is different from a prime concern for quality of product or level of cost, the management of UA has confidently proceeded to deliver what the armed services would accept at prices that were politically workable. UA, like its sister firms, practices cost-maximization and subsidy-maximization. Accounting, at UA, is not oriented primarily to hold costs down. Rather, it is operated to add up the expenditures that have been made so that a checkable bill can be sent on to the Pentagon. As the Pentagon is concerned mainly with "maintaining its industrial base," it is prepared to pay UA (subsidize) to get that result. Obviously these management practices would be suicidal in a civilian environment. Similar consequences flow from the remarkably high management costs at Universal Aerospace. For the aerospace industry as a whole, there are seventy-eight administrative, technical and clerical employees for every hundred blue-collar production and service workers. UA follows this pattern of managerial costs, which is almost twice the average for U.S. industry as a whole. Plainly, an enterprise that is operated in this fashion could not conceivably be converted to civilian operations without a drastic reshaping of management practices and probably management personnel.

Civilian enterprises need engineers and technicians, but none of them requires these people in the proportions found at UA, where more than a third of the employees are engineers and supporting technical workers. Furthermore, the engineers have become accustomed to researching, designing and producing for the Pentagon, which has permitted or even invited costs to go through the ceiling. The only problem has been a political one from time to time when some Congressman "sought publicity" by leaking one of UA's cost-maximizing "successes" as a "cost overrun." About one third of these engineers, if retrained for civilian engineering, would be employable in a converted enterprise of similar size. Their colleagues would have to either change occupation or change job location or both. Furthermore, quite a few of the men with engineering-job titles at UA have never actually obtained professional engineering degrees or professional licenses from state licensing bodies. These people would have special problems of finding new jobs. Finally, a considerable quota of the UA engineers have become highly specialized into semiadministrative jobs or technical specialties that are relevant for weaponry but have virtually no civilian counterpart. These people face the problem of major professional updating in order to have an employable engineering competence.

Of all UA's employees, the blue-collar workers in production and supporting services are best situated for conversion to civilian work. The overwhelming majority could transfer to civilian-products work with rather little change in job skills. A minority of blue-collar workers would require retraining ranging from a few weeks to a few months. In no instance would more than six months of retraining be required, even for the most demanding of the production jobs.

This does not mean that the workers at UA are gung ho for conversion to civilian work. On the contrary, they know the history of contract terminations and the management's practice of following each one swiftly with mass layoffs. The workers also know the history of UA's abortive efforts to go into civilian-products production. The more sophisticated workers appreciate the connection between that failure and the whole life style at UA, ranging from the overblown management and technical staffs to the loose standards of production performance and lack of concern about waste of materials, scrap, and quality control. The union, in UA, has reflected these understandings, and collective bargaining has had the special quality of negotiation with a nominal management that must finally get the nod from the government before major contract changes can be implemented. By and large, the officers of the union have felt a strong stake in helping to continue UA as a performer of Pentagon and Space Agency work. That is why the union has helped with, and sometimes even initiated, political campaigns to enlist the support of Congressmen and Senators on behalf of contract awards to UA.

The whole idea of conversion has definitely not been the union's cup of tea, any more than the management's or the engineer's. Like the others, the union has been less than optimistic about the feasibility of going civilian; it has not been able to see any prospect for the livelihood of its members or the continuation of the union as a bargaining entity under the banner of conversion to civilian economy. When, occasionally, a veteran trade-union officer speaks out for "peace" or in favor of "new priorities" it is perceived as a threat to UA's workers and local-union officers. Indeed, local-union officers and stewards of UA have been known to join with other aerospace local unionists to override initiatives by national officers for conversion and new-priorities legislation in favor of boosterism for another aerospace boondoggle, even one like the SST which was massively criticized and could not muster a Congressional majority approval.

Let us suppose that the Congress passes a law similar to the proposed S-2274 Bill of 1964 that was advocated by Senator George McGovern to establish a National Economic Conversion Commission. And let us further suppose that this law includes the same clause requiring every military-industry firm above a minimum size to prepare civilian conversion plans. What would happen at UA in response to this requirement?

More than likely, such a law would provoke a crisis inside the UA management. It is likely that a majority would judge that the whole move is really unfeasible and that conversion planning would be a form of play-acting. Apart from that, they would just not want it. However, the law being what it is, and a requirement for approval of the plan having been stipulated in that law, there would be no out but to go ahead, put some people in charge and do the planning as prescribed.

A conversion-planning committee for UA would have to include product designers, finance specialists, industrial-marketing men and industrial-personnel specialists, as well as representatives of all major occupations and departments of the firm. The product designers would be charged with proposing civilian products that were suited to the design and production capabilities of the firm. They would call on outside advice for accumulating a pool of possible products which are appropriate to the two main lines of UA production competence: lightweight, strong metal structures and electronic control equipment. Products that look possible on these grounds would then be checked with the marketing specialists for estimates of sales forecasts and market saturation on each of the product possibilities.

As the field of prospective products is narrowed down to a single one or a related set, the industrial engineers come into the picture to estimate the nature and the cost of the production system that would be required, taking into account work that could be subcontracted (bought in). The personnel people would then estimate the manpower requirements for the proposed production, as well as the technical and administrative staffs (including marketing) that would be required. On the basis of this information, the finance people can estimate the fixed and the working capital requirements for the proposed operations, taking into account the character and costs of the marketing function as well. The industrial engineers responsible for integrating this planning function would then prepare organization charts of functional responsibilities and estimated break-even charts and sales-expense forecasts to depict the probable prospects of the new civilian operations.

Apart from the staff specialists, the representatives of departments and employee groups on the planning committee would also play a major role. They would corral constructive ideas on all aspects of conversion planning, afford a mechanism for general participation in the planning process and, in so doing, not only alter their own occupations but also defuse well-founded fears among all military-industry employees about their job prospects beyond serving the Pentagon.

From careful studies of such planning operations it is reasonable to expect that two years are required as planning time for all the work that must be done to blueprint the changeover of sizable industrial facilities and work forces after a new product has been selected.[7] This factor of planning time is vital in considering any conversion operation. It is indispensable for ensuring deliberate consideration of new enterprise options. Absence of careful planning and reliance on crash operations usually lead to a high probability of failure. Indeed, it is the anticipation of such failure that leads the managements of aerospace firms to lay off their employees en masse when the military contract ends. To be sure, plans for a new enterprise invariably require revisions and updating, but their existence makes a big difference for the prospects of livelihood for most of the people engaged in UA and other similar enterprises.

The financing of UA-civilian could be managed under advantageous conditions. First of all, a prudent management would set aside reserves for this contingency. The requirements for such financing are defined by the requirements of UA's conversion plan. In addition, investment bankers and commercial bankers could be approached for appropriate financing on the basis of the conversion plan, coupled with the prospect of sales for civilian products. The one-year advance notice would give UA management opportunity to do a selling job on behalf of its product line. If the main conditions of economic reconstruction that I formulated in Chapter Eight are made operative, the programs of new public investment, including one of UA's civilian products (electric vehicles), would become realistic market prospects in cities and towns across the country. Among the interesting sources of possible financing that UA might conceivably draw upon would be the accumulated pension funds of the employees. During the last ten years alone, the accumulation of UA pension funds has exceeded $370 million. Obviously an infusion of money from this source would have the further effect of enlisting the group commitment of the employees of UA in successful performance of the converted enterprise, since they would have made an investment in their own future.

In order for UA to make a real try for success, major infusions of new talent would be required at critical points of the UA organization. The top management would have to get people whose main experience and orientation is civilian, and their authority would have to be made dominant among the circle of top managers. The top-management men who are unable or are unwilling to learn a civilian trade would have to leave the enterprise. For the senior officers of the firm (the president, the chairman of the board), these changes would be an unavoidable imperative for their own success. Major additions would be required in marketing and production engineering. UA and other firms like it typically operate with small marketing groups, since their market is essentially assured following "selling" efforts that have more ingredients of politics and diplomacy than of commercial marketing. Therefore, civilian-oriented marketers must be added, as well as civilian-oriented product designers. At the same time, substantial reductions would be made in administrative and engineering staffs, which at UA have become completely oversized in relation to the needs of a civilian firm.

The report of UA's conversion-planning committee really comes to life when the UA management is given notice by the Pentagon or the Space Agency, say one year in advance, that its assigned work will terminate. Then the plan becomes an operational blue-print in every one of its facets. At that point, the personnel section of the conversion committee becomes a key unit, because its responsibility includes setting up and operating a job-retraining program that is oriented to the prospective civilian operation. That would have to involve everyone in the place, from the top managers to the building-service workers. Every job would be affected in greater or lesser degree by the need to become successful in a producing and marketing environment where government subsidies are not at hand and where holding costs to plan is critical.

Under the condition of a one-year advance notice of termination of military orders there is also ample time for doing something on behalf of the one out of three UA employees who would probably have no future with UA-civilian. This condition contrasts with the practice of some military-industrial firms of posting at noon on Friday a layoff list effective that same Friday at 5 P.M. (I have been told of one firm where, on late Friday, just before 5 P.M., people were told that they were laid off and were then given a security-guard escort out of the company premises, with the parting word that their personal effects would be gathered up and sent on to their homes.) Furthermore, under the terms of reasonable schemes for occupational conversion, UA employees made surplus by conversion would have a further year to make a retraining and/or relocation adjustment, with public support, for themselves and their families.

The people made surplus by conversion would be mainly from the administrative and technical departments of UA. This expectation, even under the most favorable economic-conversion condition, is the basis for suggesting that an occupational conversion backstopping is needed. This would have to be a government-funded program to guarantee income and opportunity for job retraining and relocation for the men and women rendered surplus even by successful conversion to civilian work. (See separate discussion below.)

I have been told at UA and at other aerospace firms that this would be a bitter pill for the people involved, since it would mean a disruption of their employment, communities, social relations, children's schooling, etc. The plain truth is that the overwhelming majority of UA employees "immigrated" to its locations from other cities and states. Further, a high intensity of migration has been a sustaining feature of American economic life since World War II, particularly among military-industry employees. They could, of course, be maintained in their present locations forever if the rest of the society were prepared to subsidize them for life. Again, by reason of the characteristics of civilian as against military industries, it is unrealistic to expect full-conversion opportunity on the same site for all employees of military-industry enterprises.

If the management of UA were utterly unsuccessful in preparing a workable conversion plan, it should not be excluded that other people might think of ways of utilizing the buildings, land and facilities of UA. This option would surely require active, organized intervention by a community group which would take responsibility for either inviting other potential firms to the scene or initiating investigations for a possible new enterprise. There are government departments like the Economic Development Administration of the Commerce Department which have traditions for funding significant parts of such efforts. Under such conditions, it has often proved possible to mobilize property owners, union officers, bankers and other enterprise operators of the locality to participate in funding and taking responsibility for such local development. This latter operation, if required among the UA's of the country, would take on some of the characteristics of community organization of economic development following the closure of military bases.

So much for the details of Universal Aerospace.

Problems of Enterprise Conversion

In every military-industry firm, planning and performing conversion to civilian work involves distinctive problems for each of the main occupational groups: administrators, technicians and production workers. There are also characteristic problems of converting industrial production facilities. Having touched on these matters in a composite enterprise (UA), let us now consider them through the data of actual firms, industries and regions.

Under what management conditions may industrial conversion be expected to succeed? Apart from internal reconstruction of the enterprise, a military-industry firm can be merged into a civilian firm with the civilian top management replacing the former chiefs of the military division, thereby giving the unit an infusion of civilian-oriented managerial direction. Another scenario involves a changed top management in a military-industry division of a large multidivision civilian firm. The common feature of these circumstances is the replacement of the military-serving top management with a civilian-oriented group.

A good example of this process occurred in the merger of North American Aviation, Inc., with the Pittsburgh auto-industry supplier, the Rockwell-Standard Corporation. The resulting firm, North American–Rockwell, was given two new chief executives, both drawn from major Detroit-based automobile firms. These men proceeded to reshape the managerial criteria and control systems of North American–Rockwell and substantially expanded new civilian-product initiatives by the firm.[8]

Characteristically, however, this successful effort in converting production resources to civilian products did not precede, but rather followed, a major cutback in military activity and employment. Thus, employment at North American Aviation was slashed from 120,000 in 1967 to 73,400 in 1971. The cost-conscious civilian-oriented management was installed only after a major cutback in Pentagon and Space Agency contract work had already occurred. In the aerospace and other military-serving industries the more usual experience has been wholesale employment cutbacks following contract cancellations or completions, without the sort of serious attempt at conversion to civilian industry that took place at North American–Rockwell.

Why is the North American–Rockwell effort to convert to civilian products so unusual?[9] Civilian industrial firms of the ordinary sort periodically revise their product lines and seek out new markets. The really successful civilian industrial firms are competent at researching and developing new products, designing production systems that will turn them out at satisfactory cost and quality, and raising the capital necessary for new productive investment. Precisely these kinds of capabilities are lacking in the typical military-industrial firm, which has become oriented to maximizing costs and government subsidies. In this economy, costs and prices need only be politically acceptable—as against acceptable among competing goods in the marketplace. For civilian products, acceptable cost and price can be compared to a benefit, and the relation of cost to benefit can be compared for alternative products. In military industry, by contrast, money cost can also be calculated. But how is one to quantify a benefit? What money or other quantitative value can be assigned to the killing of a person or the destruction of a town? Since the "benefit" of a military product is statable in political rather than economic units, costs in military product that are unthinkable elsewhere are encouraged. For example, in a great array of civilian machinery the prices of the product are characteristically well under $10 per pound. In the case of the F-111, the multipurpose swing-wing fighter-bomber, the price at one point exceeded $231 per pound. At this rate a motor vehicle of modest weight (say 3,000 pounds) would cost $693,000.

Inquiries among military-industry managers on the feasibility of converting their enterprises have produced self-assessments of their capacity for conversion.

Lew Evans, chairman of the board of the Grumman Aerospace Corporation, stated in 1971, "We're not mass-consumer-market-oriented, and we're not able to function profitably under the different types of contracts and procurement processes that exist in other markets . . .   Grumman is in aerospace—and I mean 'pure' aerospace—to stay."[10]

W. P. Gwinn, chairman of the United Aircraft Corporation, had this to say to a Senate subcommittee that inquired about capability for conversion to civilian work:

> . . . aerospace companies tend to be dominated by design, develop-
> ment, manufacturing, and marketing philosophies quite different from
> those of consumer-oriented firms. The former's large engineering staffs
> and test and development facilities saddle them with high overhead;
> their manufacturing expertise is in the turning out limited production
> runs . . . ; they are accustomed to marketing to the government and
> to other aerospace companies . . . The company that had learned
> how to be successful in this environment is poorly equipped to com-
> pete with established manufacturers' mass-produced, relatively un-
> sophisticated items.[11]

Trade-union officers at a Boeing facility near Philadelphia that produced large helicopters tried to interest the Boeing management in planning for conversion to civilian work, specifically mass production of housing. The union officials consulted with architects and other specialists to develop the economic viability of their proposal. When they outlined their scheme to a Boeing official he responded, "But think how many units of housing we would have to sell to make as much money as we do on a single helicopter." He also said, "It is not easy to become established in a new field. And those fields in which Boeing's capabilities might be adapted already are occupied by reputable companies with the required technology, facilities, manpower, money and marketing outlets."[12]

Dr. Arthur Obermayer, president of Moleculon Research Corporation of Cambridge, Massachusetts, compared his firm's practices with that of civilian-product enterprises:

> We have found that military R&D is usually directed toward high-performance products requiring a significant advance in the state of the art. By contrast, commercial objectives are usually the development of a better product at a competitive price. Such commercial activities don't require the same high level of technical sophistication, but they do generally require a very practical approach, including economic evaluations, cost analysis, and market studies. In converting we have found our organization to be topheavy with scientists and engineers and deficient in sales, marketing, production, and financial areas . . . The contract negotiations with industry require personnel in our organization with much greater business judgment, since there is no well-established guideline, such as Armed Services Procurement Regulations. Accounting objectives also change; allocation of costs are not primarily for the purpose of proper billing, but rather for cost control and analysis. . . .[13]

Plainly, the top managers of military industry are themselves a major barrier to any potential conversion operations, unless they are prepared to learn the skills of civilian-industry management, or are replaced by new men who are free of the burden of unlearning a set of skills that are inappropriate in civilian economy.

A major factor that limits the conversion capability of military firms and institutions is the pattern of remarkably high managerial costs in these organizations. Joseph Hyman, president of Hycor Corporation, a small Massachusetts R&D firm, testified to a Congressional group:

> . . . part of our problem can be traced to this systems-engineering or systems-management myth that has been brought about in the aerospace industry: it keeps a lot of managers working. The counterpart company in the nondefense field does not have any of this systems

management or at least it is not called that. They call it common sense. In aerospace, it has just been given a fancy title, and there are counterparts in the Government too.

Now, unless and until the big aerospace companies get rid of perhaps three-quarters of these management people, they will never be able to compete—never—on any program which the Government is not willing to subsidize . . .[14]

Obviously, the aerospace firms, accustomed to operate with managerial methods that require twice the manpower that is conventional in civilian industry, are at an automatic cost disadvantage should they attempt to redirect the overblown managerial staff to civilian products and markets.

Military firms have also employed an extraordinary number of engineers and technicians. By 1970 in all of the nonagricultural enterprises in the United States, engineers comprised 1.2 percent of all employees. But in the military electronics industry, one third of the people employed were engineers and technicians. The special intensity of engineering employment in military work is further indicated by the fact that in the civilian-oriented part of the electronics industry, the engineering-technical component of employment has been about 11 percent.[15] As we saw in UA, for conversion to civilian economy, it is probable that about two thirds of the engineers in military electronics will have to find employment elsewhere. (We will discuss this under the general heading of occupational conversion below.) But for those who would be required for a civilian-oriented enterprise, there would have to be major retraining from cost-maximization to a design tradition where economic factors are important in the design of products and in the conduct of production. It is conceivable to do this by in-house courses of instruction, utilizing the readily available textbooks in engineering economy, together with design exercises based on civilian electronic products. Without this kind of retraining and reorientation it is implausible to expect that military electronics engineers could successfully operate in a civilian environment. I recently reviewed electrical-engineering curricula in major universities, and found that in a sampling of large schools it was possible in 1973 to obtain a degree in electrical engineering without being required to take a single course of instruction on problems of economic design of products or economic conduct of production operations. Therefore, the conversion of military-industry engineering staffs to civilian use requires intensive retraining and indoctrination in civilian design and production criteria.

These considerations are made vivid by the following account from an engineer-manager in a civilian-product electronics firm.

> We have had a number of design engineers come and go who had their training in the aerospace business. For a while I was doing the job interviews and [after a newspaper article appeared about our company] . . . there was a flood of job applications from thousands of engineers who had been working in GE-aerospace and Raytheon. We hired a few of these people—men with brilliant minds, outstanding recommendations, and very fine schooling. Without exception they all flunked out from our company because they had never really thought about designing a consumer product. . . .
>
> In aerospace you are given something to build, with a set of specifications, and that's it. If it costs you $5,000 or $50,000 you build to those specifications. . . . So as an engineer you learn to think how to achieve those design objectives at whatever price. . . . In consumer industry the design engineer . . . has to be constantly weighing, making decisions that affect the value of the product and may affect, in the end, the overall appearance of the product and its functions. He has to say: I could add this function at this cost; or, he gets around to designing the function, and, gosh, it's costing three dollars and that will reflect itself in so many dollars in selling price; is it worth it? These are kinds of decisions that a successful designer in consumer industry has to make because these are the kinds of decisions that go on in a consumer's mind: is it worth it? People from the aerospace industry haven't thought about it. . . .
>
> When you start out on a consumer project you have to be prepared to have the end product be somewhat different from what you had intended it to be . . . this interplay doesn't exist in the aerospace business, where the design process is very unidirectional. Somebody establishes an overall package. That is divided into small projects which are parceled out, and smaller projects within those projects are parceled out again. The result is one of those huge rooms of five hundred engineers poring over their benches, each one designing their own little box which fits into the next higher assembly, which fits into the next higher assembly still. There is no chance in a situation like this to say: Well, maybe the whole appearance could be a little different; we could do something slightly less effective to halve the price. After all, in aerospace the marketability is not a factor . . . The product is already sold. So what is the point of trying to make it more marketable?
>
> The design engineers from the aerospace industry came into our

firm and somebody in marketing would say: Let's make something that does the following; let's develop it, refine it and turn it into a product. What happened is the idea got taken up exactly verbatim. A product was developed which was, electronically, ungainly. Instead of doing things in subtle ways—like taking a device that was originally designed for use in clock radios and putting it into the product because it can save money—they used only that component which was traditionally specified to do that function.

In other words, the engineers we have had (from aerospace firms) have not, spontaneously, tried to figure out ways of using existing devices in novel settings. [This kind of] value engineering hasn't existed, until now at least, in aerospace . . . The colleges that train them probably never even mention value engineering—especially if they went to an Ivy League college, where even the thought of building anything was seen as evidence of a trade school mentality.

Industrial planners who undertake the blueprinting of conversion to civilian work will usually find that production workers of all classes are the ones most readily transferable to civilian product work. The basic fabrication operations are comparable, even though certain special and sometimes esoteric product requirements of military industry have no civilian counterpart. However, it is reasonable to expect problems of work standards and work load to arise in a transfer from military to civilian operations. I am advised by industrial engineers with mixed military and civilian experience that the standards of productivity that are acceptable in many military-industry firms could not be endured in civilian-products work. Accordingly, there would have to be systematic indoctrination for the whole work force in the nature of the changed work requirements for a successful move by an enterprise from military to civilian operations. Obviously, such retraining of the production work force becomes a more credible operation as the production workers can see that major alterations are being made among administrative staff and engineering departments as well.

The conversion of production workers in military industry is certain to be affected by the position and experience of their trade-union organizations. Trade unions have been important participants in the military-industry network of the United States. The following unions are the most important ones with major bargaining units in military industry: the International Association of Machinists; the United Steelworkers of America; the International Union of Electrical Workers; the United Automobile, Aerospace and Agricultural Equipment Workers Union; the Oil, Chemical and Atomic Workers Union of America. Only one of these unions, the UAW, has given affirmative attention to the conversion problem.

The trade unions, like most Americans during the 1960s, regarded military production as a new economic bonanza. When Senator George McGovern proposed legislation for establishing a national economic-conversion commission as early as 1963, only one national union, the National Farmers Union, formally endorsed the legislation.[16]

In a major departure from this pattern, in 1969 Walter P. Reuther, president of the UAW, presented a rather detailed conversion proposal to the Senate Committee on Labor and Public Welfare. The heart of the scheme was the requirement that 25 percent of military-industry firms' profits be impounded in a conversion reserve fund. This fund could be drawn upon by the management for financing, planning and performance of conversion to civilian work. Also, these funds could be drawn upon for paying unemployment benefits to the firms' employees once its military work had been terminated and new civilian work was being prepared.[17] While advancing an imaginative scheme for profit incentives to induce industrial management to undertake serious conversion planning and operations, the UAW scheme also included provisions for continuing the management's conventional subsidy-maximizing operations. The latter would be the outcome of a proposed system of government guarantees for loans to military-industry management covering 90 percent of any loan obtainable from private sources. Such a subsidy scheme would institutionalize the Lockheed type of loan guarantee that was granted by the Congress in 1971. As the subsidy is sustained it removes competitive pressure for efficient performance and for innovative activity, thus creating conditions which become the basis for further subsidy requests. Subsidy systems have the capacity to perform as "self-fulfilling prophecies."

Beyond this proposal from the UAW there is no evidence known to me of any significant initiative or attention by any national trade-

union organization or by the AFL–CIO to the problem of conversion from military to civilian economy. At a seminar at Columbia
University in 1961 I proposed that trade unions, among others,
should try to do serious forward planning for converting to civilian
economy. The response of a senior trade-union officer present was,
"When the problem comes up we will deal with it." In the nature
of the case, of course, once the problem comes up it is too late to
start dealing with it. Also, the participation of major industrial
trade unions in military industry has involved their responsible
officers in the day-to-day workings of the system and, necessarily,
in giving credence to the ideologies that justify sustained military
work. One result of this has been the generation of inner tensions
leading to the inability of trade unions to perceive the connection
between priority to military work, depletion of civilian industry
and consequent job loss in the civilian parts of their industries.

An evaluation of the physical plant and equipment is an essential part of preparing an industrial enterprise for conversion. The
physical assets include production equipment, buildings, ground
and utilities. The inventory of production equipment must differentiate between "general-purpose" and "special-purpose" equipment. Special-purpose equipment, useful only for a particular
product, may have only scrap value even though the initial cost for
its military use may have been high. General-purpose equipment is
designed to perform functions that are not specific to a particular
product. Such equipment may be transferred intact or slightly
modified for civilian application. The quality of buildings must be
assessed in terms of usefulness for diverse types of civilian industrial use.

For industrial facilities, conversion to civilian work is heavily
affected by the class of products involved in particular enterprises.
First there are the non-military-specific products. These include
the host of things purchased by the military that are also purchased in ordinary civilian activity. This ranges from containers of
milk, shoelaces, paint and light bulbs to small hand tools and other
products required by the armed forces that also correspond to
articles used in civilian life. For such enterprises the problem is
one of shifting markets on the assumption that the single large
purchaser—the Department of Defense—is replaced by a number
of civilian purchasers, distributed differently than the receiving

warehouses of the Department of Defense supply system. Stated differently, the civilian-type product will continue to be used by the same U.S. population, but marketing to that population will be through channels differing from the military purchasing organizations.

A second class of products are specific to the military, but involve production systems—machines, labor forces, factory buildings—which can conceivably be used to make other things (e.g., foundries, die-casting machines, extrusion presses, general-purpose machine tools). There the conversion problem is one of finding new products and markets for given industrial facilities and their work forces. A limiting case for conversion purposes includes those industrial processes and equipment that have no civilian use or near use. For example, test stands and related buildings and equipment for large rocket engines have no counterpart civilian applications; or the equipment for making and storing poison gases.

There is no gainsaying the fact that the transformation of an existing organization and facility is the most difficult kind of industrial-conversion operation. When an industrial enterprise is started from scratch there is none of the accompanying baggage of previous usages built into the ongoing job relations of the organization that must be overcome. Overcoming these problems requires a high degree of commitment and moral support for the whole effort from the surrounding community.

Military Bases

The conversion of military bases for civilian uses is a second principal part of conversion to peace. Within the United States, one million federal civilian employees and one and a half million uniformed military personnel are located on five hundred major military bases. A major base is one with at least one thousand people working on it. The major military bases and a large number of smaller installations are spread throughout the states of the Union and involve annual payrolls of $10 billion per year to civilian employees and $10 billion per year to the uniformed military staffs. In order to illustrate the scale of what is involved here as a conversion problem, I have prepared a table of data on employment in military industry and bases in 1971 (see Appendix 6) showing the military-industry and military-base employment within each state.

The total number of civilian and uniformed military personnel of the Pentagon's major bases and installations appears to be a modest proportion of a 1971 population of 207 million Americans and a labor force of about 87 million. The fact is, however, that the civilian and military-base personnel of the Department of Defense have great proportional importance and economic impact in the communities and regions in which they are active. Thus, in 1971 the Department of Defense had 26,985 civilian employees in New Jersey, which seems a small enough number in a population of 7,168,000; the fact is, however, that in the areas around Fort Monmouth, the Picatinny Arsenal and Fort Dix, the Department of Defense civilian employees loom large as a factor in local employment and local economy.

Some economists have held that appropriate economic conversion from a military to a civilian economy is achieved essentially by setting appropriate national fiscal and monetary policies, or by setting nationally averaged unemployment limits. Such a prescription is not responsive to the particular and concentrated problems of the communities and employees around military bases. Aggregate policies on a fiscal and monetary level do not suffice to cope with the specially intense effect owing to military bases as concentration points of regional employment.

During the 1960s it was usually possible for the Department of Defense to guarantee alternative employment within the military-base system. This could be done because of the large size of the system, the process of normal turnover and retirement and the relatively small number of people laid off in particular base areas. By March 1970 it was no longer possible to offer this sort of guarantee.

The elemental requirements for conversion of military bases to civilian uses are twofold: advanced planning of a conversion process, and organized responsibility and authority for the planning process and for its implementation in the hands of the local community.[18] Without advance planning in the range of one to three years, it is not feasible to carry out anything but crash, emergency operations. Inevitably, such accommodation to military-base closings or major reductions are bound to be costly in economic and human terms, and are fraught with high likelihood of failure. The advance-planning period is what is required to carry out the appropriate studies of the geography, natural resources, human resources and physical plant in and around military-base areas.

The military-base conversion problem can be understood as one species of general economic-development problem. It is like the problem that is faced by a major builder-developer who seeks to undertake a comprehensive, many-sided development of a given area, providing for long-term economic viability of housing, enterprises, and the community and other infrastructure needed by a durable economic society.

Local initiative is an essential feature for technical efficiency as well as being politically preferable. Central planning at a distance is not adequate to the task of weighing the locally unique combinations of physical, economic and social capabilities as well as the skills and commitment of the people on the spot. Our best information on how people become strongly motivated tells us that real authority must be linked to responsibility. Furthermore, authority for decision-making is most fruitful in alliance with competence—skills, information, resources—and participation in the decision-making process by the people most personally concerned.

One way of appreciating the importance of these considerations is to examine the consequences of little or no planning and little or no local responsibility.[19] That is the story of the New York Naval Shipyard in Brooklyn.

From 1961 to 1964 there was growing discussion of the possibility of closing this shipyard with its long history and its approximately nine thousand employees. During late 1963 and 1964 a "Save the Shipyard" committee was formed in New York City which carried out all the usual public-relations and political-pressuring operations. In November 1964 the yard was formally ordered shut, and the shutdown was completed by 1966 with the loss of nine thousand jobs in the New York metropolitan area. On February 1, 1967, the Economic Development Administration of the U.S. Commerce Department commissioned the Institute for Urban Studies at Fordham University and the consulting firm of

Tippetts-Abbett-McCarthy-Stratton to prepare a study for redevelopment of the area. These people delivered a report on "The Brooklyn Navy Yard: A Plan for Redevelopment" on May 1, 1968.

All of the classic features of the failure of planning were visible here. Instead of advance planning there was organization and expenditure of major funds for political pressure. None of the public or private parties that might be considered to be in a responsible position in this matter took any initiative whatever for advance conversion-planning operations on behalf of the New York Naval Shipyard.

From 1961 on, under my direction, graduate students in the Department of Industrial and Management Engineering at Columbia University participated in a Seminar on Problems of Conversion from Military to Civilian Economy. They prepared various research papers on the New York Naval Shipyard. In 1964 I drafted a proposal for "Utilization of the New York Naval Shipyard Area for an Ultramodern, Economically Viable Shipbuilding Enterprise." This memorandum was brought to the attention of the mayor, his Economic Development Committee, trade-union officers, bankers and others with a broad economic interest in the New York metropolitan area, including members of Congress and members of the executive branch of the federal government. None of these persons responded in any constructive way whatsoever. All the people in leadership positions who were directly or indirectly involved in the case of the New York Naval Shipyard devoted themselves to the "Save the Shipyard" committee and its political-pressure operations. One consequence is that the shipyard area and the surrounding neighborhood suffered economic deterioration, with only partial redevelopment of the shipyard area at this writing.[20]

The Importance of Planning Time

For conversion of both industrial enterprises and military bases, the availability of planning time is a crucial ingredient. For conversion of military bases the planning problem has special complications. Military bases are often set in remote areas and on tracts of land initially unsuited for civilian or commercial development.

The communities developed around military bases usually are mainly engaged in serving them. Also, military bases ordinarily have no autonomous base-management group which is likely to remain responsible when the Pentagon relinquishes the facility.

The military personnel on a given base, even the senior officers, are necessarily a transient group, subject to redeployment within their respective military organizations. The civil-service civilians involved bear major responsibilities for parts of the base, but their responsibilities have been specialized toward performance of the military-related functions. Therefore they may be perfectly fine administrators of parts of the military-serving base activity without possessing skills that are relevant to alternative civilian activities that might be operated on the base.

For these reasons base-conversion planning and implementation require significant intervention by parties outside the base proper. This means the mayor of the town, the Chamber of Commerce, the bankers, the principal shopkeepers, the officers of unions in the area—the spokesmen for all who have an economic stake in the community attached to or near military bases. These people are not base employees and they would not ordinarily meet together to consider the disposition of the base facility. Planning base conversion involves a new initiative for these people, requiring the development of a sense of community responsibility and the formation of groups that are committed and competent to discharge that responsibility. Such local groups will form in base communities only when they are all told by national leaders that this is what is expected of them and that there is no longer a prospect of securing a livelihood for their communities by Pentagon largesse which their Congressmen help to arrange.

The prognosis for military-base conversion, as for military industry, is definitely mixed. Experience with many cases of base cutbacks shows a wide range of competence for community response: from overwhelming job disappearance to the organization of new activities and investments that enlarged the base-area economy.[21] As in "Universal Aerospace" and kindred firms, it is prudent to expect that an occupational-conversion program is needed to backstop the people who are bound to discover no economic prospects in converted bases. Workable schemes to support individuals through a period of job transition are therefore a vital part of a national conversion effort.

Conversion of Occupations

What is the feasibility of retraining and transferring individuals engaged in military industry and bases to civilian pursuits? Special consideration for occupational conversion of military-economy jobs is required because, except for unemployment insurance and supplementary unemployment benefits available to some trade unions, the cost of job change, including technological change, is left to be borne by the individual workers in American economy.

Except for production workers and administrative employees doing standardized, routine tasks, military-industry jobs have been fairly specialized. This is especially visible among the engineers. A knowledgeable article in *Mechanical Engineering* emphasized that "the greater the level of experience and training, such as that of the specialist, the less adaptable he is to new industry." For example, a person with intensive training in pediatrics would not normally be expected to perform open-heart surgery. Thus, the Pentagon-serving engineer can be transferred to other technical occupations, but the inescapable requirement is training for this transfer.[22]

The employment problems of engineers are of particular interest to me as a faculty member in an engineering school. Therefore I was sensitive to the information that civilian-industry employers had been placing job ads that included the admonition that no aerospace engineers need apply.[23] The reluctance of civilian-industry managers to hire former military-industry engineers has been reported to me again and again by former students. This is confirmed by independent studies of the job problems of military engineers.[24]

If the engineer candidates for conversion to civilian industry were spread around the country, then a helter-skelter of individual adjustments, plus on-the-job training, would probably see these men through. But that kind of prospect is ruled out by the high regional concentration of military-engineering work. In one military-industry locality 33 percent of the employees in large aerospace installations are engineers and scientists. The fact is that there is no single industry or combination of industries which can conceivably require these men in this proportion. Many of these engineers and scientists must leave that particular locality. Therefore any serious effort to facilitate occupational conversion has to take into account both the change in the nature of skill and changed location of work.

On the basis of these understandings, as well as for defusing political resistance to conversion that is based upon fear of joblessness, I have formulated a Defense Industry Employees' Bill of Rights, to be incorporated into national conversion legislation:

1. One year of occupational retraining for a civilian occupation. Tuition, fees and books at any recognized educational institution (VA list).
2. Income maintenance for one year:
   $6,000 for unmarried individual
   $6,000 for chief breadwinner of family
   $2,000 for wife of married defense employee
   $1,000 for each child up to 18 years of age
3. Family relocation cost: up to $1,000 (transportation of persons and goods).
4. Health insurance for 1 year for unmarried ex-employee and for chief breadwinner and family.
5. Mortgage and credit payment moratorium; or payments by federal government for one year, to be repaid without interest within the two years following, or at 6 percent interest thereafter.
6. Loans beyond the above payments, for as much as two years beyond retraining period.
7. To be administered by state employment offices, who will also be responsible for counseling on retraining occupations.
8. Eligibility: employment by military-contractor enterprise, or on a Department of Defense base, for at least one year.
9. Registration for employment required.

Occupational conversion, however, has no meaning without a reasonable prospect of employment. The main source of new work would be new public investments (Chapter Eight).[25] For engineers and other technicians a major new job opportunity could be opened up in state, city and county government.

State, city and county governments in the United States, unlike the federal government, have not been amply supplied with engineering and allied technical talents. Accordingly, an important part of the occupational conversion of military-engineering occupations could be a program to facilitate the movement of retrained engineers to local-government employment. Limited experience with such efforts has indicated that many cities that employ outside firms or consultants to do technical planning, analysis and administrative work would be better served if they had their own professionally competent staff to perform this work for them on an ongoing basis.[26] Preliminary explorations by the federal government disclosed that "there are 15,000 to 20,000 specialists who would like to work in urban affairs," and that "cities are able to pay better salaries than is generally believed, and many of those highly skilled people are now working as bartenders or are not working at all."

The indicated requirement is for a combination of sensible technical training on technologies that are important for state, city and town governments, in combination with a major job-placement program. The latter is precisely what has been lacking until now and could be efficiently spurred by a temporary subsidy program to induce the employment of retrained engineers and others by local governments. These governments could be encouraged to employ engineering and related personnel in productive activities like municipal engineer, teacher, urban planner, etc. A subsidy to encourage such employment could be granted in inverse proportion to the income per capita in the state or locality. Thus, in the first year a high-income area hiring one of these men would receive no more than 10 percent of the annual salary to be paid, while a low-income-per-capita locality would receive 75 percent of salary as a subsidy. By the third year the subsidy in the high-income locality would be down to 5 percent and the subsidy in the low-income locality would be reduced to 25 percent. Schemes of this sort could encourage utilization of productive talent and relocate men and women who are desirous of productive careers. It would also encourage the economically less developed parts of the country, who would, by the subsidy process, receive a substantial investment in "human capital" that would further their local economic development. The crucial ingredients are a job-placement effort on a large scale, combined with appropriate occupational retraining.[27]

Blue-collar production workers are in a rather different situation from the standpoint of transferring their skills to civilian industry. Careful studies on this problem have been performed by the federal Department of Labor and the state of California's Department of Employment.[28] In major California aerospace factories 127 production occupations were examined in detail. Of these, twenty-eight occupations were of the basic craft type (electrician, plumber, carpenter) and were readily matched to counterpart occupations in other industries. Of the ninety-nine missile-industry occupations that appeared to have special relationship to defense production, all but six could be matched with at least one nonmilitary occupation. Altogether, the skills of 121 of the 127 occupations were found to be transferable to civilian industry with not more than six months of retraining being required in any instance.

Demobilization of members of the uniformed armed forces in large numbers requires a major exercise in occupational conversion. Actually, the military departments' personnel services have considerable capability for occupational and retraining counseling in terms of skill transferability from military occupational specialties to civilian jobs. This has been a continuing function in the armed forces in connection with the retirement or other termination of military personnel. The continued operation of this mechanism against a background of new civilian job opportunities would meet the job-change needs of demobilizing members of the armed forces.

Even if a heavy majority of Americans should reject the war economy and its ideologies as a way of life, there would still be the power of the government and private institutions which comprise the military economy to be overcome before a conversion to civilian economy could be achieved. The last line of defense of war economy is the organized array of occupations whose livelihood has been dependent on it. A political-economic issue of large scope is involved, for the decision power of the managements, technical groups and trade unions in military industry is not defined merely by their role in these enterprises. The top one hundred military-serving firms are also a Who's Who of American industry. Virtually every major industrial firm is included. While the proportion of their total sales[29] represented by the military-space market is a minority fraction for all except the military-specialized aerospace, ordnance, electronics and shipbuilding enterprises, the managers of the Pentagon-serving divisions of major firms do not stand alone. They draw upon the position and power of their top managements who wield considerable political and economic clout.

When the total sales of a firm amount to, say, $1 billion, then 10 percent of that to the Pentagon is $100 million, and probably the largest sales volume to any single purchaser. These are sales quantities that usually require a major effort by the firm, and their loss would make a real difference to the fortunes of the enterprise.[30] The sales to the military also carry part of the burden of overhead costs in these firms.

Similar considerations apply to the trade unions that contain substantial components of military-industry workers. They may amount to no more than 15 percent of the membership of unions whose main base is in civilian-goods industry, but this is a concentrated 15 percent whose fortunes are affected by one Pentagon top management. Consider, as a speculation, that one third of the military-industry members are rendered unemployed. Statistically, that is only 5 percent of the union membership, but that addition to a "normal" national unemployment of 5 percent adds up to a catastrophic 10 percent unemployment, which substantially depletes the members' incomes and weakens the union's bargaining position vis-à-vis its employers. Furthermore, the concentrated character of this unemployment does not afford a good prognosis for reemployment, except in the presence of substantial new civilian economic activity. For these reasons, the managements of firms and the officers of unions and of professional societies may be expected to press for maintaining the war economy. Even in the presence of a major economic-conversion effort, the resistance of important parts of these groups is to be expected.

The issue finally reduces to one of political power. The decision power of political leaders and managers is not absolute. When a sufficient part of the population refuses to yield to the self-interested coercion of these groups, then alternative public policies are conceivable. The defeat of the SST program in 1972 is just such a case in point. An environmental issue gripped the imagination of enough people to cause them and a majority of the Congress to reject the economic claims and pressures of managers and trade-union officers in the aerospace industries who mounted an all-out campaign for the SST. In my judgment, the ongoing deterioration in economy and society due to the war economy can eventually evoke self-preservation instincts among enough people to produce a political challenge to the war-economy directorate.

The role of the Congress is important here and little understood.

For the occupation of many Congressmen has become, to a degree not yet defined, an adjunct to the war economy. Representatives and Senators are called upon by local economic interests to use their good offices with the Pentagon and the Space Agency to obtain contracts, grants and base locations in their districts and states. As such efforts proceed, Congressmen have become, in effect, marketing agents for local groups and clients in relation to the principal departments of government. Obviously, a conflict of interest has developed between the agent–client functions and the constitutional responsibility of Congressmen to legislate on the executive departments with respect to their activities and their money.

The relationship between the Pentagon, the Congress and military firms has developed into a pattern of reciprocal benefits. By its long history of almost automatic acquiescence to the recommendations of the state management on military funds, the Congress supports the state management, its political policies at home and abroad and the functioning of the military-industrial system. For its part, however, the state management often recommends location of military installations and war-economy facilities in Congressional districts and states that are strategic with respect to key Congressmen in the Senate and in the House.[31] This enables members of Congress to "bring home the bacon" to constituents in terms of jobs and capital funds. In 1961 the Kennedy-Johnson administration made an innovation in the contract-awards system by the state management. It became regular practice to give members of Congress as much as twenty-four hours' advance notice on contract awards. This allowed members of Congress to take the posture—whether justified or not—of having been instrumental in arranging the work allocation. In its report on the Senate vote ending this practice on August 5, 1970, *The New York Times* reported from Washington: "Within Congress-cloakrooms there has also been recurring gossip that some members of Congress or their friends were taking advantage of advance information on Defense contract awards to speculate in the stock market." Functionally, this is similar to the grant of special rewards like stock options to executives of a firm for having concluded major deals of benefit to the firm. It will surely require a major popular revulsion to turn the Congress away from the quest for prosperity through war economy.

Ten

DOES AMERICAN CAPITALISM NEED A WAR ECONOMY?

A WAR ECONOMY is one in which military spending is a continuing, significant and legitimate end-purpose of economic activity. The consensus belief among many Americans has been that without a war economy the system could revert to some version of the Great Depression.

However, we have already shown that the war economy caused substantial modifications in the capitalist system, from the firm on up, and that war economy has become a major source of corrosion of the productive competence of the American economy as a whole. From the standpoint of its destructive effect on American society, there is certainly doubt that war economy is a highly desirable alternative to a Great Depression. Nevertheless, there is both a body of economic theory and popular belief that proclaims that war economy is the only conceivable solution to the stagnation problem of capitalism.

Does war economy in fact have that quality of inevitability? Rather than an historically inevitable outcome of capitalist dynamics, the American war economy, in my judgment, is the combined result of economic and political factors, with the latter finally determining the recourse to militarism in the American case. Other major capitalist states did not follow the American pattern.

The record of the American economy before and during the Second World War, namely that the war brought prosperity, was apparently consistent with the theory of monopoly capitalism set forth by Paul Baran and Paul Sweezy.[1] Their essential thesis is that a business economy in the stage of development called "monopoly capitalism" creates large, unusable surpluses of capital and labor. Owing to the rigidities in the way monopoly capitalism functions, depressions result that are more severe than under competitive market capitalism. The government of such a capitalist economy can only place large orders for military goods as a durable strategy for ending or limiting economic stagnation, especially among the larger firms. Military goods alone, say the "monopoly-capitalism" theorists, are salable in indefinitely large quantities, do not compete with civilian goods in any existing civilian markets, and can be made obsolete (or destroyed in combat) at will—thereby "creating" fresh demand.

From these assumptions it is inferred that American capitalism has no choices other than war economy if it is to avoid a return to the Great Depression. If this theory were sufficient to explain the main political and economic performance of major capitalist economies since World War II, it would immensely simplify the understanding and definition of limits to possible responses to war economy.

In contrast to the assumption of a static, inflexible capitalism, it is my observation that the traditional dynamics of industrial capitalism continued while state capitalism and its institutions became dominant within American economy and in its relation to the rest of the world. In the pages that follow, I shall explore the relationship between militarism and economic growth (and stagnation), showing that an economic need for war economy is specific to the state-capitalist parts of the American economy but that such a need is not an intrinsic part of civilian economy. It will be seen that the traditional role of government in capitalism as the servant of business has been in transition. During the Cold War this relationship shifted toward collaboration, a partnership between government and big business. More recently, following the great institutional changes of the Kennedy-McNamara regime, a newer pattern emerged of business as the well-rewarded servant of government.

The thirty-year-old military economy of the United States has had an evolving functional relationship with the rest of American capitalism. The development has gone through three main phases.

First, during and after the Second World War, the military economy, seen from the vantage point of economic power, helped to maintain and extend the hegemony of American capitalism against German and Japanese challengers by producing the arms for the Allies of World War II. The available evidence indicates that this function was carried out in ways that also served the enlargement of the American territorial and economic empire (for example, by trading old U.S. destroyers for British islands), in addition to laying the groundwork for the Cold War struggle which later became the central justification for the military economy. The World War II military economy consisted of a collaboration between business and government that was dominated by U.S. corporate power. War production was directed by battalions of industry managers on temporary loan to war agencies that were largely dismantled by 1946. Not surprisingly, the major firms emerged from the four-year U.S. war experience with large additions to their assets, having been favored as purchasers of government-financed plant and equipment.

The second phase in the development of American military power was the Cold War period 1950–60, from the Korean War to the close of the Eisenhower administration. This period featured the primary use of military power, now unified in one Department of Defense, for the system maintenance and competitive extension of Western capitalism as a whole as against the hegemony of the U.S.S.R. and China. This decade saw rapid development of nuclear weapons—from the 20,000-ton TNT-equivalent fission weapons to the 1-million-ton-equivalent, and larger, weapon of the hydrogen-bomb class. Intercontinental missiles and nuclear-powered submarines were invented and put into large-scale production for the first time. Major military-political initiatives included the Korean War, the Marshall Plan (1948–52), the formation of the North Atlantic Treaty Organization, the Southeast Asia Treaty Organization and related alliances, U.S. support for the Yugoslav defection from the Soviets, and the application of overt and covert U.S. power to overthrow unfriendly governments in Guatemala and Iran. By means of an intricate network of agreements, U.S. military bases were established in thirty-five countries—to "contain" the U.S.S.R. and serve as a constant threat to anti-U.S., anti-business-economy movements. At the same time, direct U.S. business investments abroad leaped forward from $11.8 billion in 1950 to $31.9 billion by 1960.

This second phase of the development of military economy was also noteworthy for implementation of the doctrine of government-business partnership as formulated by the U.S. Army Chief of Staff, General Dwight Eisenhower, in 1946. The text of the policy memorandum that defined this relationship was first published in my *Pentagon Capitalism* and constitutes the charter for what President Eisenhower in January 1961 christened the "military-industrial complex."

The third phase of the development of the American war economy, beginning in 1961, was the establishment of a formal organization for centralized management of the military economy. The government-based top management designed by Robert McNamara was thereby made the master of business-operated military industry. (This was accomplished by means of the managerial-control organization that I diagnosed in *Pentagon Capitalism*.) Once the new state managerial-control system was set in motion it exhibited the normal managerial imperative for enlarging its organization and the scope and intensity of its decision power. In accordance with the characteristics of the new state management, the military institutions and economy and the subordinate civilian economy were all utilized for the primary purpose of maintaining and enlarging the decision power of the state-capitalist (war-economy) managers.

The latest phase of the U.S. war economy involved a basic change in the mechanisms of capitalist economy by which capital investment is translated into decision power. Under business capitalism this is accomplished by a cycle that includes investment, marketing a product to regain the investment plus a profit, then ordering a new investment with the enlarged capital fund. Under the state-controlled military economy, the top management also invests capital. Here, however, it is translated directly into instrumentalities of decision power—military organizations and their equipment. From the vantage point of its top management, the

state-capitalist-controlled military economy includes no intervening market mechanism for recycling capital as in civilian economy.
Capital has only a one-time use in the military sphere, and thus the
application to decision power is direct.

Notwithstanding such changes in the institutions of capitalism,
the older business forms continued even while new ones dominated the scene. This process is a characteristic of the evolving
capitalist economy which is visible in other spheres as well. For
example, the appearance of very large firms and their domination
of many industries did not lead to the total disappearance of small
business. The growth of chain stores and shopping centers has
proceeded even while large numbers of small retail establishments
flourish. Similarly, the introduction of the new, formally structured
state capitalism did not require the disappearance of the older
functions served by military economy even though they were not
given first priority. This process of continuing older functions even
while new ones are made dominant has been visible in the U.S.
government's performance in Indochina and in the handling of a
series of other major political-economic decisions, including the
U.S. investment in Western Europe, the disposition of the Vietnam
War "peace dividend," the policy on encouraging U.S. exports, and
the Lockheed loan problem of 1971.

As the French rule was defeated in Vietnam, the United States
government sought to replace it by intervening to support conservative rulers. Historians of the Indochina War have noted that
the internal documents prepared by U.S. policy-makers from 1949
to 1960 included recurring references to a raw-materials potential
in Vietnam and neighboring states (Cambodia, Laos, Thailand)—
rice, rubber, teak, corn, tin, spices, tungsten, copra, iron ore and
oil. But the statistics of U.S. imports for 1960 and 1971 do not
confirm this portrait. In 1960 only two commodities were imported
to the U.S. from this area with a value exceeding $5 million each.
These were "rubber and allied gums" worth $48 million and "vege-
tables and preparations" worth $6.8 million. Of the rubber, $38.7
million was from Thailand and $3 million from Vietnam. In 1971,
the main commodity exports to the U.S. from Vietnam and neighboring states were $9 million of rubber and $49 million of "tin and
alloys" from Thailand.[2]

By 1973, U.S. firms had investments in Vietnam with a book
value of about $10 million. Of this, $8.5 million were the assets of

two firms distributing petroleum products. The rest was composed
of the value of branches of four U.S. banks, a U.S.-owned dairy in
Saigon and an investment in a shrimping enterprise. Two U.S. oil
companies were among four firms granted offshore petroleum-
drilling concessions by the Saigon government in 1973. I am
advised that by 1978 the oil potential of the area should be established. At this writing it's noteworthy that serious interest in an oil
potential in and around Vietnam was not indicated in oil industry
and other literature until about 1970.[3]

All this does not add up to a foreign-trade or investment stake
by American firms in and around Vietnam such as to account for a
classical imperial economic interest of a size and character to
explain the U.S. war in Indochina—direct U.S. military cost, $150
billion. An economic trade-investment explanation of the U.S. war
can be made only if the area at issue is taken to be all of Asia. But
that requires an almost limitless "domino-theory" assumption.
(Thus: if Vietnam goes, then Cambodia, Thailand, Laos; if those,
then Burma, Malaysia and then Indonesia; if all those, then India,
Japan; then, by extension, "we" will finally be fighting "them" on
the beaches of California, etc.)

Since the economic data do not support an explanation of the
U.S. war in Vietnam as a classic trade-investment imperialism
exercise, how can we account for that long, bloody and costly war
by the U.S. government?

In the classic Marxist view the U.S. war in Vietnam was a form
of "political-military overhead charge" for the operation of traditional economic imperialism. However, economic-interest poten-
tials were not in evidence from 1950 to 1970 while U.S. operations
to control the governments of Vietnam were being intensified.
From Kennedy on, there was no indication of any serious U.S.
trade or investment interest in Vietnam or the neighboring countries until 1970, when technical data became available concerning
the possible existence of large oil deposits off the coast of Indochina in the archipelago extending to the southeast. From 1954 to
1970, in the absence of current active economic interest for the
United States in Indochina, the U.S. government began vigorous
sponsorship of governments in that area to frustrate the possible
establishment of Soviet-type economies or governments that might
be ideologically oriented to the East. The U.S. government's
interventions in Vietnam have extended over twenty years, and the

American military's Vietnam War as a major operation endured from 1964 until 1973. The expenditure of over $150 billion of U.S. government funds and the operation of a major war that took more than fifty thousand American lives and an immense toll in Indochinese lives and property is best explained in terms of the requirements for enlarging the decision power of America's state managers. From 1973 on, the U.S. government's involvement in Vietnam was mainly indirect, via heavy military assistance and economic support to the Thieu regime.

In the eyes of the managers of America's state capitalism, Vietnam was the great testing ground for direct application of the new tools available to them. The methods of the new imperialism included direct wielding of military, political and economic power to checkmate leftist nationalism and to take direct political control of entire nations—without relying on, and even in the absence of, economic mechanisms of trade and investment that were basic to the older imperialism.*

---

* There is a related issue: how can we begin to account for the pattern of promises about raw-material riches for the U.S. that was repeatedly invoked by the writers of internal U.S. government policy memoranda as recorded in the Pentagon Papers? See G. Kolko, "The American Goals in Vietnam," *The Pentagon Papers,* Sen. Gravel Edition, Beacon Press, 1972, Vol. 5. With the help of Kolko's essay, we can readily identify the sources of these policy documents. Kolko's carefully documented essay accepts these statements of economic interest at face value. However, since the available data of trade and investment do not sustain that thesis, it is worth inquiring further into the origins of these documents and the function served by these statements.

The Pentagon Papers include ten major documents from 1950 to 1954 that assert a U.S. economic-strategic interest in raw materials that could originate in Vietnam and adjacent countries. No data on such raw materials are given or referred to in any of the Pentagon Papers that would indicate their possible significance to the U.S. economy or U.S. firms. Apart from one State Department document (1940) and one paragraph in an Eisenhower address (1954), the 1950–54 documents stating a U.S. raw-materials stake in Indochina came from the National Security Council, the Joint Chiefs of Staff and the special committee that controls the CIA. The main thrust of these documents was elaboration of "domino-theory" reasoning. I am reliably informed that the staffs of the National Security Council, 1950–54, were oriented to the task of avoiding a reversion to pre–World War II "isolationism." The economic case that they made in their policy memoranda was designed to exploit, simultaneously, fears of depression that were endemic in the Congress and elsewhere. Also, NSC staffers tried to make a case for the importance of an area and hence used economic rationalization for "domino-theory" political logic. It is likely that U.S. military leaders, after the Korean experience, were wary of involvement in East Asian wars.

There remains the possibility, undefined at this writing, of exploitable oil

By 1965, the new state-managerial institutions in the Pentagon and the White House were fully developed and Assistant Secretary of Defense John T. McNaughton prepared a policy memorandum on "Proposed Course of Action re Vietnam" for his immediate chief, Robert McNamara. McNaughton's formulation included the following.[4]

US aims:

70%   —to avoid a humiliating US defeat (to our reputation as a guarantor).

20%   —to keep SVN (and then adjacent) territory from Chinese hands.

10%   —to permit the people of SVN to enjoy a better, freer way of life.

ALSO—to emerge from crisis without unacceptable taint from methods used.

NOT —to "help a friend," although it would be hard to stay in if asked out.

In context, "our reputation as a guarantor" meant the decision power of the U.S. state managers. Thus the main functions served by U.S. military power and economy since the Second World War have been present in Indochina, including system competition with the U.S.S.R. and China and extension of the decision power of the chiefs of America's state capitalism. At this writing the sum of evidence sustains the conclusion that the principal factor has been the latter function of maintaining and enlarging the decision power of the state management.

The American involvement in Western European economies also illustrates the multiplicity of functions served by the military economy. The U.S. government encouraged investment by American firms in Western Europe, partly in the name of extending economic control by major American firms (function No. 1) but also in the name of shoring up the business capitalist economies of Western Europe as against the Soviet system or possible local social revolution (function No. 2). However, it was the requirement of the state management for its operations (function No. 3) that has finally come to dominate the scene.

Under the strong sponsorship of the state management, U.S.

---

reserves off Indochina. But such a development would not account for the policy formulations of 1950–54.

direct foreign investments have grown rapidly, with the result that profits from overseas operations grew from 8.8 to 15.0 percent of total corporate profits from 1960 to 1970. However, a parallel pile-up of dollars in foreign central banks, caused by sustained military spending, produced a hitherto unforeseen peril to the security of U.S. corporate investments—especially in Western European countries. Foreign governments holding over 50 billion U.S. dollars could induce "American-owned subsidiaries to sell a substantial part of their common stock to host-country residents . . ."[5] Payment would be in dollars, held in abundance by Western European central banks. In 1972 one government earmarked $100 million of its dollar holdings for a start on this process.[6] By this mechanism the war economy generated a situation that could checkmate important parts of the extension of U.S. corporate investments abroad, thereby reversing a process that the state managers had strongly fostered by tax inducements and by the worldwide implicit threat to use military power in support of U.S. policies.

Another example of how the state managers gave priority to their needs was the handling of the "peace dividend." As late as mid-1971, sophisticated economic analysts were anticipating a "peace dividend"[7] as a consequence of U.S. withdrawal from Vietnam. (The actual record of U.S. military budgets, as I showed in the first chapter, only shows signs of a permanent war economy.) For U.S. civilian economy a "peace dividend" could have been a real boon. If $25 billion of Indochina War money had been invested in neglected areas of economy and society starting in 1972, there would have been a major beginning toward reversing the trend of war economy. That would have been true even if the "peace dividend" money had been used for nothing more imaginative than an across-the-board tax reduction. But such a policy is precisely what is intolerable to the managers of the war economy, who proceeded to use up the conceivable "peace dividend" in new military projects.

Many U.S. firms have done well in foreign trade and have often received political and even military support from the U.S. government for facilitating investment and trade.[8] However, recent federal efforts to promote American economic operations abroad are contradicted by incompatible aims of the war-economy directorate.

While the federal government has been encouraging exports by making available easy credits to purchasers through the Export-Import Bank, and the president of the Export-Import Bank complains about the low-pressure attitude of many U.S. firms toward exporting, the main thrust of the federal government's military economy has been toward diminishing the export competence of U.S. civilian firms. This is accomplished by the priority given to military industry in the use of capital and talent. As between the incompatible functions of facilitating U.S. civilian industrial exports and supporting the decision power of the state management, the weight of government policy has given priority to the latter function.

A major effect of these contradictory policies is visible in the performance of the machinery and mining industries. As producers of the means of production, these industries have a nuclear importance for every industrial economy. By 1963 it was evident that for the capital-goods (machinery and mining) industries of the United States the sale of goods to the federal government far exceeded their exports to other countries. In 1963 the portion of the output of twenty-four capital-goods-producing industries going to exports was 11.1 percent, while 21.7 percent was purchased by the federal government.[9] Clearly, the military market that dominates federal machinery purchases far outweighs export sales. Moreover, as the cost- and subsidy-growth patterns of the military economy permeate the capital-goods firms they are made less competent to operate in international markets.

Priority attention to the decision-power requirements of the state management has also been visible in the handling of international balance-of-payments problems. In June 1973 the U.S. government announced that "it makes good sense with a balance of payments problem" to promote U.S. arms sales. The *New York Times* report indicated that "another reason, stressed less, is that with the decline in arms for the Vietnam war, American producers need new markets. This had led to increased pressure from American manufacturers on the Administration to adopt a more liberal attitude."[10] Officials of the state management seized upon the balance-of-payments problem (which they had been instrumental in creating) as justification for enlarging foreign orders and sales from the aerospace-industry firms (which they direct) in order to keep them occupied, thereby "maintaining the industrial base"—

their own decision power, that is. Other options for coping with balance-of-payments or military-industry problems were obviously ruled out. U.S. international-payments problems could be basically resolved by a reduction in military operations around the world, and hence in U.S. dollar spending abroad. Problems of finding activity for many military-industry firms could conceivably be resolved by converting them to civilian operations. But these options would not serve to maintain or extend the power of the state management, and were consequently ignored.

Another example of the new dominance of the state-capitalist economy and its requirements was visible in the participation of private bankers in the campaign to get the federal government to guarantee a loan of $250 million to the Lockheed Corporation in mid-1971. The Bankers Trust Company is a principal creditor of the Lockheed Corporation, and its president, William H. Moore, explained at the time, "I don't see a helluva lot of this stuff [aerospace industry] being financed out of the private sector in the future." He further stated that with respect to military industry as well as civilian-industry financing, "the banks just aren't growing fast enough to take these enormous risks."[11] Here was the president of a major private bank announcing that he and his colleagues could no longer serve their traditional bankers' function for major parts of the U.S. economy, requiring government participation in the future.

The financial crisis of the Lockheed Corporation in 1971 affords a major demonstration of how problems of war economy were dealt with in ways that at once gave priority to the requirements of the state management and served to protect the system as a whole by ensuring the profitability of a very important capitalist enterprise. When the management of the Lockheed Corporation asked the federal government for a guarantee of $250 million of further loans from private banks, this signaled the incapability of the Lockheed management to cope with the firm's ongoing problems. This could have been dealt with in many ways, including drastic replacement of the Lockheed top management, allowing the firm to go into bankruptcy and reorganizing its operations, and allowing its civilian aircraft business to be taken up by another airplane manufacturer, while separating the civilian from the military operations of Lockheed so that each could be organized and operated in a profitable way thereafter. These options were selectively rejected by the state management. As a result of the loan-supporting action approved by the Congress, not only was the Lockheed Corporation and its management preserved intact, but the bankers and airlines that had advanced funds to Lockheed were saved from financial disruption; subsidy-maximization was ensured for Lockheed and the array of associated firms. That decision served to maintain an important part of the state management's war economy and managerial team, while extending the decision power of the state management to a great network of banks, suppliers and airline customers involved with the Lockheed Corporation.

This behavior of the state management is also noteworthy for its ordinariness. It is entirely consistent with the long-standing mores of capitalist industrial management, whose fundamental rule is to operate with priority to the maintenance and extension of decision power. The state management has complied with that rule. In fact, the relentless drive for power that it has exhibited within American economy and society has only one other counterpart: the imperial expansion of U.S. economic, military and political power around the world. The addition of domestic to external imperialism, both state-propelled, is the central contribution of the state management to American society.

Some observers of industrial capitalism have focused on continuity in the thrust for decision power by corporations as a basis for the judgment that the main interior power relations of the system are not altered by the development of state-capitalist institutions. Thus the larger industrial employers and private bankers were for a long time the masters in capitalism, while governments were—literally or figuratively—their servants. But this view of industrial management's link to government does not account for the changed power relations under state capitalism. Consider, for example, the familiar pattern of government-to-industry and industry-to-government exchanges of top-management officials. Many writers have tended to view the transfer of people from top echelons of private firms to government departments as evidence of the dominance of private industrial managements over the operation of the federal government.[12] Actually, managers must perform in accordance with the criteria of the organizations that they operate. A successful manager in most of private civilian-serving industry will be a cost-minimizer. Upon his transferring to the Pentagon his success requires attention to cost- and subsidy-maximizing routines. By setting performance require- ments, the institution dominates the individual. But the inter- change of people plays an important part in the continuation of older functions even while the main thrust of the state manage- ment is on behalf of its own functional goals.

It is therefore not true that the present condition of American capitalism is merely a continuation of what was there before. The large firms are still there and their chiefs wield far more political influence than any other definable group of citizens. No govern- ment can function without their approval and cooperation. How- ever, as decision-makers over capital and technology, these firms, as institutions, take second place to the new managerial groups located at the peak of the federal government. The directorate of the Pentagon initiates policies that would ordinarily be opposed by managers of private firms on grounds of self-interest. These in- clude policies that produce domestic inflation and devaluation of the dollar, and that transfer control of capital from the chiefs of private firms to the chiefs of the federal government. None of this is to say that the chiefs of private capitalism are lacking in major political influence on the operation of government. It is to say, however, that their influence is operative within a state-capitalist- dominated economy to which they acquiesce in the name of the services rendered to them. But the state-capitalist economy has operating characteristics rather different from and often contra- dictory to those of their firms.

This bears closely on the issue of who are the final decision- makers over the military economy. The term "final decision-maker" identifies the person or group whose decision cannot be vetoed by anyone else. Is that function performed by the managers of the principal military-industry firms or is that power in the hands of the state management, whose chief is the President of the United States?

When the White House and the state-management chiefs de- cided in the early 1960s that a new bomber program was not desired, they were able to override all the pressures that derived from the Air Force and the various military-industry firms with a stake in this project. Years later, in 1971, the White House and the Pentagon chiefs decided to pursue a new heavy-bomber program. At that time, however, there was a difference of judgment among the President's advisers in the Bureau of the Budget and the military-security staff of the White House. The differences were settled by Presidential action in favor of the bomber.

There is further evidence on the location of final decision power in the war economy in the way reductions in military research and production were carried out in 1969–70. At that time I visited a number of major military-industry firms to discover from them the procedures that were followed in their relation to the Department of Defense during this period. I discovered that the cutbacks in military-industry activity were carried out without prior consultation or notification of the managements of the military-industry firms. They were given peremptory orders to curtail specific activities. The firms were dealt with as one would expect a top management to deal with the submanagements who operate divisions of the enterprise. In this case the top management is the state management of the White House–Pentagon, and the submanagements are the chiefs of the principal military-industry firms. Military firms, mayors of cities with military bases, and others with economic interests in the allocation of military work attempt to influence the decisions on allocation of military-economy funds. They can often negotiate a more desirable result for themselves, depending on their political and financial clout. What is crucial here is the definition of who is the final decision-maker in the war-economy system, whose decision cannot be vetoed. On the evidence, final decision-makers are the political chiefs of the state management.

Within the framework of the military economy itself, both primarily military enterprises and arms-producing parts of civilian firms have been tied into and made subordinate to the senior officers of government. Thus, the control over these institutions is, finally, by political means. The Pentagon-controlled military economy intertwines with the civilian economy and produces increasing dependence of the latter on the former. Thus, the one hundred largest "defense contractors" include the larger enterprises of the civilian industrial system. Each of these firms has a significant number of divisions devoted to servicing the Pentagon's state management.

In combination with the state-management control that penetrates into the military branches of larger private firms, the administrative powers of the federal government limit power for autonomous decision-making by the managements of the private (civilian) economy as well. Thus, the private firms are beholden to the federal government for approvals, licenses and permissions, which include such vital matters as the handling of taxes and the interpretation of myriad rules. Thereby the managers of nominally private firms are increasingly administered by the managers of state capitalism even in their "private" economic operations.[13] Moreover, the chiefs of the war economy, by their central control of capital and technical resources, have imposed their requirements on the civilian part of the economy and thereby have altered the characteristics of capitalism as a whole.

Characteristically, the writers of the "monopoly-capitalism" school have given primary attention to the consequences from the growth of the largest firms with the concentration of business-capitalist decision-making in their hands. The relation of a big corporation-dominated economy to government has been understood as a continuation of the pre–World War II economic era in which government was primarily the servant of its private-business master. This view of capitalism has emphasized the elements of continuity in the economy: the employment relationship, profit-taking, competition for investment opportunity and markets at home and abroad. Assumed throughout is the idea that not only was the state used to pull the monopoly capitalists' chestnuts out of the Great Depression fire by means of war economy, but the experience so gained made war economy into the monopoly capitalists' inevitably preferred alternative to a return to economic stagnation.

Moreover, the theorists of monopoly capitalism make no allowance for the growth of a new center of economic decision-making, the state management, which is endowed with all the production decision-making characteristics that should identify a capitalist ruling class in the tradition of Marx.

A managerial-hierarchical institutional network as big as a military economy has a built-in tendency for self-perpetuation and self-expansion. The larger the operation, the more specialized the jobs and the longer its duration, the stronger will be the pressures to continue it. From the standpoint of the people most directly involved, it is their competence, their living, the defining factor in their place in society. If nothing more were present, these factors would be strong incentives to continue the operation. But the military economy of the United States has a lot more going for it than the impulse of large organizations to perpetuate themselves. The Pentagon's economy has come to dominate the national economy. Its institutionalized thrust for extending its decision power at home and abroad has been fueled by annual grants of fresh capital that exceed the national product of most countries of the world. Its directors, administrators, technicians and workers are especially well rewarded. For many firms and institutions the military economy is, in fact, indispensable.

The final element of the monopoly-capitalism thesis is that the monopoly capitalists can and do enforce their preference for war economy as against a Great Depression because war economy is a competent instrument for inducing economic growth. Let us submit the monopoly-capitalism thesis to some straightforward tests of validity on its own grounds.

Assume that the thesis is valid, that war economy has been and continues to be the necessary solution for sustaining business profitability and for disposing of economic surpluses that limit growth and induce general stagnation in capitalism. If that were indeed the case, then the following effects should be observable: (1) the record of U.S. military spending, its rise and fall, should correspond with the rise and fall of corporate profits; (2) among capitalist economies, more intense war-economy activity should correspond with greater intensity in economic activity generally; and, finally, (3) business capitalist economies as a group should show greater intensity of military spending than other economies. The economic record since World War II has important bearing on these issues.

On the first effect: The rise and fall of military spending has not correlated with the rise and fall of corporate profits. The drop in U.S. military spending following World War II did not trigger the creation of vast economic surpluses. On the contrary, from 1946 to 1950 employment, general economic activity and business profits all rose. The U.S. entry into the Korean War occurred in 1950 while American corporate profits after taxes totaled $24.9 billion; after two years of this war, profits were down to $19.6 billion. Hence, the end of World War II led to an acceleration of corporate profits, and two years of the Korean War were followed by a diminution in corporate profit-taking. Corporate profits then rose as the Korean War was ended. Thereafter, profits showed uneven development until 1960, while military spending varied between $38 billion and $46 billion yearly. From 1960 to 1966 annual profits soared from $27 billion to $50 billion while Presidents Kennedy and Johnson raised military spending from $45 billion to $60 billion yearly. Thereafter the Vietnam War was escalated, with government spending on goods and services for the military being enlarged from $50 billion in 1965 to $78 billion in 1969. In parallel, corporate profits dropped from a peak of $50 billion in 1966 to $40 billion by 1970.[14]

I am advised that early in the 1950s the federal government's National Security Council made a policy decision that henceforth about 10 percent of the nation's gross national product should be regularly applied to military-security purposes. This decision was an integral part of the (second phase) main Cold War strategy of American leaders: to apply the industrial and economic power of the United States to win a worldwide contest for system maintenance versus the Soviets. Thus, the sustained high levels of U.S. military-economy activity during the 1950s and 1960s cannot be explained as a response to low profitability or to accumulating economic surpluses, but as a result of government policy. By 1965, when Lyndon Johnson began to sharply escalate military activity and war economy for the Indochina War, the U.S. economy as a whole was operating at a high level of activity. Thus the escalation of war economy on behalf of the Indochina War, like the record from 1945 to 1970, cannot be described as a response to problems of growing economic surplus, however defined. As the Pentagon Papers show in abundant detail, the U.S. war in Indochina was the power-extending enterprise of the new state-capitalist managers. The rise and fall of military spending showed no necessary correspondence with the general rise and fall of corporate profits.

The second effect inferred from the monopoly-capitalism thesis is that among capitalist economies more military-economy activity should correspond with more effective resolution of an economic-surplus problem and hence with greater economic growth. On this issue it is relevant to examine the performance of three major capitalist economies: the United States, the Federal Republic of Germany and Japan. (Together, these countries accounted for 45 percent of the world's production of electricity by 1970.) The table below shows military spending as a percent of the gross national product as of 1968 for each of these countries. This percentage depicts the intensity of war economy in those countries. Clearly, the United States leads the way in military spending. The average growth rate in output per employee-hour in manufacturing in each of these countries for 1975–80 is also given.[15]

	Military Spending as Percent of Gross National Product, 1980	Growth Rate in Manufacturing Output per Employee-Hour 1975–80
United States	5.5	1.7
Federal Republic of Germany	3.3	4.3
Japan	0.9	8.0

Here again the differences among these three capitalist economies are substantial. However, if it were the case that greater intensity of war-economic activity corresponds with less economic stagnation and hence greater economic growth, then one would expect that the largest growth rate in output per employed person would have occurred in the United States and the lowest growth rate would have occurred in Japan. The reverse was actually the case. This outcome is not consistent with the attempt to explain levels of military spending in monopoly capitalism as offsets to economic stagnation.*

* Some observers have sought to explain the more rapid growth rates of Germany, Japan and other Western capitalist economies as a result of more activist policies to encourage investment, and a "leapfrogging" effect in using new technology. True, these countries encouraged investment. But all that was on a lesser scale than the U.S. effort, which was, however, a priority investment in nonproductive military economy that had a depressing effect on American industrial productivity. Neither was there any autonomous technological factor which determined the considerable differences in growth rates between, on the one hand, the United States and, on the other, Germany and Japan. True, these countries did have to build much of their industrial capacities from scratch after World War II. But that was more than 25 years ago, and, since most machinery is usually written off for replacement in about 10 years, we are, at this writing, in the third equipment cycle since World War II. Furthermore, insofar as managers in all these countries sought to minimize cost, the selection of the preferred types and mix of machinery and manpower for doing given work was determined by the relative prices of machinery and labor. This, and not any autonomous technological factor, controls the intensity of mechanization and consequent levels of productivity. See S. Melman, *Dynamic Factors in Industrial Productivity*, Basil Blackwell, John Wiley, 1954.

The third logical consequence of the monopoly-capitalism thesis that I suggested above is that business capitalist economies as a group should show greater intensity of military-economic activity than other economies, since, by hypothesis, the business capitalist nations are notably vulnerable to self-induced stagnation and hence dependent on war economy as an accelerator of economic activity. Actually, the data of major states for 1968, 1970, and 1980 show a rather different portrait. National military expenditures in percent of gross national product appeared as follows.[16]

	1968	1970	1980
United States	9.2	7.8	5.5
U.S.S.R.	9.3	10.0	14.6
China	9.0	11.0	8.5

Ignoring the inevitable problems of variation in the quality of these data, these statistics do not support the inference from the theory of monopoly capitalism—that the United States, as the leading economy of this kind, would necessarily have a greater intensity of military spending than other types of economies. Neither is it valid, as is sometimes alleged, that levels of military economy in the U.S. and the U.S.S.R. are in fact determined by the "defense" need of each country, given the level of military initiative by the other side. Thus it has been argued that the U.S. level is owing to causes inherent in monopoly capitalism, while the U.S.S.R. must then respond to "defend" itself. But it is well established that both the U.S. and the U.S.S.R. wield military power that is far into the overkill range and hence not explicable in either country by rational military-power considerations. Similar reasoning from the limits of military power applies if one begins with the case that the U.S. is merely responding to the U.S.S.R. Moreover, these limits obtain regardless of one's opinion about which state was mainly responsible for the Cold War.

To be sure, the military establishments of the U.S. and the U.S.S.R. also serve as "umbrella" military forces for the networks of states that are allied to each of these two superpowers. Comparable information on military expenditures as a portion of gross national product is available for sixteen states allied to the United

States. This shows an average of 3.4 percent. Also, for 1968 we have parallel information for six Eastern-bloc states allied to the U.S.S.R. Here the military percent of gross national product was 4.1.[17] Since the measures that are summarized here are subject to unknown errors of estimate, I am not prepared to dwell on the possible significance of the differences that appear. This much, however, is evident: from the economic-surplus-under-monopoly-capitalism thesis one would expect a particularly high level of military expenditures as a portion of gross national product in the major and minor capitalist states as compared to the Eastern-bloc economies. There is no evidence here of such a difference.

In sum, the evidence of military spending and economic growth among countries and within the United States does not support the theory that war economy is an economically derived necessity, specific to monopoly capitalism. This conclusion is confirmed by a study of the relationship between military spending, growth and stagnation for eighteen nations by Albert Szymanski.[18] The war economy of the United States, with its great network of enterprises and employees and with expenditures of one and a half trillion dollars since 1946 cannot be explained as an offset to economic surplus in industrial capitalism. For the permanent war economy has itself become a generator of surplus capital and surplus labor (Chapter Four). The fact that the war economy of World War II was useful for ending the Great Depression became the basis for a theory that there was no other way to get a full-employment economy. Hence, from an empirical observation that war production restored prosperity, a theory of necessity, of indispensability, of war production to prosperity was derived.

Who Needs a War Economy?

Consider that many elements of economy or technology may be useful to one or another sector of a capitalist economy but still be dispensable. Child labor was once highly useful to businessmen, but it proved to be dispensable. Unorganized workers were replaced in many enterprises by unionized workers. Workers' liability for industrial accidents was replaced by systems of workmen's compensation. Unchecked freedom to pollute the natural environment is being replaced by constraints on such practices. Child labor, unorganized and uninsured employees, and freedom to pollute have indeed been serviceable and useful to businessmen. But these conditions were not indispensable for survival of the capitalist system. Primary decision power by the employer was retained as employees continued to do his now constrained bidding. The hierarchical organization of the employer's management continued, as did the managerial imperative to extend its decision power. Capitalism continued, though modified. Businessmen had to operate with new costs, and production decision-making took on qualities of bilateralism as unions were accorded a formal voice in various aspects of production decisions.

Indispensability is a quality of need that implies an unchangeable connection, without alternatives. That kind of connection between capitalism and war economy has been advanced by the theorists of "monopoly capitalism." As we have seen, that approach does not explain the incidence of war economy. Instead, I propose to identify principal occupational and industrial groups within American capitalism for whom war economy is indispensable. For whom is the need real and for whom is it illusory?

If war economy is not an inherent economic necessity of capitalism, then the American war economy stems from noneconomic political requirements of American society. I have shown that the need for war economy is differentiated by occupation, class, industry, locality and political values and that the need for war economy is economically real for a part of American society but an ideologically induced necessity for the rest. Necessity in this context means, for example, that for the highly specialized military occupations the disappearance of this employment would entail a great crisis. In the chapter on conversion I identified the military officer and the military-industry and military-base employees whose occupations are specialized in the service of military economy. The main point here is that war economy is indispensable for some occupations and institutions and is serviceable to others, and that both these groups comprise a minority of American society. For the rest, the ideological consensus about the need for war economy is an ideologically induced illusion at variance with reality.

War economy is indispensable for the directorate of the state management that controls America's state capitalism. It is indispensable, too, for the bulk of the sales and profits of the leading military-industry firms that specialize in serving the Pentagon. Dependence on the Pentagon is assured by prevention of planning for civilian alternatives at all levels. The same kind of necessity also applies to the large specialized staffs of the federal government's security agencies (the CIA and the National Security Agency), as well as the members of Congress who have become specialists in contract liaison with the Pentagon, and the corps of intellectuals who have become specialists in the ideologies that serve the war economy.

In addition, there is an array of occupations that find the military economy useful and valuable while not necessarily indispensable. Foremost among these are the industrial managements with a minority of sales to the military, either as prime contractors or as subcontractors. These firms would continue to function, perhaps at lower levels, without military contracts. (It should be recalled that there are about twenty thousand firms that "prime contract" to the Department of Defense and about five times that many subcontractors.)

Announcements by military firms place emphasis on both the direct and the indirect, or ripple-effect, employment stemming from new military-contract activity in the particular enterprise. For example, when the Grumman Aerospace Corporation announced in December 1972 that it might halt production on the F-14 fighter because it was not being paid enough by the Pentagon, Grumman said, according to a news story, that the total impact was

> far more extensive than the 136 prime Grumman subcontractors. Each prime subcontractor has itself subcontracted with anywhere from ten to twenty-five other companies and this so-called "ripple effect" is expected to land at least 2,000 corporations in the middle of the F-14 controversy . . . All told it was estimated that some ten thousand different companies including 800 on Long Island are involved in some aspect of the F-14 subcontracting and procurement.[19]

Such accounts imply that the military system is indispensable to all of the subcontracting firms.

The mercantile and service industries that cater to the multi-million armed-forces and military-industry markets obviously find the military economy highly serviceable to their business. The Army Times Publishing Company, on January 22, 1971, defined its market to potential advertisers as follows.

In 1970 military consumers bought enough color film to photograph the entire population of China, one at a time. They bought enough cosmetics to make up all the young blondes in Sweden. Enough soft drinks to fill up the *Queen Elizabeth II*. Enough frozen food to stack 9,000 miles high. The military consumer market gave "birth" to more babies than any city in America. More, in fact, than the two largest cities combined. Per household, *Army Times, Navy Times* and *Air Force Times* readers own four times as many tape recorders, three times as many dishwashers, more than twice as many movie cameras than civilians. Our market buys more food, proprietary drugs, soaps and detergents, automobiles and commercial air travel. And they probably buy more of what *you* sell. It's BIG. And it's growing.

The fact is, however, that these goods would also be sold to the same people if they were earning comparable incomes in civilian-economy occupations.

The war economy includes institutional arrangements that amplify on the themes of its necessity and usefulness and that lock in managements, stockholders and the work force to the way of life that it provides. Industrial managements are given assurance at closed-door meetings of the Pentagon's Industry Advisory Council that profits on defense contracts will be maintained and enlarged at more than satisfactory levels. The nominally private bankers of the United States have been trained to finance military-industry operations with their patterned incompetence. The banker takes little risk. He expects that whenever failure threatens a military-industry firm it will finally be bailed out by the war-economy directorate following a plea of danger to the economy as a whole. William Henry Moore, the chairman of the Bankers Trust Company, made such a plea as the Congress was considering the special legislation to underwrite $250 million of further loans to the Lockheed Corporation.[20]

My contacts with trade unions of blue-collar workers and orga-nizations of engineers in military industry have shown that con-trary to independent assessment of their convertibility, they fear-fully regard the war economy as indispensable to their livelihood, especially in the absence of serious plans for an enlarged civilian economy. To preserve their military-industry jobs they have learned to participate in mobilizing political pressures for con-tinuation of war economy. This process was brought to wide public attention during the public debates on the SST, where they lost, and on the federal underwriting of the Lockheed Corporation, where they won. By such participation, and by ignoring alternatives to war work, they make their dependency a self-fulfilling prophecy.[21]

Many scientists doing basic research have come to see their fortunes as investigators as inevitably tied to the power and budgets of the Pentagon. The number of people so involved is not counted and probably amounts to no more than a few thousand. But their qualitative importance to the military is substantial, both as sources of knowledge and as a means for recruiting bright young people for the direct and indirect services of the military establishment. The genesis of this sort of relationship between scientists and the military was in the World War II Manhattan Project that made the atomic bomb, and the allied military technology efforts in the Western world during and after that war. After their World War II victory, the armed services were able to get immense funds for research in the name of "defense" and the competition with the Soviets. Even though the money for basic research was always a minority part of these military R&D budgets, these millions of dollars were the key resources for expanding and sustaining many laboratories in the basic sciences in American universities. With this background it was feasible for the military to establish, via the Institute for Defense Analyses, the Jason Group, a team of elite scientists who consult for the Pentagon on military-technical problems. The chief administrators and staffs of universities, technical institutes and other educational and research organizations that receive large military-agency support are also part of the network of occupations for whom the military economy is serviceable. I am advised that among some of these institutions subsidy systems have operated via the simple device of loose control over generous overhead payments.

"Need" for war economy may also be viewed in terms of the vital profit-making and investment function of capitalism. During the thirty-year-long war economy, American corporations enjoyed an increase in the absolute level of corporate profits and of payments to corporate officers. From 1950 to 1972 the level of real corporate profits rose by about 10 percent, taking into account the rise in the prices of producers' goods.[22] At the same time, however, corporate tax liability (mainly federal) increased by almost 20 percent.[23] If the name of the game in capitalism is control over the investment of capital, then this development certainly spelled a diminution in the relative decision power of the traditional centers of financial and industrial control in the American economy. I made a point of inquiring of officers of a few major firms, Why was such a reduction in decision power accepted? The typical reply was that the senior officers have been essentially "bought off" with handsome salaries and fringe benefits, not to mention occasional access to the highest places of power in the federal government. Thus while the policies of the state management encouraged corporate profits, they increased their own power even more.

All the major policy orientations of U.S. governments since World War II have required the active use of military power. Therefore the chiefs of the federal government, from Roosevelt to Nixon, have all needed the armed forces and their economic base. Since World War II, U.S. governments have applied military power repeatedly to protect U.S. investments, to bolster governments committed to business economies, to suppress antibusiness movements and governments and to "contain" Soviet and Chinese influence. By means of covert or indirect force, U.S. military and quasi-military organizations (the Central Intelligence Agency) toppled governments in Guatemala, Iran, Cambodia, Vietnam, and made a try to end the Castro regime in Cuba. Crucially, there is no escaping the threat of U.S. military intervention given by the ferocity and duration of the U.S. invasion of Indochina and the swift show of force in the Dominican Republic and Lebanon. The costly nuclear strategic forces are the foundation of a worldwide military-threat system. American military assistance operations, costing over $10 billion in 1973, are a major part of the state management's effort to sustain pro-U.S. governments and economies in other countries.

All these operations used the war economy as a useful instrument. Thereby the researchers, designers, industrial managers and production workers of the military economy are tied in to the military and quasimilitary organizations of the U.S. government in a common bond of vital interest in the continuance of the war economy. And the major firms benefiting from foreign trade and investment could see a link between their position and the worldwide military power of the U.S. government.

That war economy benefits many groups and institutions in terms of employment and political-economic power is clear. That it benefits the economy as a whole is dubious on other grounds. A major aspect of military economy is its destructive effect on the elemental requirement of its host economy, any economy, to serve the productive activity of the society.

What is an economy for? It is a network of social arrangements for governing man's division of labor, for determining what should be produced for sustaining life and how the product should be shared. As our command of nature is widened, an economy must also direct the uses of science to serve the improvement of life.

Because of its economically parasitic nature—yielding products that are useful neither for consumption nor for further production—a military economy does none of these things. It operates instead to diminish productive capability by withdrawing resources from civilian economy. A war economy is, in fact, an anti-economy. Consider the anti-economy effects of inflation induced by the permanent war economy. Money is needed as a reliable store of value in every large society with a fine division of labor. Inflation destroys the currency as a store of value and burdens creditors, holders of savings, pensioners, and especially all the poor. Inflation disrupts the important economic functions of saving and investing. (If this is the result of war economy as an anti-stagnation policy, as the monopoly capitalism theorists would have us believe, then what would stagnation look like?)

From another perspective: a maximally critical stance toward business capitalism diagnoses it as a form of decision process that disenfranchises (alienates) producers, that accumulates capital and concentrates decision power without apparent limit, that shapes the design and use of technologies and products for business advantage rather than human welfare, that distributes the national product with great inequality, that entails large overhead costs for supernumerary control functions in business and government, that has imposed the compulsive instabilities of competitive aggrandizement on entire economies, that has arrayed whole communities in racial and colonial exploitive relationships, that has a long history of resorting to violence in the pursuit of decision power, and that could spawn a militarized form of state capitalism. Friends of business capitalism have been able at once to concede various parts of such critiques and to respond with the demonstration that under capitalism both the material level of living and the productiveness of economy have reached heights without precedent. In a word, they argue that the cost has been worth the economic results attained.

This case cannot even be attempted for military economy. For the economic mitigating features of civilian capitalism are not present at all, there being no economically useful product from a military economy, apart from the minor part of transferable technology—no economic return to the host society.

The illusion that military economy creates wealth is sustained by the payment of ordinary money incomes for all the work that serves the military and by the acceptance of that same money as claims on the economically useful product of the civilian economy. Under American conditions this has been justified as uniquely necessary for full employment. There is, however, no economic theory, apart from the ideological supports of war economy, to justify that conclusion. Other capitalist nations have found it possible to sustain a high level of economic activity without war economy. The illusion of creating wealth from military economy begins to fade, however, as crises of inflation, loss of jobs and industrial competence, and collapse of the value of the dollar finally compel attention to the payment that must be made by the entire society for the operation of the anti-economy. It takes time for these effects to be perceived, for the beliefs that support war economy to be weakened, for dissolution of the confident cross-society consensus that has backed the war economy.

The economic moves that are synchronized by the directorate of the military economy often blur separate interests and values of diverse groups. This blurring effect was seen when the Congress voted the legislation to guarantee loans of up to $250 million to Lockheed in August 1971.

> There was no consistent ideological pattern to the voting on both sides . . . The one pattern in the roll-call was that Senators with Lockheed installation or the plants of subcontractors in their states voted for the legislation. Senators in states with plants of the McDonnell-Douglas Corporation, makers of the DC-10 airplane, the principal competitor of the Lockheed Tri-Star, voted against the Lockheed bill, as did those whose states house the General Electric Company which makes the engines for the DC-10.[24]

In short, the Senators representing the military-industrial constituencies of the Lockheed Corporation and allied firms combined across party lines to sustain "their" military-industry firm. Those who joined forces under the banner of the war-economy legislation overrode state, occupational and political-party ideologies to get the combined support for the war economy's priorities. Thereby they acted, as required by the state management, to maintain or enlarge the scope and intensity of its decision power within American society as well as abroad.

In sum, the relation of war economy to aggregate economic growth and to principal occupations shows that there is no specifically economic necessity that stems from any productive requirement of the U.S. economy as a whole or from capitalist economic relations *per se,* which makes a war economy an indispensable feature of American society. The post–World War II American war economy was developed and sustained by political decisions. These decisions were rooted in an economic-interest base of part of the economy, but were also given political support from the rest of society that has been ideologically trained to regard war economy as necessary for the well-being of all. These sustaining political/economic features have to some degree been obscured by the evolving functions of military economy and by ambiguity as to who are the rulers of that economy, and its consequences for the rest of society.

The Ideology of "No Way Out"

A lamentable ideological convergence has appeared around the idea that war economy is essential for the economic well-being of the American economy. The thesis of the Pentagon as economic benefactor to the nation was proclaimed in a book-length report, *The Economics of Defense,* published by the Department of Defense in 1972 in time for use as a handy reference to help counter the McGovern Presidential campaign.

The political conservative case for war economy is also represented by John B. Connally, the former governor of Texas turned Republican and leading member of the Texas Establishment. In

July 1971 Connally let fly with this defense of Nixon economic policies at a White House briefing:

> "We talk in terms of a norm of unemployed being 4 percent. This is a myth, it has never happened, it has never been on an annual basis [at that rate] . . . save in wartime, not in the last quarter of a century. I don't think the American people are willing at this point to continue the war . . . in order to try to achieve a 4 percent rate of unemployment."[25]

Addressing the public that desires full employment, Connally holds this to be possible only in wartime economy. So his conclusion is: drop full employment as an economic goal.

Ideology affirming a need for large scale and continuous military spending for the economy as a whole has also come from some theorists on the American left. Paul Baran wrote: "Large scale government spending on military purposes appears essential to society as a whole, to all its classes, groups, and strata whose jobs and incomes depend on the resulting maintenance of high levels of business activity."[26] In a stronger formulation, the authors of "The Military Industrial Complex: No Way Out," advise that

> the entire capitalist economy has a stake in militarism. For military spending is responsible for most of the economic growth the country has experienced in the postwar period. Without militarism, the whole economy would return to the state of collapse from which it was rescued by the Second World War.[27]

The evidence presented in this book indicates that American capitalism of the 1970s is an altered economy from that of the Great Depression, with a dominant state-capitalist component. For thirty years the variation in that part of the U.S. economy has had a controlling effect on the system as a whole, including patterns of economic growth and employment levels. But there is no defined economic necessity inherent in capitalism which gives war economy such competence. That is a political choice. The main economic problems of state capitalism are different from those of capitalism before 1939. A sustained war economy has produced many effects that were not visible during the depression or World War II. Furthermore, war economy does not have a homogeneous effect across the economy but is differentiated in its effects by industry, region and occupational class.

It is also more informative to divide the last thirty years' growth of the American economy into productive and nonproductive growth and thereby avoid the pitfalls of assuming that money-valued output is functionally all the same. When this mode of analysis is applied to the conventional analysis of growth, one cannot conclude that "military spending is responsible for most of the economic growth the country has experienced in the postwar period." Rather, military spending is then seen to yield the military growth. Economists and others who set forth a portrait of a mechanistically determined economy which includes no role for political-economic factors are, in effect, supporting war economy.

Moreover, while American capitalism since World War II has featured the growth of war economy, this development has not been true for other capitalist states. Evidently the U.S. development has not necessarily been determined by an inherent characteristic of capitalism, but rather is owing to specifically American features that include not only the growth of a state capitalism but extra-economic considerations of a political sort. It is therefore not warranted to assume that economic factors leave the United States with no alternative to war economy except a return to the Great Depression. Other countries with long capitalist histories have moved into state-dominated economies with a civilian economic emphasis.

The doctrine that what's good for Universal Aerospace is good for capitalism (or for the U.S. economy as a whole) does not stand up well under the test of performance. The unintended effects from the financial prosperity of Universal Aerospace abridge collateral gains for other businesses (e.g., inflation penalizes holders of bonds and other certificates of indebtedness, many managers are not able to invest abroad, firms are made noncompetitive because of inability to buy new production equipment, etc.), and drain the real incomes of many groups in society. What is "good" for Universal Aerospace induces an erosion of productive competence in the rest of the U.S. economy.

In the eyes of people living and working in it, capitalism appears in the form of their own working and living experience and not as an analytical abstraction. Therefore the writings about war as necessary and good for capitalism can be reasonably read as "War is necessary for my livelihood." With that understanding the ideologies of "no way out," right, center or left, converge, intended or not, into justification for acceptance of the war economy.

In the theory of monopoly capitalism, the chiefs of the U.S. government are the loyal servants of the "Wall Street" oligarchs who control big business and are thereby the real masters of U.S. economy and society. If one ignores the development of a state management, the biggest business of all, then one cannot see the concentration of responsibility and authority for war economy that lies with the government top leaders. This has several political-ideological effects that were possibly unforeseen by the theorists of monopoly capitalism. First, final responsibility for war economy is removed from the government chiefs. Second, responsibility for war economy is assigned to private corporate chiefs whose actual positions are not subject to political checks. Thus the presumed final decision-makers are removed from significant influence, except by social revolution that would dissolve their role in society by replacing capitalism with another decision process. Since there is no present indication of the prospect of a socialist revolution, there is "no way out" of war economy if one adheres to the theory of monopoly capitalism.

A further step follows in the monopoly-capitalism perspective: even if an alternative economic strategy to war economy is conceivable for offsetting the stagnation process of capitalism and for attaining full employment, the private business chiefs would block it. But this sociopolitical inference rests on the long history of popular political support for Cold War policies, yet is not a determined result stemming unavoidably from an intrinsic economic feature of capitalism. Accordingly, the politics of an exit from war economy deserves separate examination, apart from the self-defeating assumptions of powerlessness that are part of the "no way out" orientation.

Problems of an Exit from War Economy

Imagine that a political scientist was asked during 1938, "What advice could you give on the steps necessary to terminate the Nazi rule over Germany?" Suppose his reply was, "The Reichstag has only to meet, pass the necessary legislation, vote no confidence in the Chancellor, and ask the President of the Republic to nominate a new Chancellor."

This prescription is technically proper. But it is flawed to the point of being useless by its neglect of the issue of power and how it was organized and wielded. With the Chancellor and his party in formal control of the administrative machine of government (including military and police), with their parallel centralized controls over the economy and with their support from key industrialists and important parts of the middle and working classes, the Chancellor (also President after Hindenburg's death in 1934) wielded instruments of power that determined the behavior of the Reichstag members, apart from the formal rights of members of a parliament under the constitution. Hence, the parliamentary procedural recommendation is flawed by lack of specification of the social force required to cause the Reichstag to act against the Nazi rule.

In the United States of 1974 there is no dictatorship, no totalitarian rule, the Bill of Rights prevails, and a right of independent organization for political and other purposes is operative within broad limits. Nevertheless, I draw on this fearsome history of another place and time for a lesson the Americans must learn in the 1970s: whoever wishes to diminish the warmaking institutions of the United States cannot simply prescribe a set of laws and appropriations for Congress to enact. Neither is it sensible to rely on an undefined, automatic economic dynamic of capitalism to terminate the war economy.

An abundance of evidence tells us that the directorate of the American war economy is centered in the executive branch of the federal government. Furthermore, the effective authority of the war-economy chiefs is based not only on their formal role as the largest employer in American capitalism but also on the pervasive system of ideological controls that rallies the populace to support the war economy. Therefore a movement to terminate the war economy requires competence to undo the web of ideological controls and challenge the political power of the war-economy chiefs. Such a movement must develop competence to explain the following matters to the American people: how the federal government became and sustains itself as the directorate of the largest industrial corporate empire in the world; how the war economy is organized and operated in parallel with centralized political power

—often contradicting the laws of Congress and the Constitution itself; how the directorate of the war economy converts pro-peace sentiment in the population into pro-militarist majorities in the Congress; how ideology and fears of job loss are manipulated to marshal support in the Congress and the general public for war economy; how the directorate of the war economy uses its power to prevent planning for orderly conversion to an economy of peace.

An exit from war economy requires an economic blueprint, and also a social force that is competent to compel the implementation of conversion plans. American economists, with rare exception, have held that conversion is no problem: if the Congress or the federal executive would provide new civilian markets, then managements would respond to them and the rest would follow. But this calculation of the behavior of "economic man" is flawed not only by inattention to the nature of the military-serving firm, but by neglect of the issue of power, power over the war economy and how it is organized and wielded. Will the President and his subordinate managers of war economy simply stand by as Congress, or a part of the federal executive, creates large new civilian markets?

The highly political character of the power issue with respect to war economy is illustrated by an important feature of the Vietnam War period, 1965–73. During that time *The Wall Street Journal* and *The New York Times* both took a critical editorial stance against the war. These newspapers have traditionally reflected the larger interests of the American private financial and industrial Establishment. Evidently the reservations of important parts of these economic groups toward the Vietnam War were not sufficient to produce a policy change by the political directorate of the war economy. The lesson is that even major economic decision power of itself no longer suffices to determine the larger decisions on war and peace. Political and economic power have become intertwined outside Wall Street—at the top of the federal government. The same institutions responsible for planning the military-political operation of the Vietnam War also planned the war economy of the United States and protect its continuity by preventing all serious planning for peace.

Apart from the continued allocation of funds for the military, and the ceaseless adumbration of pro-militarist beliefs, the most important steps toward making the war economy durable have been those designed to prevent the development of capability for converting from military to civilian economy. The Kennedy and Johnson administrations handled a major effort to establish a National Economic Conversion Commission in the following way.

On October 31, 1963, Senator George McGovern put into the Senate hopper a bill to establish a National Economic Conversion Commission. This legislation was co-sponsored by thirty-one members of the Senate. Parallel bills were filed in the House of Representatives, notably under the leadership of F. Bradford Morse (Republican, Massachusetts) and William Fitts Ryan (Democrat, New York). A month later, on November 22, 1963, President Kennedy was assassinated. On December 3, 1963, President Johnson had a copy of the McGovern bill. Later that month, on December 21, 1963, President Johnson appointed a Committee on the Economic Impact of Defense and Disarmament, chaired by Gardner Ackley of the President's Council of Economic Advisers. Five months later, on May 25 and June 22, 1964, brief hearings were conducted on Senator McGovern's bill (S. 2274) before the Committee on Commerce of the United States Senate, chaired by Senator Warren G. Magnuson (Democrat, Washington).[28]

At the May 25, 1964, hearing, from 10:17 to 11:22 A.M., in Room 5110 of the New Senate Office Building, Senator McGovern presented his statement on the bill and Congressman Morse testified briefly. A set of formal comments on this legislation from the principal departments of government was put into the record.

On June 22 Senator Magnuson's committee heard testimony from a series of official witnesses led by Cyrus R. Vance, Deputy Secretary of Defense. The formal position of the Pentagon on the conversion legislation had been stated by John T. McNaughton, then general counsel of the Department of Defense, in a letter to Senator Magnuson. McNaughton made a special point of objecting to that clause in Senator McGovern's bill which "would require its contractors by a contract provision to establish within their organizations committees to plan for the conversion to civilian work in the event a contract is terminated or curtailed." Said McNaughton, "If company management is convinced of the value of such an effort, it will surely undertake it as it would undertake any other planning project which is in the company interest." McNaughton simply omitted reference to the well-understood pressure on

Pentagon contractors to give priority attention to the state management and its requirements—which every military-industry manager understands to be "the company interest." Vance argued that the McGovern bill was no longer necessary, because the President's Committee on the Economic Impact of Defense and Disarmament under Gardner Ackley was going to do the required work.[29]

Cyrus Vance and his deputy also testified at length about the activity of the Defense Department's Office of Economic Adjustment, established in 1961. This unit, with a professional staff of four, plus secretaries, was described as taking a key part in facilitating conversion from military to civilian economy. (The professional staff of four for this purpose compared with the thirty thousand graduates from the Pentagon's special school for training its public-relations officers alone!)

Senator Magnuson responded with

> We thank you, Mr. Secretary. And, first of all, I think it should be understood—and I am sure you understand it, and the other witnesses—that there is no particular pride of authorship in S. 2274. Actually, it is in the nature of a working sheet, and any suggestions such as you have given us here are more than welcome to the bill. We realize that this is a broad complex subject, and on legislation to achieve the objectives, we have to be very careful that we do not inject a lot of government interference or unwarranted regulations or unwarranted costs particularly into defense contracts . . .

After this designation of legislation sponsored by thirty-one Senators and many more Representatives as a "working sheet," and the promise to abstain from government "interference" in military industry, Archibald Alexander appeared for the Arms Control and Disarmament Agency to pronounce that "enactment of S. 2274 would be inappropriate." Gardner Ackley of the Council of Economic Advisers then assured the Senate committee that all relevant matters would be dealt with by his committee.

The published texts of these remarkable hearings (three hours and thirty-eight minutes of committee time to stop planning for peace) show that no representative appeared for any industrial group, nor was any supporting statement sent to the committee by any industrial enterprise. On the trade-union side, the National Farmers Union sent a statement of support for conversion legislation to be included in the record. Beyond that, the only trade-union backing for planning for peace came from the Maryland State and District of Columbia AFL–CIO and the Baltimore Council of AFL–CIO unions. Obviously, the combined absence of important industry and union backing was a measure of the wholehearted managerial and trade-union support for war-economy planning as against planning for peace.

Owing to the publication of the Pentagon Papers by *The New York Times* in 1971, we now know something about what was happening within the federal government during May and June 1964 that illuminates the way Senator McGovern's conversion legislation was handled. In the first of the *Times's* articles on the Pentagon Papers by Neil Sheehan we find the following opening paragraph. "The Pentagon Papers disclose that for 6 months before the Tonkin Gulf incident in August 1964, the United States had been mounting clandestine military attacks against North Vietnam while planning to obtain a Congressional Resolution that the administration regarded as the equivalent of a Declaration of War." Indeed, May 25, 1964, the day of Senator Magnuson's first hearing on the conversion legislation, is listed in the Pentagon Papers as the date on which the State Department completed the "Draft Resolution for Congress on Actions in Southeast Asia."[30] This document later became the main part of the Tonkin Gulf Resolution as adopted by the Congress. Between May 25 and June 22, 1964, the second day of hearings, the Pentagon Papers show evidence of accelerated military-political planning for the Vietnam War.

Now we know why Cyrus Vance, John McNaughton, Archibald Alexander and Gardner Ackley were dispatched to kill Senator McGovern's conversion bill, and why these hearings were conducted on a restricted basis under rules permitting no public witnesses. At that very time, the Johnson administration was planning a war. Vance and McNaughton, who took a lead in putting down conversion planning, were among the main war planners.[31] Planning for peace would have detracted from the economic, military and political operations required for the war planning and war operations.

From such experiences, I conclude that an exit from war economy in the United States is definable and achievable only by combined treatment of the economic- and political-power aspects of such a process. Plans for economic conversion are essential for

assuring the military-economy population that new markets and
new jobs are in the offing to secure their economic future. But such
planning cannot come to life except as a major part of the population discards the ideological controls that harness it to the war
economy. These controls cannot be turned off at will.

From the standpoint of effect on people's awareness, it is noteworthy that the unforeseen, crisis-creating effects of war economy
have often taken a long time to register. By 1962, as I showed
earlier, it was possible to diagnose a series of principal unintended
effects owing to the burgeoning war economy. Articles discussing
this issue appeared but were given short shrift because the official
ideology excluded such perceptions. It took until 1971 for the
collapse of the value of the dollar to become visible and widely
reported. A similar lag appeared between early symptoms and
general recognition of the decline of many U.S. industries, including the erosion of power supply, the telephone system and public
transportation. In part the slowness in recognition of these processes is due to the immense accumulated wealth of the American
economy. But other factors have played an important part in the
delay between the onset of these effects and their perception.
First, the impact of depletion processes in industry and economy
has been differentiated by social groups. The upper-middle-class
and white-collar employees generally (including the important
communication industries) have been well paid during the last
decades. Ready access to high levels of consumption have encouraged short-term goals of increased consumption and inattention to
political problems, participation in which could potentially endanger one's economic position.

A second factor which has obscured awareness of the effects of
war economy is the conventional misperception of cause and effect
owing to the ideological consensus that the Cold War is politically
desirable and that war economy is necessary and good for the
United States. Thus the breakdown of the central public services
and the closing of many American factories is not usually understood as having a relation to the sustained war economy. In
conventional wisdom, these are separate occurrences which are
part of the ordinary business process of success or failure of
individual firms or industries. The same events observed from the
vantage point of the mechanisms of war economy have significant
common features. Accordingly, the ideological consensus that ap-

proves war economy has interfered with the capacity of many people to see what they are looking at.

This sort of process is visible, for example, in the behavior of many senior trade-union leaders in the United States. These men have a major professional stake in the continued operation of American industry, for the workers are the members of their unions and the closing of factories means the closing of bargaining units that are the core elements of union organizations. At the same time, however, many union leaders have long histories of public political commitment in support of a war economy and the belief system that justifies it. One result appeared in an address given by George Meany, president of the AFL–CIO, on October 26, 1972, before the Aluminum Association in New York City. Meany said:

> We in the AFL-CIO are concerned about the deterioration of America's position in the world economy—about the export of American jobs and technology. We do not believe that either business or workers can possibly prosper, in the long run, if America becomes a nation of hamburger stands, hotels, importers and international banks, without the broad base of various types of industries and production. We do not believe that American business, any more than American workers, can prosper over a period of years, if one industry after another goes down the drain.[32]

Mr. Meany's undifferentiated appeal to American business ignored the considerable stake that part of business has in the war economy and in the foreign-investment and job-exporting system that has been furthered by the state management.

These considerations indicate the importance of politics, of organized effort to affect public understanding and acceptance of war economy. The basis for politics is the expectation that the effects of that system, intended and unintended, will damage economic and other aspects of life for most people in American society. However, there is no basis in any theory of society for expecting that that damage would spontaneously produce a political response that is competent to mobilize a great movement against the dominance of the war-economy directorate in American society. That result must await a widespread process of ideological demystification that exposes the damage done by war economy to many facets of life and that debunks the network of beliefs that mobilizes acquiescence to the war economy. All this must be accompanied by plausibly formulated alternatives to the war economy and by defined processes of conversion.

Such perspectives are ruled out by belief that ordinary people cannot find ways of blocking the will of officials like a President, let alone change the principal policies of an administration. It is a responsibility of intellectuals to explain that the decision power of government, as of business, consists not only of the orders of leaders or managers, but also in the readiness of people to carry out orders. Alternatives to centralized managerial control in economy and community must be asserted and defined.

Many Americans have responded to the growing perception of a damaged economy and society with the belief and hope that the whole matter would be dealt with by a change of generation. There is some validity to the idea that generational change has brought attitude changes with respect to war economy in the United States. Opinion polls on the Vietnam War regularly showed heavier pro-peace sentiment among the young. For these reasons I asked the Bureau of the Census to answer the question "When will a majority of the U.S. population eighteen years old and over have been born after 1940?"—hence will have come to awareness and maturity in the nuclear era. The reason for this question was the assumption that the generation that came to awareness during the nuclear age would have a rather different body of life experience than the one that grew up during the Great Depression. The Census Bureau estimated that this will occur in the year 1980. Thus the election of 1980 will be the first in which the majority of the entire U.S. voting-age population will have been born after January 1, 1940. My concern is that if the matter is left to an undefined, self-acting process of generational change to be induced by 1980 and after, then the famous society of 1984, as diagnosed by George Orwell, will be made more likely of realization.

On the other hand, a population that rejects the ideology of war economy and the commands of its managers is automatically launched into a consideration of: what else to do with the resources and people that are involved; how to organize the transition to other work; how to set up and control the new activity; who should be in charge; and by what rules the new work should be governed.

The main alternatives to the war economy in public policy at home and abroad are indicated by the data and analyses of this book: instead of military nonproductive activity dominating public budgets, a concentration of public funds on reconstructing and improving vital areas of public economic responsibility; instead of operating on the assumption of a permanent war economy, thoughtful planning for conversion to other work; instead of focusing technical talent on the military, a concentration of scientific and engineering effort to raise the quality of work and its products; instead of cost-maximization and subsidy-maximization and the-public-be-damned, quality with economy as criteria for work, private and public; instead of centralism in economy and government, moves to decentralize responsibility and authority, especially through the conversion of military bases and firms; instead of managerialism unlimited in private and public economy, growing participation in decision-making by all who work; instead of economic neglect and social decay for 30 million Americans, an effort to end poverty and economic underdevelopment; instead of commitment to an unlimited arms race, armed-forces reduction by international disarmament and by singlehanded initiatives; instead of military interventionism, noninterventionism as a guiding principle in foreign policy; instead of promoting local arms races through "military-assistance" programs, a vigorous effort via multinational (UN) sponsorship to promote economic development for two thirds of mankind. These perspectives have the promise of work enough and challenge enough to preoccupy Americans until the Year 2000 and beyond.

The political-economic actions, large and small, that move away from militarized state capitalism are contributions to the termination of war economy and to the required experience for the formation of a new, post-capitalist society. Military economy, with its massive state capitalist hierarchy, is fundamentally contradictory to the formation of a new political economy based upon democracy, instead of hierarchy, in the workplace and the rest of society.

The idea that war economy brings prosperity has become more than an American illusion. When converted, as it has been, into ideology that justifies the militarization of society and moral debasement, as in Vietnam, then critical reassessment of that illusion is a matter of urgency. It is a primary responsibility of thoughtful people who are committed to humane values to confront and respond to the prospect that deterioration of American economy and society, owing to the ravages of war economy, can become irreversible. That result is assured under the following conditions: first, unavailability or unawareness of a theory that explains the deterioration caused by war economy; second, unavailability or unawareness of a theory on how to convert from a military to a civilian economy; third, unavailability of sufficient people to do the organizational and technical tasks required for conversion; and, fourth, the absence of popular will to be rid of war economy and its consequences.

BIBLIOGRAPHICAL NOTE

SINCE THE FOLLOWING NOTES to the several chapters include substantial references to the literature of the subjects dealt with in this book, a separate bibliography listing is not given. For fast access to the relevant literature see the bibliographies in S. Melman, ed., *The Defense Economy*, Praeger, 1971, pp. 463–526, and S. Melman, ed., *The War Economy*, St. Martin's Press, 1971, pp. 243–44. See also Bruce M. Russett and Alfred Stepan, *Military Force and American Society*, Harper and Row, 1973, pp. 196–371.

NOTES

Chapter One

1. U.S. Bureau of the Census, *Historical Statistics of the United States from Colonial Times to 1957*, Washington, D.C., 1960, pp. 70, 143.
2. Two books by Gar Alperovitz include data and analysis on this point and introduce the interested reader to a wider literature: *Atomic Diplomacy: Hiroshima and Potsdam*, Simon and Schuster, 1965; *Cold-War Essays*, Doubleday-Anchor, 1969.
3. John Swomley, *The Military Establishment*, Beacon Press, 1964, p. 103.
4. U.S. Bureau of the Census, *Statistical Abstract of the United States, 1971*, Washington, D.C., 1971, p. 240; *The Budget of the United States Government, 1974*, Washington, D.C., 1973, p. 40: address by Leonard Sullivan, Jr., principal Deputy Director, Defense Research and Engineering, U.S. Department of Defense, before the AFMA/NSIA Symposium, Washington, D.C., Aug. 16, 1972; Executive Office of the President, Office of Management and Budget, *Historical Tables, Budget of the United States Government, Fiscal Year 1986*, Table 5.1.
5. *Historical Statistics.*
6. Walter J. Oakes, "Toward a Permanent War Economy," *Politics*, 1944, reprinted in S. Melman, ed., *The War Economy of the U.S.*, St. Martin's Press, 1971.
7. *The Budget*, pp. 72, 89, 180, 283, 301.
8. U.S. Department of Commerce, *Annual Survey of Manufactures Industry Profiles, 1970*, Washington, D.C., 1971.
9. U.S. Arms Control and Disarmament Agency, *World Military Expenditures, 1970*, Washington, D.C., 1971.
10. See the computations on total national-security budget of the U.S. in the 1972 and 1973 *Joint Economic Report*, report of the Joint Economic Committee, U.S. Congress, Washington, D.C., 1972 and 1973.
11. *Survey of Current Business*, July 1972, p. 16.
12. U.S. Bureau of the Census, *Statistical Abstract of the United States, 1972*, Washington, D.C., 1972, pp. 245, 467.

13. William M. Magruder, "Technology and the Professional Societies," *Mechanical Engineering*, September 1972.
14. The institutionalization of a military economy under government control has been given diverse interpretation by serious students. R. Barnet, *The Roots of War*, Atheneum, 1972, has emphasized the political-military institutions at the peak of U.S. government and the origins of their chiefs. G. W. Domhoff, *Who Rules America*, Prentice-Hall, 1967, and *The Higher Circles*, Random House, 1971, defines a ruling class as composed of the top corporate controllers. In the present book central importance is assigned to the economic decision-making role of government chiefs who operate the largest firm of all. They are impelled by the normal managerial dynamic to enlarge their economic, political and military power in ways that are conditioned by the special institutional features of the military economy and its sway over the economy as a whole. The American war economy is treated here as a state-capitalist economy that evolved from a private business economy.

Chapter Two

1. R. Kaufman, *The War Profiteers*, Bobbs-Merrill, 1970, Chapter 1; P. Noel-Baker, *The Arms Race*, Atlantic Books, 1958, Chapter 4.
2. H. L. Nieburg, *In the Name of Science*, Quadrangle Books, 1966, Chapters 10–12.
3. R. McNamara, *The Essence of Security*, Harper, 1968; A. Enthoven and W. Smith, *How Much is Enough?*, Harper and Row, 1971.
4. On the idea of "control" as seen by statisticians: W. A. Shewhart, *Economic Control of Quality of Manufactured Product*, D. Van Nostrand, 1931, Chapters 1, 2; L. H. C. Tippett, *Technological Applications of Statistics*, Williams and Norgate, 1950; on the developing literature, *Journal of Quality Technology;* on the idea of control of complex industrial systems, see S. B. Littauer, "Technological Stability," *Transactions of the New York Academy of Sciences*, 1950.
5. Cited in A. E. Fitzgerald, *The High Priests of Waste*, Norton, 1972, p. 35.
6. D. W. Strull, "Parametric Cost Estimating Aids DoD in Systems Acquisition Decisions," *Defense Management Journal*, April 1972.
7. E. B. Staats, "GAO Looks at DoD Weapons Acquisition Process," *Defense Management Journal*, October 1972.
8. In response to the sort of political pressures brought to bear by Senator Proxmire and others, the Air Force, by February 13–15, 1973, sponsored meetings for its supplier firms on the idea of designing something with "Cost as a Design Parameter." An Air Force Systems Command Classified Symposium in Los Angeles described a session on this subject as follows.

The near-geometric growth in costs of weapons systems over the past decade and more has prompted the Defense Department to initiate major steps to bring this problem under control.

The session will present speakers who will discuss the evolution of the design-to-price philosophy, its implementation, and its expected impact. Selected examples of design-to-price hardware developments for both the commercial and military marketplaces will be described to highlight the effect which constrained price has on the design approach. The problem of limiting total system cost (operation as well as acquisition) will also be discussed. The session will conclude with a panel discussion directed toward encouraging audience participation.

Until a major turnabout is visible in weapons prices, it is prudent to appreciate such sessions as serving to show Congressional critics an Air Force effort to restrain costs.

Readers with an interest in the general theory of the cost- and subsidy-maximizing firm should examine N. Finger, *The Impact of Subsidy Systems on Industrial Management*, Praeger, 1971, Chapter 5. For evidence of the pervasiveness of the cost-maximizing process, see U.S. General Accounting Office, *Cost Growth in Major Weapons Systems*, report to the House Committee on Armed Services, March 26, 1973.

9. S. Melman, *Dynamic Factors in Industrial Productivity*, Basil Blackwell, Oxford, and John Wiley, New York, 1956.

10. U.S. Dept. of Commerce, *Annual Survey of Manufactures, Industry Profiles 1970*, Washington, D.C., June 1972.

11. S. Melman, "The Rise of Administrative Overhead in the Manufacturing Industries of the United States, 1899–1947," *Oxford Economic Papers*, 1950.

12. *Business Week*, July 17, 1971.

13. *New York Times*, Feb. 23, 1972.

14. For a review of Pentagon response to Congressional pressures to limit such operations, see U.S. General Accounting Office, *Further Improvements Needed in Controls Over Government-owned Plant Equipment in Custody of Contractors*, report to the Congress, Aug. 29, 1972.

15. J. W. Kuhn, "Money," *The Columbia Forum*, Spring 1972, p. 56.

16. For full discussion on this issue, see the elaborate hearings, *Emergency Loan Guarantee Legislation*, before the Senate Committee on Banking, Housing and Urban Affairs, 92nd Congress, First Session, June 7–July 7, 1971, Parts I and II. See p. 469 for discussions of PL 85–804; also, *New York Times*, April 30, 1973.

17. *New York Times*, April 19, 1972.

18. Comment by Congressman Aspin in *New York Times*, Aug. 29, 1972.

19. H. Romaine, "Henry Durham: People Threatened to Kill Me If I Testified," *Earth*, October 1971.

20. Stockton and Newman, "Another Flight of Fancy," *The Nation*, May 24, 1971.

21. *New York Times*, Dec. 26, 1971, Oct. 31, 1971; *News American*, Dec. 19 and 20, 1971; U.S. General Accounting Office, *Staff Study of the C-5A Aircraft*, February 1973.
22. *Wall Street Journal*, Dec. 9, 1971.
23. *New York Times*, Dec. 20, 1972.
24. "Washington Merry-Go-Round," in *Washington Post*, Dec. 8, 1972.
25. Article by Morton Mintz, *Washington Post*, Jan. 2, 1973.
26. S. Melman, *Pentagon Capitalism*, McGraw-Hill, 1970, Chapter 2.
27. M. J. Peck and F. M. Scherer, *The Weapons Acquisitions Process: An Economic Analysis*, Graduate School of Business Administration, Harvard University, 1962, p. 429.
28. *New York Times*, April 19, 1972.
29. U.S. Arms Control and Disarmament Agency, *World Military Expenditures, 1970*, Washington, D.C., 1970.
30. *Pentagon Capitalism*.
31. *Emergency Loan Guarantee Legislation*.
32. *New York Times*, Dec. 27, 1972.

Chapter Three

1. Many theorists of capitalism have characterized it as consisting essentially of a system of markets, of exchange relations. This is the recurring theme of the main-line literature of economics, from textbooks to scholarly journals. But wherever there is division of labor there must be exchanges of products for life to continue. It is scientifically useless to imply that capitalism corresponds to any economy that includes division of labor and necessarily associated exchange relations. For there is division of labor and exchange in feudalism and in the economics of primitive societies, and in non-managerial democratically controlled economy. See M. Herskovits, *Economic Life of Primitive Peoples*, New York, 1940.
2. J. R. Kurth, "The Political Economy of Weapons Procurement: The Follow-on Imperative," *American Economic Review*, May 1972.
3. J. R. Anderson, "The Balance of Military Payments among States and Regions," in S. Melman, ed., *The War Economy of the United States*, St. Martin's Press, 1971, Chapter 17.
4. Cited in *I. F. Stone's Weekly*, May 10, 1965.
5. Article by Jack McWethy, *Washington Post*, March 26, 1972.
6. *National Economic Conversion Commission*, hearings before the Senate Committee on Commerce, 88th Congress, 2nd Session, on S. 2274, May 25, June 22, 1964.
7. U.S. Bureau of the Census, *Statistical Abstract of the United States, 1973*, p. 337.
8. S. Melman, *The Peace Race*, Ballantine Books, Braziller, 1962, Chapter 8.

9. T. Riddell, "The $676 Billion Quagmire," *The Progressive*, October 1973.

10. B. M. Russett, *What Price Vigilance?*, Yale, 1970, Chapter 5.

In this volume I do not attempt a full assessment of the direct cost of military operations to the American economy. It would probably require a reckoning of at least three elements as a first approximation: the direct budgets; the economic use values forgone; and the capital productivity forgone. The first is the sum of Department of Defense budgets 1946–75, about $1,500 billion. The second is the money worth of the economic use-values that were forgone because the $1,500 billion was used for non-economic purposes. (Note that this is not the same as the opportunity cost concept, since the tradeoff here is not between the use of a set of inputs for one or another *economic* output. In the case of the military application of a set of inputs there is no economic use value that emerges at all. There are military or political use values. But that is not the same thing. Hence there is a social cost in the absence of the ordinarily present economic use values. This is an issue in value theory that deserves further attention.) Third, there is the estimated capital productivity gain forgone. Altogether, these would add up to more than $3,600 billion, an immense social cost, exceeding in magnitude the national wealth of the United States. (See U.S. Department of Commerce, *Statistical Abstract of the U.S., 1973*, p. 337.)

11. The regression coefficients of the effects of U.S. military spending on civilian activities are given in B. Russett, *op. cit.*, p. 140. These factors for producers' durable equipment and nonresidential structures, .178, plus an allowance of 25 percent as marginal productivity of capital in the U.S. (Russett, p. 144) were applied to actual U.S. military expenditures, 1946–73 (*The Budget of the U.S. Government, 1974*, and other years). The estimated total capital-goods output forgone as a result of the military spending of a given year was, therefore, military outlay x .178 x .25 x number of years to 1973. The sum of effects for each year from 1946 to 1973 is $661.19 billion. When allowance is further made for a compounding effect, reinvesting of 25 percent of new capital outputs, then the estimated sum of these effects from 1946 to 1973 is $1,992.7 billion. These estimates are compared with actual producers' fixed investment in the U.S. (U.S. Department of Commerce, *Survey of Current Business*, March 1973; *Business Statistics, 1971*) 1946–73, which totaled $532.6 billions of nonresidential structures, $948.6 billion of producers' durable equipment.

12. See discussion and bibliography in U.S. National Commission on Productivity, *Education and Productivity*, by T. W. Schultz, Washington, D.C., June 1971.

13. For early discussion of these developments see T. McCarthy, "The Garrison Economy," *Columbia Forum*, September 1967; also S. Mel-

man, *Our Depleted Society*, Holt, Rinehart & Winston and Dell Books, 1965, Chapter 7.

14. "Undistributed profits (after inventory valuation adjustment) and capital consumption allowances" define the internal sources of funds for U.S. "nonfarm, nonfinancial corporate business" for 1971 (Board of Governors of the Federal Reserve System, in *Economic Report of the President, 1973*, Washington, D.C., 1973, p. 282). Equivalent 1939 data from U.S. Bureau of the Census, *Statistical Abstract of the United States, 1942*, Washington, D.C., 1942, pp. 224 ff. U.S. military spending, 1939 and 1971, from *Economic Report of the President, 1973*, p. 193. Since the data for capital available to private corporate management includes the funds of nominally private military-industry firms, the 1971 ratio of military funds to private capital is understated.

15. See William M. Magruder, "Technology and the Professional Societies," *Mechanical Engineering*, September 1972.

Chapter Four

1. *New York Times*, July 25, 1971.
2. *Ibid.*, Feb. 15, 1973.
3. *Business Week*, Jan. 15, 1972, p. 49.
4. S. Robach and K. Simmonds, *International Business and Multinational Enterprises*, Richard Irwin, 1973, Chapter 4. Such ideas do play the part of ideology in justification of the export of capital and job opportunities by multinational corporations.
5. *New York Times*, Sept. 21, 1972.
6. UN General Assembly, *Economic and Social Consequences of the Armaments Race and its Extremely Harmful Effects on World Peace and Security*, report of the Secretary General, 26th Session, Agenda Item 32, Oct. 22, 1971, Appendix Table A.
7. U.S. Bureau of the Census, *Statistical Abstract of the U.S., 1972*, Tables 1198 and 1273.
8. W. N. Leonard, "Research and Development in Industrial Growth," *Journal of Political Economy*, March/April 1971.
9. U.S. National Science Foundation, *Research and Development in Industry, 1969*, Surveys of Science Resources Series, NSF 71–18, 1970, p. 3. The only industry where the DoD and NASA share did not exceed 80 percent was the chemicals industry, where 71 percent of the federal R&D contract work was financed by other agencies, primarily the Atomic Energy Commission and the Department of Health, Education and Welfare.
10. J. H. Holloman and A. E. Harger, "America's Technological Dilemma," *Technology Review*, July/August, 1971.
11. S. Melman, *Dynamic Factors in Industrial Productivity*, Basil Blackwell, John Wiley, 1956; *Decision-Making and Productivity*, Basil Blackwell, John Wiley, 1958.

12. Statement by Maurice H. Stans, Secretary of Commerce, "On
    Science, Technology and the Economy," before the Subcommittee
    on Science, Research and Development, House Committee on
    Science and Astronautics, July 27, 1971, Chart 9, U.S. Dept. of
    Commerce, Washington, D.C.
13. *New York Times,* Sept. 19, 1971.
14. Statement by Maurice H. Stans, note 12 *supra.*
15. *New York Times,* April 27, 1970.
16. *Ibid.,* July 6, 1971.
17. *Ibid.,* Nov. 21, 1971.
18. *Ibid.,* July 27, 1972.
19. See letter on prototype trains, *ibid.,* July 10, 1971.
20. *IEEE Spectrum,* September 1972, p. 40.
21. *New York Post,* Dec. 15, 1971. The BART system is a classic dem-
    onstration of the aerospace "technology and systems approach" ap-
    plied to a civilian undertaking. *The New York Times* (April 2, 1974)
    reported on the ". . . rapid transit system that was hailed as a
    miracle of the age, until the trains started running in September
    1972. One train ran off the tracks. Doors opened when a train was
    going 80 miles an hour. Doors opened on the side away from the
    station platform. The detection system, the heart of the 'automated
    train control' system, was found to be unable to detect trains
    stopped dead on the tracks. . . ." The crucial train control equip-
    ment contract was given to Westinghouse for equipment that had
    never been run through operating tests. It failed, and the price went
    up from $26.2 to $40 million for the still-not-functioning control
    equipment. An engineer member of the BART board, ". . . Dr.
    Wattenberg, a veteran of NASA consultant contracts on aerospace
    companies' conformance to design and performance stipulations,
    calls this the 'aerospace shuffle.' "
22. *New York Times,* Aug. 6, 1969.
23. *Ibid.*
24. For 1970 it was 15 percent of the U.S. market. See P. G. Peterson,
    The United States in a Changing World Economy, U.S. Govern-
    ment Printing Office, Washington, D.C., December 1971, Vol. 2,
    p. 17. By 1972 the foreign share of the U.S. market was 18 percent
    as determined by N. Goldfinger, research director of AFL-CIO,
    reported in *New York Times,* March 4, 1973.
25. American Iron and Steel Institute, *Steel Imports—A National Prob-
    lem,* 1970, p. 73.
26. *Business Week,* June 5, 1971.
27. *New York Times,* Sept. 19, 1971.
28. *Business Week,* Jan. 15, 1972, special report on "Making U.S. Tech-
    nology More Competitive."
29. *New York Times,* May 1, 1970.
30. *Business Week,* March 3, 1973.
31. *New York Times,* Aug. 25, 1972.

32. S. Melman, *Report on the Productivity of Operations in the Machine Tool Industry in Western Europe*, European Productivity Agency, Paris, October 1959.

33. H. D. Sharpe, Jr., "Machine Tools, Imports and National Security," in National Academy of Engineering, *Technology and International Trade*, Washington, D.C., 1971. Note that the salability of machine tools to U.S. buyers in the replacement market is mainly controlled by the relative costs of labor to machinery to the U.S. buyer. That relationship is not altered as U.S. machine tools are rendered more price competitive abroad, as by currency devaluations. See *Wall Street Journal*, October 15, 1973.

34. W. N. Leonard, *op. cit.*, p. 250; from a theoretical economic standpoint, see R. W. Klein, "A Dynamic Theory of Comparative Advantage," *American Economic Review*, March 1973.

35. M. Boretsky, "Concerns About the Present American Position in International Trade," National Academy of Engineering, *Technology and International Trade*, Washington, D.C., 1971.

36. *New York Times*, Aug. 18, 1973.

37. *Business Week*, July 10, 1971.

38. Statement by Maurice H. Stans, note 12 *supra;* see also J. Holloman, *op. cit.*, p. 37.

39. These estimates were presented by Dr. M. Boretsky to a seminar on problems of depletion in industry at Columbia University in spring 1972. Dr. Boretsky considered the Netherlands to be a most sophisticated country in terms of technology enhancement. In that small country, R&D expenditures were, in percent of GNP: for economic development, 2.09; for defense and space, .06; for health, welfare and general advance of knowledge, .77.

40. A. Neef, "Unit Labor Costs in the U.S. and 10 Other Nations," *Monthly Labor Review*, July 1972.

41. U.S. Dept. of Commerce, *Survey of Current Business*, December 1972, p. 38.

42. Here are some average annual percents of growth in gross national product for 1960–70: U.S., 7.2; Canada, 9.1; France, 9.3; West Germany, 9.6. U.S. Arms Control and Disarmament Agency, *World Military Expenditures, 1971*. Washington, D.C., 1972, p. 22.

43. Statement of Andrew J. Biemiller, director, Dept. of Legislation, AFL-CIO, before the Subcommittee on International Trade of the Senate Committee on Finance, March 6, 1973.

44. *Maritime*, January, March, 1972.

45. Committee in Behalf of the 2½ million people of the Textile/Apparel and Fiber Industries, in *New York Times*, Nov. 17, 1970. See also reports on factory closing in *New York Times*, March 28, 1971, and April 5, 1972, and on U.S. industrial investments in Mexico, *Business Week*, Jan. 22, 1972.

46. Transcript of *60 Minutes*, Volume IV, Number 7, broadcast over the CBS Television Network Nov. 14, 1971.

47. N. Goldfinger, *op. cit.* note 24 *supra.*
48. *New York Times,* Aug. 14, 1971.
49. *Pacific Basin Reports,* June 1970.
50. For data on the variety of arrangements and strategic considerations involved in export of capital by multinational firms, see National Foreign Trade Council, *The Impact of U.S. Foreign Direct Investment on U.S. Employment and Trade,* New York, November 1971. The views of the AFL-CIO are represented by the report *Needed: A Constructive Foreign Trade Policy,* prepared by S. H. Ruttenberg and Associates, Washington, D.C., for the Industrial Union Dept., AFL-CIO, October 1971.
51. Report of Economic Policy Committee to AFL-CIO Executive Council, Feb. 20, 1973.
52. U.S. Tariff Commission, *Implications of Multinational Firms for World Trade and Investment and for U.S. Trade and Labor,* Washington, D.C., 1973, p. 612.
53. Investment-per-employee data from National Industrial Conference Board, *The Economic Almanac,* 1968, p. 285 and 225.
54. U.S. Tariff Commission, *op. cit.* The interested reader will find considerable detail on the takeover of U.S. markets in consumer electronics by foreign-based production (including U.S.-owned) in *Electronic Market Data Book, 1972,* Electronic Industries Association, Washington, D.C., 1972. Also, the U.S. Tariff Commission has conducted numerous hearings on the consequences for U.S. market control and U.S. employment from the rising tide of radio and television imports. For illuminating reports on specific products see the following Tariff Commission publications: Nos. 329 (July 1970), 341 (November 1970), 351 (January 1971), 367 (March 1971), 376 (April 1971), 380 (April 1971), 386 (April 1971), 396 (May 1971), 436 (November 1971), 485 (May 1972).

This three-volume report is a mine of data on the operating characteristics of the U.S.-based firms that have become multinational investors. For example, from Table 8, p. 637, we learn that in 1970 the U.S. manufacturing operations of the multinational firms had at an average unit labor cost that was 35 percent greater than that of all firms in the U.S. At the same time, in their foreign operations in seven principal countries (Canada, United Kingdom, Belgium, France, West Germany, Brazil, Mexico) these firms enjoyed unit labor costs that were 29 percent less than the average for all firms of those countries. In absolute dollars, the multinationals also had lower unit labor costs abroad than in the U.S.

Chapter Five

1. Based upon 1961–70 GNP growth rates and population growth rates for U.S. and Japan. See U.S. Arms Control and Disarmament Agency, *World Military Expenditures, 1971,* Washington, D.C.,

1972. By 1973 the effects of the reduced value of the dollar in relation to other currencies had the effect of making the money-valued GNP capital of Sweden and West Germany greater than that of the U.S. This may not correspond to relative "real" income, depending on the weight given to one or another aspect of consumption—e.g., the importance assigned to housing as against car-owning. See article by J. W. Anderson, "Yanks Fall to No. 3," *Boston Globe*, July 15, 1973.

2. *New York Times*, Jan. 4, 1971.
3. *Business Week*, March 3, 1973.
4. *New York Times*, Feb. 22, 1973.
5. First National Bank of Chicago, *Gold and the Balance of Payments*, 5th ed., 1969.
6. The decline in the relative value of the dollar has a host of political consequences which I will not attempt to treat here. Certain members of the U.S. Senate have been increasingly alert to this problem. This includes Senators Stuart Symington and William Fulbright. Senator Symington has spoken on the Senate floor on these points in great detail, and the full record of his analyses is to be found in the published volumes of *The Congressional Record*. An extensive analysis of the impact of the changing value of the dollar and how this has interrelated with the major foreign policies of the war-economy directorate is found in Michael Hudson's *Super Imperialism*, Holt, 1972. *See also* T. McCarthy, "How the U.S. Went Bankrupt," *Ramparts*, June, 1973; R. W. Stevens, *The Dollar in the World Economy*, Random House, 1972.
7. I am informed that the developing experience of U.S. investment managers and sellers of new securities during the late 1960s to 1974 includes diminishing confidence by the U.S. investing public in making new investments in American firms. This has been owing to declining confidence in the integrity of government and of business firms. In each case (Watergate and other corruption, Vietnam War, inflation, devaluation of the dollar, and a series of major business failures, including insurance companies and railroads) there is a feared lessening of honest public accounting. The consequence is a weakening of "the integrity of the capital market" and a withholding of investment funds.
8. *New York Times*, April 22, 1971.
9. *Ibid.*, May 25, 1971.
10. U.S. Bureau of the Census, *Statistical Abstract of the U.S., 1971*, p. 325; Coalition on National Priorities and Military Policy, *Citizens' Hearing on an Alternative Defense Budget for the U.S.*, Statement of R. Anthony, March 25, 1970, Washington, D.C.
11. The President's Council of Economic Advisers, in its 1966 report "Strengthening Human Resources," found:

If economic and social policies could be specifically designed to lower Negro unemployment to the current unemployment levels of whites, the resultant gain in GNP would be $5 billion. . . . A further gain would result if all Negroes were able to obtain jobs which would better utilize their abilities and training . . . If the average productivity of the Negro and white labor force were equalized at the white level, total production would expand by $22 billion. If both unemployment rates and productivity levels were equalized, the total output of the economy would rise by about $27 billion—4 percent of GNP.

See Council of Economic Advisers, "Strengthening Human Resources," *Annual Report of the Council of Economic Advisers,* Washington, D.C., January 1966, pp. 109–10. There are a number of similar estimates. E.g., Siegel calculated, using 1960 figures, that the annual birthright of being a Negro costs about $1,000; see Paul M. Siegel, "On the Cost of Being a Negro," in John F. Kain, ed., *Race and Poverty,* Prentice-Hall, 1969, pp. 60–67, and other articles in the same volume. Above, cited in M. Berkowitz, *Neighborhood Expenditure Liability: A Study of the Social Costs of Human Underdevelopment in New York City,* Ph.D. dissertation, Columbia University, 1973. On characteristics of "hidden unemployment" in U.S. economy, see the set of articles in *Monthly Labor Review,* March 1973.

12. Discussion of poverty in the United States has given lesser attention to the circumstances of the 790,000 American Indians. Some aspects of the Indian condition are summarized in the following.

	American Indian	U.S. Total Population
Suicides (1970)	32.0 per 100,000	16.0 per 100,000
Life expectancy (1970)	47 years	70.8 years
Unemployment rate (1972)	45% estimated	5.8%
Median family income (1971	$4,000	$9,867
Infant mortality (1970)	30.9 per 1,000 live births	21.8 per 1,000 live births
Percent entering college (1971)	18%	50%

(SOURCE: *New York Times,* Nov. 12, 1972.)

13. U.S. Bureau of the Census, *Historical Statistics of the U.S., Colonial Times to 1957,* Washington, D.C., p. 139; U.S. Bureau of the Census, *Statistical Abstract of the U.S., 1973,* p. 315.

14. B. Russett, "The Price of War," in S. Melman, ed., *The War Economy of the United States,* St. Martin's Press, 1971, p. 156.

15. M. Tolchin, "South Bronx: A Jungle Stalked by Fear, Seized by Rage," in *New York Times,* Jan. 15, 1973. In the earlier chapters of this book I have given considerable evidence of economic and technical deterioration. Here are two reports that reflect on the deterioration of the quality of life in American society:

In March, 1971 it was announced that southwest of Houston, a 1,000-acre, limited access, electronically fortified walled "city" had been constructed. This "walled city" whose homes are in the $40,000 to $200,000 range are equipped with elaborate electronic security devices, and the promoters reported that their houses were snatched up. [*Business Week,* March 6, 1971.]

[By April 1972] 30% of college students [said] they would rather live in some other country than the United States, according to a foundation-sponsored survey of collegians' personal and political attitudes. [*New York Times,* April 11, 1972.]

One of the results of perceived insecurity for the whole society has been a break in the long-standing no-questions-asked support for military budgets and operations. By April 1971, "half of those individuals questioned in a recent poll believed that the United States should reduce spending for national defense and military purposes, the Gallup organization said." Notably, the strongest criticism of military spending was among the young, with 57 percent of voters under 30 calling for reduction in military spending, compared to 49 percent in the 30–49 age group, and 46 percent of persons 50 years and older. (*New York Times,* April 15, 1971.)

16. *New York Times,* Dec. 6, 1970, April 16, 1970, April 25, 1973. See numerous articles in the magazine *Science* on reduction in research funds and impacts in various research fields.
17. *New York Times,* May 26, 1970.
18. *Ibid.,* April 23, 1971.
19. *Ibid.,* Sept. 17, 1972.
20. *Ibid.,* April 30, 1971, Dec. 6, 1972, Feb. 24, 1971, Nov. 29, 1972.
21. *Ibid.,* Nov. 20, 1970.
22. *Ibid.,* May 20, 1970.
23. *Ibid.,* June 6 and 17, 1971, July 2, 1972, Sept. 28, 1972, Nov. 12, 1972, Jan. 10, 1972.
24. Data obtained from staff of Air Force Academy.
25. *New York Times,* July 28, 1972.
26. United Nations, *Economic and Social Consequences of the Armaments Race and Its Extremely Harmful Effects on World Peace and Security,* report of the Secretary General, October 1971, paragraph 32.
27. Center for Defense Information, *Fact Sheet on Military Assistance,* Washington, D.C., 1973.
28. U.S. Arms Control and Disarmament Agency, *op. cit.,* p. 10.
29. *New York Times,* June 14, 1972.
30. *Ibid.,* July 10, 1972.

Chapter Six

1. W. Heller, *New Dimensions of Political Economy,* Cambridge, Mass., 1967, pp. 10–11, cited in R. B. Du Boff and E. S. Herman, "The New Economics: Handmaiden of Inspired Truth," *The Review of Radical Political Economics,* Vol. 4, No. 4 (August 1972).

2. N. Glazer, "The Great Society Was Never a Casualty of the War," *Saturday Review*, December 1972.

3. Address by Spiro Agnew at the luncheon of the Joint Service Clubs, St. Louis, Mo., Sept. 20, 1972. At Congressional hearings before the House Appropriations Committee on the 1975 military budget, it was revealed that not less than $1.0 billion and as much as $5 billion had been added to the Pentagon money request as "a measure of economic stimulation," according to Defense Secretary Schlesinger (*Washington Post*, February 27, 1974).

4. S. Lens, *Poverty: America's Enduring Paradox*, Crowell, 1969, pp. 296–7.

5. President Lyndon Johnson, State of the Union Message, Jan. 4, 1965; message to the Congress of the United States on the international balance of payments and our gold position, Feb. 10, 1965.

6. From Assistant Secretary of Defense David Packard, Oct. 26, 1970.

7. From Congressman Mendel Rivers on June 12, 1969.

8. From a statement by Caspar W. Weinberger, deputy director of the Office of Management and Budget, *New York Times*, Sept. 8, 1972.

9. J. J. Clark, *The New Economics of National Defense*, Random House, 1966, cited in D. Mermelstein, *Economics—Mainstream Readings and Radical Critiques*, Random House, 1970, p. 233.

10. J. Wiesner, President's science adviser, in *U.S. News & World Report*, Feb. 3, 1964.

11. J. J. Clark, *op. cit.*

12. H. Gintis, "American Keynesianism and the War Machine," in D. Mermelstein, *op. cit.*, p. 248.

13. *U.S. News & World Report*, May 19, 1950.

14. U.S. Bureau of the Census, *Historical Statistics of the United States from Colonial Times to 1957*, 1960.

15. *The Budget of the United States Government, Fiscal Year 1974*, Washington, D.C., 1973; see also *The 1973 Joint Economic Report*, report of the Joint Economic Committee, U.S. Congress, on the January 1973 Economic Report of the President, together with Statement of Committee Agreement, Minority, and Supplementary Views, Washington, D.C., March 26, 1973, pp. 72, 73.

16. Address by Mr. Leonard Sullivan, Jr., principal Deputy Director, Defense Research and Engineering, before the AFMA/NSIA Symposium, Washington, D.C., Aug. 16, 1972 (news release: Office of Assistant Secretary of Defense, Public Affairs); see Chart 3 and explanation.

17. Department of Defense, *Cost Reduction Report*, July 12, 1965.

18. *New York Times*, July 29, 1970.

19. See G. Stigler and C. Friedland, "Profits of Defense Contractors," *American Economic Review*, September 1971; re Senator Proxmire's report, see *New York Times*, May 16, 1973.

20. Statement by G. W. Miller, president, Textron, Inc., in *Forbes*, Sept. 15, 1971.

21. See article by N. Goldfinger, "What Labor Wants on Trade," *New York Times*, March 3, 1973, Section 3.

22. For a summary of the reasoning behind these estimates, see *I. F. Stone's Bi-Weekly*, June 14, 1971. Detailed analyses of U.S. military spending, by major function, are in R. Benson and H. Wolman, eds., *Counterbudget: A Blueprint for Changing National Priorities*, Praeger, 1971, a study sponsored by the National Urban Coalition.

23. U.S. Bureau of the Census, *Statistical Abstract of the United States, 1973*, pp. 774, 775. This includes economic and technical assistance, grants and loans.

24. United Nations, *Economic and Social Consequences of the Armaments Race and its Extremely Harmful Effects on World Peace and Security*, report of the Secretary General, Oct. 22, 1971, appendix, Table A.

25. U.S. Arms Control and Disarmament Agency, *World Military Expenditures, 1971*, Washington, D.C., 1972, p. 10.

26. The following textbooks were examined: Richard Caves, *American Industry: Structure, Conduct, Performance*, 2nd ed., Prentice-Hall, 1967; James A. Chalmers and Fred H. Leonard, *Economic Principles, Macroeconomic Theory and Policy*, Macmillan, 1971; Thomas F. Dernburg and Duncan M. McDougall, *Macroeconomics*, 3rd ed., McGraw-Hill, 1968; Robert Dorfman, *The Price System*, Prentice-Hall, 1964; Otto Eckstein, *Public Finance*, Prentice-Hall, 1967; David M. Gordon, *Problems in Political Economy: An Urban Perspective*, D. C. Heath and Co., Lexington, Mass., 1971; Thomas J. Hailstones and Michael J. Brennan, *Economics: An Analysis of Principles and Policies*, South-Western Publishing Co., Cincinnati, 1970; C. Lowell Harris, *The American Economy, Principles, Practices and Policies*, 6th ed., Richard D. Irwin, Inc., Homewood, Ill., 1968; Robert L. Heilbroner, *The Economic Problem*, 2nd ed., Prentice-Hall, 1970; Campbell R. McConnell, *Economics, Principles, Problems, and Policies*, McGraw-Hill, 1969; Donald A. Nichols and Clark W. Reynolds, *Principles of Economics*, Holt, Rinehart & Winston, 1971; Willis L. Peterson, *Principles of Economics: Macro*, Richard D. Irwin, Inc., Homewood, Ill., 1971; Lloyd G. Reynolds, *Economics*, 3rd ed., Irwin-Dorsey, Limited, Georgetown, Ont., 1969; Paul A. Samuelson, *Economics*, 8th ed., McGraw-Hill, 1970; and Charles L. Schultze, *National Income Analysis*, 2nd ed., Prentice-Hall, 1967.

27. See the *Economic Report of the President, 1964*, p. 46; *Economic Report of the President, 1965*, p. 102.

28. N. Chomsky, *For Reasons of State*, Pantheon, 1973, p. xv.

29. Cited in S. Hook, *Toward the Understanding of Karl Marx*, John Day, 1933, p. 135.

30. *Ibid.*, pp. 135–36.

Chapter Seven

1. Sometimes, of course, "agreement" to such occupation is obtained with the use of or the implied threat of force. Thus the continuation of a U.S. military base on Cuban soil involves the implication of the use of force, as does the installation of major Soviet bases among populations in Eastern Europe that have been hostile to Soviet occupation.
2. D. Irving, *The Destruction of Dresden*, Holt, Rinehart & Winston, New York, 1964. Compare the photographs of bombed Dresden with those of Hiroshima and Nagasaki.
3. For U.S. and U.S.S.R. strategic-nuclear-arms data and analyses, see *The Defense Monitor*, July 1973 (Center for Defense Information, 2001 Massachusetts Avenue, Washington, D.C. 20002).
4. R. McNamara, in *Authorization for Military Procurement, Research and Development, Fiscal Year 1969, and Reserve Strength*, hearings before the Senate Committee on Armed Services, 90th Congress, 2nd Session, on S.3293, Feb. 2, 1968, chart on p. 118.
5. *New York Times*, Dec. 21, 1970.
6. *Science*, Oct. 10, 1969, pp. 95ff. See also the Pugwash monograph, "Implications of Antiballistic Missile Systems," Humanities Press, New York, 1970. The interested reader should not fail to examine E. J. Sternglass, *Low-Level Radiation*, Ballantine Books, 1972; E. J. Sternglass, "Environmental Radiation and Human Health," *Proceedings of the 6th Berkeley Symposium on Mathematical Statistics and Probability*, Vol. VI (1972). A critical evaluation of the work of Sternglass and others is presented by H. R. Hoffman and D. R. Inglis in "Radiation and Infants," *Science and Public Affairs—Bulletin of the Atomic Scientists*, December 1972.
7. See G. Hohenemser, "The Nth Country Problem Today," in S. Melman, ed., *Disarmament: Its Politics and Economics*, American Academy of Arts and Sciences, 1962. In 1962 Hohenemser made an assessment of the nuclear-weapons potential of several countries and forecast the possibilities for 1975.
8. For an excellent overview of this part of modern militarism, see S. M. Hersh, *Chemical and Biological Warfare*, Bobbs-Merrill, 1968. Mr. Hersh's book is exceptionally well researched and includes extensive chapter notes that refer any interested reader to the wider literature in this field. In *Pentagon Capitalism*, pp. 123–33, I summed up certain critical technical literature on bacteriological warfare, including tables on characteristics of infective agents for biological-warfare use.
9. S. Melman, *Pentagon Capitalism*, McGraw-Hill, New York, 1970, Chapter 6.
10. In February 1973 we learned of the resurgence of guerrilla operations in the Philippines. *The New York Times* (March 26, 1973) reported: "The military situation bears a striking resemblance to

the early day of Vietnam. The guerrillas roam freely through the countryside, with support from local villagers, and with a vast intelligence network connected by runners and walkie-talkies. The army, a replica of the United States military forces, and with all American equipment, uses conventional tactics."

11. N. Chomsky in his important volume *For Reasons of State*, Pantheon Books, 1973, pp. 84–86, has defined with exacting detail the mechanism whereby the destruction of the NLF-supporting population base became an explicit military objective of the United States.

12. R. Littauer et al., *The Air War in Indochina*, Cornell University Center for International Studies, 1971.

13. *New York Times*, Hanson Baldwin, Jan. 19, 1973.

14. There is an unresolved problem here: What happened to the North Vietnamese air defense system that made it possible for them to exact this considerable toll of B-52s in December 1972 whereas previously such aircraft were virtually invulnerable at their 30–40,000-foot altitudes? Perhaps this is explained by the fact that "more than 1,050 of the so-called 'flying telegraph poles' were fired at our planes; after the first raids, most of them were launched not singly but in salvos of multiple missiles in a kind of missile-barrage fire. Carpets of bursting flak were laid over other areas at lower altitudes." (*New York Times*, Jan. 19, 1973, article by Hanson W. Baldwin.)

15. K. Hunt, *The Requirements of Military Technology in the 1970's*, Institute for Strategic Studies, London, 1967.

16. N. Chomsky, *op. cit.*, Chapters 1, 2.

17. R. A. Stubbing, "Improving the Acquisition Process for High-Risk Electronics Systems," Jan. 30, 1969 (distributed by Clearing House for Federal Scientific and Technical Information, Springfield, Va. 22151).

18. H. York, *Race to Oblivion*, Simon and Schuster, 1970, pp. 232, 233.

19. *New York Times*, Aug. 5, 1972.

20. *Ibid.*, May 11, 1973.

21. *Ibid.*, Feb. 21 and 22, 1971. See also the editorial on the false emergency, Feb. 22, 1971.

22. *New York Times*, Nov. 15, 1972.

23. *Wall Street Journal*, June 13, 1968.

24. U.S. Atomic Energy Commission, *Report to the Atomic Energy Commission by the Ad Hoc Advisory Panel on Safeguarding Special Nuclear Material*, March 10, 1967.

25. *Wall Street Journal*, June 13, 1968.

26. J. D. McCullough, "Design to Cost Problem Definition Survey to Potential Actions and Observations on Limitations," T-928, Institute for Defense Analyses, January 1973, p. 12, cited in U.S. General Accounting Office, *Cost Growth in Major Weapons Systems*, report to the House Armed Services Committee, March 26, 1973, p. 6.

27. *Ibid.*, p. 21. It is significant that the Pentagon gave the General Accounting Office a series of performance characteristics of 13 sets of new and old weapons systems to justify a 4.2-times increase in unit cost. The performance factors that were cited included payload, range or endurance, speed, avionics function, crew comfort or safety, and delivery or navigation accuracy. All these showed increases of rather less than 4.2 times. Significantly, the Pentagon staffs omitted reference to key reliability criteria like mean time between failures.

28. Baltimore *News-American,* Dec. 19, 20, 1971.

29. *American Report,* Nov. 5, 1971.

30. U.S. General Accounting Office, *op. cit.,* p. 5.

31. *Congressional Record,* Aug. 3, 1972, p. S12593.

32. Dispatch from Moscow by Theodore Shabad, *New York Times,* Oct. 3, 1971.

33. *New York Times,* July 24, 1972, and Aug. 15, 1972.

34. *Ibid.*, March 18, 1971.

35. *Ibid.*, Nov. 6, 1972.

36. *Ibid.*, June 15, 1972.

37. See the series of articles entitled "Army in Anguish" appearing in the *New York Post,* Sept. 13–24, 1971.

38. When we define the limits of military technology, an issue of professional ethics is implied. In codes of professional ethics, the misrepresentation of a product or a service is usually prohibited. Yet, much of the recent selling of military technology partakes of misrepresentation, since it involves a stated or implied promise that it will contribute either to the physical defense of the United States or to its military superiority.

39. U.S. Department of Defense, *Statement of Secretary of Defense Elliot L. Richardson Before the Senate Armed Services Committee on the FY 1974 Defense Budget and FY 1974–1978 Program,* March 28, 1973, pp. 27, 66.

Chapter Eight

1. "Report to the President" from the Cabinet Coordinating Committee on Economic Planning for the End of Vietnam Hostilities, in the *Economic Report of the President,* transmitted to the Congress January 1969.

2. Something else happened to this program. I learned, through an inquiry at the Council of Economic Advisers in 1971, that all of the files and records pertaining to this matter had been removed from the White House by the outgoing Johnson administration.

3. Joint Economic Committee of the Congress, *State and Local Public Facility Needs and Financing,* December 1966, Vol. 1, pp. 24–25.

4. U.S. Arms Control and Disarmament Agency, *The Economic and*

Social Consequences of Disarmament, U.S. reply to the inquiry of the Secretary General of the United Nations, Publication 21 (revision of ACDA publication 6 of July 1962), released June, 1964, U.S. Government Printing Office, Washington, D.C.

5. "We Can Afford a Better America," *Fortune,* March 1969, pp. 88–91, 158–63.
6. R. Benson and H. Wolman, eds., *Counterbudget: A Blueprint for Changing National Priorities, 1972–1976,* Praeger, 1971. For other approaches to employment effects of conversion to civilian economy, see R. H. Bezdek, "The Employment Effects of Counterbudget," *Journal of Economic Issues,* December 1972; UN Dept. of Economic and Social Affairs, *Disarmament and Development,* report of the group of experts on the economic and social consequences of disarmament, New York, 1972, pp. 30–31; L. Lecht, *Goals, Priorities, and Dollars,* The Free Press, 1966.
7. M. Anderson *et al., How Michigan Pays for War: A Report to the People,* Michigan Council of Churches, Peace Education Program, Lansing, Mich., 1972.
8. Industrial Reorganisation Corporation, *Report and Accounts,* 1967–68, 1968–69, 1969–70, London.
9. U.S. Bureau of the Census, *Statistical Abstract of the United States, 1972,* pp. 305, 373, 374.
10. U.S. Bureau of the Census, *Statistical Abstract of the United States, 1970,* p. 225.
11. S. Melman, *Dynamic Factors in Industrial Productivity,* Basil Blackwell, Oxford, and John Wiley, New York, 1956; "The Rise of Administrative Overhead in the Manufacturing Industries of the United States, 1899–1947," *Oxford Economic Papers,* 1950.
12. *New York Times,* Jan. 9, 1972; *U.S. News & World Report,* July 19, 1971.
13. See S. Melman, *op. cit.;* also S. Melman, *Decision-Making and Productivity,* Basil Blackwell, John Wiley, 1956; and "Managerial Versus Cooperative Decision-Making in Israel," *Studies in Comparative International Development,* Vol. VI (1970–71), No. 3, Rutgers University, New Brunswick, N.J.
14. *New York Times,* Dec. 30, 1969.
15. *Ibid.,* Jan. 2, 1971, editorial.
16. *Newsday,* May 26, 1972.
17. *Ibid.*
18. Statement by Edward L. King to the House Armed Services Committee, March 27, 1972.
19. *New York Times,* Oct. 31, 1971.
20. *Statements and Report Adopted by the AFL-CIO Executive Council, Bal Harbor, Florida, Feb. 15–23, 1971,* p. 15
21. *Economic Report of the President, 1971,* Washington, D.C., 1971, pp. 279, 280.
22. *New York Times,* Jan. 5, 1971.

23. *Ibid.*, Nov. 28, 1971.
24. House Committee on Government Operations, 90th Congress, 2nd Session, 1968, *Federal Revenue and Expenditure Estimates for States and Regions, Fiscal Years 1965–67*, pp. 25–26, 32, cited by J. R. Anderson, "The Balance of Military Payments among States and Regions," in S. Melman, ed., *The War Economy of the United States*, St. Martin's Press, New York, 1971.
25. An important contribution to the understanding of these matters was made by Edward F. Yost in his study *The Concentration of Management in Central Offices of Industrial Firms: The Limitation of Concentrated Management Decision-Making Control*, doctoral dissertation in the School of Engineering and Applied Sciences, Columbia University, 1969; see especially his Chapter 6, "The Limits of Computerized Information Technology on Managerial Concentration" (University Microfilm, Ann Arbor, Mich.).
26. *New York Times*, April 19, 1970, and June 9, 1971.
27. *Ibid.*, April 11, 1972.

Chapter Nine

1. An extensive body of analyses and bibliography on the conversion problem is found in S. Melman, ed., *Conversion of Industry From a Military to Civilian Economy*, A Series, Praeger, New York, 1970. The series includes M. Berkowitz, *The Conversion of Military-oriented Research and Development to Civilian Uses;* A. P. Christodoulou, *Conversion of Nuclear Facilities from Military to Civilian Uses;* D. M. Mack-Forlist and A. Newman, *The Conversion of Shipbuilding from Military to Civilian Markets;* S. Melman, ed., *The Defense Economy;* J. E. Ullmann, ed., *Potential Civilian Markets for the Military-Electronics Industry;* J. E. Lynch, *Local Economic Development after Military Base Closures.* Also, U.S. Arms Control and Disarmament Agency, *The Economic Impact of Reductions in Defense Spending*, Washington, D.C., 1972.
2. Office of the Assistant Secretary of Defense for Installations and Logistics, *Second Annual Report to the President on Federal Assistance to Defense-impacted Communities*, by the Inter-agency Economic Adjustment Committee, Washington, D.C., April 29, 1972.
3. For data on these occupations and institutions, see S. Melman, *Pentagon Capitalism*, McGraw-Hill, New York, 1970, Chapter 4; on conversion, see M. Berkowitz, *op. cit.*
4. A summary of federal legislation that has been prepared to encourage economic conversion is found in J. Bergsman, *Economic Adjustment to New National Priorities*, Urban Institute, Washington, D.C., July, 1971.
5. J. E. Ullmann, ed., *op. cit.*
6. D. M. Mack-Forlist and A. Newman, *op. cit.*

7. J. E. Baird, "A Network Model of the Conversion Process," in S. Melman, ed., *The Defense Economy,* Chapter 5.
8. *Business Week,* July 15, 1972.
9. I want to underscore that conversion is an entirely different process from corporate diversification. The latter means changing the product mix or the areas of investment of the firm by merging with civilian enterprises, by buying up civilian-type subdivisions, or by simply investing corporate funds in civilian-industry securities. Diversification, in that sense, can go on without any conversion whatever of the military-serving facilities or labor force. Thereby the top management of a military-serving firm can preserve itself as a management while the bulk of its military-serving employees are simply thrown to the labor market to fend for themselves. Typically, major aerospace and related firms have been able to diversify through processes of merger, corporate acquisition and the like. Conversion of the military-servicing facilities and organization to civilian products and markets is precisely what has not been happening.
10. *Grumman Plane News,* March 12, 1971.
11. U.S. Senate, Subcommittee on Executive Reorganization and Government Research, Committee on Government Operations, *National Economic Conversion Commission, Responses to Subcommittee Questionnaire,* September 1970, p. 119.
12. J. C. Goulden, "The Helicopter Breadline," *The Nation,* Jan. 11, 1971.
13. U.S. Senate, hearings Before the Committee on Labor and Public Welfare, *Post War Economic Conversion,* March 23, April 3, 1970, Part II, p. 468.
14. *Ibid.,* p. 465.
15. U.S. Arms Control and Disarmament Agency, *op. cit.,* p. 7.
16. *National Economic Conversion Commission,* hearings before the Senate Committee on Commerce, 82nd Congress, 2nd Session, on S. 2274, A Bill to Establish a National Economic Conversion Commission, and for other purposes, May 25 and June 24, 1964, Washington, D.C., 1964, p. 148. Two local labor groups also sent letters of endorsement: the Baltimore Council of AFL-CIO unions and the Maryland State and District of Columbia AFL-CIO. None of the military-industry national unions took a hand in the formal consideration of this pioneering conversion legislation.
17. *Swords into Plowshares: A Proposal to Promote Orderly Conversion from Defense to Civilian Production,* statement and testimony of Walter P. Reuther, president of the UAW, to the Senate Committee on Labor and Public Welfare, Dec. 1, 1969, UAW of Detroit, Mich., March 1970 (publication No. 1006).
18. For a discussion of the importance of local responsibility and authority for planning and operating base conversion, see B. Stein,

The Community Context of Economic Conversion, Center for Community Economic Development, Cambridge, 1971.

19. J. E. Lynch, *op. cit.*, includes abundant data on the consequences of failure to plan for economic development in advance of closure; also my paper *Planning for Conversion of Military-Industrial and Military Base Facilities,* U.S. Dept. of Commerce, Economic Development Administration, 1973, includes material to this point.

20. *New York Times,* June 30, 1973. "A 22-Acre Industrial Park Planned at Navy Yard Site" is the headline; only after considerable unemployment had been generated and it was clear that political efforts were to no avail have planning operations been undertaken by local community groups in military-base areas. This has been a repeated pattern throughout the country. See also S. Melman, *Planning for Conversion of Military-Industrial and Military Base Facilities* (above).

21. J. E. Lynch, *op. cit.*

22. N. Robbins, Jr., "The Engineer's Knowledge: Is It Transferable from One Industry to Another?," *Mechanical Engineering,* October 1971; R. L. Turnmail, "Going Through a Career Conversion?," *Electronic Design,* Aug. 16, 1971.

23. *Wall Street Journal,* March 2, 1971, included the following item in its labor affairs column: " 'No aerospace, please' declares a help-wanted ad placed in the Houston *Chronicle* by a unit of Tulsa based Telex Corp. A Telex spokesman blames a clerk for the ad's wording, but admits that the firm has been inundated with applications from formerly high paid aerospace people who don't fit its needs."

24. U.S. Arms Control and Disarmament Agency, *op. cit.*, p. 24.

25. L. Lecht, "National Priorities, Manpower Needs, and the Impact of Diminished Defense Purchases for Vietnam," Joint Economic Committee, Subcommittee on Economic Progress, 90th Congress, 2nd Session, 1968.

26. *New York Times,* Dec. 13, 1970. Localities like Lowell, Mass., a city of about 90,000 population near Boston, had about 20 job openings at the time that could be filled by engineers with some retraining.

27. The following news reports reflect on what works and doesn't work in these spheres: *New York Times,* Aug. 7, 1971, July 16, 1972; *Newsday,* December 23, 1971; see U.S. Dept. of Labor news release No. USDL-71-270, May 10, 1971. On Long Island the Long Island Association formulated an extensive manpower retraining program, and the Long Island University Graduate School of Education has defined detailed plans for occupational retraining. Self-help programs of various sorts have been operated by jobless engineers and others. See *New York Times,* Feb. 14, 1971; *Boston Herald,* Sept. 5, 1971.

28. State of California, Dept. of Employment, *The Potential Transfer of Industrial Skills from Defense to Nondefense Industries,* April

1968; U.S. Department of Labor, *Monthly Labor Review*, J. R. Cambern, D. Newton, "Skill Transfers: Can Defense Workers Adapt to Civilian Occupations?," June 1969.

29. Across the management of manufacturing and other industries, there is variation in the proportion of output to the military. What is impressive, however, is that every major industrial group has some stake in sales to the Pentagon. For data on the proportion of industrial sales to the military, see Leontief-Hoffenberg 1958 matrix, adjusted to 1965 (table prepared by Research Program on Economic Adjustments to Disarmament), as cited in S. Melman, ed., *Disarmament, Its Politics and Economics*, American Academy of Arts and Science, Boston, 1962, p. 138.

30. For a summary of major corporate military involvement, with much detailed data, see "The Business of War: 523 Corporate Contractors for the War in Indochina," *Economic Priorities Report*, Vol. 1, No. 7, February/March, 1971, Council on Economic Priorities, New York, 1971. That study opens with two pointed statements. A GM official: "We want to be known as a car and appliance manufacturer, not a merchant of death. . . . But we also want to be ready to profit from the apparently endless series of brushfire wars in which the U.S. seems to involve itself." (*Sunday Times*, London, April 21, 1968.) A GE vice-president: "We just do what the government asks; we build what they want." (L. Rodberg, D. Shearer, *The Pentagon Watchers*, Doubleday, 1970, p. 225).

31. *Wall Street Journal*, May 3, 1973.

Chapter Ten

1. P. Baran and P. Sweezy, *Monopoly Capital*, Modern Review Press, New York, 1966.

2. For a summary of the documents and arguments for a U.S. economic stake in Vietnam and Southeast Asia, see G. Kolko, "The American Goals in Vietnam," *The Pentagon Papers*, Senator Gravel Edition, Vol. 5, Critical Essays, Beacon Press, 1972, pp. 2–7. For the details of U.S. imports from Vietnam and other countries of Southeast Asia, see U.S. Department of Commerce, *U.S. Foreign Trade, General Imports, World Area by Commodity Groupings*, for various years.

Some students of the U.S. war in Vietnam suggest that, especially from 1950 to 1954, U.S. policy makers writing in the *Pentagon Papers* were concerned about Western control over Indochina in order to assure Japan's access to Far Eastern and Southeast Asian markets and raw materials. The reasoning was that since this was Japan's natural economic area, access to it would help maintain Japan as part of the West rather than compelling her to seek economic ties to the Eastern bloc states. The 1958 and 1972 data of

Japan's exports and imports do not support the earlier arguments about the central importance of Indochinese or total Southeast Asian markets to Japan's economy. For 1958 these areas accounted, respectively, for 4.6 and 22.8 percents of Japan's exports, and 0.81 and 16.3 percent of Japan's imports. For 1972 the percents of Japan's imports from these areas were, respectively, 1.1 and 17.8 while the export percents were 2.2 and 22. Vietnam and adjacent countries had negligible importance in Japanese trade. Japan's imports and exports with all Southeast Asia have been significant. But her exports and imports with North America dominated the field with 34.8 and 29.8 percents for 1972 totals.

For the *Pentagon Papers* references to Japan, see index in Vol. 5 of the Senator Gravel Edition, Beacon Press, 1972. For data on Japanese foreign trade, see Government of Japan, Ministry of Foreign Affairs, *Statistical Survey of Economy of Japan*, 1959, pp. 34–35; *ibid.*, 1973, pp. 42–43.

3. At this writing there is evidence from preliminary geophysical surveys that an oil pool of possibly large size lies in the area extending from parts of South Vietnam and Thailand through shallow seas southeast. By the end of 1970 major oil companies were bringing in crews and equipment for offshore drilling, and the Saigon government announced on Aug. 16, 1971, that bids had been received from 18 oil companies on concession rights for offshore petroleum exploration on the continental shelf extending into the South China Sea. Since the major oil companies have been understandably reluctant to make large capital investments in the Indochina area, it is noteworthy that by March 1971 the U.S. government offered investment insurance to U.S. companies for future offshore South Vietnam oil exploration and development. See *Wall Street Journal*, Feb. 20, 1973; *New York Times*, Aug. 18, 1971; *The Nation*, March 8, 1971; *American Report*, Oct. 30, 1970. An important collection of technical and economic data is in *The Congressional Record*, May 5, 1971, pp. E1977ff., and March 10, 1971, pp. H1404ff.

4. *The Pentagon Papers*, Senator Gravel Edition, Beacon Press, 1972, Volume 3, p. 695.

5. *New York Times*, March 13, 1972.

6. *Ibid.*

7. *Ibid.*, July 7, 1971.

8. *U.S. News & World Report*, July 17, 1971.

9. "The Interindustry Structure of the United States," *Survey of Current Business*, November 1964, p. 14, November 1969, p. 21.

10. *New York Times*, June 8, 1973.

11. *Ibid.*, July 13, 1971.

12. The following are some of the key data on this interchange: *New York Times*, Jan. 8, 1972, Nov. 12, 1972; *Business Week*, Jan. 15, 1972; *Congressional Record*, March 24, 1969, p. S30272.

13. One byproduct of the Watergate investigations of 1973 was a body

of data on the extraction of major political contributions for the Committee to Reelect the President from major corporations. The files of this committee included "memorandums containing information about enforcement and rate cases involving large corporations." (*New York Times,* Sept. 16, 1973.) The memorandums were from such federal agencies as the Internal Revenue Service, the Securities and Exchange Commission and the Civil Aeronautics Board. Judging from the listed agencies, these materials went beyond the range of problems involving competitively advantageous privileges, like rights to airline routes.

14. *Economic Report of the President, 1973,* Washington, D.C., 1973, p. 278.
15. U.S. Dept of Commerce, *Statistical Abstract of the United States, 1984,* pp. 883, 873.
16. U.S. Dept. of Commerce, *Statistical Abstract of the United States, 1973,* p. 831; *ibid., 1970,* p. 814; *ibid., 1984,* p. 883.
17. *Ibid., 1970,* p. 814.
18. A closely related set of analyses, covering the performance of 18 countries, is found in A. Szymanski, "Military Spending and Economic Stagnation," *American Journal of Sociology,* July 1973.
19. *New York Times,* Dec. 15, 1972. Such news stories are usually available in rich detail with respect to military-industrial work, but only rarely are similar data compiled for civilian industrial work or for civilian activity that is publicly sponsored. Plainly, the Pentagon's state management sees to it that a wide public is informed about the connection between specific war work and employment or unemployment. This reinforces belief in the Pentagon as an economic benefactor.
20. *New York Times,* July 13, 1971.
21. The armed forces themselves have a program of public relations designed to enlist support for their activities and hence encourage the belief that these are essential for the economy. Thirty thousand persons have passed through the Defense Information School in Indianapolis, a training center for military public relations. As described by one knowledgeable officer, "The essential fact is that we give people training in how to be slippery before the press and how to develop good community relations."
22. *Economic Report of the President, 1973,* p. 278.
23. *Ibid.*
24. *New York Times,* Aug. 3, 1971.
25. *Washington Post,* July 11, 1971, column by H. Rowen.
26. P. Baran, *The Political Economy of Growth,* Modern Review paperback, 1968, p. 119.
27. M. Reich and D. Finkelhor, "The Military Industrial Complex: No Way Out," in T. Christoffel, D. Kinkelhor, D. Gilborg, eds., *Up Against the American Myth,* Holt, 1970, p. 82.
28. U.S. Senate, 88th Congress, 2nd Session, Committee on Commerce,

National Economic Conversion Commission, hearings on S.2274, May 25 and June 22, 1964.

29. Vance further testified, "We can encourage large defense contractors to do the necessary long-range planning to anticipate changes in military procurement and make appropriate and timely adjustments. To this end on March 6, 1964, we changed the Armed Services Procurement Regulations to allow as reimbursable costs a reasonable and allowable part of the expense of long-range management planning which is concerned with the future overall development of the contractor's business and which may take into account the eventual possibility of economic dislocations or fundamental alterations in those markets in which the contractor currently does business." From 1964 to this writing there is no evidence of any industrial long-range planning *out* of military economy.

30. *The Pentagon Papers,* as published by *New York Times,* Bantam Books, 1971, p. 286.

31. See, *The Pentagon Papers,* Senator Gravel Edition, Vol. 5, the Name Index, pp. 13 and 19, on J. McNaughton and C. Vance.

32. From an address by AFL-CIO President George Meany to the Aluminum Association in New York City, Oct. 26, 1972.

Appendix 1 SELECTED MACHINES WHOSE PRICE INDEX (BASED ON 1957–59) EXCEEDED 150.0 BY MARCH 1970*

Agricultural Machinery and Equipment	
Agricultural Machinery Excluding Tractors	
Planting and Fertilizing Machinery	
Corn Planter, drawn, 4-row	152.8
Grain Drill, fertilizer type	157.9
Cultivators	150.9
Cultivator, rear-mounted, 4-row	156.4
Harvesting Machinery	
Corn Picker, mounted, 2-row	154.7
Haying Machinery	
Mower, mounted	164.0
Construction Machinery and Equipment	
Construction Machinery for Mounting	
Ripper	155.5
Dozer, hydraulic-controlled	157.6
Cable Power Control Unit	152.2
Mixers, Pavers, Spreaders, Etc.	
Concrete Finisher	158.1
Tractors, Other than Farm	
Crawler Type	
Diesel, 90-129 Net Engine HP	158.7
Diesel, 130-199 Net Engine HP	154.7

SOURCE: U.S. Department of Labor, Bureau of Labor Statistics, July 1970, *Wholesale Prices and Price Indexes for March 1970.*

* Index of average hourly earnings in manufacturing in March 1970 is 156 (base 1957–59).

Metalworking Machinery and Equipment
  Machine Tools
    Cutting Type   153.7
      Hobbing Machine   157.2
      Surface Grinder, 8 x 24   169.1
      Turret Lathe, ram type   160.5
      Bar Machine, automatic, 6-spindle   158.8
      Broaching Machine   159.5
    Forming-type
      Mechanical OBI Press, 32-35 Ton   156.0
  Power-driven Hand Tools
    Production-line   150.6
  Welding Machines and Equipment
    Gas Welding Machines and Equipment
      Welding Tip, acetylene   159.6
  Industrial Process Furnaces and Ovens   151.8
    Electric
      Heat-treating Furnace—factory built   162.1
    Fuel-fired*   160.8
      Atmosphere-controlled Furnace, gas*   175.9
  Cutting Tools and Accessories
    Small Cutting Tools
      Keyway Broach   157.5
      Twist Drill   153.1
      Milling Cutter, side   178.9
      Milling Cutter, plain   174.2
      End Mill   162.5
      Hand Tap   177.1
      Round Adjustable Die   172.4
    Precision Measuring Tools
      Snap Gauge, adjustable   155.9
General-purpose Machinery and Equipment
  Pumps, Compressors and Equipment
    Stationary Air Compressor, 100HP   172.2
  Scales and Balances
    Portable Dial Scale   161.2
  Miscellaneous General-purpose Equipment
    Valves and Fittings
      Gate Valve, iron, 6-inch   155.0
    Plain Bearings   165.6
      Connecting and Bearing, automotive   163.5

* Index base: January 1961.

° Index base: January 1961.
† Index Base: December 1965.

Textiles (including apparel)	12%*
Steel	15%†
Flatware	22%*
Footwear (nonrubber)	30%*
Leather gloves	30%*
Sewing machines	49%*
Black-and-white televisions	52%†
Amateur motion-picture cameras	66%*
Radios	70%†
Calculating machines	75%†
Hairworks, toupees and wigs	85%*
Magnetic tape recorders	96%†
35-mm. still cameras	100%†

* By value.
† By volume.
SOURCE: P. G. Peterson, *The United States in the Changing World Economy*,
Executive Office of the President, 1971, Vol. II, Chart 26, p. 18.

Appendix 3 DATA ON THE CLOSINGS OR REDUC-
TION IN SIZE OF U.S. FACTORIES, WITH INDICATIONS OF
RELOCATION OF FACTORIES ABROAD

These data were compiled by Mr. Nathan Spero, Research Director of
the United Electrical, Radio and Machine Workers Union and are used
here with his permission. Information also came from the International
Union of Electrical, Radio and Machine Workers, and other information
was drawn from trade journals and the daily press, as indicated.

P&M means Production and Maintenance; Sal. means Salaried; N.A.
means Not Available.

A. SHUTDOWNS, LAYOFFS AND TRANSFER OF PRODUCTION

(1) IUE Shops

Company	Date	Former Employment	Current Employment	Number Laid Off	Products	New Site
Warwick Electronics Forrest City, Ark. Local 1106	10/70	1969: 2,300	1,000	1,300	Color TVs	Mexico or Taiwan
Zion, Ill. (shutdown) Local 1022	12/70	1967: 2,000	0	2,000	Color, b&w TVs	Mexico, manufacturing facilities
Sylvania Entertainment Products Batavia, N.Y. Local 352	11/70	1966: 1,900	600	1,300	12″ b&w TV portables; DC portable sets	Initially to Smithfield, N.C., then to Hong Kong and Mexico
Sessions Clock Forestville, Conn. (shutdown) Local 261	6/70	50	0	50	TV tuners, made for RCA	RCA probably buys from Oak Electro/Netics' overseas facilities
Westinghouse Edison, N.J. Local 401 Local 491	11/70	1965: 2,300 P&M 400 Sal.	400 P&M 85 Sal.	1,900 P&M 315 Sal.	TVs, radios and phonographs	Canadian Westinghouse and a Japanese firm

Company	Date				Product	Notes
General Electric Syracuse, N.Y.	11/70	? ? ?	? ? 0	700 400 250	Color TVs B&w TVs B&w TV picture tubes	
Local 320		1968: 600 1968: 2,000	250 1,400	350 600	TV cameras Semiconductors	Japan
Emerson Radio and Phonograph Jersey City, N.J. (shutdown) Local 480	1966	approx. 1,000 in radio line	0	1,000	Radios	
	6/70	1,250	0	1,250	TV sets	Transferred to Admiral, which transferred to Taiwan
RCA Corporation Memphis, Tenn. (shutdown) Local 730	12/70	1,600	0	1,600	B&w TV sets TV antennas	Some equipment installed in Taiwan
Cincinnati, O. Local 771	6/71	5/70: 1,000	Shutdown planned	1,000	TV tubes, solid-state components	Orders for tuners were given to Oak Electro/Netics for manufacture overseas, probably Hong Kong

335

A. SHUTDOWNS, LAYOFFS AND TRANSFER OF PRODUCTION (*Cont.*)

Company	Date	Former Employment	Current Employment	Number Laid Off	Products	New Site
Philco-Ford Philadelphia, Pa. Local 101	4/70	?	?	1,300	TV's, Components	Probably Philco-Taiwan Corp. or Philco-Ford Micro-Electronics, Taiwan
IRC, Division of TRW, Inc. Philadelphia, Pa. Local 105	12/70	1969: 615	475	140	Electronic components	TRW Electronics Components Co., Taipei, or Mexico, or Puerto Rico
Standard Components Div. of Kollsman Industries Oshkosh, Wis. Local 1003 (shutdown)	5/70	1/69: 1,100	0	1,100 (shutdown)	TV tuners	Mexico

(2) *Other than IUE Shops*

Company	Date	Former Employment	Current Employment	Number Laid Off	Products	New Site
General Instrument F. W. Sickles Div. Chicopee, Mass. (shutdown)	9/69	1967: 3,000	0	3,000	TV components & tuners	Taiwan; Lisbon, Portugal; Sydney, Nova Scotia
Ludlow, Mass. (shutdown)	9/69	900	0	900	TV components & tuners	Taiwan; Lisbon; Sydney, Nova Scotia
Warwick Electronics Niles, Ill.		1966: 1,800	30	1,770	Color, b&w TV's	Mexico
General Electric Utica, N.Y.		N.A.	N.A.	2,000 in two years	Radios	N.A.
Advance Ross Electronics El Paso, Tex.		250+	approx. 15	235+	TV yokes TV components TV antennas	Transferred to Advance Ross Electronics de Mexico, S.A., Juárez, Mexico

337

A. SHUTDOWNS, LAYOFFS AND TRANSFER OF PRODUCTION (Cont.)

Company	Date	Former Employment	Current Employment	Number Laid Off	Products	New Site
Sprague Electric Worcester, Mass.	1970	900	500	400 Total company reduction of 2,400 since 1/70	Integrated circuits	N.A.
Sylvania Woburn, Mass. (shutdown)	12/70	500	0	500	Semiconductors (integrated circuits, diodes and rectifiers)	N.A.
Bangor, Maine (shutdown)	12/70	100	0	100	Semiconductors	N.A.
Hillsboro, N.H. (shutdown)	12/70	450	0	450	Semiconductors	N.A.
Sylvania Electronic System Needham, Mass. (shutdown)	12/70	228	0	228	Semiconductors	N.A.

RCA Corporation Rockville Rd. Plant, Indianapolis	12/70	N.A.	N.A.	Phonographs, TV's, components such as tuners, amplifiers	Some to main Indianapolis plant; rest to Taiwan and possibly Oak E/N
Bloomington, Ind.	12/70	N.A.	N.A.	Large-screen b&w TVs	Transfer to Taiwan, which already makes small sets; but Bloomington may pick up production from Memphis shutdown
Motorola Semi-Conductor Products, Inc. Mesa and Phoenix, Ariz.	11/70	N.A.	1,700 to 2,000	Transistors, rectifiers, IC's etc.	N.A.

B. STATUS OF FOREIGN INVESTMENT IN TAIWAN'S ELECTRONICS INDUSTRY, JUNE 30, 1968

Investment Already Approved

Name of Foreign Investor	Products	Date of Approval	Employment	Plant Site	Remarks
1. General Instrument Corp. (TEC)	IFT, tuners, deflection yokes, etc.	5/1/64	6,350	Hsintien	Operation started in November 1964
2. First Capacitor Mfg. Co., Ltd.	Capacitors	12/11/64	94	Hsinchuan	Operation started in February 1965
3. E. J. Rehfeldt	Coils	2/6/65	88	Taipei City	Operation started in October 1965
4. Philco-Ford Corp.	Radios, TVs, Phonographs	11/4/65	1,089	Chumei, Tamshui	Operation started in June 1966
5. TRW, Inc. (Thompson Ramo Wooldridge, Inc.)	Variable condensers, IFT, ceramic condensers, peaking coils	4/14/66	1,000	Shu-Lin	Operation started in October 1966
6. Philco Micro-Electronics, Inc.	Integrated circuit transistor	4/23/66	837	KEPZ	Operation started in October 1966
7. Electronic Building Element Industries	Matrix plane	4/22/66	187	KEPZ	Operation started in April 1967
8. Taiwan Nobel Electronic Co., Ltd.	Switch, resistor	5/10/66	85	Kweishan	Operation started in December 1965

No.	Company	Products	Date	Number	Location	Remarks
9.	IBM Corp. (Tatung Electronics Corp.)	Memory plants, IBM memory units	8/8/66	402	Peitou, Taipei Hsien	Operation started in October 1966
10.	Sunetics Ltd. (Eorgflo Corp.)	Magnetic-pole pieces	10/13/66	59	KEPZ	Operation started in May 1967
11.	Admiral Overseas Corp.	AM radios, stereo chassis, phonograph chassis	11/7/66	706	Chungho, Taipei Hsien	Operation started in September 1967
12.	Far East Electronics, Inc.	Earphones	12/20/66	93	KEPZ	Operation started in November 1966
13.	Cornell Dubillier Electronics Co.	Mica and electrochemical capacitors	1/24/67	250	Taoyuan	Operation started in September 1967
14.	Parsons Electronics (The Ramsey Ind. Taiwan)	Magnetic tape recorder, electric modules, cards, assemblies, etc.	1/24/67	2	KEPZ	Suspended production since March 1, 1968
15.	Taryo Communication Industrial Co.	Polyester condensers	1/28/67	30	Taipei	Workers under training
16.	Taiwan Toko Electronic Co., Ltd.	IFT, OSC coils	2/15/67	270	KEPZ	Operation started in June 1967

B. STATUS OF FOREIGN INVESTMENT IN TAIWAN'S ELECTRONICS INDUSTRY, JUNE 30, 1968 (Cont.)

Name of Foreign Investor	Products	Date of Approval	Employ- ment	Plant Site	Remarks
17. Consolidated Merchandising Corp.	Transistor radios, tape recorders, recorder phonographs	4/3/67	200	Taipei	Applying for bonded factory, workers under training
18. Radio Corp. of America (RCA Taiwan Ltd.)	Memory planes	5/11/67	156	Taoyuan	Operation started in February 1968
19. Econ Electronic Co. Ltd.	Electronic condensers	5/20/67	34	Puli, Taichung	Operation started in April 1968
20. Fox Electronic Co.	Electrolytic capacitor, printed circuit boards	5/29/67	—	Taoyuan	Suspended production since June 20, 1968
21. Yamatake Honeywell Co., Ltd.	Electronic self-balance tape recorder indicator	6/8/67	13	Taipei	Factory construction finished, workers under training
22. Channel Master Corp. (Trans World Electronics)	Television apparatus	6/19/67	67	KEPZ	Operation started in December 1967
23. Ampex Corp.	Printed circuit boards, cable harness, memory units	3/28/68	—	Kweishan	Factory under construction

24. Televac, Inc.	Receiving tubes	4/13/68	—	Hsing Shan	Machinery under installation
25. Thomas L. Higgins	Magnetic head coils, transformers for electronic use, electronic components for computers, semi-finished hearing-aid products	5/25/68	—	Hsin Chu	

C. U.S. ELECTRONICS FIRMS ON THE MEXICAN BORDER

Western Gear de Mexico, S.A.
(Western Gear, Los Angeles)

Heussen Aircraft

Electormex de Tijuana
(Fairchild Semi-Conductors,
Mountain View, Calif.)

Marshall de Mexico
(Marshall Industries, Monrovia,
Calif.)

Triad de Mexico
(Litton Industries, Venice, Calif.)

Treces, S.A.

Hatch International, S.A., de C.V.
(Hatch Control Device, El Paso,
Tex.)

Electronica Atlas, S.A.

Transitron Mexicana, S.A.
(Transitron Electric Corp.,
Wakefield, Mass.)

Sarkes Tarizan Mexicana, S.A.
(Sarkes Tarizan, Inc. Blooming-
ton, Ind.)

Cal Pacifico, S.A.
(Cal-Pacifico, Newport Beach,
Calif.)

Zaphiro, S.A.
(Topaz, Inc., San Diego, Calif.)

Internacional Manufacturera,
Electronica y Consultas, S.A.
(Republic Corp., California)

Curtis Mathes de Mexico, S.A.
(Curtis Mathes Mfg. Co., Athens,
Tex.)

Tecate Internacional, S.A.
(Temple Industries, Inc., Tecate,
Calif.)

Electronica del Noroeste, S.A.
(Fox Electronics, El Cajon,
Calif.)

Electronic Control Corp. de
Mexico, S.A.
(Electronic Control Corp.,
Eucless, Tex.)

C.T.S. de Mexico, S.A.
(C.T.S., Elkhart, Ind.)

Varo Mexicana

Border Electronics
(Hunt Electronics, Texas)

Industrial Motorola Mexicana,
S.A.
(Motorola, Inc., Phoenix, Ariz.)

Ensambladores Electronicos de
Mexico, S.A.
(Solitron Devices, Tappan, N.Y.)

Electronica Intercontinental, S.A.

Switch Luz, S.A.
(Transformer Engineers, San
Gabriel, Calif.)

Semiconductores de Baja Cali-
fornia, S.A.
(Raytheon Co., Mountain View,
Calif.)

Goleta Coil, S.A., de C.V.
(Ratel, Inc., Goleta, Calif.)

Ratel Internacional, S.A.
(Ratel, Inc., Goleta, Calif.)

Maquiladora Electronica, S.A.

Maquiladora Monterey, S.A.

Radio y Television California,
S.A.

Fairchild Controls
(Fairchild Camera and Instrument Corp., Syosset, N.Y.)

Industrias Mega
(Mega, Ind., Encino, Calif.)

Mexivend de Mexico, S.A.

Motorola Semiconductors
(Subsidiary of Motorola, Inc.,
   Franklin Park, Ill.)

Video Craft

R.C.A.

Standard Components Division

Standard Kollsman Industries

Electronica Atlas, S.A.

Certron Audio, S.A.
(Certron Corp., Anaheim, Calif.)

Tecnica Magnetica, S.A.
(Pulse Engineering, Santa Clara,
   Calif.)

Electronica de Baja California
(Warwick Electronics, Chicago,
   Ill.) (Silvertone TV)

Components de Mexico
(Fairchild, Hickville, Calif.)

C. P. Clare, S.A.
(General Instruments)

Aqua Prieta Electronica
(Ensign Coil, Chicago, Ill.)

Dickson Mexicana, S.A.
(Dickson Electronics Corp.,
   Scottsdale, Ariz.)

Sprague Capacitors
(Sprague Electric, Worcester,
   Mass.)

Lear Jet
(Lear-Siegler, California)

January 4, 1971

D. EXAMPLES OF FOREIGN OPERATIONS OF U.S. COMPANIES IN THE ELECTRONICS INDUSTRY

(Material from newspapers and business and trade magazines)

FAIRCHILD CAMERA

Set up a 5,000-worker plant in Hong Kong in 1965 to produce transistors and diodes with low-cost labor. The installation was followed by a plant in Seoul, South Korea, and one in Tijuana, Mexico. (Source: *New York Times,* May 24, 1967, in column "Market Place")

CONTROL DATA CORP.

The South Korean government authorized the company to set up a subsidiary in Seoul to produce computer memory plans for reexport to the U.S. Company plans to invest $500,000 initially, $2,500,000 in the future.

Control Data is the fifth major American electronics manufacturer authorized to produce in South Korea, following Fairchild Semiconductor, Signetics, Oak Electronics, and Motorola. (*Electronic News,* June 26, 1967)

GENERAL ELECTRIC

Began to produce electronic components in Shannon, Ireland, in 1963 and employs 1,200 people. In 1963, General Electric began a second Irish operation at Dundalk through a subsidiary, ECCO Ltd. It expects to employ 2,000 workers. (*Christian Science Monitor,* Feb. 16, 1970)

This item from *Japan Economic Journal,* Tokyo, Nov. 25, 1969 (weekly English-language edition of *Nihon Keizai Shimbun,* Japanese equivalent of the *Wall Street Journal*):

> Sanyo Electric and Tokyo Sanyo Electric have reached a basic agreement with General Electric . . . to establish an international division of labor setup in the field of cassette tape recorders. The two Japanese . . . manufacturers have for some time been exporting color and black and white TV sets, radios and tape recorders, etc., to GE. According to agreement, General Electric will cease completely production of cassette tape recorders from next spring, and Sanyo Electric and Tokyo Sanyo Electric will supply all cassette tape recorders the U.S. firm needs from then on. These tape recorders will be marketed in the United States under General Electric's brand name.

Details: Sanyo and Tokyo Sanyo will supply all GE needs, 840,000 per year. GE will not buy from anybody else. Final volume will be decided in a three-year contract. Prices will be modified every six months. GE exports of cassette tape recorders will be procured from Sanyo and Tokyo Sanyo "and will be directly shipped to these areas from Japan." Export prices will not be changed even if there should be price fluctuations in Japan.

There are no cassette recorders for civilian use produced in the U.S. by any company.

DATA PRODUCT CORP., CULVER CITY, CAL.

Produces magnetic cores and other components of electronic computers near Dublin. (*Christian Science Monitor,* Feb. 16, 1970)

TECHNICON INSTRUMENTS CORP., NEW YORK

Manufactures automated analytical systems for industrial applications near Dublin. (*Christian Science Monitor,* Feb. 16, 1970)

PHILCO TAIWAN CORP., A UNIT OF FORD MOTOR CO.

Came to Taiwan three years ago to make television sets, radios and other electronic components, exporting all it produces to the U.S. Says William B. Scott, managing director, "We came to compete with other countries that had grabbed up to 45 percent of the U.S. radio market and were making inroads in the television market." (*Wall Street Journal*, March 27, 1969)

MOTOROLA CO.

Has an electronic-component assembly plant on the outskirts of Seoul, South Korea. George A. Needham, director of the plant, told visitors that production costs in Korea were one tenth of costs for similar production at Motorola's plant in Phoenix, Ariz. He said it takes two weeks less time to train Korean girls to assemble semiconductors and transistors than to teach American girls the same jobs. Mr. Needham explained, "These girls here are more motivated. Life is tough in this country. These people really need this work." (*New York Times*, May 12, 1970)

ZENITH RADIO CORP.

Zenith is responding in the same way that most other electronic companies already have. It is building its first plant where labor is cheap, in Taiwan. Even the Japanese, hunting for cheaper labor, have been putting up electronic plants here. In the last decade, more than 475 corporations invested $433 million in Taiwan. Most of this money was from the U.S. ($235 million) and Japan ($116 million), and most of it was spent by electronic companies. Nearly $100 million worth of electronic products were made last year in Taiwan.

To date, Admiral, Motorola, Philco-Ford, Bendix, Arvin, RCA, Consolidated Electronics, Texas Instrument, IBM and Ampex have established plants in Taiwan. General Instrument Corp. was the first big U.S. electronic company to build in Taiwan, only six years ago.

Wages are half those in Hong Kong, a third of Japan's, a tenth of West Germany's, and a twentieth of those in the U.S. (*Business Week*, July 1, 1970)

[*U.S. News & World Report* also carries the following items on Zenith.]

The TV market. Television sets, as well as radios, are being manufactured abroad for U.S. consumption. Imports will get more than 50 per cent of the American market for black-and-white television sets in 1970—up from a nominal share in 1962, according to Joseph S. Wright, chairman of Zenith Radio Corporation.

Color TV? "Rapidly going the same way," says Mr. Wright. He adds: "It is not at all difficult to project . . . that 80 per cent or more of the U.S. home electronics industry will be produced in foreign countries within three or four years unless there is a major change in our trade policy."

And U.S. electronics producers have set up plants in Taiwan, Hong Kong, South Korea, and the Mexican border zone, or have licensed Japanese firms to use basic American technology. Zenith is starting construction on a big new plant in Taiwan.

Zenith's Mr. Wright estimates his company's U.S. employment was down 4,000 in 1969, "because of the competitive necessity of making, or having made offshore, products which we had planned only a year and a half ago to produce here in the U.S." (*U.S. News & World Report,* July 6, 1970, p. 44)

GENERAL INFORMATION ON FOREIGN RUNAWAY PLANTS

Trouble spots. Two fields in particular—electrical equipment and electronics production—are targets of labor's growing opposition to multinational companies. Three unions list 19 companies that have shut down or curtailed U.S. operations since mid-1969. According to the unions, a Westinghouse color television plant in Edison, N.J., transferred production to Japan and Canada this year, a Sperry Rand computer plant shifted assembly operations to Germany and Japan, and Emerson—which has imported all its radios since 1966—arranged with Admiral Corp. to have TV sets manufactured in Taiwan for sale in the U.S. [Note: 1,250 workers in Jersey City lost their jobs as a result of the Emerson action in closing down its TV plant.—Nat Spero]

The unions say that Taiwan's largest employer with 12,000 workers, is now General Instrument Corp., which has shut down operations in Massachusetts and Rhode Island during the past two years. Other companies on the unions' list include Singer, IBM, General Electric, Ampex, Raytheon, Motorola, Sylvania, and Philco-Ford.

The AFL-CIO points a specially accusing finger at Mexico, where some 200 plants employing about 20,000 workers "just south of the Mexican border" assemble everything from TV components to clothing. It cites as one example a $7-million plant built by RCA Corp. in Juarez, where 3,000 Mexicans are putting together electronic components for shipment to the U.S. (*Business Week,* Dec. 19, 1970, pp. 95, 98)

SYLVANIA ELECTRIC PRODUCTS CO.

The *Electronic News* of Feb. 4, 1970, carried an item headlined, "Bond with the Orient—After wetting its feet with some entertainment semiconductor manufacture in Hong Kong, Sylvania is thinking of following Fairchild and Signetics into South Korea. It would be an assembly operation, probably for integrated circuits, taking advantage of the inexpensive labor for bonding operations. Sylvania may wait for the outcome of the value-added controversy in Washington before making any moves." This value-added controversy refers to the tariff item mentioned above where the company needs only to pay the tariff on the value added on components partially fabricated abroad and then brought into this country.

Sylvania announced in October 1970 that it was closing down plants in Maine and Massachusetts producing integrated circuits, diodes and rectifiers, laying off 1,235 employees. It says its moves were dictated by declines in defense spending and price competition. (*New York Times,* Dec. 5, 1970)

[It would appear from the earlier story in *Electronic News,* cited above, that an expansion of its foreign operations may also be a key factor in its shutdowns.—Nat Spero]

RADIO CORPORATION OF AMERICA

In its house organ, *RCA Family,* November 1970, p. 12, the company speaks of expanding its semiconductor expansion both in the U.S. and abroad:

"We are planning," Mr. Hittinger [William C. Hittinger, vice-president and general manager, Solid State Division] said, "to focus our attention on opportunities within RCA for building a strong semiconductor operation, the outcome of which will help us by having better devices to sell on the outside market."

Expansion overseas also fits into the Solid State Division's future. "We are all quite optimistic that we will see other areas of the world in which we can expand and increase our sales," Mr. Hittinger said.

"By expanding Solid State product capabilities here in the United States," he said, "and by taking advantage of growth opportunities overseas, in the European area in particular, we will be able to achieve the goals that RCA's planners have set for us."

The Solid State Division has already begun establishing its European semiconductor capabilities with a plant in Liège, Belgium, and an applications laboratory and test facility in the United Kingdom.

Mr. Hittinger has recently announced the appointment of a Division Vice-President, Solid State–Europe, with responsibility for engineering, marketing, manufacturing, distribution and sales, further emphasizing RCA's intention to expand its overseas opportunities.

On the home front, a new national solid state sales organization has been formed which "is geared to grow with the rapidly expanding technologies of the semiconductor industry."

But the company recently announced it planned to phase out solid state operations at its Cincinnati, Ohio, plant in February. Initially some 220 workers would be affected. Domestic production would be continued at five other semi-conductor plants. An RCA spokesman described the action as the phasing out of older, less efficient plants. (*New York Times,* Dec. 5, 1970)

RCA also announced it was closing down its black and white TV tube plant in Memphis, Tenn. Employment in this plant has dwindled from a high of 4,000 in the late 1960's to about 1,600 at present, and these 1,600 employees will also be laid off. In mid-September it halted production of color TV picture tubes at Lancaster, Pa. The company says it is continuing to produce tubes in Scranton, Pa. and Marion, Ind. (*New York Times,* Dec. 9, 1970)

SCOTLAND

There are now 17 U.S. electronic companies in Scotland with a total investment of $100-million, triple the 1964 figure. Signetics is setting up a $3.6-million integrated circuit operation to employ 500 workers. Honeywell now employs 6,000 workers to turn out computers and microswitches. Motorola has opened a new $10-million semi-conductor plant that will employ some 1,500 persons by 1975. Labor costs are 30 per cent to 40 per cent cheaper than in the U.S., and in addition there are rebates on plant and equipment spending. (*Business Week,* July 4, 1970, pp. 26–27)

MEXICAN OPERATIONS

More than forty companies have invested about $10 million in assembly plants in Baja, Cal. It is estimated that between 3,000 and 3,500 people, mostly women, are employed in such plants in Tijuana alone, the major center of the movement. Several thousand more Mexican workers in Mexicali, Tecate, and the mainland border cities of Juarez and Nuevo Laredo. The majority of plants are engaged in electronic assembly.

Companies involved in these operations include Litton Industries, Fairchild Camera, Solitron Devices, Transitron, and Raytheon.

The American companies pay duty only on the value that is added to products in the Mexican plants. Consequently none of the work is initially manufacturing, but rather components are shipped over the border for assembly and the completed product is shipped back to the U.S. (*Los Angeles Times,* Nov. 19, 1967)

TWIN MEXICAN PLANTS

In the *Wall Street Journal* of Jan. 26, 1970, there appeared an advertisement of the Development Authority for Tucson's expansion stating, "Mr. President: Don't be embarrassed at your next board meeting when the question asker on the board asks: "What's going on in

Tucson, Arizona, that caused Motorola, Control Data, Kimberley-Clark, Lear Jet Stereo, and Philco-Ford to establish plants there?' "

The Authority's answer appears to the right of this question: "Twin plants in Nogales, Mexico, only one hour away . . . 30¢ per hour labor . . . more profitable than Japan, Hong Kong or Taiwan."

DUMPING

The Treasury Department has ruled that Japanese are selling capacitors, ferrite cores, tuners, and television sets at less than fair value prices in the U.S. In a hearing on the ferrite cores, "the Japanese countered that competition in this product came from overseas-based U.S. firms. They claim that the products at issue, cores used in radio and television sets, are now virtually never exported to this country by Japan." (*Electronic News*, Dec. 14, 1970, pp. 1, 14)

The following material relates particularly to plants under contract to U.E. (United Electrical, Radio and Machine Workers of America).

GENERAL ELECTRIC

G.E. announced a new manufacturing facility in Singapore is planned for construction, beginning late this year, for the production of timing devices to serve Far Eastern clock radio and other manufacturers, according to Cecil S. Semple, vice president of General Electric Company and general manager of the Housewares Division.

Timers for consumer electronics and other original equipment manufacturers are currently produced at the Company's Specialty Appliance Department plant here in Ashland.

The new plant in Singapore, expected to be completed in the summer of 1971, will supplement domestic production of timers to "serve expanding markets throughout the world and especially in the Far East," it was explained by William E. Newing, department general manager.

He pointed out that the increasing demand by Far Eastern customers for Telechron timers makes it imperative that a subsidiary plant be located nearer to this market.

"The planned Singapore facility represents an opportunity to continue to compete effectively in an area where manufacturing of consumer electronics and other electrical products has been growing rapidly," he said.

Newing said a growth in domestic demand for timers, which will continue to be made in Ashland, and for clocks, which are also made at the Ashland plant, should enable General Electric to sustain production levels in Ashland.

Accordingly, Newing said he does not expect that the proposed Singapore facility will have any appreciable impact on employment in Ashland. The Ashland plant will have basic responsibility for timer engineering and marketing at both locations. (*G.E. Employee Bulletin*, Ashland, Mass., Aug. 17, 1970.)

GENERAL ELECTRIC, ERIE, PA., LOCOMOTIVE DIVISION

Our UE Local reports that G.E. established a locomotive plant in Sao Paulo, Brazil, and is presently building a large plant in South Africa to build locomotives for the export trade formerly produced in Erie. However, so far, there has been no impact upon employment in the Erie plant.

GENERAL INSTRUMENT CO.—JERROLD ELECTRONICS PLANT

(Under contract to UE Local 158.)

This plant has not been closed, but the company laid off 200 workers assembling printed circuits for use in cable television. This work goes to a warehouse in Texas, shipped across the border into Mexico where the printed circuits are now assembled, shipped back to Texas and thence back to Philadelphia where the printed circuit is assembled into the overall product. Our Local claims that one printed circuit costs about 75¢ to 80¢ when produced in Philadelphia, about 13¢ in Mexico.

The following material is from trade-union sources, the International Union of Electrical Workers, the Machinists, and the International Brotherhood of Electrical Workers

ADVANCE ROSS ELECTRONICS

In moving its operation to Juárez, Mexico, the company had reduced its El Paso labor force from 250 down to 14.

TRANSITRON

It has 1,500 workers in its Laredo, Mexico, plant and only management personnel in its Laredo, Texas, facility.

GENERAL INSTRUMENT

It has closed down several of its New England plants plus Canadian facilities, laying off 3,000–4,000 workers. Its Portugal plant absorbed 500 jobs, while at Taiwan, where it is the largest employer its plant grew to 12,000 workers.

SPRAGUE ELECTRIC CO.

Had 2,700 factory workers in North Adams, Mass. This number was reduced to 2,000 early this year. Last year it opened a plant in Metamoros, Mexico, and transferred capacitor lines to it.

GENERAL ELECTRIC, SCHENECTADY, N.Y.

Shipped 285 turbine buckets to Japan for machining, to be returned to Schenectady.

The following material is from a speech by Senator Vance Hartke describing loss of jobs in this country as a result of runaway foreign plants.

"Philco in Philadelphia lost 1,300 jobs.

"Warwick Electronics lost 1,000 jobs in its Illinois and Arkansas plants to Mexico.

"Emerson Radio in Jersey City closed down with a loss of 1,250 jobs. Its TV production will be produced for it by Admiral with a plant in Taiwan.

"Zenith Radio laid off 3,000 workers with 4,000 additional jobs moving to Zenith's Taiwan plant in 1971. . . ."

(*Congressional Record*, Aug. 6, 1970, pp. S12888-12889)

Appendix 4 EXCERPT FROM TESTIMONY BY LIEU-
TENANT COLONEL EDWARD L. KING (RET.) ON MILI-
TARY MANPOWER PLANNING IN THE FY 1974 DEFENSE
DEPARTMENT BUDGET REQUEST BEFORE THE U.S. SEN-
ATE ARMED SERVICES COMMITTEE, JUNE 7, 1973

. . . The Department of Defense Authorization Bill (H.R. 6722)
which the Committee is considering contains what I believe to be excessive end-strength authorizations for each of the military departments.
These end-strengths are based on the type of embellished commitment
and threat evaluation that I have discussed, but they are also based on
wasteful and low combat productive doctrines and management techniques.

The FY 1974 budget outlays for military manpower will exceed $30
billion. What amount of combat defense will the American taxpayer
receive for his money? Let us examine the specifics of how some of this
costly military manpower will be used during FY 1974:

—According to a press statement of the former Comptroller of the
Department of Defense, about 77.5% of the fiscal 1974 active military
force of 2.2 million men and women will be serving as officers or non-
commissioned officers—a ratio of about 3 supervisors or health care specialists for each private, seaman and airman.

—In the 2.2 million active duty force being proposed for authorization
in FY 1974 only the following percentage of each military department
will be serving in combat-skill jobs that directly fire on an armed enemy
of the U.S.:

Army	24% of a requested end-strength of 803,806
Navy	12% " " " " " " 566,320
Marines	28% " " " " " " 176,219
Air Force	8% " " " " " " 666,357

—Despite the end of most short tours to Vietnam and a smaller planned force, Department of Defense manpower projected for non-productive transient status will number 89,000 (3.7% of the total force) in FY 1974. This represents an increase of 7,000 military personnel over the number of transients required in FY 1973. And the 89,000 non-productive man-spaces represents enough personnel to man 5½ combat divisions. The cost of FY 1973 transient manpower was $1.5 billion. In FY 1974 the Department of Defense is projecting 2,269,000 Permanent Change of Station (PCS) moves among its total 2,200,000 active military force, more than one PCS move per military individual.

—Military "grade creep" continues unchecked in the FY 1974 force. In a peacetime environment there will continue to be over 200,000 officers serving on active duty in higher "temporary" wartime rank (no program has reverted officers to permanent peacetime rank since the end of World War II). Despite the implied and intended restrictions contained in the Officer Personnel Act of 1947 and the Officer Grade Limitation Act of 1954, to maintain a balanced officer corps, the 2.2 million FY 1974 force will contain more 4- and 3-star officers (182) than were required on active duty in 1945 (139) to command over 12 million. In the FY 1973 armed force there is one general/admiral to command each 1,800 other military personnel. On June 30, 1945, at the peak of World War II, there was one general/admiral to command each 5,000 other personnel, and we won that war. On that same date in 1945 there were 14,898 colonels/Navy captains on active duty; on June 30, 1973, there will be 16,650 colonels/Navy captains on active duty in a 2.3 million force. There are also more lieutenant colonels/commanders in the FY 1973 force than there were in the 2.6 million FY 1964 force.

A comparison of FY 1964 and FY 1973 officer strengths shows 18,698 fewer captains, lieutenants and warrant officers in the smaller FY 1973 force, but an increase of 6,907 in the number of general/flag and field grade officers. It is difficult to relate these figures to a recent Army announcement which stated that the Army would involuntarily release approximately 4,900 reserve officers in the grade of major and below from active duty by October 1, 1973. It would appear that again token forced reduction is going to take place at the bottom rather than the bloated top of the officer corps. And it should be remembered that in terms of combat productivity, about 80% of active duty U.S. field grade officers are assigned to noncombat duties.

—The Defense Authorization bill contains an end-strength request for an active Army manpower level of 803,806 personnel. But less than 220,000 of those soldiers will be serving in the 13 combat divisions the Army will field in FY 1974 to fight in defense of our national security. And within each 16,000-man division over two-thirds of the personnel will be serving as officers or non-commissioned officers—only one-third as privates.

—In FY 1973 there are nearly 70,000 U.S. military personnel scattered about in 46 countries that include the following: Argentina, Australia, Brazil, Bermuda, Denmark, Dominican Republic, Ethiopia, Great Britain, Greece, Iceland, Italy, Indonesia, Iran, Jordan, Liberia, Morocco, Netherlands, Norway, Nigeria, Portugal, Paraguay, Pakistan, Spain, Saudi Arabia, Taiwan, Turkey, Tunisia, and Zaire. The FY 1974 Department of Defense requests give no indication of any lessening of this scattered U.S. military manpower deployment. It is difficult to understand how the security of these countries significantly impacts on our own security to a degree to justify stationing this number of our costly military manpower there.

—In FY 1974 the Department of Defense will train more administrative specialists and clerks (311,100) than they will infantry, guncrew, and seamanship specialists (215,700). The Department of Defense will also pay for 24,845 career officers to attend graduate education courses during FY 1974. And it is interesting to note that in FY 1974 the Air Force (with a requested end-strength of 660,357) will need to send 3,589 more officers to obtain graduate degrees in business management than the Army (which will have a requested end-strength of 803,806). Why does the Air Force need twice as many officers with graduate degrees in business management to manage 143,449 fewer personnel?

Mr. Chairman, I believe that if there is serious interest in reducing defense manpower costs and still adequately defending our national security, then some hard decisions still remain to be made.

Foreign "threats" must be more realistically perceived and evaluated on intent rather than "worst case" analysis. Overseas commitments must be more carefully weighed against actual treaty obligations and the priorities and best interests of this country, and troop deployments and overseas bases curtailed to more effectively relate to U.S. national security objectives. We must cease scattering our military manpower about the globe with combat missions they often cannot reasonably hope to accomplish. And in this regard we should face up to the fact that it is virtually impossible to make needed reductions in defense spending without first making substantial reductions in our over-commanded and over-supported forces stationed in Central Europe.

Present costly and unnecessarily lavish armed forces combat and support doctrines can no longer be tolerated. Our defense leadership and the Joint Chiefs of Staff must be more strongly encouraged to stop parochial log-rolling, and be required to streamline force structures by austerely revising current Tables of Organization and Equipment (TO&E) and Tables of Distribution (TD).

I believe now is the time to return to a traditional peacetime permanent officer rank structure, to reduce the excessive number of permanent change of station moves and unnecessary unit rotations that waste our manpower. It is time to eliminate duplicative rank-justifying headquarters and lavish support commands, and return to time-tested principles of armed forces planning and support doctrines within the parameters of new national priorities and austere common-sense combat requirements.

When these steps are taken, America can be even more adequately defended by more efficient armed forces and at far less cost in men and money. . . .

Appendix 5 EXAMPLES OF CIVILIAN–MILITARY
TRADE-OFFS*

TRANSPORTATION

1. Construction of Washington, D.C., Metro subway system (phone interview with Office of Community Services, Washington Metropolitan Area Transit Authority, Washington, D.C.) = $2.98 billion = cost of nuclear aircraft carrier *and* its aircraft, guided missiles, frigates and other support costs (remarks by Senator Allen Ellender, "The President's Defense Budget for Fiscal Year 1973," *Congressional Record*, Vol. 118, No. 6, Jan. 25, 1972, p. S409).

2. Proposal of Mayor Thomas Lukens of Cincinnati for federal subsidies for urban transportation systems to pay deficits and operating costs (Jack Eisen, "Cincinnati Mayor Urges U.S. Subsidy for 'Dying' Urban Transit Systems," *Washington Post*, Feb. 18, 1972) = $150 million per year = approximate cost of each Airborne Warning and Control System plane, to counter nonexistent Soviet bomber threat (estimate from Department of Defense publication "Weapon System Status," January 1972).

HOUSING

1. One Huey helicopter = $1 million (estimate from Department of Defense publication "Weapon System Status") = 66 low-cost houses with two bedrooms each, at $15,000 each (SANE "pie" chart, 1971).

* These military–civilian trade-off data were researched by economist Tom Riddell and were first published in May 1972 by SANE as a bulletin titled *What Could Your Tax Dollars Buy?*

2. Unfunded applications for assistance in housing programs in the state of Arkansas, as of November 1971 (Senator J. W. Fulbright, *Congressional Record*, Nov. 10, 1971) = $100 million = one DD-963 destroyer (remarks by Congressman Les Aspin, "Defense Cost Rise Because of Military Gadgetry," *Congressional Record—Extension of Remarks*, Vol. 118, No. 6, Jan. 25, 1972, p. E425; statement contained in letter to Melvin Laird, dated Jan. 5, 1971).

3. One Navy A-6E "Intruder" aircraft (estimate from Department of Defense publication "Weapon System Status") = $9 million = construction of 257 average New York City apartments at $35,000 each (Seymour Melman, professor of industrial engineering, Columbia University).

4. One Vulcan 20mm. cannon used extensively in Indochina (estimate from Department of Defense, "Weapon System Status") = $200,000 = average cost of 8 single-family houses at $25,000 each (Joseph D. Fried, "Any Hope for Housing?," *Saturday Review*, Feb. 12, 1972).

5. Funds for public housing impounded by Nixon Administration in fiscal year 1972 (Carl Holman, president, National Urban Coalition, testimony before Senate Appropriations Committee on the budget, Feb. 4, 1972) = $130 million = 8 Navy F-14 air superiority fighters at $16 million each (Senator William Proxmire, "The U.S. Navy Jet That Shot Itself Down, and Other Pentagon Lemons," *Potomac Magazine*, *Washington Post*, Dec. 5, 1971).

ENVIRONMENT

1. EPA program to clean up pollution in the Great Lakes vetoed by Office of Management and Budget in January 1972, due to large federal budget deficit (Elsie Carper, "Budget Office Bans EPA's Program to Save Lakes," *Washington Post*, Feb. 22, 1972) = $141 million for 1973 = 1973 request for funds for new Boeing 747s to be equipped as the President's airborne command post for the executive staff in case of nuclear attack (Richard P. Levine, "Increased Pentagon Spending Promises a Boost for Defense Industry," *Wall Street Journal*, Jan. 25, 1972).

2. Unfunded applications for HUD Water and Sewer grants ("The Federal Budget and the Cities: A Review of the President's 1973 Budget in Light of Urban Needs and National Priorities," National League of Cities and U.S. Conference of Mayors) = $4 billion plus = the overrun to date on the F-111 aircraft program = $4.7 billion (remarks by Senator William Proxmire, "Cost Data for Major Weapons Systems," *Congressional Record*, Vol. 117, No. 168, Nov. 8, 1971, p. S17802; data

abstracted from June 30, 1971 *Selected Acquisition Reports—SARS—* prepared by the Department of Defense).

3. Estimated cost of abatement of water pollution between 1970 and 1975 by President's Council on Environmental Quality = $38 billion = overrun of current Pentagon cost estimates above original planning estimates for 45 weapons systems as of June 30, 1971, $35.2 billion (remarks by Senator William Proxmire, "Cost Data for Major Weapons Systems").

4. Estimate for abatement of air pollution for same period (President's Council on Environmental Quality) = $23.7 billion = the cost of "exoticism" of weapons system (oversophistication and technical frills) which hasn't panned out, estimated by Senator Mike Mansfield = $20 to $30 billion (remarks by Senator Mike Mansfield, "The Military Budget," *Congressional Record*, Vol. 118, No. 17, Feb. 9, 1972, p. S1463).

5. Estimate for adequate solid-waste treatment programs (President's Council on Environmental Quality) = $43.5 billion = possible total cost of the B-1 bomber program to completion, with fully equipped planes—bombs, SCADs (subsonic-cruise armed decoys), SRAMs (short-range attack missiles) and avionics (estimate of Office of Management and Budget as reported in Berkeley Rice, "The B-1 Bomber: The Very Model of a Modern Major Misconception," *Saturday Review*, Dec. 11, 1971).

6. Total cost of environmental cleanup (President's Council on Environmental Quality) = $105.2 billion—eventual cost of all weapons systems now in development or procurement (remarks by Senator John Stennis, "The Military Budget," *Congressional Record*, Vol. 118, No. 17, Feb. 9, 1972, p. S1462).

RURAL DEVELOPMENT

1. A new high school for Toledo-Newport, Oregon (Senator Mark Hatfield's *Newsletter*, fall 1971) = $6.25 million = the amount Lincoln County, Oregon, paid to support military spending in fiscal year 1971 (Senator Mark Hatfield, fall 1971).

2. Congressional legislation proposed to upgrade life in rural America —federal financing to provide opportunities for employment and progress (*Washington Post*, Feb. 20, 1972) = $300 million per year = five C-5A aircraft at $60 million each (Senator William Proxmire, "The U.S. Navy Jet That Shot Itself Down, and Other Pentagon Lemons," *Potomac Magazine, Washington Post*, Dec. 5, 1971).

3. Unfunded applications for Farmers Home Administration grants and loans for development of water and sewer systems in small com-

munities in Arkansas, as of November 1971 (remarks of Senator J. W. Fulbright, "Special Foreign Economic and Humanitarian Assistance Act of 1971," *Congressional Record*, Vol. 117, No. 170, Nov. 10, 1971, p. S18066) = $20 million = 10 Sprint missiles in the Safeguard ABM system at $2 million each (Ralph Lapp, Senate Foreign Relations Committee ABM hearings, spring 1969).

4. Funded applications for assistance in housing programs in Arkansas as of November 1971 (remarks of Senator Fulbright, "Special Foreign Economic Humanitarian Assistance Act of 1971") = $100 million = approximate cost of 2 months' bombing in Laos (John Kerry in UAW *Solidarity*, March 1972).

5. National Health Service Corps to improve delivery of health services to rural areas—funding was decreased $4 million in 1973 budget; was $22 million below the Congressionally authorized level (Dr. James R. Kimmey, executive director, American Public Health Association, testimony before Senate Appropriations Committee on the 1973 budget, Feb. 3, 1972) = $22 million = ½ of the increase in funding for 1973 ($44 million) for the Lockheed Cheyenne helicopter, a program previously halted by Congress (Richard P. Levine, "Increased Pentagon Spending Promises a Boost for Defense Industry," *Wall Street Journal*, Jan. 25, 1972).

INCOME SECURITY AND WELFARE

1. Decrease in funding for the child nutrition programs of the Department of Agriculture in the proposed 1973 budget (*Special Analyses of the U.S. Budget*, Office of Management and Budget) = $69 million = two DE-1052 Destroyer escorts at $34 million each (remarks by Congressman Les Aspin, "Defense Cost Rise Because of Military Gadgetry," *Congressional Record—Extension of Remarks*, Vol. 118, No. 6, Jan. 25, 1972, p. E425; statement contained in letter to Melvin Laird dated Jan. 5, 1971).

2. Decrease in funding of the Special Milk program of the Department of Agriculture in the proposed 1973 budget (*Special Analyses of the U.S. Budget*, Office of Management and Budget) = $1 million = 1 Main battle tank (Senator William Proxmire, "The U.S. Navy Jet That Shot Itself Down, and Other Pentagon Lemons," *Potomac Magazine*, *Washington Post*, Dec. 5, 1971).

3. Decrease in grants to states from HEW for public assistance in the proposed 1973 budget (*Special Analyses of the U.S. Budget*, Office of Management and Budget) = $567 million = 3 nuclear-power attack

submarines at $175 million each (*Business Week,* "Stopping the Incredible Rise in Weapons Costs," Feb. 19, 1972).

4. November 1971 Census Bureau estimate of amount necessary to bring all poor American families (25.5 million people) above the poverty line (Peter Milius, "The Poor in America: Who They Are," *Washington Post,* Feb. 20, 1972) = $11.4 billion = current Pentagon estimate of the costs of producing the B-1 bombers, minus equipment (Berkeley Rice, "The B-1 Bomber: The Very Model of a Modern Major Misconception," *Saturday Review,* Dec. 11, 1971).

5. Elimination of hunger in the United States (Urban Coalition) = $4 to $5 billion per year = current estimate of the total final cost of the C-5A construction program (remarks by Senator William Proxmire, "Cost Data for Major Weapons Systems," *Congressional Record,* Vol. 117, No. 168, Nov. 8, 1971, p. S17802; Data abstracted from June 30, 1971, *Selected Acquisition Reports—SARS*—prepared by the Department of Defense).

DAY CARE AND CHILD DEVELOPMENT

1. The Federal Child Care Program for child nutrition, health and day care approved by Congress but vetoed by President Nixon in December 1971 (*Washington Post*) = $2.1 billion = the overrun to date on the B-1 bomber program in which not even one prototype has been completed yet ($2.2 billion) (remarks by Senator William Proxmire, "Cost Data for Major Weapons Systems," *Congressional Record,* Vol. 117, No. 168, Nov. 8, 1971, p. S17802; data abstracted from June 30, 1971, *SARS*).

EDUCATION

1. A $10,000 salary for 100,000 elementary-school teachers = $1 billion = construction costs of one nuclear-powered aircraft carrier, *minus* equipment (remarks by Senator Allen Ellender, "The President's Defense Budget for Fiscal Year 1973," *Congressional Record,* Vol. 118, No. 6, Jan. 25, 1972, p. S409).

2. Construction of two suburban high schools in the Midwest (SANE "pie" chart, 1971) = $32 million = the cost of current loaning of Navy destroyers and submarines to Turkey, Greece, Spain and Korea (Legislative Memo, Coalition on National Priorities and Military Policy, March 6, 1972).

3. Deficit of Philadelphia school board for running the school system in 1971 (Philadelphia *Inquirer*, Feb. 26, 1972) = $40 million = Pentagon estimate of the cost of one B-1 bomber (Berkeley Rice, "The B-1 Bomber: The Very Model of a Modern Major Misconception," *Saturday Review*, Dec. 11, 1971).

4. Cost to reopen the main branch of the New York Public Library on Saturdays, Sundays and holidays for one year (Herbert Mitgang, "The Nonwar War," *New York Times*, Sept. 27, 1971) = $900,000 = approximate operating costs of six Huey helicopters for one year in Indochina (*The Air War in Indochina*, Cornell University Center for International Studies, pp. 5–9).

5. Keeping the New York Public Library's Science and Technology Division, threatened with closing, open to the public (*Science*, Oct. 8, 1971) = $1 million = approximate cost of one Huey helicopter (Department of Defense, "Weapon System Status").

6. Construction of 28 school projects in Philadelphia, shelved for lack of funds (Philadelphia SANE *Newsletter*, winter 1972) = $17 million = one Navy F-14 air superiority fighter ($16 million) (remarks by Congressman Les Aspin, "Defense Cost Rise Because of Military Gadgetry," *Congressional Record—Extension of Remarks*, Vol. 118, No. 6, Jan. 25, 1972, p. E425; statement contained in letter to Melvin Laird dated Jan. 5, 1971).

7. School system budgets:

Gary, Indiana (*Washington Post*) = $42 million = 5 Air Force F-15 air superiority fighters ($45 million) (remarks by Congressman Les Aspin, "Defense Cost Rise Because of Military Gadgetry").

Washington, D.C. (*Washington Post*) = $141.7 million = 5 Boeing 747s for the President's airborne command post to be used by executive staff in nuclear war, at $28 million each (Richard P. Levine, "Increased Pentagon Spending Promises a Boost for Defense Industry," *Wall Street Journal*, Jan. 25, 1972).

New York City (*Washington Post*) = $1.7 billion = 1973 Safeguard funding ($1.5 billion) (Richard P. Levine, "Increased Pentagon Spending Promises a Boost for Defense Industry").

Independence, Missouri (*Washington Post*) — $10 million = projected cost of one Air Force F-15 fighter ($9 million) (remarks by Congressman Les Aspin, "Defense Cost Rise Because of Military Gadgetry").

Philadelphia (*Washington Post*) = $330 million = projected cost of proposed new "tactical cruise-missile attack submarine" ($300 million) (Richard P. Levine, "Navy Wants to Build New Class of Nuclear Subs, but Cost of $300 Million Each May Deter Move," *Wall Street Journal,* March 15, 1972).

Dayton school system, in November 1971, needed $12.6 million to reopen its schools (*Washington Post*) = 4 Spartan missiles for the Safeguard ABM system (Ralph Lapp, Senate Foreign Relations Committee ABM hearings, spring 1969).

8. $2,050 college scholarships to 20 American students = $41,000 = the operating cost of *each* B-52 sortie in Southeast Asia (sortie = one plane, one mission) (*The Air War in Indochina,* Cornell University Center for International Studies).

9. Loss of 6,000 aircraft in Indochina as of October 1969, valued at (Washington Labor for Peace, *Rich Man's War, Poor Man's Fight*) $6 billion = an equipped elementary school for 1,000 children, a junior high school for 1,300 children, a senior high school for 1,500 children in *each* of 250 communities, plus paying a starting salary of $7,000 to each of 35,714 teachers (Washington Labor for Peace, *Rich Man's War, Poor Man's Fight*).

10. Decrease in 1973 federal funding for graduate fellowships (Roger Heyns, president, American Council on Education, testimony before Senate Appropriations Committee on the 1973 budget, Feb. 3, 1972) = $175 million = one nuclear-power attack submarine ("Stopping the Incredible Rise in Weapons Costs," *Business Week,* Feb. 19, 1972).

11. Decrease in 1973 federal funding for library acquisitions (Roger Heyns, president, American Council on Education, testimony before Senate Appropriations Committee on the 1973 budget, Feb. 3, 1972) = $14 million = 7 Sprint Missiles for the Safeguard ABM system at $2 million each (Ralph Lapp, Senate Foreign Relations Committee hearings on ABM, spring 1969).

URBAN DEVELOPMENT

1. City of New Orleans, Louisiana, unfunded applications for grants-in-aid from federal government for urban development, open space, housing rehabilitation, and law enforcement (Mayor Moon Landrieu, testimony before Senate Appropriations Committee on the 1973 budget, Feb. 3, 1972) = $94 million = approximate cost of 2 months' bombing in Laos (John Kerry, UAW *Solidarity,* March 1972).

2. The Nixon administration's shortfall in requests for funds for urban renewal below 1972 Congressional authorization ("The Federal Budget and the Cities: A Review of the President's 1973 Budget in Light of Urban Needs and National Priorities," U.S. Conference of Mayors and

the League of Cities) = $465 million = increase in funding in 1973 for the F-15 Air Force fighter plane = $491 million (Richard Levine, "Increased Pentagon Spending Promises a Boost for Defense Industry," *Wall Street Journal*, Jan. 25, 1972).

3. Funds impounded in 1972 by Nixon for housing rehabilitation (Mayor Moon Landrieu, testimony before the Senate Appropriations Committee on the 1973 budget, Feb. 3, 1972) = $50 million = 3 Navy F-14s ($48 million) (remarks by Congressman Les Aspin, "Defense Cost Rise Because of Military Gadgetry," *Congressional Record—Extension of Remarks*, Vol. 118, No. 6, Jan. 25, 1972, p. E425; statement contained in letter to Melvin Laird dated Jan. 5, 1971).

4. League of Cities and U.S. Conference of Mayors estimate of urban centers' needs for modernizing hospitals and building new ones (Mayor Kenneth Gibson, testimony before Senate Appropriations Committee on the 1973 budget, Feb. 3, 1972) = $18 billion = low-range estimate of possible total cost of the underwater long-range missile system (ULMS) (Richard Levine, "Increased Pentagon Spending Promises a Boost for Defense Industry").

5. Funds needed for urban renewal in Newark, New Jersey, to trigger commercial, residential, institutional and industrial development on 625 acres of land (Mayor Kenneth Gibson, testimony before Senate Appropriations Committee on the 1973 budget, Feb. 3, 1972) = $125 million = four DE-1052 destroyer escorts ($132 million) (remarks by Congressman Les Aspin, "Defense Cost Rise Because of Military Gadgetry").

6. League of Cities estimate of additional funds needed to continue to physically rebuild blighted areas in the nation's cities (Mayor Kenneth Gibson, testimony before Senate Appropriations Committee on the 1973 budget, Feb. 3, 1972) = $3 billion = the cost of a fully equipped nuclear aircraft carrier with its planes, escort ships and necessary support (remarks by Senator Allen Ellender, "The President's Defense Budget for Fiscal Year 1973," *Congressional Record*, Vol. 118, No. 6, Jan. 25, 1972, p. S409).

7. Detroit's budget deficit for 1971 (Mayor Roman S. Gribbs, testimony before Senate Appropriations Committee on the 1973 budget, Feb. 3, 1972) = $30 million = 3 Air Force F-15s ($27 million) (remarks by Congressman Les Aspin, "Defense Cost Rise Because of Military Gadgetry").

8. *Cuts* in urban categorical grants managed by HUD in President Nixon's proposed 1973 budget ("The Federal Budget and the Cities: A Review of the President's 1973 Budget in Light of Urban Needs and National Priorities," U.S. Conference of Mayors and the League of Cities):

Urban renewal = $465 million = $491-million increase in funding for Air Force's F-15 (Richard Levine, "Increased Pentagon Spending Promises a Boost for Defense Industry").

Water and sewer = $700 million = $800-million increase in funding for ULMS (Richard Levine, "Increased Pentagon Spending").

Section 236 housing = $50 million = $44-million increase in funding for the Cheyenne helicopter (Richard Levine, "Increased Pentagon Spending").

Rehabilitation loans = $90 million = $74 million increase in funding for the B-1 bomber (Richard Levine, "Increased Pentagon Spending").

Rent supplements = $7 million = $9.3 million funding for procurement of Vulcan 20mm. cannons for fiscal year 1973 (Department of Defense, "Weapon System Status").

HEALTH

1. Health center in Baton Rouge, Louisiana ("Representative Construction Costs of Hospitals and Related Health Facilities," Department of Health, Education and Welfare, Facilities Engineering and Construction Agency) = $1.5 million = the operating costs of 10 Huey helicopters in Indochina for one year (*The Air War in Indochina*, Cornell University Center for International Studies).

2. Federal heart-disease-prevention program to establish research centers and clinics, proposed by Senator Schweiker ("Schweiker Asks 5-Year War on Heart Disease," *Washington Post*, Feb. 21, 1972) = $425 million over 5 years = $404 million 1973 funding for converting Polaris submarines to Poseidon MIRVed configuration (Richard Levine, "Increased Pentagon Spending Promises Boost for Defense Industry," *Wall Street Journal*, Jan. 25, 1972).

3. Coalition of Health Funding estimate of shortcoming of Nixon's health budget versus American health needs for research programs, manpower, construction, health services and mental health (Stuart Auerbach, "Coalition Assails Nixon's Health Budget as Far Too Small," *Washington Post*, Feb. 18, 1972) = $2.3 billion = the combined overruns on the C-5A and Main battle tank weapons programs (remarks by Senator William Proxmire, "Cost Data for Major Weapons Systems," *Congressional Record*, Vol. 117, No. 168, Nov. 8, 1971, p. S17802; data abstracted from June 30, 1971, *Selected Acquisition Reports—SARS—* prepared by the Department of Defense).

4. Funding-increase proposals of Coalition (Stuart Auerbach, "Coalition Assails Nixon's Health Budget as Far Too Small": NIH receive in-

crease of $300 million instead of $139 million increase in budget = $161 million = 1973 funding for procurement of F-111 aircraft (Richard Levine, "Increased Pentagon Spending Promises Boost for Defense Industry"); or, overrun to date on the Cheyenne close-support-helicopter program ($167 million) (remarks by Senator Proxmire, "Cost Data for Major Weapons Systems"); health manpower programs receive $1 billion more rather than $141 million *cut* in budget = $1.1 billion (Senator Proxmire, "Cost Data . . . = overrun to date on the Safeguard ABM system; increase of $343 million for mental health instead of $612 million stand-pat request in budget = increase in funding in 1973 for the Airborne Warning and Control System (AWACS) program ($331 million) (Richard Levine, "Increased Pentagon Spending Promises Boost for Defense Industry").

5. Decrease in funding of Health Services and Mental Health Administration and National Institutes of Health from 1972 to 1973 budget (Dr. John Cooper, Association of American Medical Colleges, testimony before Senate Appropriations Committee on the 1973 budget, Feb. 2, 1972) = $65 million = one C-5A aircraft ($60 million) (Senator William Proxmire, "The U.S. Navy Jet That Shot Itself Down, and Other Pentagon Lemons," *Potomac Magazine, Washington Post,* Dec. 5, 1971).

6. Decrease in funds for education and training of health personnel from 1972 to 1973 budget (Dr. John Cooper, testimony before Senate Appropriations Committee on the 1973 budget = $140.9 million = one DE-1052 destroyer escort and one DD-963 destroyer ($134 million) (remarks by Congressman Les Aspin, "Defense Cost Rise Because of Military Gadgetry," *Congressional Record—Extension of Remarks,* Vol. 118, No. 6, Jan. 25, 1972, p. E425; statement contained in letter to Melvin Laird dated Jan. 5, 1971).

7. Decrease in funds for health-services planning and development (Dr. John Cooper, testimony on the 1973 Budget) = $139.5 million = 15 Air Force F-15 fighters (remarks by (Congressman Aspin, "Defense Cost Rise Because of Military Gadgetry").

8. Funds needed for full implementation of authorization for Comprehensive Health Manpower Training Act construction grants to expand capabilities of nation's medical schools (Nixon requested no funds in 1973 budget) (Dr. John Cooper, testimony on the 1973 budget = $250 million = current overrun on the M60 Sheridan tank program ($245 million) (remarks by Senator Proxmire, "Cost Data for Major Weapons Systems").

9. Funds for medical facilities construction grants at 1972 level to rebuild and renew hospital physical plants (an increase of $145 million over Nixon request) (Dr. John Cooper, testimony on the 1973 Budget,

= $230 million = 4 C-5A's ($240 million) (Senator Proxmire, "The U.S. Navy Jet That Shot Itself Down, and Other Pentagon Lemons").

10. *Cut* in Hill-Burton hospital construction grants ("The Federal Budget and the Cities: A Review of the President's 1973 Budget in Light of Urban Needs and National Priorities," U.S. Conference of Mayors and the League of Cities) = $72 million = Office of Management and Budget estimate of ultimate cost of one B-1 bomber with its bombs, SCADs, SRAMs, and avionics = $80 million (Berkeley Rice, "The B-1 Bomber: The Very Model of a Modern Major Misconception," *Saturday Review*, Dec. 11, 1971).

11. Additional federal health funding deemed necessary by the Coalition for Health Funding (testimony of Dr. Michael DeBakey before Senate Appropriations Committee on the 1973 budget, Feb. 4, 1972); $100 million more for programs of National Cancer Institute to bring to fully authorized spending level for 1973 = one DD-963 destroyer (remarks by Congressman Aspin, "Defense Cost Rise Because of Military Gadgetry"); $100 million more for National Heart and Lung Institute = 11 Air Force F-15s (Congressman Aspin); $100 million for construction of community mental-health centers (this is the authorized level; Nixon requested nothing) = 6 Navy F-14s (Congressman Aspin); $900 million more for health manpower training and nurse training set to bring to fully authorized level = $838-million increase in Department of Defense R&D (Richard Levine, "Increased Pentagon Spending Promises Boost for Defense Industry"); $90 million more for maternal and child-health and crippled children's services to continue to reduce infant-mortality rate and provide needed services to the newborn and to crippled children, and to increase training of nurse midwives, pediatric nurses and physician's assistants = two B-1 bombers ($80 million) (Berkeley Rice, "The B-1 Bomber: The Very Model of a Modern Major Misconception"); $6 million more needed for screening and detection to reach virtually all children afflicted with lead-based paint poisoning (testimony of Dr. Michael DeBakey on the 1973 budget = 146 B-52 sorties in Southeast Asia (*The Air War in Indochina*, Cornell University Center for International Studies).

12. Construction of general hospital, equipping with beds and supporting services ("Representative Construction Costs," HEW): 300-bed hospital at $52,000 per bed = $15.6 million = one Navy F-14 (remarks by Congressman Aspin, "Defense Cost Rise Because of Military Gadgetry"); four 300-bed hospitals = $60 million = one C-5A (Senator William Proxmire, "The U.S. Navy Jet That Shot Itself Down, and Other Pentagon Lemons"); 50-bed hospital at $47,000 per bed = $2.35 million = 2 Huey helicopters (Department of Defense, "Weapon System Status"); 100-bed hospital at $44,000 per bed = $4.4 million =

4 Main battle tanks (Senator Proxmire, "The U.S. Navy Jet That Shot
Itself Down . . .").

13. Construction of two-story public-health center in Decatur, Ala-
bama ("Representative Construction Costs," HEW) = $1 million = one
Huey helicopter (Department of Defense, "Weapon System Status").

14. Construction of a 584-bed general hospital in San Francisco
("Representative Construction Costs," HEW) = $41 million = one B-1
bomber (Berkeley Rice, "The B-1 Bomber: The Very Model of a Modern
Major Misconception").

15. Construction of a 228-bed general hospital in Granite City, Ill.
("Representative Construction Costs," HEW) = $12 million = 3 Huey
helicopters and one Air Force F-15 fighter (remarks by Congressman
Aspin, "Defense Cost Rise Because of Military Gadgetry," and "Weapon
System Status," Department of Defense).

16. Construction of a 22-bed nursing home in Estill, South Carolina
("Representative Construction Costs," HEW) = $446,000 = approxi-
mate cost of ten B-52 bombing sorties in Indochina, or approximate op-
erating costs of 3 Huey helicopters in Southeast Asia for one year (*The
Air War in Indochina*, Cornell University Center for International
Studies).

IMPOUNDED FUNDS

1. Congressionally authorized funds for highway construction, low-
rent public housing, Model Cities, water and sewer grants, urban renewal, regional economic development, farm credit, and mass transportation by President Nixon in 1971 (George Wilson, "Pentagon Fears
Reliance on U.S. Word Is Imperiled," *Washington Post*, Nov. 2, 1971)
= $12 billion = the overruns to date on the Main battle tank, the M60
tank, Safeguard ABM, B-1 bomber, F-111, Cheyenne, DD-963 destroyer,
and C-5A (remarks by Senator Proxmire, "Cost Data for Major Weapons
Systems").

Appendix 6

EMPLOYMENT IN MILITARY INDUSTRY AND BASES, 1971

State	Military Industry	Bases Military Personnel	Civilian Personnel
Alabama	19,000	23,000	25,000
Alaska	8,000	26,000	6,000
Arizona	23,600	28,000	9,000
Arkansas	5,500	9,000	5,000
California	322,400	227,000	149,000
Colorado	12,100	47,000	17,000
Connecticut	64,150	5,000	3,000
Delaware	1,800	6,000	2,000
Florida	63,400	69,000	29,000
Georgia	44,000	53,000	38,000
Hawaii	6,700	37,000	21,000
Idaho	2,400	5,000	1,000
Illinois	38,950	38,000	24,000
Indiana	43,800	7,000	16,000
Iowa	8,800	1,000	1,000
Kansas	18,750	32,000	6,000
Kentucky	8,300	24,000	16,000
Louisiana	17,700	27,000	8,000
Maine	2,500	6,000	2,000
Maryland	41,850	47,000	45,000
Massachusetts	74,550	19,000	18,000
Michigan	26,050	14,000	12,000
Minnesota	24,250	3,000	3,000

370

State	Military Industry	Bases Military Personnel	Civilian Personnel
Mississippi	30,850	20,000	8,000
Missouri	96,600	27,000	21,650
Montana	12,700	6,000	2,000
Nebraska	5,250	12,000	4,000
Nevada	1,400	9,000	3,000
New Hampshire	7,650	5,000	7,000
New Jersey	60,400	41,000	27,000
New Mexico	8,400	16,000	10,000
New York	182,400	23,000	26,000
North Carolina	27,700	87,000	13,000
North Dakota	3,550	13,000	2,000
Ohio	63,352	15,000	36,000
Oklahoma	12,500	25,000	32,000
Oregon	3,800	2,000	4,000
Pennsylvania	75,000	11,000	61,000
Rhode Island	5,950	9,000	11,000
South Carolina	8,550	56,000	18,000
South Dakota	2,550	6,000	1,000
Tennessee	21,000	12,000	7,000
Texas	137,650	153,000	69,000
Utah	9,150	5,000	26,000
Vermont	1,850	less than 500	1,000
Virginia	62,000	96,000	96,000
Washington	56,350	34,000	22,000
West Virginia	2,800	less than 500	2,000
Wisconsin	19,550	1,000	3,000
Wyoming	1,300	4,000	1,000

SOURCE: *Staff Study of the Economic Impact of the McGovern Defense Budget,* Congressman John Rhodes, October 17, 1972. The data was probably obtained by the Congressman from the Department of Defense.

INDEX

ABRES, 176–77
Accounting manipulations, 49–50
Ackley, Gardner, 293, 294
Administrative costs, 35*ff*.
Advance Ross Electronics, 337, 352
Aerospace industry, 254*ff*.
  accounting manipulations in, 50
  conversion of, 230, 232*ff*.
  managerial problems of, 243–44
  research and development in, 94
AFL-CIO, 98, 102, 295, 297
Agnew, Spiro, 130
Agricultural-machinery prices, 329
Agricultural products, 112–13
Air Force Systems Command, 30
Airframe industry, 230
Air power, 171–72
Alexander, Archibald, 294
Alperovitz, Gar, 303
American Hospital Supply, 99
American Machinist, 82*n.*
Amtrak, 93
Anderson, J. R., 306
Anti-economy, 285, 286
Appropriations Committee, 49
Armed forces, 158*ff*.
  bases, 222, 249*ff*., 370–71
  civil liberties and, 184
  demobilization of, 257
  "grade creep" in, 355
  officers/enlisted men ratio, 354,
    355
  popular support for, 184–85
  reduction of, 190
  size of, 15, 354–56
Armed Services Committees, 159

*Armed Services Procurement
  Regulations,* 53
Arms. *See also* Nuclear weapons.
  production, profit-taking in, 29
  sales, 108, 109, 269
Arms Control and Disarmament
  Agency, 194
Army. *See also* Armed forces.
  supertank program of, 49
Army Research Office, 64
Army Times Publishing Co., 281
Ash, Roy, 50
Assistant Secretary of Defense, 53
Atomic Energy Commission, 95, 180
Atomic weapons. *See* Nuclear
  weapons.
Automobile industry, 75–76, 87,
  101–2

Balance of payments. *See* Trade
  deficit.
Ball bearings, 93
Bankers, 270–71, 282
Baran, Paul, 261, 288
Barnet, R., 304
BART System, 85, 309
Benefit, cost relation to, 241–42
Berkowitz, M., 321
B-52 aircraft, 172, 178
Bidding for contracts, 36–37
Biological warfare, 169
Black and Decker Company, 78
Blacks, unemployment and, 312–13
Blue-collar workers, conversion and,
  235, 256–57, 282

373

Contract allocations, 61–62
Control Data Corporation, 345
Conversion, 226*ff.*
  of aerospace industry, 230, 232*ff.*
  blue-collar workers and, 235,
    256–57, 282
  diversification vs., 322
  engineers and, 234–35, 244–46,
    254–56
  financing of, 237–38
  flexibility for, lack of, 51–52
  legislation for, 65, 236, 293–94
  local initiative and, 251–52, 253,
    255–56
  managerial problems in, 238,
    240–41, 243–44
  mergers and, 240–41
  of military bases, 249*ff.*
  new products and, 229–30, 236–
    237, 249
  of occupations, 254*ff.*
  physical plant and, 248
  planning for, 236–37, 250*ff.*
  product class and, 248–49
  unions and, 235–36, 246–48, 258,
    282
Corporations. *See* Firms, military-
    industry.
Cost
  benefit relation to, 241–42
  estimates, 28*ff.*
  growth, 85, 140
  of unit of output, 43–44
Cost Estimating Procedures, 30
Cost-maximization, 21, 51, 140
  in administration, 38–39
  aerospace example of, 234
  centralism and, 215
  civilian inefficiency and, 69
  cost growth and, 140
  as design parameter, 304–5
  historical costing and, 28, 31
  limitations on, lack of, 32
  Litton and, 49
  loans and, 205
  Lockheed and, 44*ff.*
  logic of, 34
  machinery and, 41
  production management and,
    43–45
  raw materials and, 41–42
  research and, 39

Cost-maximization (*continued*)
  standardized unit of output and,
    43–44
  wages and, 40
Cost-minimization, 32–33
  self-correction and, 57–58, 205
Cost overrun, 51. *See also* Cost-
    maximization.
Council of Economic Advisers, 65,
    150–51
Currie, Malcolm R., 175

Data Product Corporation, 346
Day care, 362
DC-3 airplane, 89
Decentralization, 218–19, 223–24
Decision-making power, 52–54, 56,
    263*ff.*
  balance of payments and, 269–70
  capital translated into, 263–64
  centralized, 52–54, 56, 210–11
  changes proposed for, 206–7
  of corporations, 271
  decentralization and, 218–19
  expansion of, 64–65, 107
  exports and, 269
  final, 272–73
  private economy and, 274
  production and, 59
  profits and, 284
  Vietnam War and, 266–67
Defense spending, 17, 138. *See also*
    Budget, defense; Military
    spending.
Delivery systems, 163, 165
Department of Defense. *See also*
    Military spending; Pentagon.
  convertibility and, 232*ff.*
  cost-reduction program, 139
  decision-making by. *See* Decision-
    making power.
  employment in, 250
  limits of power and, 159–60
  price estimates and, 28
  profit decisions of, 56
  responsibility in, 139–40
  security clearances and, 37
Depletion, 24, 25, 86–88
  of capital supply, 79
  Cold War and, 20
  in productivity, 83, 204